Language and the Law: International Outlooks

ŁÓDŹ
STUDIES IN LANGUAGE

Edited by
Barbara Lewandowska-Tomaszczyk

Vol. 16

PETER LANG
Frankfurt am Main · Berlin · Bern · Bruxelles · New York · Oxford · Wien

Krzysztof Kredens
Stanisław Goźdź-Roszkowski
(eds.)

Language and the Law: International Outlooks

PETER LANG
Internationaler Verlag der Wissenschaften

Bibliographic Information published by the Deutsche Nationalbibliothek
The Deutsche Nationalbibliothek lists this publication in the Deutsche Nationalbibliografie; detailed bibliographic data is available in the internet at <http://www.d-nb.de>.

ISSN 1437-5281
ISBN 978-3-631-57447-8

www.peterlang.de

TABLE OF CONTENTS

NOTES ON CONTRIBUTORS

Susan Blackwell is a Lecturer in English Language at the University of Birmingham, where her research and teaching interests include child language, corpus linguistics and forensic linguistics. She has recently completed her Doctoral dissertation on the acquisition and use of personal pronouns in English and Dutch. She runs the forensic-linguistics electronic discussion list.

Luciana Carvalho is a lawyer specialized in contract law. She holds an MA in linguistics from Universidade de São Paulo and teaches legal translation at Pontifícia Universidade Católica de São Paulo. She also works in and outside of courts of law as an expert in legal language issues.

Le Cheng is a Doctoral candidate at City University of Hong Kong. He graduated from China University of Political Sciences and Law, received his Master's degree in law at Southwest University of Political Sciences and Law, his Master's degree in English linguistics at Zhejiang University and passed the Bar examination. His main academic interest is in discourse analysis of legal documents.

Jan Chovanec is Assistant Professor of English Linguistics at the Department of English and American Studies, Masaryk University in Brno. His main interests involve language in the media and language and law, with a focus on interpersonal aspects of communication, word play, and the interface between verbal and visual channels.

Burns Cooper has taught linguistics and English at the University of Alaska Fairbanks since 1990. His current research interests include courtroom language, authorship analysis, and forensic speaker identification. He has also done research on linguistic poetics, as shown in his book *Mysterious Music: Rhythm and Free Verse* (Stanford University Press 1998), and on the relationship of intonation to dialect.

Ioana Costache got her BA in philology from the University of Bucharest in 2002. She went on to do a Master's degree in applied linguistics and ELT at the same university (2003), followed by an MSt in General Linguistics and Comparative Philology at Oxford University. Between 2002 and 2006 she taught aspects of linguistics at the University of Bucharest and in October 2006 went back to Oxford to research 17th-century Romanian.

Richard L. Creech is an attorney and director of ESQ Language Services, LLC, a legal translation company based in Washington, DC. He has a Bachelor's degree in linguistics from Harvard University and law degrees from the Northwestern University School of Law and the University of Utrecht. He has written numerous works on the interaction of legal and linguistic systems, including *Law and Language in the European Union: The Paradox of a Babel "United in Diversity"* (Europa Law Publishing 2005).

Agnieszka Doczekalska received both her LLM and Diploma in translation from the University of Lodz. She also holds a Diplôme d'Université de traduction professionnelle from Université des Sciences Humaines de Strasbourg. She is now a Doctoral candidate at the Law Department of the European University Institute, Florence, where her research centres on legal multilingualism.

Lorna Fadden is a Doctoral candidate at Simon Fraser University in British Columbia, Canada. Her research focuses on the discourse and prosody of police interviews as well as the institutional discourse of Canada's Aboriginal people. During her MA studies, she examined various morphosyntactic properties of indigenous languages of the Americas. She assists the Métis Nation with the preservation of Michif.

Maurizio Gotti is Professor of English Linguistics at the University of Bergamo, where he is director of CERLIS, the research centre on specialized languages. From 1999 to 2001 he was President of the Italian Association of English Studies. From 2000 to 2004 he was President of the European Confederation of University Language Centres. His main research areas are English syntax and lexicography, and the features and origins of specialized discourse.

Chris Heffer has a PhD in forensic linguistics from the University of Birmingham and is co-director of the MA in Forensic Linguistics at Cardiff University. He has written and presented extensively on jury instruction and the language of legal professionals in court, including *The Language of Jury Trial: A Corpus-aided Analysis of Legal-Lay Discourse* (Palgrave 2005). He has also published in the areas of stylistics, translation, lexicography and legal evidence.

Georgina Heydon is a Post-Doctoral Research Fellow in criminal justice in the School of Humanities, Communications and Social Sciences at Monash University. Her published research is largely focussed on the investigation of interactions between participants in police interviews, although she also maintains an interest in the broader field of sociolinguistics, discourse analysis and narrative structure.

Syûgo Hotta is Associate Professor of Linguistics at the College of Law and the Graduate School of Language Education and Information Science, Ritsumeikan University, Japan. He got a PhD in linguistics from the University of Chicago, USA, and an LLM from Osgoode Hall Law School, York University, Canada. His research interests include a model-theoretic approach to linguistic phenomena in legal contexts and word-formation in Japanese and English.

Anne Lise Kjær received her PhD in legal language from Copenhagen Business School. She is now a Postdoctoral Research Associate in the Faculty of Law, University of Copenhagen. Her principal research interests are in the area of law and language (legal language and translation, legal interpretation, multilingualism and European legal integration). She teaches upper-level courses in Law and Language.

Aleksandra Matulewska got her PhD in linguistics from Adam Mickiewicz University, where she now lectures. Her research areas are those of specialised translation and legal language. She is the author of numerous articles on legal translation and the monograph *Lingua Legis in Translation* (Peter Lang GmbH 2007).

Willem Meijs received his PhD in English linguistics from Amsterdam Free University, where he lectured before moving to Amsterdam University to do research in computational linguistics, corpus linguistics and lexicology. He is a founding member of ICAME, the International Computer Archive of Modern English. In 1991 he moved to Birmingham (UK), where he set up a small company, Language Consultancy Desk, specialising in translation and linguistic advice.

Ruth Morris is a lecturer at Bar-Ilan University and also works as a freelance conference interpreter. She has an MA in communications from the Hebrew University of Jerusalem and a PhD from Lancaster University. Her primary research area is the field of court interpreting, but her interests include community interpreting and language policy. She is co-author (with Joan Colin) of *Interpreters and the Legal Process* (Waterside Press 1996).

Víctor M. González Ruiz got his PhD from the Universidad de Las Palmas de Gran Canaria, Spain, where he is now a Lecturer in Legal Translation. His research areas are those of specialised (legal and audiovisual) translation, legal language and cultural studies.

Jess Shapero got her BSc (Hons) in computer science from Wolverhampton Polytechnic. She also received an MSc in cognitive science and, with a thesis on punctuation, an MPhil in English, both from Birmingham University, where she is currently writing a Doctoral thesis on suicide notes.

King Kui Sin received his PhD from the Southern Illinois University. He is Associate Professor at City University of Hong Kong. He worked in the Judiciary as a court interpreter and served on the Bilingual Laws Advisory Committee from 1990 to 1997. His research interest and publications are in the areas of language and the law, and the philosophy of language.

Godfrey A. Steele is Senior Lecturer in Communication Studies at the University of the West Indies, St. Augustine, Trinidad and Tobago, where he developed, and teaches on, undergraduate programmes in business communication, health communication and communication studies. He is currently developing a language and the law course and researching the use of witness statements and links among communication and culture.

Susan Šarčević is Professor at the Faculty of Law, University of Rijeka, where she teaches legal German, legal English and EU terminology. She also teaches a postgraduate course on translation of the EU *acquis* in Zagreb. She has published widely on legal translation and legal lexicography, given plenary lectures at conferences worldwide and is a partner in national and international projects on legal translation and terminology.

Anne Wagner is a Senior Lecturer in LSP affiliated with Université du Littoral Côte d'Opale, France. She is Editor-in-Chief of the International Journal for the Semiotics of Law and of the new series Legal Semiotics Monographs (Deborah Charles Publications). She presides over The International Roundtable for the Semiotics of Law. Her main research interests include legal interpretation and discourse, law and culture and semiotics of law.

Iwona Witczak-Plisiecka received her MPhil in linguistics from Trinity College, Dublin University, and her MA and PhD in English studies from the University of Lodz, where she currently teaches and researches. Her main academic interests are in philosophy of language, semantics and pragmatics; they also include issues of linguistic relativism, language policy and politics, and legal discourse and translation. She is Associate Editor of *Łódź Papers in Pragmatics*.

Jarosław Wyrembak got his PhD in law from Warsaw University, where he now lectures at the Institute of Penal Law. He is interested in the law-making process, aspects of criminal law and the semantic and pragmatic interpretation of legal instruments. He is the author of numerous publications in these areas.

Diana Yankova has a PhD in linguistics and teaches legal English and culture studies at the Applied Linguistics Department, New Bulgarian University. Her research interests include language and the law, discourse analysis, and approximation of legislation. She is the author of *Legal Language Made Simple: Statutory Provisions in English and Bulgarian* (Tip-Top Press 2004).

INTRODUCTION

Scholarship in the area of language and the law has undergone rapid growth in the last three decades, eventually acquiring a social presence it had long been due. While the majority of the research has originated in English-speaking countries or in environments otherwise influenced by Anglo-Saxon academic concerns, numerous interesting developments have also been reported elsewhere. These days the field is very much a global phenomenon, a state of affairs attested to by this collection, which offers a glimpse into the work of scholars investigating the ways in which legal substance intersects with language description in a variety of legal contexts and linguistic systems. The contributions come from researchers working in 19 countries on five continents: Australia, Brazil, Bulgaria, Canada, Croatia, China, Czech Republic, England, France, Hong Kong, Israel, Italy, Japan, Poland, Romania, Spain, Trinidad and Tobago, USA and Wales.

Language and the Law: International Outlooks is of necessity an eclectic volume, what with the different legal and linguistic systems discussed and diversity of perspectives offered, though it is eclectic in other capacities as well. The 23 papers come from both linguists and lawyers, distinguished scholars and researchers in the early stages of their careers, common and civil law jurisdictions. While we are aware that we have not avoided all the dangers inherent in managing such great diversity, the decisions we made in the few cases where we resolved to sacrifice depth to gain scope were conscious ones.

The contributions span a wide range of reassuringly familiar topics, which we have grouped into seven parts. Part I deals with multilingualism. MAURIZIO GOTTI's paper (*Legal discourse in multilingual and multicultural contexts*) discusses some wide-ranging implications of globalization for legal discourse. Drawing on several examples from arbitration texts, he examines how the complex interplay between an international perspective on legislation and the specific local conditions affects the legal field and legal language. SUSAN ŠARČEVIĆ (*Making multilingualism work in the enlarged European Union*) analyzes the effectiveness of efforts made by the European Commission's Directorate-General for Translation (DGT) to draft Community legislation in all official languages of the enlarged EU. In her contribution, Šarčević advocates the need for an increased emphasis on improving the quality of Community acts by encouraging greater interaction between drafters and translators. In a similar vein, AGNIESZKA DOCZEKALSKA (*Production and application of multilingual law: The principle of equality of authentic texts and the value of subsequent translation*), focuses on the phenomenon of subsequent translation and its significance in the context of the principle of equality of authentic texts. More specifically, she seeks to analyze the value of subsequent translation, attempting to determine how subsequent translation is and should be produced, and whether it contributes or should contribute to the common meaning of a single instrument as far as the interpretation of multilingual law by courts is concerned.

Part II investigates various aspects of legal translation and interpreting. ANNE LISE KJÆR (*Legal translation in the European Union: A research field in need of a new approach)* provides a critique of the current state of translation studies in respect of legal translation within the framework of the European Union. She argues that translation and multilingual drafting should be accorded the recognition they deserve due to their unique nature. Kjær calls for a new approach which would result in establishing an independent interdisciplinary research field with a focus especially on features of law and language characteristic of the multilingual and multi-legal system of the European Union. Reflecting on different approaches to the study of terms, DIANA YANKOVA (*How harmonious is harmonization of legislation? On the concept of term equivalence*) describes terminological aspects related to the process of standardizing legal terminology. She analyzes various options available to the translator in the EU context against the background of Bulgaria's legal culture. The analysis is based on 120 pages of selected EU directives on intellectual property, copyright and related rights and their translations from English into Bulgarian. LUCIANA CARVALHO (*Translating contracts and agreements from a corpus linguistics perspective*) explores the usefulness of using a corpus linguistics methodology to provide naturally occurring Brazilian Portuguese translation equivalents for binomial expressions commonly found in legal agreements originally written in English. The intended legal effect in the target language can only be attained, the author insists, if the translator treats binomial expressions as units. RUTH MORRIS (*Monoglots and polyglots, or principles and application: Dealing with linguistic diversity in English-speaking legal systems*) provides a comprehensive, diachronic and comparative description of dominant attitudes to the provision of interpreting services in English-speaking legal systems. She describes the switch from multilingualism to monolingualism in English law and how this process has affected contemporary courtroom practice.

Part III consists of five contributions centred on the issue of courtroom and legal discourse. CHRIS HEFFER (*Judgement in court: Evaluating participants in courtroom discourse*), in the longest paper of this collection, explores the relation between factual evidence and subjective judgement. He provides a corpus-based analytical overview of the linguistic construal of judgement by legal professionals in court. This is accompanied by a reflection on methodology, whereby Heffer combines corpus methodologies and a systematic analytical framework to provide empirical grounding for the study of evaluation. IWONA WITCZAK-PLISIECKA (*Linguistic aspects of deontic* shall *in the legal context*) in her contribution addresses the problem of deonticity in the legal context, focusing on the function of the English modal verb *shall* found in normative texts. It is argued that the deontic *shall*, which in the legal domain is used mainly to impose obligation or confer legal rights, can be approached as a vehicle for deontic speech acts, i.e. indirect speech acts where the verb *shall* carries illocutionary directive force. IOANA COSTACHE (*Nineteenth-century Romanian contracts for works: a case study*), in another empirically-oriented study, presents a diachronic description of Romanian contracts for works in which she attempts to trace their specific structural and pragmatic features. JAN CHOVANEC (*The same though different: Tobacco health warnings in European Community Member States*) compares the wording of tobacco health warnings in several European countries in order to highlight the existence of subtle differences between the various language versions. By providing several illustrative examples, he convincingly demonstrates how the differences result in a reduced degree of equivalence and, consequently, consumers in various countries may be warned of the same fact in a significantly different manner. Finally, VICTOR M. GONZÁLES RUIZ (*Changing the law on marriage: The semantics of tolerance*) describes linguistic changes caused by the introduction of a new act passed by the Spanish Parliament which recognizes the right of same-sex couples to get married. The author focuses on specific strategies employed by the legislator to effect a profound change in social policy and the law on family and marriage.

Part IV is devoted to statutory interpretation. ANNE WAGNER (*Mapping legal knowledge*), by focusing on the impact exerted by the French government and the legal profession, explores the different ways in which users of law tend to apply or modify it. She argues that a thorough understanding of legal discourse inevitably involves an in-depth analysis by means of three different methods: a linguistic one, that of legal conceptualization, and the method of socialization. JAROSŁAW WYREMBAK (*Exploring the limitations of statutory interpretation: some remarks on Polish Supreme Court's approach to the interpretation of selected criminal law provisions*) examines the extent to which the textual, linguistic perspective affects the interpretation of legislative provisions. This is firmly grounded in a careful analysis of decisions handed down by Poland's Supreme Court.

Part V targets selected aspects of police interviews. GEORGINA HEYDON (*The importance of being (in)formal: discourse strategies in police interviews with children*) describes the methods used by police interviewers to elicit response and manage interactions in child witness statements. By referring to the Video and Audio Taping of Evidence (VATE) project, which has been in operation in Victoria, Australia since 1993, this contribution vividly demonstrates the considerable pressure on police officers under these circumstances to balance the requirements of the courts with the needs of the child, and that the result can only be a unique and at times innovative blend of formality and informality. LORNA

FADDEN (*Discourse differences of Aboriginal and Caucasian suspects in police interviews*) offers an empirical, corpus-based study in which she richly illustrates major differences between Canadian Aboriginal and non-Aboriginal suspects in terms of testimonies elicited in the course of police interviews. Fadden demonstrates how Aboriginal suspects' discourse behaviour could be misinterpreted by those ignorant of particular discourse features typical of the varieties of English spoken by Aboriginal people.

Part VI consists of two contrastive studies. In the first one, CHENG LE and KING KUI SIN (*Contrastive analysis of Chinese and American court judgments*) provide a corpus-based genre analysis of Chinese and American judgments. The authors do not stop at comparing and contrasting the linguistic aspects (macrostructures, rhetorical moves) of the respective legal instruments but they set their study against the wider backdrop of different legal cultures and institutions. ALEKSANDRA MATULEWSKA (*The macrostructure and register of English and Polish* testaments) adopts a similar data-based, genre-oriented methodology to explore the differences and similarities between English (British and American) and Polish wills, and reflects on the implications the study carries for legal translation.

Part VII deals with the semantics of trade names and, more specifically, distinctiveness of trademarks. RICHARD CREECH (*Missing the mark: Assessing trademarks for distinctiveness and descriptiveness in Europe's multilingual environment*) discusses this issue by describing and commenting upon the decisions of the European Court of Justice given in the multilingual environment of contemporary European Union. The author traces the development of a methodology for assessing trademarks. It is argued that before any decision concerning a disputed trademark is reached, the court should examine how the mark is understood by speakers of all the different languages spoken in the Community. So far, the argument goes, the judicial institutions of the European Union have preferred to take an easier route and have generally considered the meaning of a mark in only one language. SYÛGO HOTTA (*Morphosyntactic structure of Japanese trademarks and their distinctiveness: A new model for linguistic analysis of trademarks*) in his paper continues pursuing the complex nature of distinctiveness in trademarks by proposing a new analytical model for the morphosyntactic structure of trademarks. Aided in his analysis by the well-known linguistic concept of markedness, Hotta discusses a Japanese trademark infringement case in which the morphosyntactic structure of two trademarks was at issue.

Part VIII groups three contributions exploring various aspects of forensic linguistics. SUE BLACKWELL, WILLEM MEIJS and JESS SHAPERO (*Texts of murder and martyrdom*) set out to discuss a new type of texts – possibly a new written genre – which has recently appeared in the public domain. The authors attempt at a linguistic description of what they call "martyrdom texts", i.e. texts written by Islamic extremists before carrying out acts of violence during which they expect to die. It is demonstrated how this category of texts differs from the related categories of suicide and murder texts. BURNS COOPER (*Idea density as a marker of authorship: A preliminary study*) offers a preliminary investigation of the possibility of using a psycholinguistic measure, "idea density," for forensic linguistic work. The paper implies a long-term relationship between idea density (which in the paper is referred to as propositional density) and neurology. This is considered as potentially very useful for authorship studies because the basic problem of whether writers maintain elements of their style over time could thus be overcome. Finally, GODFREY A. STEELE (*Course content for language of the law and the interpretation of the law*) focuses on the pedagogical aspects of language and the law. He provides a detailed description of a course on legal language and law interpretation. Importantly, this is accompanied by a student needs analysis and a rationale for adopting a particular teaching methodology.

We like to think that by opening doors to an array of unique linguistic and legal realities, this collection is capable of enriching the investigative perspectives of researchers interested in language and the law, and also of inspiring them to embark on new scholarly endeavours. We owe a debt of gratitude to Barbara Lewandowska-Tomaszczyk, the Łódź Studies in Language series editor, for recognizing the urgency of the subject and helping us throughout the editorial process. We offer a word of thanks also to the Contributors, who have helped to make that process a labour of love.

Krzysztof Kredens
Stanisław Goźdź-Roszkowski

Łódź, July 2007

Part I

MULTILINGUALISM

Maurizio Gotti
Università di Bergamo
Italy

LEGAL DISCOURSE IN MULTILINGUAL AND MULTICULTURAL CONTEXTS

1. Globalisation in specialized contexts

In recent years, the dismantling of cultural, disciplinary and national barriers, especially in the context of co-operation and collaboration in international trade, has accelerated moves towards the globalisation of socio-cultural, business and communication issues. This process of globalisation offers a topical illustration of the interaction between linguistic and cultural factors in the construction of discourse, both within specialized domains and in wider contexts. Domain-specific languages are prone to the pressures of intercultural variation, as it is not only the sociocultural factors inherent in a text but also the interpretive schemata that deeply affect its realisation and interpretation within the host professional community (cf. Gotti 2003).

This process of globalization has certainly favoured English, and in the last century English undoubtedly became the language of international communication in most international contexts. Indeed, now English is the main language of international business and academic conferences, and is commonly used in a variety of domains: from science to technology, from diplomacy to sport, from pop music to advertising. On a worldwide level English is perceived as having the highest "utility and exchange values" (Coulmas 1991), as it offers the possibility of making use of the language for the widest range of purposes and in the largest number of places all over the world.

The use of English by non-native speakers is quickly spreading also in non-working contexts. In spite of the multilingual policy adopted by the EU authorities, English is actually becoming the *lingua franca* of Europe, as this often proves to be the only language common to the two interlocutors.[1] Not only do ordinary people in Europe communicate with one another in English, but this language is the one frequently used by European Union officials to communicate with one another and with EU citizens. A confirmation can be found in a sentence taken from the call for tenders for a European Union programme:

---

[1] The same situation is found in Asia, where international trading among Asian countries relies on Asian varieties of English, rather than on Asian languages themselves (Yano 2001).

> Proposals may be submitted in any Community language. In order to facilitate assessment by evaluators drawn from various EEA countries, an English translation should preferably accompany any proposals made in another language. (INFO 2000)

2. Globalization in the legal field

The globalising trend has also affected the legal field, where an international perspective is becoming more and more widespread. Legal discourse is thus another significant area where intercultural factors may be investigated. Although legal discourse is often thought to be less likely, in respect to other professional genres, to display strong cross-cultural variations, since law texts are commonly aimed at practitioners closely linked to national legal contexts, cultural aspects do represent an important conditioning factor on its construction and interpretation. Indeed, legal discourse – which used to be employed in narrow professional and local milieus and thus more closely geared to specific cultural values and identity systems – is now more and more frequently involved in globalization processes, which have relevant consequences on the discourse produced by both native and non-native practitioners working in intercultural and cross-cultural settings. Nowadays many of the texts in use at a local level are the result of a process of translation or adaptation of more general documents formulated at an international level. This is the consequence of the fact that in the context of co-operation and collaboration in international trade, law too is fast assuming an international perspective rather than remaining a purely domestic concern. The increasing need at an international level for accurate and authoritative translation of legal texts and documents across languages relies on the need for them to convey appropriately in both languages the pragmatic and functional intentions and implications of the original text (Šarčević 1997).

An excellent example of this trend is the need for a common European legal framework; this task is much more complex than simply translating common normative documents into all the languages of the European Union, because this newly created framework is meant to be interpreted within the contexts of a diversity of individual legal systems and tongues. Significant differentiations may arise in the various member countries of western Europe, especially when one needs to interpret such issues as human rights, international agreements and contracts, freedom of speech, freedom of trade, protection of intellectual property, all of which have very strong socio-political and cultural constraints. Although all legal documents in all languages address these issues, they do so in distinctive and also in overlapping ways, because of the different languages in which they are constructed and the cultural differences of the societies in question and of their legal systems. Indeed, legal terminology is so culture-bound (the reasons being at the same time historical, sociological, political and jurisprudential) that a satisfactory translation of all the legal terms of one text from one context to another is at times impossible.[2] David underlines this difficulty with a few examples:

> To translate into English technical words used by lawyers in France, in Spain, or in Germany is in many cases an impossible task, and conversely there are no words in the languages of the continent to express the most elementary notions of English law. The words *common law* and *equity* are the best examples thereof; we have to keep the English words [...] because no words in French or in any other language are adequate to convey the meaning of these words, clearly linked as they are to the specific history of English law alone. (David 1980: 39)

The adoption of a particular term instead of another may give rise to ambiguity and misinterpretation. Several examples of this are given by Fletcher (1999), who examines the translation into various languages of the English text of the European Convention on Human Rights. For instance, the translation provided for the expression *fair and regular trial* into *juicio justo y imparcial* (Spanish) and *procès juste et équitable* (French) is not satisfactory, as the use of the non-equivalent adjectives *regular* (English) / *imparcial* (Spanish) / *équitable* (French) can easily show. The same could be said for the rendering of the concept of *reasonableness*, basic in common law systems, where expressions such as *reasonable steps*, *reasonable measures*, *reasonable person* and *proof beyond a reasonable doubt* frequently occur. This concept, instead, when translated into languages spoken in countries adopting a civil law system is considered too vague and its rendering as *ragionevole*, *raisonnable* or *vernünftig* often gives rise to criticism and dissatisfaction.

Other excellent examples of translation discrepancies can easily be found in texts relating to the process of building a common European legal framework. For example, translators into English find it difficult to express such culturally-specific French collocations as *acteurs sociaux, acteurs économiques, acteurs institutionnels, acteurs publics, acteurs politiques*, which have no direct equivalent in the target language (Salmasi 2003: 117), and they sometimes transliterate terms or create calques from one language into another, relying on the false premise of a very close relationship between similar lexemes in different languages (see the examples of *transmettre / transmit* and *prévoir / foresee* in Seymour 2002). Indeed, in Europe the legal drafting issue has become extremely important with the elaboration of a multilingual legislation concerning the

[2] This also applies to different contexts using the same language. As Nadelmann and Mehren rightly exemplify, "Even in the same language the meaning of a legal term may differ from system to system. Thus, "domicile" has one meaning in English law and quite different meanings in American jurisdictions." (1967: 195). As Nida aptly remarks, "competent translators are always aware that ultimately words only have meaning in terms of the corresponding culture" (Nida 2001: 13).

European Union. This depends on the fact that the official languages of the European Union are those of its Member States, and as new countries join the Union, their languages are added to the number. This is part of a precise policy aiming to build a community of peoples respecting and safeguarding at the same time the existing variety of customs and cultural identities, a principle based on the conviction that the languages of Europe are part of its immense and diverse cultural heritage, and therefore it is considered the duty of the Union to guarantee their preservation.

As European Union legislation must be published in all Member States' official languages in order to be valid also at a national level, in the elaboration of European legislation and its introduction into the various national contexts a fundamental role is played by legal drafting and translation. As regards the former, the elaboration of the texts is carried out in a parallel fashion by the various teams, making use of a common multilingual terminological database and relying on shared Community concepts and institutions. This procedure, however, encounters problems mainly due to the presence of different legal systems in the various countries and the existence of a specific tradition of the legal register in each Member State. Indeed, closer co-operation between the various legal systems of the EU members has not been achieved through creation of a new legislative framework to replace the existing one. Such systems are still in use and only in very few cases have the more evident discrepancies been eliminated.

The European authorities are aware of these problems and greater and greater emphasis is being laid on the quality of legislation drafting at supranational level. An example of this is the "Declaration on the Quality of the Drafting of Community Legislation", which is an important part of the Treaty of Amsterdam (1998); this document explicitly states that "the quality of the drafting of Community legislation is crucial if it is to be properly implemented by the competent national authorities and better understood by the public and in business circles". This has led to much greater uniformity in the translation of European directives into the various languages of the Union and to more marked homogeneity and interdependence of the resulting texts. Translators work in single-language units of approximately twenty people and translate, almost without exception, into their mother tongue. Their command of foreign languages is expected to be backed up by a good general knowledge and some competence in at least one specialized area such as law, technology, economics, etc. Translators are also assumed to possess word processing and other computer skills such as database interrogation, as they frequently rely on terminology and documentation available in electronic versions.

This new approach to the translation of European directives has also served a harmonising function, in the sense that from the adoption of the texts of the European Union greater uniformity has derived in the use of terminology as well as a higher degree of conceptual homogeneity, which is then transferred into local legal practices. A typical example of this influence of European legislation on the local legal language is the frequent adoption of equivalent definitions of legal concepts deriving directly from European regulations and directives. However, these efforts and initiatives in better drafting procedures have not solved all discrepancy problems, as the final texts are also conditioned by the different rhetorical traditions pertaining to the cultural systems involved, thus often leading to diverging constructions and therefore to conflictual interpretations, with the risk of raising legal controversies. Moreover, in the translation process there is often an addition to and/or alteration of the semantic value of the original, due to the fact that the interpreter brings his/her own experience, knowledge and attitude to the text he/she is translating into another language. For this reason it is commonly suggested that translators working in this field should have two different types of competence: not only linguistic but also legal.[3]

Moreover, as has often been remarked, the adoption of a *lingua franca* may have important consequences on the approach adopted locally. Indeed, when the language chosen for the international arbitration procedure is English, there is a tendency to adopt procedures typical of common law countries:

> Frequently the presence of American (or British) lawyers in a procedure normally leads to the de facto use of US (or English) procedures. (Lazareff 1999: 37)

The influential role played by this language is much more significant now that English is so frequently used also in cases in which no native English-speaking party is involved. The frequency of this situation is confirmed by Taniguchi's testimony:

> There are very many different arbitral practices associated with different legal and commercial cultures. However, the world has been unmistakingly proceeding toward a single commercial culture. Japanese businessmen, for example, are negotiating business in the English language not only with English speaking businessmen but also Korean, European and middle eastern businessmen. This is one of the realities of international trade today. (Taniguchi 1998: 39)

The increasing role of English as a *lingua franca* can also be seen at the European Union level, where the use of English has become prevalent. Indeed, at the Translation Service of the European Union, nearly three-fifths of the documents sent for translation are drafted originally in English. This is nearly double the quantity of material drafted in French, which for decades was the dominant language. The great increase in the use of English in this context is due to the fact

[3] For example, the Court of First Instance and the Court of Justice of the European Communities have eleven translation divisions (one for each of the Community languages) averaging fifteen "lawyer/linguists" each (cf. Weston 1995).

that English is often adopted as a "relay language" for translations between combinations of languages, such as the Baltic languages and almost any other, for which the EU institutions are unlikely to find enough translators who can bridge the gap directly: the first translation is into English and from this a text in another language is then produced.

3. International commercial arbitration

An excellent example of the globalising process taking place in the legal system is constituted by international commercial arbitration. In the last few decades, all over the world arbitration has become more and more common as a legal instrument for the settling of commercial disputes. The high recourse to this mediating procedure has given rise to a widely felt need for greater harmonisation of the procedures followed, which has led to the elaboration of the UNCITRAL document approved by the United Nations to be used as a model by most of the member countries in the construction of their own individual statutory provisions for commercial arbitration. However, in spite of the growing globalisation of arbitration culture, the elaboration of the UN Model Law has not guaranteed complete uniformity among the various national legislations, as the different countries have used this model in different ways, depending upon their national requirements, concerns, cultures, legal systems, languages, and other constraints. Indeed, in the process of adoption of this model, the English language text of the UNCITRAL has often had to be translated into the local languages, a procedure which has implied not only the adaptation of the original discourse to the typical features and resources of the national tongues, but also its adjustment to the cultural needs and legal constraints of each specific country. In the following sections examples of discrepancy in the formulation of arbitration concepts in different languages will be taken into consideration so as to identify the various motivations that have determined such diverging outcomes.[4] The examples will be drawn from legislation on international arbitration based on the Model Law on International Commercial Arbitration (ML) and the UNCITRAL Arbitration Rules (AR) issued by the United Nations and later integrated into the laws of several countries with varying constitutional, sociocultural and economic

[4] The analysis presented here derives from an international research project entitled *Generic Integrity in Legislative Discourse in Multilingual and Multicultural Contexts* (http://gild.mmc.cityu.edu.hk/). The project has investigated the generic integrity of legislative discourse by analysing the linguistic and discoursal properties of a multilingual corpus of international arbitration laws drawn from a number of different countries, cultures, and socio-political backgrounds, written in different languages, and used within and across a variety of legal systems. Some of the results of the project are presented in Bhatia et al. 2003, Bhatia, Candling and Gotti 2003, and Bhatia, Candling and Engberg (forthcoming).

conditions. In particular, a comparison will be made with Italian arbitration law from the Code of Civil Procedure (arts. 806-840) and with regulations drafted by the arbitration chambers of Milan, Bergamo and Venice.[5]

In the last two decades the UNCITRAL provisions have been used as a model by a large number of countries. As the Model Law and its connected arbitration rules were created with the purpose of achieving the highest degree of harmonisation, the single countries have been recommended to make as few changes as possible when incorporating them into their legal systems. However, the adoption of this Model Law has not guaranteed complete uniformity among the various national legislations, as this process has implied not only the adaptation of the original discourse to the typical features and resources of the national tongues, but also its adjustment to the socio-cultural needs and legal constraints of each specific country.

Indeed, the socio-economic environment in which legal provisions are introduced may greatly influence the style adopted in drafting the normative texts. An example can be seen in the regulations enacted in the Italian context by the Milan, Bergamo and Venice Arbitration Chambers. These institutions are situated in one of the most highly industrialized areas in Northern Italy, where a large number of small enterprises operate successfully on foreign markets. Their sets of rules are intended for a number of business people running small and medium-sized companies and wanting clear indications on how to resolve commercial disputes without recourse to ordinary justice. This explains the higher degree of user-friendliness encountered in their texts, which can be noted in several cases. One instance is the fact that two of them (BAC and MAC) include standard arbitration clauses – such as the clauses for a sole arbitrator, for an arbitral tribunal and for a multi-party arbitration – which can be adopted verbatim and completed easily by the reader, as can be seen from the following examples:

> 1) *Arbitration agreement* [a)]
> The undersigned [b)] ....and .... considering that a dispute has arisen on the subject [c)] .... agree to defer this dispute to the decision of [d)] .... to be appointed in accordance with the Rules of the National and International Arbitration Chamber of Bergamo, which the parties expressly declare they know and which they accept in full.

[5] The texts taken into particular consideration are: articles 806-840 of the Code of Civil Procedure (an English translation, offered by the Milan Chamber of National and International Arbitration, is available from www.camera-arbitrale.com/eng/rifarb.htm; it is the version referred to in this article), UNCITRAL Arbitration Rules, the UN Model Law on International Commercial Arbitration, and also the regulations enacted by Milan Arbitration Chamber, Bergamo Arbitration Chamber and Venice Arbitration Chamber.

The arbitrators / the sole arbitrator shall decide according to the rules and regulations ……………..... / fairness (specify what is relevant).
The language of the arbitration shall be ………………………

Notes

[a] The arbitration agreement is a document that is stipulated when the dispute has already arisen between the parties and in the absence of a precautionary arbitration clause.

[b] Specification of the name and residence, or in the case of companies, the head offices of the parties.

[c] Reference, also expressed in general terms, of the subject under dispute, with possible reference to the contract out of which the dispute originated.

[d] Specification of the number of arbitrators (one or three). (BAC, Arbitration agreement)

2) *Clause for Sole Arbitrator*
All disputes arising out of the present contract [1], including those concerning its validity, interpretation, performance and termination, shall be referred to a sole arbitrator according to the International Arbitration Rules of the Chamber of National and International Arbitration of Milan, which the parties declare that they know and accept in their entirety.
The sole arbitrator shall decide according to the norms ...[2].
The language of the arbitration shall be ...

Notes

[1] Where the arbitration clause is contained in a document other than the contract to which it pertains, the contract referred to shall be indicated.

[2] The parties may indicate the norms applicable to the merits of the dispute; alternatively, they may provide that the arbitrator decide ex aequo et bono. (MAC, Clause for Sole Arbitrator)

The texts above have the form of ready-to-use specimens and are thus very easy to copy and complete. Instead, the UNCITRAL arbitration rules, on which the Italian texts are modelled, are mainly informative and imply some sort of adaptation on the part of the user of the clauses presented (cf. quotation 26). This is in line with the results of Salmi-Tolonen's (2003) analysis of the Finnish Arbitration Act compared with the UNCITRAL Model Law, which confirm her hypothesis that the functions of national legislation and the international model law are slightly different: expository and descriptive in the case of the model law, and directive in the case of national legislation.

3) *Model arbitration clause*
Any dispute, controversy or claim arising out of or relating to this contract, or the breach, termination or invalidity thereof, shall be settled by arbitration in accordance with the UNCITRAL Arbitration Rules as at present in force.

Note
Parties may wish to consider adding:
a) The appointing authority shall be ... (name of institution or person);
b) The number of arbitrators shall be ... (one or three);
c) The place of arbitration shall be ... (town or country);
d) The language(s) to be used in the arbitral proceedings shall be ... (AR 1)

AR's adherence to a more traditional legal style is also demonstrated by the lengthy and complex structure of most of its sentences, in line with the features of legal discourse (Mellinkoff 1963, Gustafsson 1975, Solan 1993, Tiersma 1999, Gotti 2003). As can be seen from Table 1, the average sentence length is higher in AR than in the other three texts:

Table 1. Average sentence length in the corpus analysed (From Belotti 2003: 33)

	Average sentence length
AR	43.1
MAC	37.0
BAC	34.4
VAC	29.8

The more complex structure of legal discourse in AR is confirmed by the data concerning sentence types. As Table 2 shows, AR has more complex sentences than the Italian texts; MAC, BAC and VAC, on the contrary, contain more simple and compound sentences.

Table 2. Distribution of sentence types (From Belotti 2003: 34)

	AR		MAC		BAC		VAC	
Simple	5	17%	9	19%	15	28%	4	33%
Compound	1	3%			2	4%	5	42%
Complex	24	80%	36	77%	37	68%	3	25%
Complex-compound			2	4%				

The shorter sentence length and the higher average number of simple and compound sentences determine a positive impact on the level of readability of the Italian texts and make them easier to process, which strengthens their greater degree of user-friendliness. This greater attention to reader's competence and expectations is confirmed by the use of lexis. Indeed, AR contains many Latinate and French forms, some of which already found in ML: *ex aequo et bono, amiable compositeur, de iure, de facto, ipso iure, in camera*. These, instead, do not occur at all in some of the Italian arbitration rules (such as BAC) or are very few in others (MAC and VAC). The same can be said for archaic words, as can be seen in Table 3:

Table 3. Type and number of occurrences of archaic words (From Belotti 2002:132)

	AR	MAC	BAC	VAC
Forthwith		1		
Hereinafter	1			
Therefore	2	2		
Therefor	2	2		
Therein		1		
Thereof	2	3		3
Thereon	2			
Thereto	2			
Total	*11*	*9*	*0*	*3*

4. Conclusion

As has been seen, the recent strong moves towards globalisation have implied relevant consequences in socio-cultural and communication terms. As language is inseparable from set cultural implications and is deeply involved in new social changes, local discourse often demonstrates that culture is not only ignored but at times even rejected or distorted. Thus intercultural communication is shown to affect the strategies themselves whereby discourse is negotiated and where social practices are shaped by cultural diversity and a strong need for a language for mutual comprehension. Also the role and status of English in increasingly numerous communities and domains constitute a complex issue, especially because the adoption and influence of this language often has controversial political, social and economic implications. As a result, elements of linguistic and intercultural conflict are bound to arise, determining changes in the forms and uses of both the donor and receiving languages. Although the use of English as a common language is an important tool in increasing our opportunities for mutual understanding and international cooperation, its spread at times creates conflicts, stemming from the diverging interests of monolingual and multilingual societies, an issue which seems to be more a question of social identity than linguistics.

The globalising trend pervading all specialized domains has also affected the legal field, where an international perspective is becoming more and more widespread. However, in spite of the growing efforts of the international community to guarantee greater and greater harmonisation in legislation and procedures, local constraints and specific cultural aspects still represent a relevant conditioning factor. This is clearly visible in the normative texts in use in the various contexts which show discrepancies deriving not only from differing legal and cultural systems, but also from the use of different linguistic codes. Indeed, nowadays many of the texts in use at a local level are the result of a process of translation or adaptation of more general documents formulated at an international level. The formulation of legal concepts in normative texts in a multilingual/multicultural context is greatly conditioned by specific sociocultural and economic factors strictly depending on the different cultural, linguistic and legal environments in which it takes place. The investigation of the process of adaptation of the international legislation to different national realities has pointed out several cases in which the source text offers the input on the basis of which new autonomous texts are created taking into consideration the needs of the final users, a result in line with the findings of other scholars (e.g. Vermeer 1996).

The analysis of arbitration texts has shown that, although the Model Law has been created with the purpose of achieving the highest degree of harmonisation (the single countries have been recommended to make as few changes as possible when incorporating them into their legal systems), total harmonisation has not been realized, with the consequence that it is no longer unanimously perceived as a final and attainable goal. Indeed, the current prevalent interpretation of the harmonisation process emphasizes a common understanding of the meaning of terms and practices rather than total adoption and blind acceptance of proposed models (Borris 1999: 11). In spite of the desire to make international arbitration procedures "unbound" (Paulsson 1981) by local constraints, cultural aspects still represent an important conditioning factor on the construction and interpretation of the legal discourse concerning this mediating practice.

In particular, cultural constraints have proved to be detectable in texts which are the result of a translation or a re-writing process such as those deriving from the process of adjustment and adaptation of a text issued by an international organisation to the legal and socio-cultural features of the various national target users. These international documents have been shown to possess clear traits of "hybrid" (Trosborg 1997: 146) discourse; indeed, the differentiations between the source and the resulting texts are the outcome of the conscious and deliberate decisions taken by the drafters of the local documents, and their final form shows that they "are arrived at as an outcome of negotiations between cultures and the norms and conventions involved" (Trosborg 1997: 146).

Although the analysis reported in this paper has primarily concentrated on the discoursal properties of arbitration documents located in two specific contexts, its results may contribute to a wider understanding of how legal texts are constructed, interpreted and used in multilingual and multicultural contexts.

According to this more general perspective, the discussion of certain linguistic and textual features has provided interesting insights, for example, into how sociocultural factors are influenced by common law systems on the one hand and civil law systems on the other, or by different target readers with their own legal culture and professional expectations. In this way, even a limited investigation of a specific case such as the one presented in this paper may be of help for a better knowledge of legal language seen from an international perspective and for a more detailed understanding of linguistic and textual phenomena closely linked to cross-cultural traits.

References

Belotti, U. (2002). "The language of Italian arbitration rules in English: some measurable aspects". *Linguistica e Filologia* 15, 113-141.

Belotti, U. (2003). "Generic integrity in Italian arbitration rules". In: V. Bhatia, C. Candlin and M. Gotti (eds.), *Legal Discourse in Multilingual and Multicultural Contexts: Arbitration Texts in Europe.* Bern: Peter Lang, 19-40.

Bhatia, V., Candlin, C. and J. Engberg (eds.) (Forthcoming). *Legal Discourse across Cultures and Systems*, Amsterdam: Benjamins.

Bhatia, V., Candlin, C. and M. Gotti (eds.) (2003), *Legal Discourse in Multilingual and Multicultural Contexts: Arbitration Texts in Europe.* Bern: Peter Lang.

Bhatia V., Candlin, C., Engberg, J. and A. Trosborg (eds.) (2003). *Multilingual and Multicultural Contexts of Legislation: An International Perspective.* Frankfurt am Main: Peter Lang.

Borris, C. (1999). "The reconciliation of conflicts between Common Law and Civil Law principles in the arbitration process". In: S. N. Frommel and B. Rider (eds.), *Conflicting Legal Cultures in Commercial Arbitration: Old Issues and New Trends.* The Hague: Kluwer Law International, 1-18.

Coulmas, F. (1991). "The language trade in the Asian Pacific". *Journal of Asian Pacific Communication* 2/1, 1-27.

David, R. (1980). *English Law and French Law.* London: Stevens.

Fletcher, G. P. (1999). "Fair and reasonable: a linguistic glimpse into the American legal mind". In: R. Sacco and L. Castellani (eds.), *Les multiples langues du droit européen uniforme.* Turin: L'Harmattan Italia, 57-70.

Gotti, M. (2003). *Specialized Discourse. Linguistic Features and Changing Conventions.* Bern: Peter Lang.

Gustafsson, M. (1975). *Some Syntactic Properties of English Law Language.* Turku: University of Turku, Department of English.

Lazareff, S. (1999). "International arbitration: towards a common procedural approach". In: S. N. Frommel and B. Rider (eds.), *Conflicting Legal Cultures in Commercial Arbitration: Old Issues and New Trends*. The Hague: Kluwer Law International, 31-38.

Mellinkoff, D. (1963). *The Language of the Law*. Boston: Little, Brown and Co.

Nadelmann, K. and A. von Mehren (1967). "Equivalences in treaties in the conflicts field". *The American Journal of Comparative Law* 15, 195-203.

Nida, E. (2001). *Context in Translating*, Amsterdam: Benjamins.

Paulsson, J. (1981). "Arbitration unbound: award detached from the law of its country of origin". *International and Comparative Law Quarterly* 30, 358-387.

Salmasi, S. (2003). "English as a *Lingua Franca* at the European Union: the undertakings of pride?". *Recherches Anglaises et Nord-Américaines* 36, 113-120.

Salmi-Tolonen, T. (2003). "Arbitration law as action: an analysis of the Finnish Arbitration Act". In: V. Bhatia, C. Candlin and M. Gotti (eds.), *Legal Discourse in Multilingual and Multicultural Contexts: Arbitration Texts in Europe*. Bern: Peter Lang, 313-332.

Šarčević, S. (1997). *New Approach to Legal Translation*. The Hague: Kluwer Law International.

Solan, L. (1993). *The Language of Judges*. Chicago: The University of Chicago Press.

Taniguchi, Y. (1998). "Is there a growing international arbitration culture? An observation from Asia". In: A. J. van den Berg (gen. ed.), *International Dispute Resolution: Towards an International Arbitration Culture*. Dordrecht: Kluwer Law International, 31-40.

Tiersma, P. (1999). *Legal Language*. Chicago: The University of Chicago Press.

Trosborg, A. (1997). "Translating hybrid political texts". In: A. Trosborg (ed.) *Text Typology and Translation*. Amsterdam: Benjamins, 145-158.

Vermeer, H. (1996). *A Skopos Theory of Translation (Some Arguments For and Against)*. Heidelberg: Textcontext Wissenschaft.

Weston, M. (1995). "Translating at the European Court of Human Rights". *Terminologies et tradition* 3, 121-134.

Yano, Y. (2001). "World Englishes in 2000 and beyond". *World Englishes* 20(2), 119-131.

Susan Šarčević
University of Rijeka
Croatia

MAKING MULTILINGUALISM WORK IN THE ENLARGED EUROPEAN UNION

1. Introduction

When welcoming the staff members from the new Member States, Juhani Lönnroth, Director General of the European Commission's Directorate-General for Translation (DGT), called the May enlargement of 2004 a "truly historic event" marking the "disappearance of the old, divided Europe and the beginning of a new era on our continent". Calling upon the newcomers to help "build the 'New Europe'", he expressed confidence that they would succeed in translating the Commission's documents "with quality, precision and speed", thus ensuring that "the Union can work efficiently" (Lönnroth 2004: 1) in 20 official languages, soon to become 23.

Focusing on legal translation, this paper examines what the Commission has done to meet its obligation to "draft" Community legislation in all official languages of the enlarged EU. Regarding the challenge of enlargement mainly as "organizational" in nature (McCluskey 2001: 7), the DGT had hoped to bridge the transitional period by implementing a series of actions to match supply and demand. After the date of accession, however, it soon became clear that quantity control in itself was insufficient to enable the DGT to return to "business as usual" within the targeted time period. From the legal point of view, the main challenge of enlargement is safeguarding the uniform interpretation of Community law in the new multilingual setting; however, this is possible only if the authentic texts of Community legislation are reliable in all language versions. Shifting the emphasis from quantity to quality control, this paper argues that the key to making multilingualism work in the enlarged EU is to improve the quality of the basic texts of draft legislation by implementing the interinstitutional drafting guidelines designed to take account of the multilingual aspects of Community legislation. This will not only facilitate the translation process but also improve the quality and thus reliability of the authentic texts in all language versions, ultimately promoting the uniform interpretation of Community law in the enlarging Union.

2. Legal basis of multilingualism in the EU

The language policy of the European Union is truly unique, not just because of the unprecedented number of official languages but also because it guarantees equal rights for all official languages, regardless of the percentage of population of Union citizens speaking each language. The languages of the EU are part of its immense and diverse cultural heritage and are regarded as the most distinguishing feature of the national identity of the Member States. As such, it is sometimes claimed that the principle of absolute language equality is non-negotiable on the basis of the Treaty. Technically speaking, this is not correct.

Article 6, which was incorporated into the Treaty establishing the European Union, obliges the Union to respect the national identities of its Member States but does not explicitly mention language. Moreover, the very first Treaties laid down no rules on language matters and did not even mention multilingualism. Instead, there was (and still is) a provision empowering the Council, acting unanimously, to determine the rules governing the languages of the institutions of the Community (now Article 290, EC Treaty). On the basis of that Article, the Council of Ministers adopted Council Regulation No. 1 of 1958, which provided that the official languages and the working languages of the institutions of the Community shall be Dutch, French, German and Italian (Article 1) (see Appendix I).

As to the difference between official and working languages, it is generally accepted that the "official languages are those used by the institutions in their relations with the Member States and their nationals", whereas the working languages are "those used internally by the respective institutions for the adoption of documents" (Berteloot 2001: 7-8). Article 6 of Council Regulation No. 1 empowers the institutions to stipulate in their rules of procedure which of the languages are to be used in specific cases. For example, according to the Commission's Rules of Procedure, in formal meetings, instruments adopted in the course of a meeting, by written procedure or the empowerment procedure are to be submitted in the authentic language or languages, i.e. all the official languages of the Communities in the case of instruments of general application and the language or languages to whom they are addressed in other cases. (Article 18, Rules of Procedure of the Commission, 2001). As a rule, the working languages of the Commission in informal meetings are English, French and occasionally German (see Schübel-Pfister 2004: 59-67; Creech 2005: 24).

Pursuant to Regulation No. 1, regulations and other documents of general application shall be drafted in all official languages (Article 4), and the *Official Journal* shall be published in all official languages (Article 5). As a manifestation of the principle of absolute language equality, the texts of Community instruments are equally authentic in all language versions. The authentic texts are identified in the language clause in the final provisions of the particular instrument. For example, the standard language clause of treaties states that the particular treaty is "drawn up in a single original" in all the official languages (plus Irish), "the texts in each of these languages being equally authentic". The principle of equal authenticity is important because it puts all language versions – the basic text(s) and authoritative translations – on an equal footing for the purpose of interpretation in the sense that no single text should prevail in the event of an ambiguity or textual diversity between the various language versions. From the legal point of view, all the authentic texts are regarded as originals. Although all but the basic text are produced by translation, they are not indicated as translations, and lawyers even refrain from referring to them as translations, so as to avoid any implication of inferiority (see Šarčević 2000: 20, 64; Wagner, Bech and Martínez 2002: 7-8).

3. The linguistic regime and enlargement

Fearing that the translation mechanism would become unmanageable and too costly, the language question has been raised at each of the previous waves of enlargement and negotiated anew in each Act of Accession (see summary in Moratinos Johnston 2000: 55-59). When Denmark, Ireland and the United Kingdom acceded to the European Communities in 1973, it was even uncertain whether English would become an official language and whether the English texts would be accorded equal authenticity (Akehurst 1972: 21). With this question positively resolved, the number of official languages rose to six, then to seven and nine with the accession of Greece in 1981, followed by Portugal and Spain in 1986. In 1992, Jacques Delors, then president of the European Commission, went so far as to question the feasibility of retaining the principle of absolute language equality (*The Economist*, 11 April 1992: 32). Again in 1994, during the French Presidency of the Council, a proposal was launched to restrict the number of official and working languages to five, as in the Community Trade Mark Office. Such attempts, however, resulted in political conflict. Thereafter, the established language policy was reaffirmed and the number of official languages climbed to eleven with the accession of Finland, Sweden and Austria in 1995.

On the eve of the 2004 enlargement, serious doubts were again raised, at least unofficially, about the feasibility of retaining the old language policy (e.g. at the conference "Multilingualism and EU Enlargement", held in Brussels on 10 February 2000). In addition to the usual fears about the high cost, inconvenience and inefficiency of multilingualism, concerns were expressed because of the large number of candidate countries and the fact that all of the new languages are "small" and relatively little known in the existing Member States (see Šarčević 2002: 243 and Manners 2000: 124). While all proposals to reduce the number of official languages were flatly rejected by politicians, support grew in certain circles for renewed proposals to reduce the number of working languages to a group of five, three or two core languages (see Schübel-Pfister 2004: 484-500); some even envisaged a European Union with one official language (Dupont 1998: 165, Moréteau 1999: 156-161; see also the comments by Creech 2005: 39-45). Although Kapteyn and VerLoren acknowledged that it was becoming all the more pressing "to apply more widely the practice of using one or two languages", they identified three situations in which the principle of language equality should be retained:

> In so far as Community acts have legal effect, it is important that they be available to Community citizens in their own language. Similarly, it is important to safeguard the use of a person's own language in the European Parliament and, in so far as litigants are concerned, before the Court (Kapteyn and VerLoren 1998: 107).

As regards Community legislation, one should keep in mind that the Community *acquis* is legally binding and most Community acts have general application, i.e. they are applicable in all Member States. Moreover, Community law has precedence over national law. Since the rights and obligations arising from the treaties and Community acts are binding on all of the Union's citizens and business organizations, it follows that all have the democratic right to have access to the law in their own language. Moreover, Community law must be enforced not only by the European Court of Justice but also by the national courts of all Member States. Hence, the importance of the principle of equal authenticity comes into play. Theoretically, national judges are bound by all authentic language versions; however, in practice they tend to rely primarily on the relevant text in their own language when interpreting Community law, unless an ambiguity or obscurity "forces" them to consult one or more of the other language versions.

By the same token, the objective of language equality is to guarantee equality before the law to all of the Union's citizens. Ironically, the very objective of multilingualism is endangered by the undeniable fact that linguistic diversity poses a constant threat to the uniform interpretation of Community law. Although all the equally authentic texts of a single instrument are presumed to have the same meaning, lawyers are the first to admit that this is a legal fiction and that legal translation is at best approximation (Kuner 1991: 958). In this context, Braselmann had earlier warned that there can be no uniform law for all in all EU languages (1992: 73). In regard to the growing number of authentic texts of a legal instrument, Tabory once remarked that "[t]he probability of confusion, errors and discrepancies is multiplied in direct proportion to the number of authentic texts" (1980: 146). For our purpose, this would mean that the threat to the uniform interpretation of Community law increases with each additional authentic language version.

Despite the disadvantages of multilingualism, the EU continues to remain firmly committed to its founding principle of multilingualism based on language equality. Since a reduction in the official and/or working languages would require a unanimous vote of the Council of Ministers, any radical change was clearly out of question. Moreover, any change in the official status would amount to an outright act of discrimination, undoubtedly against the least populous Member States. In light of the political sensitivity of the language issue, the politicians willingly agreed to retain the old language policy, which can now be considered non-negotiable.

Proof of this came in April 2005 with the signature of the Act of Accession between the Republic of Bulgaria and Romania and the Member States of the European Union, in which Romanian and Bulgarian are recognized as authentic languages of the Treaties (see Appendix II), as well as official and working languages to be used by the EU institutions from the date of their accession. Not to be outdone, Ireland requested a change in the status of Irish, which has been a Treaty language since 1973. Under a special agreement with the government of Ireland, only primary legislation and certain other pieces of legislation have been translated into Irish. On 13 June 2005, the Council amended Regulation No. 1 to include Irish as the 21st official and working language of the European Union (OJ 2005 L156/3). For practical reasons, the Council decided that only regulations adopted by the European Parliament and the Council under the co-decision procedure will have to be available in Irish. Other legislative acts will be exempted for a transition period of five years to allow time to train and recruit translators.[1]

4. Incorporating nine new languages

Incorporating nine new languages – Czech, Estonian, Hungarian, Latvian, Lithuanian, Maltese, Polish, Slovak and Slovene – in one go created an unprecedented challenge for EU institutions. At the same time, they have had to cope with a significant increase in demand for translation, which has grown steadily with the expansion of the scope of EU activities. Since the institutions are empowered to stipulate which of the languages are to be used in specific cases, it was left to each of them to find ways of making concessions to make the new system work. Generally speaking, most of the concessions have affected the working languages used in various situations. The Commission and, in particular,

[1] This arrangement is similar to the agreement reached with the government of Malta. At the request of the Maltese authorities, the Council adopted a derogation by which for a period of three years, beginning on 1 May 2004, the European Union does not have to publish all legislative acts in Maltese in the EU *Official Journal* (OJ 2004 L169/1).

the DGT have had to adopt some innovative measures in order to meet their legal obligations.

The Commission commenced preparations for the latest enlargement back in 1996 by creating the Technical Assistance Information Exchange Office (TAIEX), whose mandate was later extended to assist the candidate countries of Central and Eastern Europe in harmonizing their laws with European law and setting up national Translation Coordination Units to translate the Community *acquis* into the national language of each country. As usual, the Herculean task of translating existing primary and secondary Community legislation was the responsibility of the governments of the candidate countries, not the EU. For its part, TAIEX organized translation courses, provided technological assistance and helped terminologists in the candidate countries find proper terminology for concepts of Community law (see Gozzi 2001: 24-28).

The most extensive reforms were carried out within the Commission itself by adopting a series of action plans to match supply and demand for translation. In 2001 the Commission's action plan for the simplification and rationalization of the linguistic regime introduced a number of modernization measures, including better planning and coordination among services, establishing a permanent dialogue between the language services and their clients, better use of support staff, new technologies and external resources, as well as the reduction of translation work on draft documents (Commission press release IP/01/1869 of 20/12/2001). In particular, the Commission attempted to curb demand by implementing actions to streamline the production, translation and legal revision of documents within its decision-making process. As before, the working languages of the Commission, i.e. its procedural languages used internally for the adoption of documents, remain English, French and German; however, the practice of examining documents on the basis of three language versions only (the so-called "oral" procedure) has been extended to the "written" decision procedure used for documents of a more technical nature. As a result, documentation is no longer required in all working languages for the "written" decision procedure. Upon finalization, however, all documents of a general legislative or regulatory nature must be translated into all official languages before being sent to the other institutions (Commission press release IP/01/1869 of 20/12/2001).

Under an Action Plan adopted in 2002, the terminological databases developed in the candidate countries were incorporated into the existing EU databases and language support was provided for legal revisers from the candidate countries who work with the Commission on producing authentic versions of Community legislation in their national languages. Recruitment for in-house and freelance translators for the new languages began in 2003, when field offices of the DGT were set up in the capitals of all ten accession countries except Cyprus.[2]

---

[2] See http://www.europa.eu.int/comm/dgs/translation/enlargement/2004.

Despite extensive preparations, the DGT found itself in a precarious position on the date of accession. Among other things, its high hopes that technological innovations would significantly increase productivity failed to meet expectations. Already plagued by a translation backlog of some 60,000 pages, the DGT and the Commission in general were forced to adopt more stringent measures to match supply and demand (Commission press release, IP/04/679 of 26/5/2004). With new funds appropriated, the DGT stepped up its campaign to increase the translation capacity by recruiting and training internal and external translators for each of the new languages. By the end of December 2004, 296 full-time translators were in place in Luxembourg and the field offices; by the end of June 2005, the number had increased to 429 (Commission press release, Memo/05/269 of 20/07/2005).[3] However, the productivity of the translators for the new languages was "not fully in line with expectations". According to the press release, this was due mainly to "the high training and technical coaching needs among the newly recruited translators, who had good language skills but little professional experience or knowledge of EU procedure and terminology" (Memo/05/269 of 20/07/2005).

For the first time, translators are required to translate not only into their principal language but also out of their principal language into a relay or pivot language, usually English, French, German, Italian and Spanish (cf. Creech 2005: 27). The message is then translated by another colleague into the requested target language. The so-called relay method is used for uncommon language combinations such as from Latvian into Greek. As of January 2005, 245 translators of the old EU-15 languages were studying the new languages and a number of them are already sufficiently proficient to translate from their "new" language into one or more of the "old" languages (Commission press release, Memo/05/10 of 13/01/2005). As before, however, all Community legislation is translated by DGT translators from the language of the basic text, either English or French,[4] into their principal language.

As a demand management control, the Commission set priorities on the documents to be translated, first priority being given to documents for which it has a legal obligation or political commitment to translate. These include all

[3] The recruitment of translators per language by the end of June 2005 is as follows: CS-45, ET-51, HU-51, LT-63, LV-47, MT-22, PL-50, SK-51, SL-49.

[4] It is estimated that 80% of the Commission's documents were originally drafted in French, until the 1990's, when the balance began to swing in favour of English. In 1997, 45.4% of the Commission's documents were drafted in English, 40.4% in French and 5.4% in German; in 2000, 55% were drafted in English, 33% in French and 4% in German; in 2004, 62% were drafted in English, 26% in French and 3.1% in German (*Translating for a Multilingual Community*, 2005).

proposals for legislation, public messages to European citizens and companies,[5] autonomous acts of the Commission, and all merger, state-aid and competition decisions. For non-obligatory translation requests, realistic deadlines are negotiated, which are often longer than those set for the previous 11 official languages. As a result, the Council and the Parliament may in some cases "start their internal procedures with documents in the EU-15 languages only, knowing that the remaining (EU-10) versions will be provided at a later stage". This situation should be back to normal when recruitment is completed by the end of the transition period.

Another effective measure of demand control is the requirement to shorten the length of certain documents. For example, the maximum length of a Commission Communication has been reduced from an average of 37 pages to 15 (Commission press release, Memo/05/10 of 13/01/2005). The insistence on length control has also helped improve the clarity of the original message, thus facilitating the task of the translators. Even prior to the most recent enlargement, special attention was devoted to improving the linguistic quality of original documents drafted primarily in English or French. In response to continued complaints about the "contaminated" English or French of original documents drafted by non-native speakers, the DGT established an Editing Service in 2002, entrusting it with the task of revising original texts in English and French before they are sent for translation.

5. Improving the quality of Community legislation

The basic texts of legislation are originally drawn up by politicians and subject experts, redrafted by lawyer linguists of the Legal Service of the Commission and translated by translators of the Commission's DGT into the other official languages. All language versions of draft legislation are revised by lawyer linguists of the Legal Revisers Group of the Legal Service of the Commission before being sent to the Council and the Parliament. The lawyer linguists of the Legal Service of the Council are responsible for the final editing and verification of the concordance of all language versions prior to publication.

The Legal Services of the three institutions involved in the legislative process – the Commission, the Council and the Parliament – have played an important role in proposing and implementing guidelines on the quality of drafting Community legislation. Improving the quality of the basic texts of draft legislation is bound to have an impact on the work of the translators, ultimately

[5] Pursuant to Article 21 of the EC Treaty, every citizen of the Union has the right to write to any of the EU institutions in one of the EU official languages and to receive an answer in the same language.

bringing about a marked improvement in the quality of the authentic texts of all language versions. One of the main elements of the campaign for better lawmaking, as it is now called, is the emphasis on clarity (Commission Report to the European Council, Better lawmaking 1999: 5).[6] It is well known that the quality of a translation often depends on the quality of the original document, in particular its clarity. It goes without saying that the translator must understand the source text in order to produce a correct and accurate translation that will be understood by the target citizens and business organizations affected by the particular instrument, as well as by the judges, officials and others responsible for interpreting and enforcing the law. A well-drafted basic text has numerous benefits: citizens and business organizations are able to identify their rights and obligations, thus promoting legal certainty and reducing the number of disputes. Furthermore, and perhaps more important, uniform law is promoted, thus ensuring the equality of all the Union's citizens before the law, regardless of the language version of Community law applied. The campaign for improving the quality of Community legislation dates back to 1992; however, the drafting guidelines proposed were not put into practice until much later. In the end, it appears that the new drafting guidelines can be instrumental in making multilingualism work in the enlarged EU.

Some sources attribute the difficulties experienced during the ratification of the Treaty on European Union mainly to language. Although the Treaty existed in all the official languages, the language used was considered "too obscure to convey the substance of the concepts and ideas central to the Union" (Berteloot 2001: 9). Responding to the growing demand for transparency, the Edinburgh European Council of 1992 recognized the need for clearer and simpler acts complying with principles of good legislative drafting. Thereafter, the Council passed the Resolution of 8 June 1993 on the quality of drafting of Community legislation (OJ C 166, 17.6.1993), in which concrete suggestions were made for simplifying and clarifying the language of legislative texts without changing the substance. In 1995, the Commission issued a document on General guidelines for legislative policy (SEC(1995) 2255/7,18.1.1996), followed in 1996 by its first SLIM pilot project for improving, simplifying or even repealing existing Community legislation (COM (96) 559 final). These soft law rules found a more authoritative source in the Declaration on the quality of drafting annexed to the Treaty of Amsterdam. By virtue of that Declaration, the Parliament, Council and Commission adopted the Interinstitutional Agreement of 22 December 1998 containing common guidelines to improve the quality of drafting Community

[6] The *Fight the Fog* campaign, initiated in the Directorate-General for Translation in 1998, should also be mentioned in this context. While both campaigns emphasize the need for clarity in legislative texts, the Fight-the-Fog campaign goes further by encouraging drafters to use plain language. See examples in Cutts 2001.

legislation (OJ C73, 17.3.1999) (see Timmermans 1998: 39-50). To aid in the implementation of those guidelines, the three Legal Services issued the *Joint Practical Guide* (last updated in 2003), which is to be used in conjunction with other more specific instruments, such as the Council's *Manual of Precedents* (as last updated in July 2002), the Commission's *Manual on Legislative Drafting* (as last updated in 1997), the *Interinstitutional Style Guide* (1998) or the models in *LegisWrite* (drafted by the Commission in 1999).

The common guidelines are significant for translation because they make drafters aware of the effects of multilingualism on drafting quality and the need to take account of the hybrid character of Community law when drafting legislation. While Community law is a supranational law distinct from the national laws of the Member States, it is also distinguished by the meeting of the diverse legal traditions of the Member States, each with its own concepts and terminologies. Moreover, Community law is negotiated to a much greater degree than national law and is thus the result of political compromise or *droit diplomatique*, as it is often called (Timmermans 1997: 41). As such, the basic text often contains a number of intentional ambiguities, obscurities and vague points. In such cases, any attempt by drafters and translators to clarify the text runs the risk of upsetting the delicately achieved compromise and misrepresenting the intent of the lawmakers (Šarčević 2000: 204). Therefore, lawmakers are also called upon to contribute to clarity by expressing their intent as clearly as possible. Otherwise, provisions that are not clear may be interpreted restrictively by the Community courts. If that happens, the result could be just the opposite of what was actually intended by the lawmakers.

6. Respecting multilingualism when drafting Community acts

Formulated in mandatory language, the guidelines in the *Joint Practical Guide* take on the appearance of binding rules rather than recommendations. For example, Guideline 1 reads: "Community legislative acts shall be drafted clearly, simply and precisely." This is further explained in point 1.1:

> The drafting of a legislative act must be:
> - clear, easy to understand and unambiguous;
> - simple, concise, containing no unnecessary elements;
> - precise, leaving no uncertainty in the mind of the reader.

The first reference to multilingualism in point 1.2.1 stresses the importance of the principle of drafting clear, simple and precise legislation in Community legislative acts, "which must fit into a system which is not only complex, but also multicultural and multilingual".

6.1. Additional requirements when drafting multilingual legislation

Dealing with multilingualism, Guideline 5 admonishes drafters to take account of the multilingual nature of Community legislation, reminding them that respecting multilingualism "entails additional requirements beyond those which apply to the drafting of a national legislative text" (5.1). The general rule in Guideline 5 reads:

> Throughout the process leading to their adoption, draft acts shall be framed in terms and sentence structures which respect the multilingual nature of Community legislation; concepts or terminology specific to any one national legal system are to be used with care.

By way of explanation, point 5.2 requires the original text to be "particularly simple, clear and direct, since any over-complexity or ambiguity, however slight, could result in inaccuracies, approximations or real mistranslations in one or more of the other Community languages". While the use of lists in provisions is effective to emphasize individual points, if misused it can create confusion or unintended ambiguity, leaving the provision open to contradictory interpretations. This is the case in the following definition of market prices, which is cited in the *Joint Practical Guide* as an example of drafting to be avoided.

> The market prices of [product X] shall be the prices ex-factory, exclusive of national taxes and charges:
>
> a) of the fresh product packages in blocks;
> b) raised by an amount of [EUR X] to take account of the transport costs necessary.

The ambiguity can be avoided by restructuring the provision in two paragraphs. In the preferred text below, the misplaced modifier in point a) is incorporated into the first paragraph following "prices ex-factory", thus achieving correct word order which is essential for comprehension in English. The main ambiguity, however, is caused by point b), which could be interpreted as meaning that the market price includes the price ex-factory plus transport costs. To clarify this matter, the information in point b) is placed in a separate paragraph, leaving no doubt that the market price does not include transport costs. The use of the mandatory *shall* eliminates any discretion as to whether or not the transport costs are to be added:

> The market prices of [product X] shall be the prices ex-factory of the fresh product packaged in blocks, exclusive of national taxes and charges.

> Those prices shall be raised by an amount of [EUR X] to take account of the transport costs necessary.

6.2. The plea for simplification

Highlighted in Guideline 4, the plea for simplification plays a central role in respecting multilingualism. In this sense, drafters are advised to facilitate translation by avoiding "overly complicated sentences, comprising several phrases, subordinate clauses or parentheses (interpolated clauses)" (5.2.2). This, of course, is not new; neither is the recommendation in Guideline 4 that each sentence should express one idea only and that there must be a logical link between the ideas expressed in an article (4.4). Furthermore, each article should contain only one provision or rule and "its structure must be as simple as possible" (4.5). This is very similar to the basic drafting rule in Switzerland, known as the Eugen Huber Rule after the father of the Swiss Civil Code of 1907 (see Šarčević 2005: 288). It is not by chance that clarity has long been the main drafting principal of Swiss legislation, which is drawn up in three equally authentic language versions.

The example of drafting to be avoided cited in the *Joint Practical Guide* violates the above rule. Written in one sentence, the provision expresses two ideas, the second of which is introduced by the often problematic phrase "subject to":

> All parties to the agreement must have access to the results of the work, subject to the understanding that research institutes have the possibility to reserve use of the results for subsequent research projects.

In the preferred text below, the idea expressed in the "subject to" phrase is formulated in a separate sentence and placed in a new paragraph. Since the main purpose of the enacting terms of an instrument is to set forth obligations and prohibitions, grant permissions, establish rights and confer authorizations, it is essential that drafters and translators use the proper conventional drafting forms in each language to achieve the intended effect. The words *have the possibility* are inappropriate and thus are replaced in the preferred text with the modal *may*, making it clear that the permission expresses an exception to the general rule in paragraph 1:

> All parties to the agreement must have access to the results of the work.
>
> However, research institutes may reserve use of the results for subsequent research projects.

6.3. Using proper language to express obligations and prohibitions

Like drafters, translators must always take account of the type of act concerned and, in particular, whether it is binding or not. Similarly, they must be aware of the purpose of the various parts of each act and use proper language accordingly. As stressed in point 2.3.1 of Guideline 2, "[t]he choice of verb and tense varies between different types of act and the different languages, and also between the recitals and the enacting terms". Particularly problematic is the use of *shall* to express obligations in English, whereas French uses the present tense (point 2.3.2). *Should* is not mandatory and thus is to be used only in the preamble of binding acts. Since different languages use different forms to express obligations, in my opinion, this is one of the main sources of mistranslations and one of the most sensitive, as any ambiguity in this regard leads to different results in practice, thus threatening the uniform interpretation of Community law. As for prohibitions, the weaker form *may not* is sometimes interpreted as discretionary, whereas *shall not* makes it clear that any violation of the prohibition is subject to sanction. To clarify this issue in the provision concerning actions of members of the Commission, the Treaty establishing a Constitution for Europe provides in paragraph 2(3) of Article III-347 that "[t]he members of the Commission shall not, during their term of office, engage in any other occupation, whether gainful or not", thereby replacing the weaker "may not" in Article 213 of the EC Treaty. Translators should follow this example when formulating prohibitions in the other language versions.

6.4. Clarifying the grammatical relationship between different parts of the sentence

The basic drafting rule in Guideline 1 admonishes drafters to respect the rules of grammar and punctuation as this "makes it easier to understand the text properly in the drafting language as well as to translate it into the other languages" (1.4.2). As a means of respecting multilingualism, this issue is taken up again in point 5.2.3 of Guideline 5, which reads:

> The grammatical relationship between the different parts of the sentence must be clear. There should be no doubt, for example, as to whether an object relates to the verb in the main clause or to that in a subordinate clause.

Another grammar-related problem is the difficulty to recognize whether a modifying clause or phrase necessarily restricts the meaning of the word it modifies. Differences in syntax can lead to semantic divergences between the various language versions and thus to different interpretations, sometimes resulting in litigation. This occurred in *Bayerische Hypotheken v. Wechselbank AG*, in which the German *Bundesgerichtshof* requested the European Court of Justice (ECJ) to clarify the meaning of Article 1(1) of the EEC Directive 85/577 of 20 December 1985, which defines the scope of application of the doorstep selling directive. Greatly simplified, the question at issue was whether a guarantee (*suretyship*, *Bürgschaft*) under German law falls within the scope of the Directive. While the wording of the English text suggests that the Directive does not apply to a guarantee because a guarantee is not a contract "under which a trader supplies goods and services to a consumer", the wording of the German text favours a broader interpretation that allows the Directive to apply to all contracts concluded between a trader who supplies goods or services and a consumer: "Diese Richtlinie gilt für Verträge, die zwischen einem Gewerbetreibenden, der Waren liefert oder Dienstleistungen erbringt, und einem Verbraucher geschlossen werden [...]." In its decision of 17 March 1998, the ECJ favoured the broad sense of the German text, ruling that, in principle, a guarantee could fall under the Directive on the basis of its accessory character (Schulte-Nölke 1999: 150-152).[7] A comparison of the other authentic texts at that time reveals that the German text coincides with all the other language versions, with the exception of the Swedish and Finnish texts, which were subsequent translations based on the English "translation" (see Šarčević 2002: 260-261).[8]

6.5. Terminological considerations

As regards terminology, drafters and translators alike are called upon to respect terminological consistency as a means of promoting the uniform interpretation of Community law. In this sense, Guideline 6 reads: "The

[7] However, the ECJ went a step further by restricting the application of the Directive to guarantees for non-commercial loans.

[8] The other authentic language versions of the disputed provision (except Greek) read as follows: FR: La présente directive s'applique aux contrats conclus entre un commerçant fournissant des biens ou des services et un consommateur... ; IT: La presente direttiva si applica ai contratti stipulati tra un commerciante che fornisce beni o servizi e un consumatore... ; NL: Deze richtlijn is van toepassing op overeenkomsten die tussen een handelaar die goederen levert of diensten verricht, en een consument worden gesloten... ; DA: Dette direktiv gaelder for aftaler indgaaet mellem en erhvervsdrivende, der levereer varer eller tjenesteydelser, og en forbruger... ; ES: La presente Directiva se aplicará a los contratos celebrados entre un comerciante que suministre bienes o servicios y un consumidor... ; PT: A presente directiva é aplicável aos contratos celebrados entre um comerciante que forneça bens ou serviços e um consumidor... ; SV: Detta direktiv skall gälla för avtal där en näringsidkare tillhandaller en konsument varor eller tjänster, när besöket inte äger rum pa konsumentens uttryckliga begäran...; FI: Tätä direktiiviä sovelletaan sellaisiin elinkeinonharjoittajien ja kuluttajien välisiin sopimuksiin tavaran toimittamisesta tai palvelun suorittamisesta, jotka on tehty...[.]

terminology used in a given act shall be consistent both internally and with acts already in force, especially in the same field. Identical concepts shall be expressed in the same terms, as far as possible without departing from their meaning in ordinary, legal or technical language." Since the use of synonyms in legislative texts causes confusion and encourages litigation, drafters and translators are required to repeat the same terms over and over again and to use standard formulae whenever appropriate (Šarčević 2000: 118). Similarly, citations from existing texts (treaty, regulation, directive etc.) must be clearly indicated and the authentic wording of the particular provision used in each language version (5.5.1).

To facilitate translation by promoting clarity of the basic text, point 5.2.4 of Guideline 5 advises drafters to avoid "jargon, certain vogue words and Latin expressions used in a sense other than their generally accepted legal meaning". In particular, as Heikki Mattila has shown, Latin expressions must be used with care as their meaning sometimes differs between the common law and civil law systems (2005: 77-83). Above all, drafters should avoid the use of expressions and phrases – legal and otherwise – which are "too specific to the author's own language or legal system" as this "increases the risk of translation problems" (5.3). For example, the French *sans préjudice* is cited in the *Joint Practical Guide* as a common expression to avoid. Having "no equivalent in other Community languages", it can be translated only by using "circumlocutions and approximations, which inevitably result in semantic divergences between the various language versions" (5.3.1). Although the translation equivalents of *sans préjudice* had already become well established in the EU-15 languages, its literal equivalent in English *without prejudice to* caused considerable confusion for those who translated the Community *acquis* from English into the new languages.

Due to the inherent conceptual incongruence of legal terms between legal systems, the greatest threat to the uniform interpretation of Community law is the use of "legal terms which are too closely linked to national legal systems" (5.3.2). This warning applies to both drafters and translators. For their part, translators are advised to avoid using national terms of their own legal systems which are only partially equivalent with the source concepts, as this inevitably leads to misinterpretations by national judges (Šarčević 2001: 83). On the other hand, using linguistic equivalents also causes interpretation problems since national judges are unfamiliar with the underlying concepts, thus resulting in diverse interpretations which can adversely affect the rights and obligations of the Union's citizens. Therefore, neutral terms should be used whenever possible (cf. Šarčević 2000: 255; also Akehurst 1972: 260). As pointed out in the *Joint Practical Guide*, the concept of *faute* is well known to French law; however, "there is no direct equivalent in other legal systems, in particular in English and German law". Therefore, depending on the context, drafters are advised to use neutral terms such as *illégalité* or *manquement* (in relation to an obligation), which can easily be translated into other languages as *illegality* or *breach* (5.3.2).

6.6. Achieving fidelity to the target language

Traditionally, it was believed that accuracy could be achieved in translations of legislation only by imitating the letter of the law in the source text, i.e., by reproducing the words and even syntax as closely as possible. Having rejected the old principle of fidelity to the source text, the DGT encourages its translators to produce legislative texts that are faithful to the target language instead. According to Pescatore, former judge of the Court of Justice, the ideal translation of EU documents is written as if it were originally formulated in the target language (1999: 92), so as not to alienate national judges, lawyers and officials who interpret Community law in each of the Member States (Šarčević 2001: 88-89). This principle is considered so important that it has been incorporated into Guideline 5 on respecting the multilingualism of Community legislation. For the sake of clarity and better lawmaking, point 5.4 acknowledges that "those called on to apply or interpret the act in each Member State… must perceive it not as a 'translation' in a negative sense – but as a text which corresponds to a certain legislative style". In particular, translators are warned that "[t]exts peppered with loan words, literal translations or jargon which are hard to understand are the source of much of the criticism of Community legislation which is, as a result, regarded as alien".

To avoid such criticism, the Director-General of the DGT calls upon translators from the new Member States to be inventive with language (Lönnroth 2004: 2). However, such inventiveness requires considerable intuition, which presupposes both legal and linguistic competence: A skilled translator of legislation must know how, when and where he/she can be inventive and still respect the restrictions of legal translation. As regards the old EU-15 languages, Weyers comments that the Dutch translators of Community legislation generally fail to recognize and take advantage of their *Handlungsspielraum*, as a result of which the basic unit of translation is still the word or phrase and not the sentence or paragraph (1999: 173). With the recent emphasis on simplifying legislation, it is hoped that translators will take advantage of this opportunity to produce legislative texts that convey the legislative intent not only accurately and clearly but also in the spirit of the target language.

7. Outlook

As the number of official languages continues to grow, so does the strain on the principle of absolute language equality and the threat to uniform Community law. While the actions taken by the DGT to match supply and demand have undoubtedly helped the DGT to meet its legal obligations, it is above all the emphasis on achieving clarity in the basic texts that is instrumental in making multilingualism work by facilitating translation and ultimately improving the quality of Community acts in all official languages (cf. Flückiger 2005: 357-358). In my opinion, taking this development a step further could provide the key to the future in an even larger EU, in particular by encouraging greater interaction between drafters and translators. Traditionally, the translation of legislation has been an act of one-way communication without any participation on the part of the translators. However, experience in other jurisdictions has shown that the quality of multilingual legislation can be considerably improved by incorporating the translators into the legislative process at an earlier stage, preferably before adoption of the basic text (cf. Pescatore 1999: 94). On the one hand, this acquaints translators with the "true" legislative intent. More important, however, is the opportunity to allow the translator to become a reviser of the original text or *Mitredaktor*, as the Swiss call it (Šarčević 2000: 97-98). Forced to analyze every detail of the basic text, a critical translator tends to detect unclear or ambiguous formulations, misleading logical connectors and other linguistic defects that obstruct comprehension. If detected prior to adoption, such defects can be corrected, thus improving the basic text and the other language versions as well. Recognizing the merits of this strategy, point 5.5.2 of the *Joint Practical Guide* confirms that "comments from translators and, more generally, all departments which carry out a linguistic check of the text can be extremely useful" in identifying any errors and ambiguities in the original text. In many cases, "the best solution will be to alter the original, rather than the translation".

This can be regarded as the first step in converting the translator into a co-drafter. The process of co-drafting, i.e., producing legislation simultaneously or parallel in more than one language has been successfully introduced in Canada, Switzerland and Hong Kong (Šarčević 2005: 281-288 and 2000: 100-103). As for the feasibility of producing Community legislation by co-drafting, Tito Gallas, Head of the Legal Service of the Council, believes that this would be unmanageable due to the large number of official languages (2001: 115). On the other hand, an initial attempt at multilingual drafting has already been undertaken in the European Central Bank, where lawyer linguists of the "large" languages have been incorporated into the process of drafting ECB legal acts, which are then translated into the other official languages. This so-called "cradle to grave" approach involving lawyer linguists from initial drafting to final publication is relatively new but has already produced visible improvements in the quality of the basic text (Weenink-Griffiths 2005).

While the volume of legal acts produced by the ECB is considerably smaller, the practice of involving several languages in an early stage of the drafting process could be tested in the other institutions in the preparation of more important acts. Whereas an attempt to introduce a limited form of multilingual drafting would be ideal, any action taken to ensure interaction between drafters and translators in the preparation of Community legislation is bound to improve the quality of the basic text and ultimately the texts of the other language versions as well, thus making multilingualism work in an enlarging EU.

References

Akehurst, M. (1972). "Preparing the Authentic English Text of the E.E.C. Treaty". In: B. A. Wortley (ed.), *An Introduction to the Law of the European Economic Community*. Manchester: Manchester University Press, 20-31.

Berteloot, P. (2001). "Language Policy in the European Union". In: S. Šarčević (ed.), *Legal Translation, Preparation for Accession to the European Union*. Rijeka: Faculty of Law, 1-22.

Braselmann, P. (1992). "Übernationales Recht und Mehrsprachigkeit, Linguistische Überlegungen zu Sprachproblemen in EuGH-Urteilen". *EuR* (*Europarecht*), 55-74.

Creech, R. (2005). *Law and Language in the European Union, The Paradox of a Babel "United in Diversity"*. Groningen: Europa Law Publishing.

Cutts, M. (2001). *Clarifying Eurolaw*. High Peak, UK: Plain Language Commission.

Dupont, P. (1998). "A Single Language for Europe?". *The Linguist* 37(6), 162-167.

Flückiger, A. (2005). "Le multilinguisme de l'Union européenne: un défi pour la qualité de la législation". In: Gémar, J.-Cl and N. Kasirer (eds.), *Jurilinguistique entre langues et droits / Jurilinguistics Between Law and Language*. Montréal: Editions Thémis / Bruxelles: Bruylant, 339-361.

Gallas, T. (2001). "La rédaction législative multilingue dans l'Union européenne : bilan et perspectives". *LeGes (Gesetzgebung und Evaluation)* 12(3), 115-129.

Gozzi, P. (2001). "Translation of the *Acquis Communautaire*: Recent Experiences in Countries Preparing for Membership". In: S. Šarčević (ed.), *Legal Translation, Preparation for Accession to the European Union*. Rijeka: Faculty of Law, 23-34.

Joint Practical Guide of the European Parliament, the Council and the Commission (for persons involved in the drafting of legislation within the Community institutions) (2003).
Available online at http://www.europa.eu.int/eur-lex/lex/en/techleg/index.htm.

Kapteyn, P.J.G. and P. Verloren Van Themaat (1998). *Introduction to the Law of the European Communities.* The Hague/London/Boston: Kluwer Law International.

Kuner, C. (1991). "The Interpretation of Multilingual Treaties: Comparison of Texts versus the Presumption of Similar Meaning". *Comparative Law Quarterly* 40(4), 953-964.

Lönnroth, J. (2004). "Videomessage to the DGT Staff: Welcoming the Staff Members from the New Member States". Available online at www.europa.eu.int/comm/translation/reading/articles/enlargement_en.htm.

Manners, I. (2000). "Small States and the Internal Balance of the European Union: Institutional Issues". In: Gower, J. and J. Redmond (eds.) *Enlarging the European Union. The Way Forward.* Aldershot (UK): Ashgate, 123-135.

Mattila, H. (2005). "Jurilinguistique et latin juridique". In: Gémar, J.-Cl and N. Kasirer (eds.) *Jurilinguistique entre langues et droits / Jurilinguistics Between Law and Language*, Montréal: Editions Thémis / Bruxelles: Bruylant, 71-89.

McCluskey, B. (2001). "Respecting Multilingualism in the Enlargement of the European Union – the Organisational Challenge". *Terminologie et Traduction* 2, 7-21.

Moratinos Johnston, S. (2000). "Multilingualism and EU Enlargement". *Terminologie et traduction* 3, 5-70.

Moréteau, O. (1999). "L'anglais pourrait-il devenir la langue juridique commune en Europe ?" In: R. Sacco and L. Castellani (eds.), *Les multiples langues du droit européen uniforme.* Torino: L Harmattan Italia, 143-162.

Pescatore, P. (1999). "Das Konzipieren übersetzungsgerechter juristischer Dokumente". In: G.-R. de Groot and R. Schulze (eds.), *Recht und Übersetzen.* Baden-Baden: Nomos, 91-99.

Schübel-Pfister, I. (2004). *Sprache und Gemeinschaftsrecht.* Berlin: Duncker and Humblot.

Schulte-Nölke, H. (1999). "Elf Amtssprachen, ein Recht? Folgen der Mehrsprachigkeit für die Auslegung von Verbraucherschutzrichtlinien". In: R. Schulze (ed.), *Auslegung europäischen Privatrechts und angeglichenen Rechts.* Baden-Baden: Nomos, 143-160.

Šarčević, S. (2005). "The Quest for Legislative Bilingualism and Multilingualism: Co-drafting in Canada and Switzerland". In: Gémar, J.-Cl. and N. Kasirer (eds.), *Jurilinguistique entre langues et droits / Jurilinguistics Between Law and Language*, Montréal: Editions Thémis / Bruxelles: Bruylant, 277-292.

Šarčević, S. (2002). "Problems of interpretation in an enlarged European Union". In: R. Sacco (ed.), *L'interprétation des textes juridiques rédigés dans plus d'une langue*, Torino: L'Harmattan Italia, 239-272.

Šarčević, S. (2001). "Translation Procedures for Legal Translators". In: S. Šarčević (ed.), *Legal Translation,Preparation for Accession to the European Union.* Rijeka: Faculty of Law, 75-109.

Šarčević, S. (2000). *New Approach to Legal Translation.* The Hague/London/Boston: Kluwer Law International.

Tabory, M. (1980). *Multilingualism in International Law and Institutions.* Alphen aan den Rijn: Sihthoff and Noordhoff.

Timmermans, C.W.A. (1998). "How to improve the quality of Community legislation: the viewpoint of the European Commission". In: A. Kellermann, G. Ciavarini Azzi, S. Jacobs and R. Deighton-Smith (eds.), *Improving the Quality of Legislation in Europe.* The Hague: Kluwer Law International, 39-59.

Translating for a Multilingual Community. Directorate-General for Translation of the European Commission, last updated in March 2005, available at http://www.europa.eu.int/comm/dgs/translation/bookshelf/brochure_en.pdf.

Wagner, E., Bech, S. and J. Martínez (2002). *Translating for the European Union Institutions.* Manchester: St. Jerome.

Weenink-Griffiths, J. (2005). "Optimal use of multilingual resources in legal drafting". In: B. Pozzo (ed.), *The Language Policies of EU Institutions after the Enlargement* (proceedings of conference held 15-16 April 2005 in Como)

Weyers, G. (1999). "Das Übersetzen von Rechtstexten: eine Herausforderung an die Übersetzungswissenschaft". In: G.-R. de Groot and R. Schulze (eds.) *Recht und Übersetzen.* Baden-Baden: Nomos Verlagsgesellschaft, 151-174.

Appendix I

Council Regulation No. 1 of 1958 determining the languages to be used by the European Economic Community

(*Official Journal* No. 17 of 6 October 1958; English special edition, Series-I, as amended)

THE COUNCIL OF THE EUROPEAN ECONOMIC COMMUNITY,

Having regard to Article 217 of the Treaty which provides that the rules governing the languages of the institutions of the Community shall, without prejudice to the provisions contained in the rules of procedure of the Court of Justice, be determined by the Council, acting unanimously;

Whereas each of the 4 languages in which the Treaty is drafted is recognised as an official language in one or more of the Member States of the Community,

HAS ADOPTED THIS REGULATION:

Article 1
The official languages and the working languages of the institutions of the Community shall be Dutch, French, German and Italian.*

Article 2
Documents which a Member State or a person subject to the jurisdiction of a Member State sends to institutions of the Community may be drafted in any one of the official languages selected by the sender. The reply shall be drafted in the same language.

Article 3
Documents which an institution of the Community sends to a Member State or to a person subject to the jurisdiction of a Member State shall be drafted in the language of such State.

Article 4
Regulations and other documents of general application shall be drafted in the 4 official languages.

Article 5
The *Official Journal of the European Communities* shall be published in the 4 official languages.

Article 6
The institutions of the Community may stipulate in their rules of procedure which of the languages are to be used in specific cases.

Article 7
The languages to be used in the proceedings of the Court of Justice shall be laid down in its rules of procedure.

Article 8
If a Member State has more than one official language, the language to be used shall, at the request of such State, be governed by the general rules of its law.

This regulation shall be binding in its entirety and directly applicable in all Member States.

** With each enlargement this Regulation has been amended to incorporate the new official languages - English and Danish in 1973, Greek in 1981, Spanish and Portuguese in 1986, Swedish and Finnish in 1995, and Czech, Estonian, Hungarian, Latvian, Lithuanian, Maltese, Polish, Slovak and Slovene in 2004.*

Appendix II

Accession Treaty between the Member States of the European Union and the Republic of Bulgaria and Romania

(*Official Journal of the European Union* L 157/19 of 21.6.2005)

Article 6

This Treaty, drawn up in a single original in the Bulgarian, Czech, Danish, Dutch, English, Estonian, Finnish, French, German, Greek, Hungarian, Irish, Italian, Latvian, Lithuanian, Maltese, Polish, Portuguese, Romanian, Slovak, Slovenian, Spanish and Swedish languages, the texts in each of these languages being equally authentic, shall be deposited in the archives of the Government of the Italian Republic, which will remit a certified copy to each of the Governments of the other Signatory States.

Agnieszka Doczekalska
European University Institute
Italy

PRODUCTION AND APPLICATION OF MULTILINGUAL LAW: THE PRINCIPLE OF EQUALITY OF AUTHENTIC TEXTS AND THE VALUE OF SUBSEQUENT TRANSLATION

1. Introduction

The phenomenon of multilingual law stems from official multilingualism, which usually requires not only that the law should be enacted in all official languages, but also that the texts of a single legal instrument expressed in the official languages should be treated as equally authentic. Owing to this equal authenticity of official language versions of a legal act, these versions are called authentic texts of this act.[1] Such texts can be simultaneously drafted in all official languages (the so-called "co-drafting model"[2]) but much more often one authentic text is drafted in one official language and then translated into the remaining official languages (the "translation model"). I would like to focus on a particular case of the latter situation, namely subsequent translation.

We deal with the case of "subsequent translation" when two cumulative criteria are present: the first one is that not all language versions of a single multilingual legal act are drafted at the same time. The second one is that a translation is prepared and authenticated once the drafting and authentication process for the particular legal act has been completed (see Šarčević 2000: 93). Such a situation is related to the expanding number of official languages. It takes place, for instance, within the European Union (EU) after each enlargement as

[1] For the concept of "equally authentic legal texts" see Šarčević 2000, and also Rosenne 1983, Tabory 1980 (in international organizations), Wagner, Bech and Martínez 2002, Truchot 2003 (in the European Union), Revell 2004 (in Canada), and Sin 1989 (in Hong Kong).

[2] In the co-drafting model, that includes different methods (see Covacs 1982); there is one drafter for each language version and the time and place of drafting of all language versions are combined. For instance, co-drafting methods have been applied in Canada at the federal level since 1978, when the Department of Justice introduced bilingual co-drafting (Levert 1995), and they were adopted at the provincial level by the government of New Brunswick in the 1980s (Keating 1995).

well as in multilingual countries when a new language is raised to an official one.[3] Apart from such situations, when subsequent translation is justified, sometimes it is used as an irregular authentication procedure (Tabory 1980: 193, Rosenne 1983: 783, Šarčević 2000: 93). Although no new language is granted the status of an official language, and hence the number of official languages remains unchanged, a text in one of the official languages cannot be submitted before the adoption. It is usually due to practical or technical difficulties (e.g. lack of time, lack of qualified translators). Examples of the latter situation can be found as far as legal drafting at national (in some multilingual countries)[4], international (in international organizations)[5] and supranational level (in the European Community)[6] is concerned.

I will analyse the issue of the value of subsequent translation attempting to find an answer to two main questions: i) how subsequent translation is and should be produced, and ii) whether it contributes or should contribute to the common meaning of a single instrument as far as the interpretation of multilingual law by courts is concerned. In order to answer these questions, I have based my analysis mainly on the legal drafting and judicial interpretation of EU law[7]. As brought up

---

[3] Enactment of a new language version of already adopted legal acts could be observed for instance in Hong Kong, where until 1989 statute law was enacted only in English. However, after the signing of the *Joint Declaration on the Question of Hong Kong* by the UK and China in 1984, the *Royal Instructions* (in 1986) and the *Official Languages Ordinance* (in 1987) were amended to enable laws to be enacted also in Chinese (Law Drafting Division Department of Justice 2001). Another example can be found in Switzerland, where Italian became a new official language in 1902.

[4] An example of such a situation within a multilingual country can be found in Switzerland, where the Italian version of a legal act was usually not ready at the time of adoption. Such practice was forbidden in 1974, when the requirement for the Italian version to be present prior to adoption was introduced into *The Federal Act of 1962 on the Procedure of the Federal Assembly and the Promulgation and Entry into Force of Legislation* (see Dessemont and Asnay 1995, Šarčević 2000).

[5] Examples are given by e.g. Tabory (1980).

[6] For instance, although the *Treaty establishing the European Economic Community* states that it was "drawn up in a single original in the German, French, Italian and Netherlands languages" (Article 248), when it was signed on 25 March 1957, only the German and French versions were ready and compared by jurists and linguists. There were only rough drafts of the Italian and Dutch versions at that moment. Work on them was finished at the end of April (see Maas 1968-1969).

[7] In this paper I use the term "the European Union" (EU) to denote the organization created in 1992 by the *Treaty on the European Union* (TEU) and founded on the three Communities (i.e. the European Economic Community (EEC), renamed by the TEU as "the European Community" (EC), the European Coal and Steel Community (ECSC) and Euroatom). These European Communities nowadays form Pillar I of the EU. Since mainly Pillar I (the so-called EC Pillar) produces legally binding acts, I use the terms "EU law", "EC law" or "Community law" interchangeably. When I use the term the "European Communities" I refer to the Communities that existed before the EU was created.

above, the case of subsequent translation may come about in national, international as well as supranational multilingual legal systems. Each legal multilingualism is characterized by its own specific features, such as: reasons for official multilingualism, its legal basis, rules and methods of drafting, adopting and judicial interpretation of multilingual law. Some noteworthy characteristics of EU law can be specified. The distinctiveness of EU legal multilingualism has to do not only with the large number of official languages but also the fact that some countries share the same official language (e.g. German – an official language of EU institutions – is the official language in Germany, Austria and Belgium; French - in France and Belgium, English - in the United Kingdom, Ireland and Malta; Dutch – in the Netherlands and Belgium). Each national legal system uses its own "terminology that does not necessarily correspond with the legal languages of other countries" (López-Rodríguez 2004: 110). Legal language also differs in countries having the same language (Heutger 2003). Hence, a uniform German, French, English, or Dutch legal terminology[8] does not exist (De Groot 1996: 156). Consequently, EU languages of the law should be distinguished from Member States' (MS) languages of the law. Moreover, the importance of EU legal multilingualism and equality of language versions arises from the fact that the laws of the EU are in some cases directly applicable (i.e. they take effect within the MS, without the need for incorporation or implementation by national authorities) or have a direct effect[9] (i.e. provide rights and obligations to individuals enforceable in national courts).[10] Thus, EU laws should be also uniformly applicable.

I have decided to base my analysis on the EU case not only because of the specific characteristics of its law and multilingualism but mainly because of the significance of subsequent translation in this setting.

2. Translation

Before I examine the issue of subsequent translation in the EU, some clarifications concerning the term "translation" should be made. This term or expressions including the word "translation" have been used so far in this paper, but the term "translation" should not be applied in reference to authentic texts. Although there is no doubt that language versions of a legal act are prepared by translation, in legal language it is improper to use the term "translation" (Šarčević 2000: 64). It is a consequence of official multilingualism that consists not only in the coexistence of two or more languages but also in the equality of these

[8] That is, uniform terminology does not exist for each of the mentioned languages taken separately.
[9] See *Van Gend en Loos v Nederlandse Tariefcommissie*, C-26/62, 1963 ECR 3.
[10] For further details on direct applicability and direct effect, see Davies 2001.

languages (Wagner, Bech and Martínez 2002: 1). It means that legally all language versions have equal power and authority. Consequently, one version cannot be regarded as a translation of another. Hence, from the legal standpoint, all authentic texts are originals regardless of the way of production. This statement is the main assumption behind the theory of original texts (Šarčević 2000), which recognizes some legal fictions, like those of equivalent originals, presumption of simultaneous drafting of all language versions, and identicalness of authentic texts. These fictions create a paradox that Correia (2003: 41) described with regard to the EU as follows: "In practice, Community law is inconceivable *without* translation, whereas in strictly legal terms Community law is inconceivable *with* it". However, thanks to this paradox and legal fictions linguistic equality and multilingual law can exist.

3. The principle of equality of authentic texts (PEAT)

In law, the aforementioned fictions are expressed by the principle of equality of authentic texts, whereby the legal effect of equal authenticity of all texts of a single legal act can be achieved. PEAT presumes that all authentic texts of the same legal act have common meaning ("presumption of the unity of multilingual legal act"). Consequently, all the authentic texts of a single legal act contribute to the common meaning of this act (Šarčević 2000: 64). Thus, no single text should prevail for the purpose of interpretation" (*ibid.* 20). PEAT influences the method of production of all language versions of a single legal act and the methods of interpretation of multilingual law.

I consider the value of subsequent translation from both a normative and descriptive perspective in order to demonstrate how PEAT should work in theory, and how it works in practice. With this two-sided analysis in place, I tackle the question of whether all language versions are actually treated as equally valid authentic texts. I focus, first, on the production of subsequent translation, and, second, on the application and interpretation of multilingual European law in the European Court of Justice (ECJ) and the Court of First Instance (CFI).

4. Production of EU multilingual law – case of subsequent translation

As regards the EU, each enlargement generally causes an increase in the number of official languages. In order to be allowed to join the EU, candidate states must adopt, implement and enforce all of the *acquis communautaire*. However, in order to adopt the *acquis,* a candidate state whose national official language is to become an official language of the EU, has to translate the *acquis* into this language. Hence a new language version of legal acts that have already been adopted is prepared. This is a typical case of subsequent translation. The *acquis communautaire* is enacted in all official languages of the European Union and all language versions of a single act contribute to its meaning. Therefore, a new language version should be prepared on the basis of all language versions of a particular legal act.

That was possible during the first enlargement when only four language versions had to be considered.[11] Before the enlargement in 2004, there were eleven official languages, which is why in the preparation of a new language version eleven authentic texts should have been considered. Nowadays 23 language versions contribute to the meaning of a single legal act. Because of the great number of official languages and therefore of authentic texts of single acts, considering all language versions during subsequent translation is practically impossible. Thus, the following question arises: which language(s) a new version should be translated from? Should it perhaps be the language(s) in which the act was drawn up? Such a solution was chosen for example by Finland when it was joining the EU in 1995. Presuming that French was the language that EU legislation had been mainly drafted in, Finland selected this language as a source language for translation of the *acquis*, considering the texts that were not in French unreliable (Nartis 1997: 22). However, it is often the case that subsequent translation is based on a text that had been subsequently translated itself. For instance, in the translation of the *acquis communautaire* by the candidate states before the enlargement in 2004, the source languages were English, French and German[12]. While English and French are nowadays the main working and drafting languages in EU institutions[13], it should be taken into account that French and German have been official languages since the European Communities were established, whereas English – the language of most source texts and, in some countries the only one, became official language of the EC in 1973 when the UK became a member. Hence, legal acts drawn up before this date were not drafted in English.

Although, given the value of PEAT, it is not justified to rely only on one language version, practical factors (like time pressure, organizational problems, lack of qualified translators who have not only linguistic but also legal

[11] See Akehurst (1972), who describes the preparation of the English version of the *EEC Treaty* and points out that all four language versions were considered.

[12] For instance, see *Evaluation of Phare Programmes in Support of EU Integration and Law Approximation* Final Reports of May 1999 for Estonia, Hungary and Poland. The report for Estonia only mentions translation of legislation and other EU materials from English into Estonian. Similarly, the report for Hungary makes a mention of translation from English into Hungarian. The Polish report states that source languages for the translation of secondary legislation were English, French and German.

[13] Until the beginning of the 1990s, French was the dominant language of EU institutions. For the issue of use of official languages in EU institutions see Truchot 2003.

knowledge, and economical or financial restrictions) make translation based on all language versions impossible.

Nevertheless, according to translation theory, the drafting of a target text, in our case the drafting of a new language version, is not the last stage of the translation process. Different approaches to and classifications of translation stages aside, three essential stages specific to the process of translating can be pointed out for the purposes of this paper: analysis, synthesis and revision. During analysis the source text is read and analysed by the translator. During synthesis the target text is produced. During revision, the draft translation (target text) is evaluated, edited and adjusted to meet the standards of translation (Bell 1997: 187). In my opinion, during synthesis, when a new language version of a legal act is produced, it is acceptable to limit the number of language versions taken into consideration. However, during the stage of revision, all authentic texts should be compared in order to ensure legal and linguistic consistency of the legal instruments (acts) in all the official languages of the Communities.

Sometimes, such a comparison of different versions of authentic texts during drafting or revision processes can help to notice and explain divergences and ambiguities of existing language versions of a legal act. If an ambiguity is present in the compared texts, it should be retained in the target text (new language version). Very often, ambiguities are the result of very difficult negotiations and delicate political arbitration.[14] When we speak about the EU we have to remember that legislative procedures are very complicated and complex, consisting of many stages and involving institutions representing different interests[15]. Noteworthy is also the fact that different translators are involved in drafting legal acts, because each of the institutions participating in the legislative procedure has its own translation service. Since ambiguity is often the result of a compromise, the translator does not have the right to improve the legal act (Akehurst 1972: 25, Correira 2003: 42).

5. Interpretation of multilingual law – interpretative value of texts produced by means of subsequent translation

It is the role of the ECJ, which since 1989 has been assisted by the CFI, to harmonize legal meaning and ensure uniform interpretation and application of EU law.[16] Moreover, the ECJ has the jurisdiction to give preliminary rulings on the

[14] See e.g. Hartley (1996) on the so-called "deliberate uncertainty" that occurs when the representatives of the MS cannot achieve agreement and therefore use vague terms.

[15] The Commission represents interest of the Community as the whole, the Council - of the MS, the Parliament – of the citizens.

[16] See art. 220 of the *EC Treaty*.

interpretation of the Treaty and secondary legislation, when requested by national courts.[17] In accordance with PEAT, the Court has to determine one meaning for all language versions. Hence, regardless of the large number of language versions, the ECJ should compare all texts of a given legal act, even those that were produced by means of subsequent translation. There is settled case law that expresses this rule. In the judgement in the CILFIT case the ECJ stated that:

> Community legislation is drafted in several languages and that the different language versions are all equally authentic. An interpretation of a provision of Community law thus involves a comparison of the different language versions.[18]

The practice of the Court confirms that when the ECJ has to determine the meaning of a term, especially when differences between language versions exist, it takes into consideration all language versions, also those that were produced after the adoption of the act in question had been completed.[19] In another judgement the ECJ stated that:

> "The different language versions of a Community text must be given a uniform interpretation and hence in the case of divergence between the versions the provision in question must be interpreted by reference to the purpose and general scheme of the rules of which it forms a part".[20]

What is more,

> "the uniform application of Community rules requires that they be interpreted in accordance with the actual intention of the person who drafted them and the objective pursued by that person, in particular in the light of the versions drawn up in all languages"[21].

Does this last statement challenge the interpretative value of versions subsequently translated? We should keep in mind that texts created before the adoption of a legal act are as well very often produced by means of translation. Usually, a legal act is not drafted simultaneously in all official languages but in one language (most often in English and French) and then translated into the remaining official languages. Translators working in the translation services of EU institutions do not participate in debates and negotiations and so do not know "the actual intention of the person who drafted" the act. Moreover, one should not

---

[17] See art. 234 of the *EC Treaty*.

[18] *CILFIT v. Ministry of Health*, par. 18, 1982 ECR 3415.

[19] See, e.g., the recent judgements: C-192/04, 2005 ECR 00; C-257/00, 2003 ECR I-345; C-305/01, 2003 ECR I-6729.

[20] Case 30/77, *Regina v. Bouchereau*, par. 1, 1977 E.C.R. 1999.

[21] Judgement in the case C-268/99 *Jany v Staatssecretaris van Justitie*, para. 47, 2001 ECR I-8615.

determine in advance that the text in which the act had been originally drafted should prevail, because the source of the interpretative problem might be included in that particular text. Moreover, in its statement the ECJ required that interpretation should be made "in particular in the light of the versions drawn up in all languages". According to the theory of original texts and the related fiction of simultaneous drafting of all language versions, also the version that was prepared as *de fac*to subsequent translation, from the legal point of view is regarded as a version in which the act was drawn up.

To sum up, as far as the interpretation of multilingual law by the ECJ is concerned, it seems that theory meets practice. The ECJ in fact makes an effort to compare all or most of the language versions and although the Court sometimes refers to *travaux preparatoire* to find out the actual intention of those who drafted the act, it does not ignore language versions prepared by subsequent translation.

6. Conclusion

The European Union regards equality among the languages of the member states as crucial to its unity. Its respect for linguistic diversity and promotion of multilingualism is expressed in a range of provisions of the Treaties. In addition, legal certainty and equality requires that "all those governed by EU law are bound to the same behaviour and know what that is" (Shelton 1997: 617). For these reasons, EU legal acts are required to be enacted in all official languages. The use of the word "official" in the notion "official languages" means that all legal texts are published in all these languages and that all these texts are considered equally authentic (Dessemont and Asnay 1995: 11). Thus, the principle of equality of authentic texts is the very basis of official and legal multilingualism. There is a strong correlation between the value of subsequent translation and the principle of equality of authentic texts. If we deny equal status to texts produced before and after the adoption of a legal act we cannot preserve the concept of authentic texts. Therefore, I think we should be very careful in challenging the value of subsequent translation. Legally, texts produced by subsequent translation are as authentic as the those produced before the adoption and authentication stages. Since texts are authentic as long as they have been authenticated in the prescribed way (Rosenne 1983: 782), from the legal point of view it is not the way or time of drafting a text that is decisive for its value but the adoption and authentication of that text. Practically, the value of a text produced after the moment of adoption, in my opinion does not depend on the means or time of production but rather on the quality of that text. Hence, everybody involved in the production of a text, when the adoption of a legal act is completed, should make an effort to ensure high quality of translation.

References

Akehurst, M. (1972). "Preparing the Authentic English Text of the EEC Treaty". In: B. A. Wortley (ed.), *An Introduction to the Law of the European Economic Community*. Manchester: Manchester University Press, 20-31.

Bell, R. T. (1997). "Psycholinguistic/cognitive approaches". In: M. Baker (ed.), *The Routledge Encyclopedia of Translation Studies*. London and New York: Routledge, 185-190.

Brown and Kennedy (2000). *The Court of Justice of the European Community*. London: Sweet and Maxwell.

Correia, R. (2003). "Translation of EU Legal Texts". In: A. Tosi (ed.), *Crossing Barriers and Bridging Cultures. The Challenges of Multilingual Translation for the European Union.*Clevedon: Multilingual Matters, 38-44.

Covacs, A. (1982). "La réalisation de la version française des lois fédérales du Canada". In: J.-C. Gémar (ed.), *Langage du droit et traduction. Essais de jurilinguistique*. Montréal: Linguatech Collection Langues de spécialité et Conseil de la langue française, 83-100.

Davies, K. (2001). *Understanding European Union Law*. London and Sydney: Cavendish Publishing.

De Groot, G.-R. (1996). "Law, Legal Language and the Legal System: Reflections on the Problems of Translating Legal Texts". In: V. Gessner, A. Hoeland, and C. Varga (eds.), *European Legal Cultures*. Dartmouth, 155-160.

Dessemontet, F. and T. Ansay (1995). *Introduction to Swiss Law*. The Hague-Boston-London: Kluwer Law International.

Hartley, T. C. (1996). "Five Forms of Uncertainty in European Community Law". *Cambridge Law Journal* 55(2), 265-288.

Heutger, V. (2003). "Law and Language in the European Union". *Global Jurist Topics* 3, 1-15.

Keating, J. (1995). "La corédaction et l'expérience néo – brunswickoise". In: G. Snow and J. Vanderlinden (eds.), *Français juridique et science du droit*. Bruxelles: Bruylant, 255–266.

Law Drafting Division Department of Justice (2001). *Legislative Drafting in Hong Kong. Crystallization in Definitive Form*. 2nd edition. Available at http://www.doj.gov.hk/eng/public/pdf/ldhkv2e.pdf, last accessed September 2005.

Levert, L. (1995). "Bijuridisme et bilinguisme législatifs: un enjeu et un pari". In: G. Snow and J. Vanderlinden (eds.), *Français juridique et science du droit*. Bruxelles: Bruylant, 203-217.

López-Rodríguez, A. M. (2004). "Towards a European Civil Code without a Common European Legal Culture? The Link between Law, Language and Culture". *Brooklyn Journal of International Law* 29(3), 1195-1220.

Maas, H. H. (1968-1969). "The English Version of the Treaty of Rome". *Common Market Law Review* 6, 205-209.

Nartis, Raul (1997). "The Role of Language Cognition in Legal Method". *Juridica International* 1, 14-24.

Revell, D. L. (2004). "Authoring Bilingual Laws: the Importance of Process". *Brooklyn Journal of International Law* 29(3), 1085-1105.

Rosenne, S. (1983). "The Meaning of 'Authentic Text' in Modern Treaty Law". In: R. Bernhardt et al. (eds.), *Völkerrecht Als Rechtsordnung Internationale Gerichtsbarkeit Menschenrechte: Festschrift für Hermann Mosler*, 759-784.

Šarčević, S. (2000). *New Approach to Legal Translation*. The Hague: Kluwer Law International.

Šarčević, S. (2003). "General Guidelines for Translating the Acquis Communautaire/Opće upute za prevođenje pravne stečevine Europske zajednice (prijevod)". *Priručnik za prevođenje pravnih akata Europske unije*. Zagreb: Ministarstvo za europske integracije Republike Hrvatske, 9-22.

Shelton, D. (1997). "Reconcilable Differences? The Interpretation of Multilingual Treaties". *Hastings International and Comparative Law Review* 20, 611- 637.

Sinn, K. K. (1989). "Meaning, Translation and Bilingual Legislation". In: P. Pupier and J. Woehrling (eds.), *Langue et Droit. Actes du Premier Congrès de l'Institut international de droit linguistique compare*. Montréal: Wilson and Lafleur Ltée, 509-515.

Tabory, M. (1980). *Multilingualism in International Law and Institutions*. Alphen ann den Rijn: Sijthoff and Noordhoff.

Truchot, C. (2003). "Languages and Supranationality in Europe: The linguistic Influence of the European Union". In: J. Maurais and M. A. Morris (eds.), *Languages in a Globalising World*. Cambridge: Cambridge University Press, 99-110.

Evaluation of Phare programmes in support of EU Integration and Law Approximation - 05/1999 - ref. 951483 – Final Reports:

for Estonia available at:
http://www.eu.int/comm/europeaid/evaluation/reports/cards/951483_est.pdf,
for Hungary available at:
http://www.eu.int/comm/europeaid/evaluation/reports/cards/951483_hun.pdf,
for Poland available at:
http://www.eu.int/comm/europeaid/evaluation/reports/cards/951483_pl.pdf,
last accessed June 2007.

Part II

LEGAL TRANSLATION AND INTERPRETING

Anne Lise Kjær
University of Copenhagen
Denmark

LEGAL TRANSLATION IN THE EUROPEAN UNION: A RESEARCH FIELD IN NEED OF A NEW APPROACH

1. Introduction

At the time of writing, the European Union has 27 Member States and 23 official languages. The language policy implies that EU legislation must be drafted and published in all 23 languages and that all 23 texts of a legislative act are equally authentic and authoritative language versions. As co-drafting of texts in 23 languages is impossible in practice, legal translation is a key activity in the EU, offered by the translation services of the various EU institutions.

According to the "Facts and Figures" given on the web site of the Commission's Translation Service, the service produced no fewer than 1,541,518 pages in 2006. If one includes the other institutions and bodies of the EU (notably the Council, the Parliament, the Court of Justice, and the European Central Bank), the number of translated pages must be several millions. In terms of quantity alone, one may safely assert that the importance of translation is not greater in any other institutional context in Europe than in the EU. Moreover, Europe's extreme degree of linguistic and legal pluralism makes the complexity of legal translation in the EU unparalleled in the world. Nevertheless, translation studies are surprisingly silent as regards accounting theoretically for the special features and difficulties of translating EU law.

I complained to that effect in an article some years ago (Kjær 1999b), and even though there is evidence of an increasing interest in translation and multilingual drafting in the EU (see e.g. Berteloot 2001 and 2004; Burr/Gallas 2004; Doczekalska, this volume; Mulders 2006; Sandrini 2004a and 2006; Šarčević 2001, 2006, and this volume), the subject has not been established as an independent research field based on its own theoretical framework. How can one explain this relative lack of interest in the EU on the part of translation researchers?

One explanation is that translation within a multilingual legal system like the EU is commonly regarded as considerably simpler than translation between two legal systems. In the case of multilingual translation there is only one legal system in play – source text and target text refer to the same legal system. Consequently, the argument goes, the most difficult aspect of legal translation, viz. the divergence between the legal systems involved in the translation process, is not present in the multilingual legal system of the EU. This is a view that many translation theorists seem to endorse – see especially the work of de Groot (1988, 1991, 1999 and 2002), Stolze (1992 and 1998) and Sandrini (1998, 1999a and 2004a).

Another explanation for the relative lack of interest in developing a translation theory focussing especially on EU law may be that translation within the EU is regarded as just an example of a more general type of translation, "translating international legal instruments" (Cao 2007b) or that it is possible to describe it adequately in terms of translation and co-drafting methods developed in multilingual legal systems like Switzerland and Canada. Thus, the reason why translation in the EU has not established itself as a research field in its own right seems to be that translation theorists generally agree that it is possible to account for it by means of already existing categories and theories.

In my opinion, however, legal translation within the framework of the European Union is not only much more complex than appears from the existing theories, but also qualitatively different from translation in other contexts due to the special character and organisation of the legal system. Two points are generally overlooked in the existing contributions:

1) The interplay with the domestic legal systems of the Member States. By treating EU translation as translation in international organisations or translation in multilingual national legal systems, the analyses fail to account for the fact that EU law comprises features of both international law and domestic law, a fact which makes translation in the EU particularly complicated.
2) EU law is not an established legal system. It is a system of incoherent legal rules and principles developing into a more coherent legal system. Legal translators and specialists in law and language often point out that legal translation cannot be described properly without taking the mechanisms and functions of law into consideration. However, in the case of EU law, a legal system under development, they generally fail to explain what impact the process of legal development has on the way legal translation works.

The question is whether translation in the EU can be accounted for adequately by well-known translation methods and strategies or by notions such as co-drafting or standardisation of texts and terminology. In this paper I shall try to explain why I do not think they can, and why, in a wider perspective, problems of legal translation in the EU system cast new light on established principles of language and translation in the field of law. In my opinion, an independent research field focussing especially on legal translation in the EU should be established.

In the following, I shall first present an overview of typologies of legal translation developed within translation studies during the past decades (section 2). Then, I shall discuss the applicability of those typologies in a description of legal translation within the EU (section 3). Next, I shall comment on some special features characterizing translation within the EU which taken together call for a new theoretical approach (section 4). Moreover, I shall consider the interpretation methods adopted by the European Court of Justice in order to cope with multilingualism and indicate the gloomy perspective for translators (section 5). Finally, I shall offer an alternative and more optimistic perspective and encourage translation theorists and specialists in legal linguistics to contribute to the development of a multidisciplinary research field on language, law and legal integration, especially focussing on the role that language and translation play in the development of the legal system of the EU (section 6).

2. Types of legal translation

Theories of legal translation as a subject field of legal linguistics (Luttermann 1999) are based on knowledge from both theories of law and theories of language and combine insights of general translation studies and LSP research with legal knowledge (see e.g. the work of Cao, Gémar, de Groot, Kjær, Madsen, Šarčević, Sandrini, and Stolze). While for many years, translation studies did not distinguish between translations within various LSP subject fields (science, technology, economics, medicine, law etc.) there has been an increasing recognition of the special character of legal translation making it necessary to treat it separately (see e.g. Kjær 2004a).

The interdependency of law and language is commonly stressed in legal theory, comparative law, and legal linguistics. "Legal language has developed its characteristics to meet the demands of the legal system in which it is expressed" (Cao 2007b:28), and "bound to a particular legal system, each language of the law is the product of a specific culture and history" (Gémar 2006, in Šarčević 1997: 9). Thus, it is widely acknowledged that translation in the field of law should be based on an interdisciplinary approach which takes as its starting point the legal systems in which source text and target text are to be applied. Profound knowledge of the legal systems and legal languages involved and the difference between them is of paramount importance.

Theories of legal translation generally take the interdependency of language and legal system as their starting point in descriptions of the characteristics of translation in the field of law and base categories of legal translation on that relationship. Three interrelated classifications of legal translation are relevant for the argument in this paper:

1) Classification of legal translation based on degrees of difference or similarity of the legal systems involved;
2) Classification of legal translation based on legal text types and purpose of the target language legal text; and
3) Classification of legal translation based on the distinction "between" or "within" legal systems

In the following survey, I shall first give an overview of the basic translation types that are distinguished in translation theory. Then, in section 3, I shall attempt to apply the existing typologies to translation within the EU.

2.1. Translation and degrees of difference / similarity of the legal systems

De Groot (1988: 409-410) classifies the difficulty of legal translation according to the similarity or difference between the legal systems involved in the translation process:

> The fact that comparative law is the basis of translating legal texts, justifies the supposition that the degree of difficulty is not primarily determined by linguistic differences, but by the extent of affinity of the legal system in question. The extent of affinity of the languages in question is a secondary factor which influences the degree of difficulty of the translation.

Against this background de Groot distinguishes between the following categories:

1. Easiest translation: legal systems and legal languages are closely related, e.g. legal translation in the relation Denmark – Norway or Spain – France.
2. Easy translation: the legal systems are closely related, but the languages have few similarities, e.g. legal translation in the relation France – the Netherlands or Germany – Japan.
3. Difficult translation: the languages are closely related, but the legal systems are very different, e.g. legal translation in the relation England – the Netherlands.
4. Most difficult translation: legal systems are very different and legal languages are hardly related, e.g. legal translation in the relation England – China.

De Groot's thesis that the degree of difficulty of translation depends on the relatedness of the legal systems concerned is widely accepted in translation theory

– see e.g. Šarčević (1997: 13), Cao (2007b: 23-32), Sandrini (1998), or Stolze (1992) – and cannot be rejected. From my point of view, however, taking comparative law as the starting point of any discussion of legal translation often prevents one to take a broader view and makes it difficult to account for all relevant factors of language use in the field of law.

2.2. Translation, legal text types and purpose of the target language legal text

Another relevant classification of translation is the one applied in Cao (2007b), with reference to Kelsen's well-known distinction between performative and informative, prescriptive and descriptive legal texts in his "General Theory of Norms":

1. Translating Private Legal Documents
   a. For performative purposes (e.g. contracts stipulating that both or all language versions have legal force)
   b. For informative purposes (e.g. legal certificates such as marriage, divorce, birth and death)
2. Translating Domestic Legislation
   c. For performative purposes (in bilingual and multilingual countries)
   d. For informative purposes (from one monolingual country into another)
3. Translating International Legal Instruments
   e. With binding legal effect (e.g. treaties, conventions and agreements)
   f. Without binding legal effect (e.g. resolutions, declarations, guidelines)

Private legal documents are "documents that are drafted and used by lawyers in their daily practice on behalf of their clients", including contracts, wills and court documents (Cao 2007b: 83), domestic legislation are statutes (Cao 2007b: 101), and international legal instruments, as stated, treaties and other international texts concluded by contracting states on the basis of bilateral or multilateral negotiation, or set up by an international organisation such as the UN or the European Union (Cao 2007b:134).

Again, this classification is thoroughly meaningful and is recurrently used in translation theory, see Šarčević (1997: 8ff) with further references. Nevertheless, for reasons to be elucidated below, it is difficult to apply it to translation of legal texts within the European Union.

2.3. Translation between or within legal systems

It already follows from the categories of translation mentioned in section 2.2 that translation theorists often distinguish between the following two main types of legal translation: 1) translation "between" legal systems, and 2) translation "within" legal systems. The distinction is based on the general assumption that any legal language, including its concepts and genre conventions, is the language of one particular legal system. It follows that legal translation may in fact involve only one language, in cases where that language is the official language of more than one state, say translation from the German legal language of Germany into the German legal language of Switzerland and Austria or into the German legal language applied in the autonomous Province of South Tyrol (Sandrini 1999b), or in the German Community of Belgium (Šarčević 1997: 52-53). As de Groot (1999: 13) points out:

> Es existieren innerhalb einer Sprache so viele Rechtssprachen, wie es Rechtssysteme gibt, die sich dieser Sprache als Rechtssprache bedienen.

2.3.1. Translation between legal systems

In the case of translation between legal systems, legal texts referring to and functioning within one legal system are translated into another legal language which belongs to another legal system. One example of this category is translation of "private legal documents". Another example would be domestic legislation of a monolingual country being translated into a foreign language for information purposes (Cao 2007b:101). Characteristically, translation of this kind must be based not only on a contrastive analysis of the source language and the target language, but also requires a comparison of the two legal systems. Because legal systems differ, there will always be instances of conflicting terminology and concepts and, depending on the degree of affinity or difference between the two legal systems, translation between legal systems involves profound problems of how to transfer culture-bound concepts, conceptions or institutions belonging to the source language system into the target language text. As pointed out by de Groot (1988: 409-410) the difficulty of legal translation of this kind depends on the distance between the legal systems concerned, not the relatedness of the languages (see section 2.1).

2.3.2. Translation within legal systems

Translation *within* legal systems occurs in countries or international organisations with more than one official language and is required because legislative acts and legal instruments of the system must appear in all official languages. This category covers what Cao calls "[t]ranslating domestic legislation" – in bilingual and multilingual jurisdictions (2007b: 101f) and "[t]ranslating international legal instruments" (2007b: 134f). The dominant feature of legal translation of this kind is that only one legal system is involved. Therefore, no comparison of legal systems is required, and the translation process does not involve any cultural transfer of concepts. The concepts are the same, irrespective of the language. Translating in this case is only a matter of changing languages and therefore, in the classification of de Groot (1988), should be relatively easy.

Hand in hand with this understanding of translation, therefore, goes the assertion that the real problem of legal language in multilingual legal settings is not translation, but standardisation of legal terminology. As Šarčević (1997: 267) states:

> "Overburdened" by their own legal background, language, and culture, lawyers tend to resist any interference or change. [Since adopting a common nomenclature] requires a considerable amount of tampering with established definitions, it is easier to create new legal regimes with a new conceptual system.

Closely connected with the problem of standardising bilingual and multilingual legal concepts and legal terminology, is the question of how to produce bilingual or multilingual texts. The ideal way of formulating the different language versions is a co-drafting procedure on the basis of standardised concepts and terminology. Formally, co-drafting is multilingual text production and does not entail translation at all. It presupposes the existence of ready-made ideas, concepts, and conceptions, enabling legal drafters to draft all text versions in all official languages simultaneously. The problem is, however, that the ideas, the concepts, and conceptions to be conveyed in the legal instrument are all expressed in language. Even if the drafters of the various language versions sit side by side, they will probably communicate in just one language, which will then be the basis of text production in the other languages. Furthermore, what regularly happens is that the drafters write a draft version, and that this draft version is translated into the other languages.

3. The applicability of the general typology on legal translation in the European Union

Let us now turn more specifically to translation in the multilingual system of EU law and discuss the applicability of the general typology outlined above. On the face of it, translation in the EU is translation *within* a legal system. The system of reference of all 23 language versions of Community law is the same. There is no change of legal systems, only change of languages. Therefore, in the classification of de Groot, translation in the EU belongs to the category of relatively easy translation. Moreover, as presumed by Cao (2007b: 151f), the appropriate textual category of EU translation seems to be "translating international legal instruments". However, there are a number of reasons why these assumptions do not hold.

3.1. Translation in the EU is both translation within and between legal systems

The European Union is not like any other political system. Existing theories of constitutional law cannot account for the peculiarities of the system. Even if the European Union resembles a federal state like The Federal Republic of Germany or the United States of America, theoretically and practically it is not (or not yet). Neither can it be accounted for as merely a confederation of sovereign nation states like the United Nations. In political science, the unparalleled development of the European Union as compared to other international organizations has led to its designation as a *sui generis* geopolitical entity. It is neither a "Bundesstaat" (federation), nor a "Staatenbund" (confederation); it is a "Staatenverbund", a category of its own.

Similar problems arise when one wants to characterize the legal system of the EU. It is often described as a legal system of its own. While this is true to a certain degree, this is not the whole story. EU law is not and will never be an independent legal system. It owes its existence to the national legal systems in which it is applied. In some areas of law (competition law as one prominent example), EU law does make out a self-sufficient system or a unified set of rules which is identical in all national legal systems. Importantly, however, EU law in most fields is only harmonized law, i.e. it is best described as harmonized national law that has to meet some common standards laid down in EU directives.

The difficulty of defining the legal character of the European Union also applies to legal translation carried out within the Union. Like the EU system itself, legal translation in the EU system is something special, requiring theoretical categories of its own.

One important distinction to be made applies to what one might call supranational translation (translation within the institutions of the EU) as opposed to national translation (translation of EU legislation in the Member States). Due to the interplay with the national legal systems, a full description of translation within the legal system of the EU should include the intralingual translation involved when EU directives are transformed into domestic legal instruments.

On the whole, one should distinguish between several discrete contexts in which legal translation is undertaken within the framework of the European Union, including e.g.:

1. Supranational translation of EU law: Translation in the EU institutions:
   a. Translation of legislation at the Commission, the Council and the European Parliament
   b. Translation at the European Court of Justice (ECJ):
      i. Translation of judgements of the ECJ
      ii. Translation of questions of interpretation of Community law for preliminary ruling (from a national court to the ECJ)
2. National translation of EU law: Translation in the Member States: Implementation of directives – intralingual translation into the national legal language)

The distinction between national and supranational translation is important for at least the following reasons:

1. The recipients of the translated texts are not the same.
   In the case of intralingual translation of directives, the translated text is meant for a domestic readership, including (ideally) the general public. In the case of interlingual translations at the EU institutions, the readership is primarily, if not exclusively, an international interpretive community consisting of lawyers, legal scholars, and judges with special knowledge of EU law, even if some of the texts (especially regulations) have direct effect in the Member States.

2. The texts are meant to fit into different conceptual frameworks.
   Intralingual translations have to be adapted to the conceptual framework of domestic law and legal language. Interlingual translations at the EU institutions have to be adapted to the conceptual framework of EU law and established EU terminology, i.e. the words and phrases that have been applied previously for the same concepts in other EU texts both across the 23 official languages and within the individual language (linguistic precedents).

The special treatment of translation at the European Court of Justice is based on the fact that the language versions of judgements are not equally authentic. French is the language in which the judgements are drafted, whereas the authentic language version is the language of the case (any of the official languages).

In the case of questions for preliminary rulings, the text to be translated at the Court is a source text with foundation in the national legal system of one of the Member States. During proceedings before a national court a question of the proper interpretation of Community law arises, and the national court refers the question to the European Court of Justice for a ruling. In essence, the national court asks the European Court a very specific question: How is this particular piece of Community legislation to be understood in relation to circumstances like those dealt with in this particular case? In other words, the text to be translated is a source text in the sense of an original text and hence a text with a determinate source text meaning (as opposed to source texts when translating EU legislation – see below).

3.2. Translation in the EU is neither translation of domestic legislation nor translation of international legal instruments

In the typology applied by Cao (2007b), EU translation is described as an instance of "translating international legal instruments" and hence treated like multilingual translation in international law. Even if the European Union, as stated above, is not comparable to international organisations such as the UN, this could be a relevant category to choose when one wants to account for translation of primary legislation of the EU, i.e. treaties and other agreements set up and signed by the Member States in their own right. But as far as secondary translation is concerned, the proper category would rather be "translating domestic legislation" as secondary legislation may have direct effect in the Member States. Indeed, in some respects, EU translation does resemble legal translation in multilingual countries like Switzerland and Canada. Nevertheless, it is fairly clear that EU law cannot simply be regarded as domestic law.

In most cases, EU law is expressed by way of indirectly applicable directives which have to be implemented in domestic law before having effect. In the process of implementation, EU directives are transposed into national law – and in some cases translated into the national legal languages. Therefore, due to the complex character of the EU legal system – the interactions between national and European levels of law – legal translation in the EU can be accounted for properly only if one recognizes the fact that EU translation is neither translation of domestic legislation nor translation of international legal instruments, but combines elements of both categories.

3.3. Translation in the EU is not "easy translation"

As stated above, it seems reasonable at first sight to treat translation in the EU as an example of a relatively easy translation task in de Groot's classification. Even though the European Union has, at the time of writing, 23 official languages of equal standing, only one legal system, EU law, is involved in the translation process. It follows that, on the face of it, EU concepts are expressed equally and with identical meanings in all 23 languages and that, correspondingly, all language versions refer equally and only to EU law. Likewise, any legal translation in the EU seems to be just a question of changing languages; no transfer of legal content takes place, or so it seems.

Formally, all language versions of EU legislative instruments refer only to EU law. In reality, however, the reference is more complex, because EU law has no language of its own. EU law is expressed in the 23 national languages which have been declared official languages of the systems: Bulgarian, Czech, Danish, German, Estonian, Greek, English, Spanish, French, Irish, Italian, Latvian, Lithuanian, Hungarian, Maltese, Dutch, Polish, Portuguese, Romanian, Slovak, Slovene, Finnish, and Swedish. The problem is that the legal terminology of the 23 official languages is rooted in, and derives its meaning from, the national legal systems of the Member States. Hence, it is too simple to say that only one legal system is involved in the translation of EU texts. The national laws of the member states are definitely also present. When EU concepts are expressed in the 23 official languages which are at the same time the national legal languages of the Member States, it is impossible to avoid using concepts which belong to the national legal systems.

4. Problems of legal translation in the EU caused by the special character of the legal system

The conclusion of the above considerations is that, for many reasons, legal translation in the EU is much more complex than assumed in general theories of legal translation. The EU legal system involves not only the EU system itself (and its 23 official languages), but also the 27 domestic legal systems of the Member States and their legal languages. Moreover, the speciality of EU law is that legal instruments are *produced* within the EU system, but *applied* in each of the 27 domestic legal systems of the member states. Therefore, in any legal text of the EU there is an inherent tension between the common European law and the domestic laws in which the common rules are being implemented and in which the rules are put to work.

But it is not only the interaction with the Member States that gives rise to idiosyncrasies of translation in the European Union. Another factor that makes legal translation in the EU a translation type *sui generis*, is the dynamics of EU law, the fact that EU law is a legal system under development. Taken together:

1. the interplay with the domestic legal systems of the Member States; and
2. the constant development and dynamics of EU law

make it difficult to apply the traditional theories of legal translation to the translation of legal texts in the EU. In the following survey I shall try to give an overview of a number of interrelated problems that a new approach to legal translation focussing especially on EU law would have to take into account.

4.1. The problem of multiple or unclear references of legal concepts

By "multiple references of legal concepts" I mean the problem whereby EU law is an independent legal order without an independent legal language, without a language of its own. Legal concepts of EU law are expressed in the 23 different national legal languages of the Member States. So, what translation strategy should translators apply in order to cope with the problem of multiple references which inevitably arises? In the translation process, there is not only one legal system involved, but at least three: The national legal system of the source language, the national legal system of the target language, and the EU legal system, besides, not infrequently, one additional legal system, when the text to be translated is itself a translation from a draft version written in one of the *de facto* working languages of the EU institutions (English, French, and to a lesser degree, German).

Unclear reference of legal concepts is another problem caused by European multilingualism. Two interrelated aspects should be mentioned. First, the draft version of EU texts is more often than not written by non-native speakers who are not in full command of the draft language. Consequently, the draft language text regularly contains much hidden translation or inference from the native language of the drafter (Frame 2005: 22). In other words, the terminology chosen by the drafter may not correspond to the content that he or she intended to convey. Moreover, English is often the language in which legal texts are drafted. But what kind of English is that? Certainly not the Common law legal English of Great Britain with established legal meaning, but international English applied as a *lingua franca*, a neutral linguistic code that can cross language barriers. It is a variety of English devoid of any cultural content and any established meaning. Second, during negotiations of EU legislation, meaning production takes place in an intercultural dialogue between legal actors belonging to different legal systems and traditions. Therefore, their mutual understanding is constantly challenged by the lack of equivalence between their legal languages, the impossibility of reproducing the exact meaning and intention of the speaker. Frequently, the dialogue stalls, because the arguments of the other parties suddenly seem incoherent or out of place. So a representative of the Danish Consumer Council, participating in a Commission committee preparing legislation in the field of consumer protection, once told me.

As a result, the meaning of the concepts applied in the texts produced in the EU institutions will often be unclear (see, likewise, Weston (1995: 122-123), on translation at the European Court of Human Rights). But even if we ignore the communicative problems just described, the short history of EU law makes the meaning of the legal texts inherently indeterminate. As mentioned, the legal system of the EU is under development, and there are still many uncovered branches of law with no legal terminology or with no established legal terminology. Furthermore, as EU law is a young legal system, the case law of the European Court of Justice is still in fluctuation. In other words, EU legal concepts are generally lacking the deep level structure of meaning otherwise characteristic of legal semantics. This renders the meaning of EU concepts inherently unstable, fuzzy, and vague. Thus, at the time of translation, it is often unclear to the translator what the intended meaning of the source language concepts is, and he or she will regularly be on insecure ground when he or she translates.

Is it not possible to solve the problems caused by multiple and unclear reference of legal concepts? In theories of legal translation and legal interpretation three solutions are repeatedly suggested: standardisation of terms and concepts, definitions in legislation, and judicial control (interpretation) by the European Court of Justice.

Uncertainty of EU legal terminology seems to make standardisation imperative (see e.g. Sandrini 2004a:145). But standardisation of terms and concepts in the field of law is almost a contradiction in terms, due to the development of law vis-à-vis social and cultural change. The meaning of legal concepts is never forever fixed, but "tends to be in a constant state of flux, being redefined by lawmakers, judges or scholars" (Sandrini 1996: 345). If this reservation applies to legal language in general, it is even more relevant in the case of EU law, due to its dynamic nature. Thus, it is fair to say that standardization, if it is possible at all in the field of law, can never keep up with the constant development of EU law. In the meantime, the translation services of the EU institutions must do their job and translate hundreds and hundreds of pages of EU legislation.

Sometimes the argument is put forward that definitions eliminate uncertainty of the concepts applied in legislation (Šarčević 2006: 142, 147). In fact, influenced by Common law statutory style, definitions are increasingly employed in EU legislation. However, definitions are written in language as well, i.e. in just as many languages (23) as the legislative text itself, and even though the extra words may help diminishing uncertainty, they may also add to the complexity and obscurity, by additional divergence (see likewise Šarčević 2006: 141). A similar reservation must be made as regards interpretation of Community law in the case law of the European Court of Justice. According to Article 234 of the EC Treaty, the Court has the sole competence to interpret Community law. This is to secure uniform interpretation and to avoid the pluralism of understanding and application of Community law which would inevitably arise if the national law courts had the last say. The exclusive jurisdiction of the Court is often highlighted as a measure that contributes to eliminating uncertainty in Community law (see, for instance, Šarčević 1997: 222ff).

The meaning of legal concepts is normally established through legal interpretation by judges in case law. However, apart from the fact that in many areas of law, EU case law is not well-established, it should be borne in mind that the Court functions in a multilingual, multicultural context itself. Even though the judges are excellent jurists, they, too, are subject to the difficulties involved in interlingual, intercultural communication. What is more, many judgments of the Court are compromise judgments, phrased in a language that seeks to obscure the difference in meaning that often occurs during the debates of the judges when they consider the judgement. Some years ago, an ECJ judge revealed to me that the obscure language of the Court is also due to the fact that many judges do not speak French as fluently as required in order to pass judgments. And even if they do: What variety of French is it? The French of the French legal system, or that of Belgium or Luxembourg? Or perhaps an international variety of French with no clear cultural content?

4.2. Translation in the EU is translation without a source text

It follows from the language policy of the European Union that, as a rule, every piece of EU legislation with general applicability has to be drawn up in all 23 official languages. Each text is regarded as being an authentic version of the legislative act; no single language version is furnished with the status of an original text. Hence, there is no distinction between draft version and translations, and it follows from the case law of the European Court of Justice that interpreters are not allowed to refer to the draft version of a text as an especially authoritative legal source. Furthermore, the translations are not marked as such, and it is indicated nowhere from which language version the texts were translated.

In the work of the translator, as he or she will experience it, there is, of course, a source text and a target text, and correspondingly (with the reservations described in section 4.1.) a source language meaning which she transfers into the target language. From a legal point of view, however, there is no distinction between the texts. They are both original versions of the legislative instrument with equal authenticity, like all the other official versions. Thus, one might maintain that the translator should treat both texts as source texts - as equally important sources to Community law! He or she is not allowed to make a literal translation of the source text, thereby giving priority to the legal language conventions of the source text; neither is he or she allowed to translate the text idiomatically, thereby giving priority to the target language conventions. Somehow, the translator must use a legal language lying in between: a more neutral, a more general language, a language of common denominators (see Šarčević 1997: 255).

Both the source text and the target text refer *per definitionem* to the concepts of the EU legal system, and must be understood independently from any national legal system. Therefore, the translators should avoid as much as they possibly can using terminology which is rooted in the national laws of the Member States. This view is expressed in the "Joint Practical Guide of the European Parliament, the Council, and the Commission". The guide comprises 6 general principles that should be met with by persons involved in the drafting of Community legislation, including principles 1 and 5 on the clarity and multilingual nature of Community legislation:

> Principle 1: "Community legislative acts shall be drafted clearly, simply and precisely."
> Principle 5: "Throughout the process leading to their adoption, draft acts shall be framed in terms and sentence structures which respect the multilingual nature of Community legislation; concepts or terminology specific to any one national legal system are to be used with care."

The guide does not go into much detail as regards the practical implementation of the drafting principles. However, the guide does give some advice that may help the drafter and may be of inspiration to the translator as well. Thus, the principle of simplicity may be achieved by the use of "everyday language", as made clear in the following passage:

> 1.4.1: The author should attempt to reduce the legislative intention to simple terms, in order to be able to express it simply. In so far as possible, everyday language should be used.

As regards legal concepts, the guide gives one example of how to circumvent national terminology, the French legal concept of "faute" which has no equivalents in the other official languages of the Community:

> 5.3.2: As regards actual legal terminology, terms which are too closely linked to national legal systems should be avoided.

Example:
The concept of *faute*, which is well known in French law, has no direct equivalent in other legal systems (in particular, English and German law); depending on the context, terms such as *illégalité, manquement* (in relation to an obligation), etc., which can easily be translated into other languages ("illegality", "breach" etc.) should be used instead.

Again, it seems to be suggested that the legal drafter should apply, if not "everyday language", then at least "everyday legal language", a general legal language which may bridge the gap between the national legal concepts. Otherwise, however, the guidelines leave it to the Community translators to decide how they should actually proceed in order to fulfil the desired principles. What is worse, translation theory is silent, too.

4.3. Translation in the EU requires absolute equivalence

In the theory of legal translation, one basic assumption is that the translator's task is to transfer the meaning of the source language legal text into the target language in a way that makes it possible for the target language recipient to understand the text. In order for the translator to achieve that goal, they will have to compare both the two languages concerned, i.e. their syntactical, lexical, pragmatic, and textual peculiarities, and the two legal systems involved: the target language legal system and the source language legal system. Hence, legal translation should always be based on contrastive linguistics and comparative law which will enable the translator to find the closest equivalents in the target language.

Moreover, as regards legal concepts in particular, it is assumed that it is generally not possible to find equivalents in the target language that covers the meaning of the source language concepts. Due to the interdependency of legal language and legal system, what can be hoped for, at best, is partial equivalence. However, in the case of legal translation in the EU, the question of equivalence is a delicate one. Formally, absolute equivalence is required. Even if this is a contradiction in terms as far as legal translation is concerned, each authentic text is presumed to have identical meaning. This is due to the fact, referred to in section 4.2 above, that all language versions of Community legislation are equally authoritative, "original" texts; none of them are "just" translations. They all have the force of law.

Theories of legal translation have developed a whole range of methods to be employed in order to compensate for the lack of equivalence between legal concepts belonging to different legal systems: lexical expansion, descriptive paraphrases, definitions, borrowings, literal equivalents, neologisms etc. (see e.g. Šarčević 1997: 250-269). All methods are based on the assumption that there is a source text concept with a clear, determinate meaning which is to be translated into the target language. However, as we have seen above, the presumption that legal translation is about conveying the source language legal concepts into the target language does not hold in the case of EU law. With 23 official languages of equal standing, the intended meaning cannot be ascribed to any of the texts. None of the languages, none of the texts, and none of the legal systems have priority over the others. Consequently, the usual translation methods are of limited use in EU law.

The "identical-meaning-principle" and the equality of all language versions also apply to international legal instruments and to domestic legislation in bilingual and multilingual legal systems (Tabory 1980, Cao 2007b, Šarčević 1997). In this respect there is no difference between Community law and multilingual law in other contexts. However, in the case of Community law, the extreme number of equally authentic language versions makes it difficult or impossible to make use of the solutions to the problem of absolute equivalence introduced elsewhere. Thus, multilingual text production and co-drafting techniques as those invented in Canada and Switzerland with a view to preserving equivalence and equality of both/all official languages, including their linguistic and pragmatic conventions, cannot be and are not applied in Community law.

The practical reason for this is that it is simply not possible to co-draft 23 original texts. The interlingual and intercultural dialogue between 23 drafters needed in order to produce 23 texts simultaneously is impracticable. The formal reason is that, even though EU translators are allowed to translate idiomatically in the non-substantive parts of legislative acts and thus to adapt the target language text to the target language linguistic and legal conventions (Šarčević 1997: 224, quoting Koutsivitis), they have to follow the rule of interlingual identity as far as the substantive parts of legislation are concerned.

Terminological consistency within and across language versions is safeguarded by a number of drafting principles laid down in the Joint Practical Guide. The primary principle is principle 6.2 concerning "formal consistency":

> **Formal consistency**
> 6.2. Consistency of terminology means that the same terms are to be used to express the same concepts and that identical terms must not be used to express different concepts. The aim is to leave no ambiguities, contradictions or doubts as to the meaning of a term. Any given term is therefore to be used in a uniform manner to refer to the same thing and another term must be chosen to express a different concept.
> 6.2.1. This applies not only to the provisions of a single act, including the annexes, but also to provisions of related acts, in particular implementing acts and all other acts in the same area. In general, terminology must be consistent with the legislation in force.

But other principles of the guidelines also aim at securing terminological consistency:

> 5.5. [...] as to the relationship between the original text and translations of it
> 5.5.1. [...] the author must ensure that translators can immediately identify the sources drawn on in the original text. If a passage in the original text has been taken from an existing text (Treaty, directive, regulation, etc.) that must be clear from the text [...]. There is a risk that any hidden citations without a reference to the source will be translated freely in one or more languages, even though the author specifically intended to use the *authentic wording* of an existing provision. [italics added]
> 12.2. [...] repetition of passages or articles of the Treaties or other acts] is dangerous, since any departure from *the original wording* may give the impression that a different result was intended, and even give rise to a sort of presumption to that effect. [italics added]
> 18.12. Amendments are made in the form of text inserted into the act to be amended. Amendments must fit seamlessly into the basic text. In particular, the structure and terminology of the basic text must be maintained.

The legal background of the terminological restrictions on legal drafters and translators in the EU is the two factors that we have repeatedly referred to:

1. The fact that EU law is not an established legal system: legal concepts of the EU are still in the process of being established and furnished with autonomous legal meaning, distinguishable from domestic concepts and conceptions.
2. The fact that the EU legal order owes its existence to the interaction with the national legal orders of the Member States: The texts are produced in the EU institutions, but applied locally by national officials, lawyers, and judges. The best way to ensure that EU concepts are not misinterpreted by national lawyers is to apply terminology which is not genuine national terminology.

Or in the words of the Joint Practical Guide:

> 5.4: The aim is that, as far as possible, and taking account of the specific nature of Community law and its terminology, those called on to apply or interpret the act in each Member State ... must perceive it not as a "translation" in a negative sense — but as a text which corresponds to a certain legislative style.

The requirement of absolute equivalence between the 23 language versions puts tremendous constraints on translators in the EU. In the absence of established legal concepts, the only thing to do for legal text producers and legal translators is to cling to reproduction of the exact same words and phrases within and across language versions. Theoretically, this is an interesting aspect of legislative drafting in the EU: As the meaning of concepts is inherently indeterminate and cannot be ascribed to any of the languages involved, the best drafters and translators can obtain, is what one might call "relative equivalence" in the sense that identical terminology applied across languages from time to time signals identical meaning. So whatever the legal translator chooses to write, and for the reasons listed above, he or she often writes in the dark, the presumption is that if there is interlingual reproduction of terminology, there is conceptual equivalence between the language versions.

4.4. Translation in the EU is not translation!

As co-drafting techniques are not applied in EU law, translation remains an integral part of the legislative process. The production of Community texts relies heavily on translation. This is of course true in the sense that thousands and thousands of pages are translated by the Translation Services of the EU institutions each year. But if translation of legislative acts in the EU does not comply with the core principles underlying theories of legal translation, as we have seen above, the question arises if one can still meaningfully talk about translation?

The primary concern when translating legislation in the EU is not the target language legal conventions and the target language recipient, but rather the reproduction of words and phrases that can ensure coherence and consistency within and across the 23 equally authentic language versions. Therefore, it seems fair to say that translation in the EU is not translation in the strict sense of the word. It is interlingual text reproduction! Obviously, reproduction of terminology is not the same as standardization of terminology. Standardization of terms according to the principles laid down by the International Organization for Standardization is based on definitions of the concepts for which they stand (ISO standards 704 and 1087). In EU law, terms applied in the legislative acts may be defined in the acts themselves; but otherwise it is for the European Court of Justice to define the meaning of the terms.

5. Multilingual interpretation of the European Court of Justice

I could have written another story about multilingualism in the EU, quite a sad story, in fact. I could have described the meaninglessness of legal translation in the EU system, which is as absurd as the work of a man who has been told to dig a hole in the ground, and when finished is told to cover it up again. The fact is that in the legal practice of European lawyers only two language versions really count, the English and the French ones, although all 23 languages are formally defined as equally authoritative (Braselmann 2002: 253). One might even say that the texts drawn up in French and English do not count either. In the case law of the EC Court it has repeatedly been ruled that no language version must be given priority over the others, because all texts are of equal standing. Any interpretation of EU law must be based on a comparison of all 23 language versions. Nobody is allowed to rely on the version drawn up in his own language, as will appear from the following landmark decisions by the Court.

> The different language versions of a Community text must be given a uniform interpretation and hence in the case of divergence between the versions the provision in question must be interpreted by reference to the purpose and general scheme of the rules of which it forms a part. (Case 30/77, Regina v. Bouchereau).

> The elimination of linguistic discrepancies by way of interpretation may in certain circumstances run counter to the concern for legal certainty, inasmuch as one or more of the texts involved may have to be interpreted in a manner at variance with the natural and usual meaning of the words. Consequently, it is preferable to explore the possibilities of solving the points at issue without giving preference to any one of the texts involved.(Case 80-76, North Kerry Milk v. Minister for Agriculture and Fisheries).

> When a single decision is addressed to all the member states the necessity for uniform application and accordingly for uniform interpretation makes it impossible to consider one version of the text in isolation but requires that it be interpreted on the basis of both the real intention of its author and the aim he seeks to achieve, in the light in particular of the versions in all four languages. (Case 29/69, Stauder v. City of Ulm).

Thus, in the case of linguistic diversity between the language versions of an EU legislative act, the interpreter is really not allowed to rely on the texts at all, but has to await the EC Court's interpretation. And what does the Court do? It sets the texts aside, dismisses the actual wording of the texts and interprets them teleologically, according to the purpose of the act and with a view to furthering the general goals of the European Union. One conclusion to be drawn from the interpretation method adopted by the Court is that the translators in the EU are permitted to be more creative in their choice of words than translators of international treaties (see Šarčević 1997: 224). However, another, more pessimistic, conclusion could read as follows: "It is not very important for the translators of the EU system to be particularly accurate and careful. Whatever they write does not matter in legal practice!" Although this statement may be an exaggeration, it is more in accordance with the actual functioning of EU law than both translators and translation theorists would like to believe. As a Danish expert on EU law once said to me: "The texts of EU legislation are like the banister of a staircase: You are glad it is there, but you don't really use it."

6. Conclusion: Call for a new approach

Even if the statement by professor Rasmussen was meant to be a provocation, he is not the only one to conclude that the wording is of limited use when interpreting Community legislation. In an opinion of Advocate General Cosmas, delivered on 17 November 1998 in Case C-216/97, he considered the interpretation methods to be applied when constructing the Sixth Directive of Value Added Tax (often the subject of preliminary rulings):

> 9. It is worth making the preliminary point that, when the Community legislature laid down the rules on the harmonisation of the laws of the Member States relating to taxes, it did not formulate the relevant provisions of the Sixth Directive in a manner that was wholly clear and consistent. Responsibility should not be attributed to the legislature itself, but to the inherent incapacity of the terminology – where synonymous terms are sought in many different languages – to express a constantly changing reality and to stamp legal concepts with a clear inter-State and durable character. ...
>
> 11. The above observation is of some significance. It allows us to pinpoint the substance of the question under examination and the appropriate method to deal with it. That cannot consist in drawing arguments from the wording of the provisions at issue and comparing them with each other. Instead of adhering to the superficial content of the Sixth Directive, it is preferable to seek its true meaning by treating it as an aggregate rational system of rules.

From the point of view of translation theory, Advocate General Cosmas' observation is commonplace. Translators know that absolute equivalence between "clear inter-State" legal concepts is an illusion. This is a conclusion that follows naturally from the theory of legal translation and its fundamental categories and principles. Nevertheless, absolute equivalence is the formal requirement of EU legislation, the result of a multilingual legal system which is based on the principle of equal authenticity of all 23 languages, irrespective of the number of their speakers, their diffusion, and international importance.

Therefore, instead of concluding, like Advocate General Cosmas, that the wording of a legislative act is of no importance (as Šarčević 1997 does), translation theory should develop a new approach to legal translation in the EU which would be able to account *theoretically* for the role that language and translation, irrespective of the lack of absolute equivalence, actually play in establishing the meaning of Community legislation.

Theories and categories usually applied in translation studies cannot account adequately for translation problems, translation solutions, and interpretation methods adopted within the legal framework of the EU. This is why I call for the need to establish an independent interdisciplinary research field that focuses especially on features of law and language characteristic of the multilingual and multi-legal system of the EU. Interestingly, as follows from the case law of the EC Court, equivalence between the equally authentic language versions is sought for not by relying on the wording of the provision in question, but "by reference to the purpose and general scheme of the rules of which it forms a part" (Case 30/77, Regina v. Bouchereau). Therefore, the first challenge for translation theory is to define how the wording and terminology chosen in the individual language versions contribute to identifying the purpose and the general scheme that is the object of the teleological, dynamic interpretation by the Court.

What translation methods can the translators of EU law adopt in order to obtain the "teleological equivalence" strived for in EU law? And what new categories does translation theory need to account for the fact that legal translation and legal interpretation do in fact function in the context of the European Union, even if the theoretical assumptions of translation theory point in the opposite direction? The presuppositions underlying dominant theories of legal translation entail a view on the relationship between language and the law which needs to be reconsidered; otherwise, one will have to conclude that legal translation is an impossible task in the case of a multilingual legal system like the EU, or that legal translation in the EU is not translation at all or that it differs radically and profoundly from legal translation in all other cases. Translation studies generally refer to the necessity of taking the legal context into account when dealing with translation of legal texts both in theory and practice. However, if one wants to understand the way legal translation functions in the EU, it is not sufficient to apply translation theory and comparative law and legal theory; one also has to take into account integration theories that can explain the dynamics of European legal integration and the ways that interlingual communication of national and international interpretive communities contribute to that process.

Without abandoning comparative law and translation theory, the research field should take its point of departure somewhere else. As suggested in Kjær (2004b), a meaningful place to start is Habermas' theory of communicative action and Wittgenstein's functional approach to meaning.

References

Berteloot, P. (2001): "Der Rahmen juristischer Übersetzungen". In: Gerard-René de Groot and Reiner Schulze (eds.), *Recht und Übersetzen*. Baden-Baden: Nomos, 101-113.

Berteloot, P. (2004): "Die Europäische Union und ihre mehrsprachigen Rechtstexte". In: F. Müller and I. Burr: *Rechtssprache Europas. Reflexion der Praxis von Sprache und Mehrsprachigkeit im supranationalen Recht*. Berlin: Duncker and Humblot, 179-193.

Braselmann, P. (2002): "Gleiches Recht für alle – in alle Sprachen?". In: U. Hass-Zumkehr (ed.), *Sprache und Recht.* Jahrbuch des Instituts für deutsche Sprache 2001. Berlin and New York: de Gruyter, 240-254.

Buerstedde, W., Christensen, R. and M. Sokolowski (2001): "Leaving Babel. Die Aufgabe des Übersetzens als Chance für die Arbeit des EuGH". In: Friedrich Müller and Rainer Wimmer: *Neue Studien zur Rechtslinguistik.* Berlin: Duncker and Humblot, 119-172.

Burr, I. and T. Gallas (2004). "Zur Textproduktion im Gemeinschaftsrecht". In: F. Müller and I. Burr (eds.), *Rechtssprache Europas. Reflexion der Praxis von Sprache und Mehrsprachigkeit im supranationalen Recht.* Berlin: Duncker and Humblot, 195-242.

Cao, D. (2007a). "Inter-lingual uncertainty in bilingual and multilingual law". *Journal of Pragmatics* 39, 69-83.

Cao, D. (2007b): *Translating Law.* Clevedon: Multilingual Matters.

Caussignac, G. (2004). "Empirische Aspekte der zweisprachigen Redaktion von Rechtserlassen". In: F. Müller and I. Burr (eds.), *Rechtssprache Europas. Reflexion der Praxis von Sprache und Mehrsprachigkeit im supranationalen Recht.* Berlin: Duncker and Humblot, 157-178.

Charrow, V. R., Crandall, J. A. and R. P. Charrow (1982). "Characteristics and Functions of Legal Language". In: R. Kittredge and J. Lehrberger (eds.), *Sublanguage. Studies in Restricted Semantic Domains.* Berlin and New York: de Gruyter, 175-190.

Christensen, R. and F. Müller (2004). "Mehrsprachigkeit oder das eine Recht in vielen Sprachen" In: F. Müller and I. Burr (eds.), *Rechtssprache Europas. Reflexion der Praxis von Sprache und Mehrsprachigkeit im supranationalen Recht.* Berlin: Duncker and Humblot, 9-21.

Christensen, R. and Sokolowski, M. (2004). "Juristisches Entscheiden unter der Vorgabe von Mehrsprachigkeit". In: F. Müller and I. Burr (eds.), *Rechtssprache Europas. Reflexion der Praxis von Sprache und Mehrsprachigkeit im supranationalen Recht.* Berlin: Duncker and Humblot, 113-137.

de Groot, G. R. (1988): "Problems of legal translation from the point of view of a comparative lawyer". In: P. Nekeman (ed.), *Translation, our future.* Proceedings of XI World congress of the FIT. Euroterm Maastricht, 407-421.

de Groot, G. R. (1991): "Recht, Rechtssprache und Rechtssystem. Betrachtungen über die Problematik der Übersetzung juristischer Texte". *Terminologie et Traduction* 3, 279-316.

de Groot, G. R. (1999). "Das Übersetzen juristischer Terminologies". In: G.-R. de Groot and R. Schulze (eds.), *Recht und Übersetzen.* Baden-Baden: Nomos, 11-46.

de Groot, G. R. (2002). "Rechtsvergleichung als Kerntätigkeit bei der Übersetzung juristischer Terminologies". In: U. Hass-Zumkehr (ed.), *Sprache und Recht*. Jahrbuch des Instituts für deutsche Sprache 2001. Berlin and New York: de Gruyter, 222-239.

Engberg, J. (2002). "Legal Meaning Assumptions – What are the Consequences for Legal Interpretation and Legal Translation?" *International Journal for the Semiotics of Law* 15, 375-388.

Engberg, J. (2004). "Statutory Texts as Instances of Language(s): Consequences and Limitations on Interpretation". *Brooklyn Journal of International Law* 29(3), 1135-1166.

European Commission (2007a). *Translating for a Multilingual Community*. Brussels, March 2007.

European Commission (2007b). *Translation Tools and Workflow*. Brussels, March 2007.

Frame, I. (2005). "Linguistic oddities in European Union legislation: don't shoot the translator". *Clarity* 53, 21-24.

Gémar, J.-C. (2006). "Traduction spécialisée et droit. Langages du droit, styles et sens". In: M. Gotti and S. Šarčević (eds.), *Insights into Specialized Translation*. Bern: Peter Lang, 79-106.

Gerzymisch-Arbogast, H. (2003). "Das Zusammenspiel von Sprache und Fach beim Übersetzen. Beitrag der Übersetzung und Übersetzungswissenschaft zur Vielfalt und Einheit in Europa", In: I. Burr and G. Gréciano (eds.), *Europa: Sprache und Recht. La construction européenne: aspects linguistiques et juridiques*. Baden-Baden: Nomos, 127-139.

Glanert, S. (2006). "Zur Sprache gebracht: Rechtsvereinheitlichung in Europa". *European Review of Private Law* 2/2006, 157-174.

Habermas, J. (1981). *Theorie des kommunikativen Handelns, Bde 1–2*. Frankfurt/Main: Suhrkamp.

Kjær, A. L. (1995). "Vergleich von Unvergleichbarem. Zur kontrastiven Analyse unbestimmter Rechtsbegriffe". In: Kromann, H.-P. and Kjær, A. L. (eds.), *Von der Allgegenwart der Lexikologie. Kontrastive Lexikologie als Vorstufe zur zweisprachigen Lexikographie*. Tübingen: Niemeyer, 39-56.

Kjær, A. L. (1999a). *Recht und Sprache in der Europäischen Union. Zur Rolle der Mehrsprachigkeit des EU-Rechts im integrationsrechtlichen Prozess*. Copenhagen Research Project on European Integration, Institute of Political Science, University of Copenhagen.

Kjær, A. L. (1999b). "Überlegungen zum Verhältnis von Sprache und Recht bei der Übersetzung von Rechtstexten der Europäischen Union". In: P. Sandrini (ed.), *Übersetzen von Rechtstexten. Fachkommunikation im Spannungsfeld zwischen Rechtsordnung und Sprache*. Tübingen: Narr, 63-79.

Kjær, A. L. (2002). "'Eurospeak' – 'Eurotexte' – 'Eurobegriffe': Zur Pluralität von Sprachen und Rechten bei der Produktion und Rezeption gemeinschaftsrechtlicher Texte". In: L. Eriksen and K. Luttermann (eds.), *Juristische Fachsprache*. Münster: LIT-Verlag, 115-131.

Kjær, A. L. (2004a). "Sprachwissenschaftliche Aspekte der Übersetzung sozialwissenschaftlicher Texte". In A. P. Frank et al. (eds.), *Übersetzung, Translation, Traduction. Ein internationales Handbuch zur Übersetzungsforschung*. Berlin and New York: de Gruyter, 641-649.

Kjær, A. L. (2004b). "A Common Legal Language in Europe?". In M. van Hoecke (ed.), *Epistemology and Methodology of Comparative Law*. Oxford: Hart, 377-398.

Loehr, K. (1998). *Mehrsprachigkeitsprobleme in der Europäischen Union*. Frankfurt/Main, Berlin, Bern: Peter Lang.

Luttermann, K. (1999). "Übersetzen juristischer Texte als Arbeitsfeld der Rechtslinguistik". In: G.-R. de Groot and R. Schulze (eds.), *Recht und Übersetzen*. Baden-Baden: Nomos, 47-57.

Madsen, D. (1997a). "A model for translation of legal texts". In: M. Snell-Hornby, Z. Jettmarová and K. Kaindl (eds.), *Translation as Intercultural Communication*. Amsterdam and Philadelphia: John Benjamins, 291-299.

Madsen, D. (1997b). "Towards a Description of Communication in the Legal Universe. Translation of Legal Texts and the Skopos Theory". *Fachsprache* 19, 17-27.

Mattila, H. (2006). *Comparative Legal Linguistics*. London: Ashgate.

Mulders, L. (2006). "Translation at the Court of Justice". Paper presented at the "Binding Unity and Divergent Concepts in EU Law" conference, Tilburg University, 12-13 January 2006.

Pescatore, P. (1999). "Das Konzipieren übersetzungsgerechter juristischer Dokumente". In: G.-R. de Groot and R. Schulze (eds.), *Recht und Übersetzen*. Baden-Baden: Nomos, 91-99.

Revell, D. L. (2004). "Authoring Bilingual Laws: The Importance of Process". *Brooklyn Journal of International Law* 29(3), 1085-1105.

Robinson, W. (2005). "How the European Commission drafts legislation in 20 languages". *Clarity* 53, 4-10.

Sandrini, P. (1996). "Comparative Analysis of Legal Terms: Equivalence Revisited". In: C. Galinski and K.-D. Schmitz (eds.), *Terminology and Knowledge Engineering (TKE'96)*. Frankfurt/Main: Indeks Verlag, 342-351.

Sandrini, P. (1998). "Übersetzung von Rechtstexten: Die Rechtsordnung als Kommunikationsrahmen". In: L. Lundquist, H. Picht and J. Qvistgaard (eds.), *LSP: Identity and Interface. Research, Knowledge and Society*. Proceedings of the 11th European Symposium on Language for Special Purposes, Copenhagen, August 1997. Copenhagen Business School, 865-875.

Sandrini, P. (1999a). "Translation zwischen Kultur und Kommunikation: Der Sonderfall Recht". In: P. Sandrini (ed.), *Übersetzen von Rechtstexten. Fachkommunikation im Spannungsfeld zwischen Rechtsordnung und Sprache*. Tübingen: Narr, 9-43.

Sandrini, P. (1999b). "Deutsche Rechtssprache für Italienisches Recht: Der Fall Südtirol". In: G.-R. de Groot and R. Schulze (eds.), *Recht und Übersetzen*. Baden-Baden: Nomos, 198-199.

Sandrini, P. (2004a). "Transnationale interlinguale Rechtskommunikation: Translation als Wissenstransfer". In: F. Müller and I. Burr (eds.), *Rechtssprache Europas. Reflexion der Praxis von Sprache und Mehrsprachigkeit im supranationalen Recht*. Berlin: Duncker and Humblot, 139-156.

Sandrini, P. (2004b). "Globalisierung und Mehrsprachigkeit: Translation im Wandel?". In: L. Zybatow (ed.), *Translation in der globalen Welt und neue Wege in der Sprach- und Übersetzerausbildung*. Frankfurt/Main: Peter Lang, 165-177.

Sandrini, P. (2006). "LSP Translation and Globalization". In: M. Gotti and S. Šarčević (eds.), *Insights into Specialized Translation*. Bern: Peter Lang, 107-118.

Šarčević, S. (1988). "Translation of legislation - with special emphasis on languages of limited diffusion." In: Paul Nekeman (ed.), *XI World Congress of FIT: Proceedings: Translation, our future*. Euroterm Maastricht 1988, 455 - 462.

Šarčević, S. (1997). *New Approach to Legal Translation*. The Hague: Kluwer.

Šarčević, S. (2000). "Legal Translation and Translation Theory: a Receiver-Oriented Approach", at http://www.tradulex.org/Actes2000/sarcevic.pdf.

Šarčević, S. (ed.) (2001). *Legal translation. Preparation for accession to the European Union*. Rijeka: Faculty of Law.

Šarčević, S. (2006). "Die Übersetzung von mehrsprachigen EU-Rechtsvorschriften: Der Kampf gegen Sprachdivergenzen". In: M. Gotti and S. Šarčević (eds.), *Insights into Specialized Translation*. Bern: Peter Lang, 121-152.

Schäffner, C. (2003). "Translation and Intercultural Communication: Similarities and Differences". *Studies in Communication Sciences* 3(2), 79-107.

Stolze, R. (1992). "Rechts- und Sprachvergleich beim Übersetzen juristischer Texte". In: K.-D. Baumann and H. Kalverkämper (eds.), *Kontrastive Fachsprachenforschung*. Tübingen: Narr, 223-230.

Stolze, R. (1998). "Die Rolle von Fachsprachen im Kontakt von Einzelsprachen III: Fachübersetzung in den Geistes- und Sozialwissenschaften". In: L. Hoffmann, H. Kalverkämper and H. E. Wiegand (eds.), *Fachsprachen. Ein internationales Handbuch zur Fachsprachenforschung und Terminologiewissenschaft*. Berlin and New York: de Gruyter, 784-791.

Tabory, M. (1980). *Multilingualism in International Law and Institutions*. Alphen and den Rijn: Sijthoff and Noordhoff.

Weenink-Griffith, J. (2005). "The European Central Bank's approach to drafting legislation in 20 languages." *Clarity* 53, 11-14.

Weston, M. (1995). "Translating at the European Court of Human Rights". *Terminologie et Traduction* 3, 121-134.
Wittgenstein, L. (1984). *Philosophische Untersuchungen.* Werkausgabe in 8 Bänden, Band 1. Frankfurt/Main: Suhrkamp.

Diana Yankova
New Bulgarian University
Bulgaria

HOW HARMONIOUS IS HARMONIZATION OF LEGISLATION? ON THE CONCEPT OF TERM EQUIVALENCE

1. Introduction

Countries seeking accession to the European Union, such as Bulgaria and Romania, were not long ago in the process of harmonizing existing institutions and bodies, creating new ones and finding the language to communicate adequately within a unified Europe. Approximation of legislation entails the arduous and demanding task of standardizing legal terminology.

Some terminological aspects in this process are considered in this paper, reflecting on different approaches to the study of terms. The various mechanisms available to the translator are examined within the EU context and against the background of Bulgaria's legal culture. The analysis is based on 120 pages of selected EU directives[1] on intellectual property, copyright and related rights and their respective translations from English into Bulgarian, highlighting some felicitous choices and techniques employed, as well as some recurring inconsistencies.

At present there is great instability in Bulgarian legal terminology. New terms are coined rather ad hoc without regard to uniformity even in one and the same legal instrument. Terms are not evaluated according to the conceptual system of the particular field under codification. There is a process of replacement of Bulgarian terms due to the demand of international lexis and a marked shift of content of some native words under the influence of the languages in contact (cf. Yankova and Vassileva 2002).

2. The setting

Community law is a prime example of supranational law and, given the now 23 official languages, presents quite an idiosyncratic legal, linguistic, social and cultural setting. The Acquis communautaire or the collection of EU legislation encompasses primary legislation (the Treaties), secondary legislation (deriving

[1] Council Directives 91/250/EEC, 92/100/EEC, 93/83/EEC, 93/98/EEC, and 96/9/EC.

from the Treaties) and case law. There are five types of secondary EU instruments: regulation, directive, decision, recommendation, and opinion, of which the first two are the most important and most recurrent. It is essential for the translator to be aware of the parts that compose each instrument, the functions it performs and whether and to what extent it is binding.

EU directives are one of the means for achieving the aims and purposes of the European Community and are binding on all Member States, who have the discretion to determine how to incorporate them in the respective national legislation. Non-member States seeking membership are also in the process of harmonization of their national laws.

What are some of the characteristics of the specific EU context and how do they shape the linguistic and cognitive structure of the produced texts? The distinctive nature of the EU setting lies in the fact that a Member State translates and incorporates Community legislation into its own national law and language whereas in traditional cases nations draft their own laws, rather than adopt them from the outside.

The supranational environment in which EU legal instruments are drafted and the absence of a single culture are defining features of this setting. EU's multilingualism is a challenge for translation of legislative texts since the legal systems are not comparable. Terms that are used in one Member State sometimes cannot be easily rendered into the languages of another (e.g. summary judgement in English law is non-existent in the German legal system). Other realities that bear upon the way texts are shaped are the recommendations of the "fight the fog" campaign, the non-binding observance of age-long linguistic and legal traditions (as is the case in Britain for instance), the equal footing of all the official languages, the aspiration to draft legislation that will be comprehensible to the public at large and that can easily be translated into different languages, the fact that sometimes legislation in English is drafted by non-native speakers. Supranationality and multilingualism are the two most salient features of Community law. At least in theory.

In practice, some languages like Greek or Danish hardly ever function as source languages. Most documents are drafted in French, German, English or Spanish (cf. Robertson 2001: 699 or Trosborg 1997: 150) with a marked predominance of English. The English text of a document is often used for negotiations between delegations and in the accession procedures with non-member countries. According to a 2001 public opinion survey in the then 15 Member States conducted by INRA-Europe, although the proportion of EU population speaking English as a mother tongue is 16% (24% for German) the total proportion speaking this language both as mother and non-mother tongue is 47% (32% for German), making it the most widely used language in the European Union.

Notwithstanding the existing linguistic diversity, the working groups which try to institute a common European legal framework, choose English as the language of communication. From a practical point of view, this precludes the necessity to elaborate uniform terminology in each language and facilitates concentrating more on the legal issues to be tackled. Concurrently, it aggravates potential language problems since English legal language is closely related to English legal concepts, which can sometimes essentially depart from civil law notions.

EU citizens that speak regional languages like Catalan do not enjoy the same linguistic rights as those speaking the national languages of the member States. More people speak Catalan than those who speak the official languages Swedish, Portuguese, Greek, Danish and Finnish (Forrest 1998). Jacques Delors (1992: 32), among other EU officials, has expressed concern about the feasibility of maintaining language equality in an expanded and expanding European Union. Furthermore, at its 2667th meeting on 13 June 2005 in Luxembourg, the Council of the European Union decided to amend the 1958 Regulation No. 1 to grant Irish full status as official and working language and authorized the limited use at official EU level of languages recognized by member States other than the official languages.

What are the implications of this supranational, multilingual, multicultural context on professional interaction within EU institutions and more specifically on the communicative situation?

3. The specific multilingual communicative situation

Let us consider some features of the genre of statutory legislation from the point of view of the communicative situation, namely the participants in the communication, the purpose of communication, the production strategies.

In the context of a national legislation process the legal draftsman does not as a rule participate in parliamentary discussions, he is only the writer of the document and not the actual author of legislation. To make matters more complicated, legislation is multi-authored prose and often time-pressured. In codification the link between addresser and addressee is mediated. The law is intended for each individual in the society, but is interpreted by the specialist. Its illocutionary force holds no matter who the participants in the communication are. The main function of statutes is directive - it imposes obligations and confers rights.

The principal concern in legal drafting is the expression of the intent of the legislative body, not the facilitation of text comprehension. The ultimate concern of statutes is to regulate behaviour and not so much to inform and impart knowledge.

In many other types of text, the author often expresses an idea and then reformulates it in a different way so as to give the reader sufficient means and time to digest it. In legislation, sentences are over-compact and arranged in lists: the interpreter has the task to determine which ideas are important. The draftsman always has to keep in mind that he is writing for a hostile audience - the text will be interpreted by warring sides in the courtroom. Statutory writing strives to be precise and at the same time all-inclusive.

In the context of Community law we are witnessing a remarkable communicative situation where standard concepts of sender-receiver of message, medium, text type, have become rather fuzzy, giving rise to hybrid texts (cf. Trosborg 1997: 146) that derive from languages and cultures in contact, from intercultural communication. In addition to the traditional participants in legislative communication – the text producers (initiators and authors of statutory instruments) and text receivers (specialists who interpret the law and the general public) in this supranational and multilingual environment, there is another set of participants: that of translators and revisers who make certain that the produced texts are legally flawless and best suited to the local context. Translators are considered acting as mediators between text producers and receivers but can also be regarded as producing a new text and whose primary concern is target text receivers.

4. Translation problems that surfaced in the translated EU directives

In principle, Bulgarian legal language is not much different from other types of formal language. Bulgarian Acts can, as a rule, be read like ordinary prose with ordinary words with familiar meaning and ordinary grammar: they are easy to apprehend. Being part of the Continental tradition, the stress is on general principle at issue (or the "ratio legis") resulting in brevity of expression.

The Bulgarian translation of the Directives under examination, however, demonstrates a marked deviation from this tradition, especially in the numerous Preambles and the long and complex sentences. Certainly, a point to consider is the standardization of texts produced in the Union. All the different versions have to be uniform not only regarding the content, but also regarding the organization of the text. The layout, articles, paragraphs, sentences have to match completely in order to facilitate reference to the document in any of the official languages. The full stop rule requires "an equal number of full stops in source text and translations" (Trosborg 1997: 152). The translator, though constrained by EU requirements for standardization and uniformity of legislation, should observe the natural word order in the target language, making the sentence sound as naturally as possible.

Some of the terminological problematic areas encountered in the translation of the directives into Bulgarian can be systematized as follows:

Conceptual non-equivalence. Since translation is a form of cross-cultural communication, one of the difficulties translators most often encounter is institutions or concepts which do not exist in one of the cultures. For instance, the Bulgarian terms *предварително следствие* (*predvaritelno sledstvie*, preliminary investigation)[2] or *дознание* (*doznanie*, preliminary inquest) do not have conceptual equivalents in Britain. The National Investigation Service, an independent body in Bulgaria, does not exist in other law systems. The work of the *дознател* (*doznatel*) is performed by a police inspector in England. Another such term is *възпитателна работа* (*văzpitatelna rabota*) which is usually rendered by a loan translation in English as "educative work".

Specificity/Generality of terms. A greater or lesser degree of lexical density on the semantic continuum poses great demands on the work of the translator. Concepts in one language may have multiple meanings in another. More often than not Bulgarian legal terms have broader meaning than the corresponding English terms. A case in point would be *адвокат* (*advokat*) which corresponds to advocate, barrister, solicitor, counsel, lawyer and attorney. The English enactment in the sense of a legal document codifying the result of deliberations of a committee or society or legislative body is rendered in Bulgarian with *закон* (*zakon*, act), *нормативен акт* (*normativen akt*, enactment), *правно предписание* (*pravno predpisanie*, regulation), *постановление* (*postanovlenie*, ordinance), *указ* (*ukaz*, decree).

Faux amis or false cognates. Superficial resemblance conceals their different meanings, e.g. "third country" instead of "non member state", process of law is not *законен процес* (*zakonen proces*) but *законна процедура* (*zakonna procedura*). One of the most glaring examples of a semantic deviation of international lexis in the analysed texts is the translation of "public" as *публика* (*publika*). The word in Bulgarian means "audience". The correct rendition of "public" is *общество* (*obštestvo*) or *обществеearност* (*obštestvenost*).

Collocational semantic variation. Discrimination between the diverse meanings of one and the same word depending on the immediate context: e.g. legal – *правен* (*praven*), *юридически* (*juridičeski*), *съдебен* (*sădeben*), *законен* (*zakonen*).

Positive or negative latent value attribution to words or phrases in particular contexts. These are occurrences when past semantics hinders the adoption of loan words owing to negative connotation. The word "directive", for instance, is a term associated with the former totalitarian regimes in Eastern bloc countries with negative overtones. It has seemingly undergone a motivated shift of

[2] All examples in the Cyrillic script are followed by a transliteration in italics and a translation in regular font in brackets

content, however, and is currently freely used in relation to the institutional discourse of the European Union.

5. Selecting adequate translation strategies

In establishing equivalencies different criteria can be considered depending on the purpose of the translation. Equivalents can be communicative, linguistic (literal), or functional. A communicative translational equivalent is one that is directed to the recipient of a text. The purpose is to facilitate the specialist in the target language in understanding the concept behind the term. Secondly, a translational equivalent can be oriented towards the source-language term, giving primary importance to linguistic form. Thirdly, the translator can opt for an equivalent that is a legal term in the target language (for a discussion of types of conceptual equivalence cf. Yankova 2003: 57 ff.).

Of paramount importance in translating statutory texts is focusing on the content of the message and the precision and accuracy in meaning which override considerations of style. The prescriptive, authoritative character of legislation as a rule calls for literal translation in order for the translated text to achieve an effect identical to that of the source text. Therefore, functional equivalence is of utmost concern in legal translation. It is also recipient oriented in that it should correspond pragmatically to the source text.

In the absence of adequate conceptual equivalents in the target language there are several possibilities the translator can resort to. If we take as example the Bulgarian *касационен съд* (*kasacionen săd*) or Cour de Cassation in French, it can be translated as Supreme Court, in which case a communicative translational equivalent would be employed, focusing on the concept. The aim would be to make a foreign lawyer understand that it is the highest court in the Bulgarian system. The other option would be for the term to be translated as Court of Cassation, whereby it would be source-language oriented and faithful to the linguistic form. It would also convey the foreign nature of the concept it refers to. However, it might hamper text comprehension unless the foreign lawyer is well versed in French or Latin or is acquainted with the Franco-Germanic legal system, on which the Bulgarian one is based.

The Anglo-American term "trust" has no equivalent in Bulgarian civil law. First, the translator can supply additional information to explain that trust is a right of property, real or personal, held by one party for the benefit of another. Another possibility would be to preserve the source term. There has been an increasing tendency to use anglicisms in the Bulgarian language. Most young professionals feel comfortable with the English language and the untranslated usage of English terms would eliminate mis-translation. However, the primary purpose of translation is to make the source text accessible to people who do not know the source language. Moreover, non-translation renders an already hard-to-unpack legal text even more difficult for ordinary citizens. A third solution would be to find a short but sufficiently explanatory phrase, e.g. in the case of "trust": *опека и управление на имущество* (*opeka i upravlenie na imushtestvo*). A fourth option would be to create a neologism. In my opinion, in most similar cases the best solution is the third option - finding a short, explanatory phrase that would be both relatively succinct and sufficiently descriptive. In Šarčević's view (1997) the most adequate rendering in cases of terminological incongruity is the attempt to convey the intended meaning in neutral language.

The creation of new lexical entities (neologisms) in cases of terminological incongruity can be of two types: totally new creations and borrowings from other languages. Neologisms should not be selected in an arbitrary way; they should show to a certain degree the content of the source term and be understandable by the target audience. When choosing neologisms the translator should also take into consideration the choice of earlier translators. Borrowings can be of three types: direct borrowing, e.g. компютър (kompjutăr) > computer; b) loan translation (calquing), e.g. *Бялата книга* (*Bjalata kniga*) > White Paper; c) internationalisms (Latin or Greek basic root forms, e.g. *магистрат* (*magistrat*) > magistrate. Direct borrowing can be recommended when the source language term can be easily integrated into the phonemic, graphemic, and morphological structure of the target language and if it permits derivatives. The use of Latin or Greek word elements produces internationalisms which facilitate text comprehension: e.g. jurisprudence > *юриспруденция* (*jurisprudencija*), ministry > *министерство* (*ministerstvo*), restitution > *реституция* (*restitutziya*). Loan translation is generally used for complex or compound terms and phrases, e.g. common law jurisdiction > *обичайно-правна юрисдикция* (*običajno-pravna jurisdikcija*) and is generally preferred to direct borrowing but neither form of term creation is acceptable if it violates the natural word-formation techniques of a linguistic community.

When the term is transparent or semantically motivated a good choice is a literal translation (Community law, Green Paper > *право на Общността* (*pravo na Obštnostta*), *Зелената книга* (*Zelenata kniga*). There are instances of description of the terms, as in collecting society rendered as *организация за колективно управление на права* (*organizacija za kolektivno upravlenie na prava*).

Another approach would be to extend the meaning of an existing term to encompass that of a new concept, e.g. piracy now refers also to audio piracy, something that could not have been foreseen when the word was first created. Many terms are coined by the use of simile, i.e. the naming of a concept in analogy to another, familiar one. When a special concept (belonging to a target domain) is designated by the name of a general concept (belonging to a source domain) because of some resemblance between the two, then we have metaphorical term formation and its motivation can be found in similarities of form, function and position (e.g. "mouse" in computing, "control arm" in engineering, "bedrock" in geology). A term in one field can also be re-used in another field for a different concept (e.g. "hardware" in computing and general language).

When a concept in the source language has several equivalents in the target language, i.e. when it manifests differences along the semantic continuum, the felicitous choice would be effected through descriptive terms in order to make this distinction.

Most important of all before attempting translation, however, is to look closely at the system of concepts and concept relationships in each individual language. Acknowledging that concept systems are logical hierarchies in which concepts are subordinated, superordinated or juxtaposed to each other, of special importance for terminological work is the study of these hierarchical relationships. Conceptual differences between two (or more) languages are especially manifest in legal terminologies.

Let us take as an example the English legal term "defamation". Black's Law Dictionary gives the following definition: "holding up of a person to ridicule, scorn or contempt in a respectable and considerable part of the community. Includes both libel and slander". Under "libel" we find: "a method of defamation expressed by print, writing, pictures, or signs" and under "slander": "the speaking of base and defamatory words tending to prejudice another in his reputation, office, trade, business, or means of livelihood".

Within the conceptual system of British law, libel and slander are both methods of defamation; the former being expressed by print, writing, pictures, or signs; the latter by oral expression or transitory gestures; and defamation is the generic term. Or, in linguistic terms, defamation is the superordinate term for the co-hyponyms libel and slander. The semantic characteristics look like this:

> defamation: (+false), (+defamatory), (+(or) -permanent form), (+ (or) -transient form)
> libel: (+false), (+defamatory), (+permanent form)
> slander: (+false), (+defamatory), (+transient form)

If we consider the conceptual system of Bulgarian law, we only find the term *клевета* (*kleveta*) which corresponds in semantic features to the generic term "defamation":

> клевета: (+false), (+defamatory), (+(or) -permanent form), (+ (or) -transient form).

In an English-Bulgarian translation, the appropriate choice is a descriptive equivalent (e.g. a phrase that is equivalent to oral defamation and defamation in a permanent form). When translating such terms from Bulgarian into English, translators should be careful in choosing the pertinent co-hyponym.

In cases of collocational variation, Jacobs's (1995) assignment of thematic roles can be very useful in delineating the diverse meanings of a word. Undoubtedly a componential analysis is indispensable in the choice of translation procedure. The term and its concept have to be identified, delineated in the source language in order to find the appropriate term in the target language. Semanticians have resorted to analysing the meaning of a single word (word-internal semantics) and the meaning that word has with other parts of a sentence (external semantics). The legal terms under consideration in this study constitute a semantic unit, their definition is a proposition consisting of a predicate and arguments that fulfill varying semantic or thematic roles. Fillmore (1968) explains the propositional content (the deep structure) of a simple sentence through deep cases (relations) such as: Agentive, Instrumental, Objective, Factitive, Locative, Benefactive, which are converted into surface representation of sentences. Jacobs (1995) talks of the following thematic roles that the predicate assigns to its arguments: Agent, Instrument, Theme, Experiencer, Source and Goal, Benefactive, Location and Time.

> - Agent: a mind-possessor who acts intentionally;
> - Instrument: the thing with which the action is done;
> - Theme:
> a) inert entity, which is in a certain state or position or is changing state or position,
> b) affected mind-possessing entities (or Patient);
> Experiencer: the one who experiences a mental state or process such as thinking, knowing, believing, understanding, fearing, etc.;
> - Source and Goal: source refers to the location from which someone or something originates and goal to the location that serves as the destination;
> - Benefactive: the role of the individual for whose benefit some action is undertaken;
> - Location and Time: these are thematic roles for nonargument noun phrases. (Jacobs 1995: 22-29).

All the different ways of rendering legal terms in Bulgarian included the thematic roles: +Agent, +Instrument, +Theme. However, the various uses demonstrated a different thematic role as the salient one in the four cases, or even additional thematic roles, besides the essential ones:

legal and noun:

правен (praven) and noun: +Agent: legal protection > правна закрила (pravna zakrila), legal implications > правни последствия (pravni posledstvija);

юридически (juridičeski) and noun: +Instrument in the salient role: legal entity > юридическо лице (juridičesko

lice) legal residence > юридическо местожителство (juridičesko mestožitelstvo);
съдебен (sădeben) and noun: +Locative: legal costs > съдебни разноски (sădebni raznoski), legal opinion > съдебно становище (sădebno stanovište);
законен (zakonen) and noun: +Theme as the salient role: legal duties > законен дълг (zakonen dălg), legal right > законно право (zakonno pravo).

Another example is "(un)authorised and noun" (e.g. an authorized person, unauthorized removal), where depending on the presence of the semantic roles +Theme or +Patient, the respective Bulgarian terms are: *упълномощено лице* (*upălnomošteno lice*), *непозволено отстраняване* (*nepozvoleno otstranjavane*).

6. Conclusions

A basic difficulty in translating legal (or any other specialized) texts is the lack of equivalent terminology. A successful translation is one that relays the content of the source text achieving adequate semantics and pragmatics in the target language. Searching for terminological equivalence entails constant comparison between the legal systems of the source and target languages. Legal traditions and cultures are so diverse that concepts in one system are alien to another system; therefore the cultural dimension of the concept should also be taken into account when looking for terminological equivalents. Some authors hold the view that full equivalence can only occur when the source and target language relate to the same legal system. "In principle, this is only the case when translating within a bi- or multilingual legal system, such as that of Belgium, Finland, Switzerland and - to some degree – Canada" (de Groot 2000:133). The on-going process of establishing a uniform legal system and institutions across Europe would mean that terminological equivalence is both necessary and possible. The issue is how to achieve this equivalence? What conceptual and linguistic resources to employ? The analysis of the objective form of language, the outsider view or the "etic" aspects in conjunction with how language functions for users in real-life coupled with the insider view, or the "emic" aspects can offer insights into both the common, shared meaning and the culturally specific facets of meaning.

To summarize, I would like to provide a list of suggestions that have resulted from the present study as guidelines for further legal translations from Bulgarian into English and from English into Bulgarian:

- each term should be evaluated with regard to the conceptual system of the particular field under codification;
- a componential analysis of the semantic features of the concept is indispensable in finding the most appropriate translational equivalent of a term;
- in the absence of adequate equivalents the possible choices are: non-translation (preserving the source term), finding a short explanatory phrase (paraphrase), creating a neologism;
- preserving the source term is the least desirable option unless it concerns established Latinisms in one of the languages;
- paraphrase is a very useful technique for non-existing legal terms. It should be short, but sufficiently explanatory;
- neologisms cannot be chosen in an arbitrary way. They should be somewhat transparent to the target audience and should not violate the natural word formation of the target language. They should also allow for derivatives;
- in choosing neologisms, the choice of earlier translators should be taken into account in order to achieve continuity and avoid confusion.

References

Delors, J. (1992). Article in *The Economist*, April 11.

Fillmore, C. (1968). "The Case for Case". In: E. Bach and R. T. Harms (eds.), *Universals in Linguistic Theory*. New York: Holt, 1-88.

Forrest, A. (1998). "The Challenges of Languages in Europe". *T and T* 3, 101-121.

de Groot, G-R. (2000). "Translating Legal Information". In G. Zaccaria, *Journal of Legal Hermeneutics. Translation in Law*, 5. Münster-Hamburg-London: Lit Verlag, 131-149.

Jacobs, R. (1995). *English Syntax: a Grammar for English Language Professionals*. Oxford: Oxford University Press.

Robertson, C. (2001). "Multilingual Law: A Framework for Understanding LSP within the EU". In: F. Mayer (ed.), *Language for Specific Purposes. Perspectives for the New Millennium*, vol. 2., Tübingen: Gunter Narr Verlag.

Trosborg, A. (1997). "Translating Hybrid Political Texts". In: A. Trosborg (ed.), *Text Typology and Translation*. Amsterdam/Philadelphia: John Benjamins.

Šarčević, S. (1997). *New Approach to Legal Translation*. The Hague: Kluwer Law International.

Yankova, D. and I. Vassileva (2002). "Supranational Legislative Texts: a New Challenge for Translators in Europe". In: H. P. Kelz (ed.), *Die sprachliche Zukunft Europas. Mehrsprachigkeit und Sprachenpolitik*. Baden-Baden: Nomos-Verlag, 145-158.

Yankova, D. (2003). “Towards Achieving Equivalence in Bulgarian-English Translation of Statutory Writing”. *Чуждоезиково обучение* [Foreign Language Teaching] 3, 52-63.

Luciana Carvalho
Pontifícia Universidade Católica de São Paulo
Brazil

TRANSLATING CONTRACTS AND AGREEMENTS FROM A CORPUS LINGUISTICS PERSPECTIVE

1. Introduction

The goal of this study is to provide naturally occurring Brazilian Portuguese translation equivalents for binomial expressions in legal agreements originally written in English. I have attempted to provide translators with the necessary linguistic and cultural elements to enable them to render a natural translation, that is, to translate legal language into legal language.

Binomial expressions are formed by two words belonging to the same grammatical category and joined by *and* or *or*. Some examples are: *terms and conditions*, *any and all*, *executed and delivered*, *due and payable*, *action or proceeding*, *agreement or obligation*. Binomials are an integral part of English legal language, and as such have attracted a considerable amount of study (Mellinkoff 1962, Bhatia 1993, Vystrcilova 2000, Kwok 2000, and Rossini 2005, among others). On the other hand, the same does not apply to Brazilian Portuguese legal language, in which binomial expressions are not as common. Therefore, when dealing with binomial expressions, Brazilian translators tend to translate all the elements of a binomial literally (Carvalho 2006 and 2007) and, consequently, in many cases fail to attain the "intended legal effect" (Šarčević 2000: 12) of the communicative event.

For this reason, to study binomials in English legal language and help determine their translation equivalents in Brazilian Portuguese, I compiled and explored a bilingual comparable corpus made up of authentic *agreements* and *contratos*, totalling, approximately, one million words – 705,744 in English and 289,984 in Brazilian Portuguese.

The choice of text type is due to the fact that *agreements* and *contratos* are among the most difficult documents to translate (Mayoral Asensio 2003), they also have an incredibly high concentration of binomial expressions (Carvalho 2007), and are among the most translated documents in the Brazilian market.

Exploring such a corpus greatly depended on the tools and methods of Corpus Linguistics. Tagging was carried out with UCREL's CLAWS 7 (*the Constituent Likelihood Automatic Word-tagging System*), and the chosen corpus exploration software was Scott's (1996) *WordSmith Tools*.

2. Definitions, origin, roles and classification of binomial expressions

Binomial expressions are also termed *binomials* (Bhatia 1993), *doublets* (Mayoral Asensio 2003), and *doublings* (Mellinkoff 1963). These units have been the object of study both in unspecialized (Malkiel 1957, Tagnin 1989 and 2005, among others) and specialized language (Mellinkoff 1963, Bhatia 1993, Vystrcilova 2000, Kwok 2000, and Rossini 2005, among others). For the purposes of this corpus-based research a binomial is considered *a sequence of two words belonging to the same grammatical category and joined by* and *or* and *occurring three or more times in at least two documents in the corpus.*

These units are reported to have emerged in the Early Modern English period – a period marked by the production of binomials representing new terminology in English Law – and were usually formed by the combination of an existing term in Old English and its synonym in French (Nevalainen 1999: 363). Binomials such as *bargain and sale* and *breaking and entering* are examples of this phenomenon (Barleben 2003). On the other hand, the proliferation of binomials has also been attributed to the fact that lawyers and notaries, at a certain time in the history of English Law, were paid according to the number of pages they wrote, which resulted in the considerable use of superfluous words (Mellinkoff 1963: 190).

The literature assigns various roles to binomial expressions. Among them you can find: "precision and all-inclusiveness" (Bhatia 1993: 108), "a convenient linguistic device for adding weight to the end of the sentences" (Gustafsson 1984: 133), and "a distinct style marker of legal English" (Gustafsson 1984: 133).

Gustafsson (1984), Malkiel (1959) and Mellinkoff (1963) have classified binomials according to the semantic relationship of their elements. To Gustafsson (1984: 133), binomials can be classified as: a) *synonymous* (last will and testament), b) *antonymous* ([be present] in person or by proxy), or c) *complementary* (shoot and kill). Malkiel (1959) classifies them as a) *near synonyms* (null and void), b) *complementary* (assault and battery), c) *opposite* (assets and liabilities), d) *subdivision* (months and years) or e) *consequence* (shot and killed). Finally, Mellinkoff (1963) uses the terms a) *worthless doubling* (force and effect) and b) *useful doubling* (full faith and credit).

3. Why study binomials?

The importance of studying binomial expressions is not only because they are a distinct mark of legal discourse and extremely common in legal English, as Mellinkoff (1963) and Crystal and Davy (1969) put it, but also because there are many different kinds of binomials, meaning that they represent a challenge and a trap to the legal translator (Mayoral Asensio 2003: 96-7, Kwok 2000: 3).

Moreover, binomial expressions are not easily found in bilingual legal dictionaries (Carvalho 2006: 316).

However, in English, binomial expressions are found in virtually any kind of legal genre, such as statutory provisions, decisions, orders, opinions, formbooks, boilerplate, formulas, deeds, and especially in contracts and agreements. This study is concerned with the occurrence and translation of binomials in contracts and agreements because they are among the most difficult documents to translate and to understand (Mayoral Asensio 2003: 93), besides representing a considerable share of the amount of work of legal translators.

4. But what is a contract?

To determine which kind of documents would be included in our corpus, the definition of *contrato* (contract) in the Brazilian Legal System was adopted. Therefore, in this study a *contract* is considered "an agreement involving the manifestation of will between two or more parties, according to the law, and aimed at regulating interests in acquiring, modifying or terminating legal property relationships" (Diniz 1999: 9).

In the definition above, there is no mention of *consideration,* which is a common law requirement for determining whether an agreement is a contract or not. This is not the same for the Brazilian legal system. Thus, the concept of *contrato* encompasses both what the common law considers a *contract* and an *agreement.*

5. Legal translation: respecting linguistic conventions

Some authors (Parr 1997: 18, in Kwok 2000: 29) believe it to be impossible to find enough synonyms in the target language reflecting all the components in a binomial in the source language and attribute the challenge of translating such units to this shortcoming. However, the translator's role does not merely consist in finding the same number of equivalents in the target language, but also in making sure s/he is translating *legal language* into *legal language* (De Groot 1998: 23). In our case, Brazilian legal language, unlike English legal language, is not characterized by such abundant use of binomial expressions. For this reason, the translator must be familiar with the language and cultural conventions of each legal system involved in the translation activity in order to attain the "intended legal effect" (Šarčević 2000: 12) and "this presupposes legal competence and a basic knowledge of the characteristics of legal texts" (Šarčević 2000: 4). However, when dealing with binomial expressions, studies show that Brazilian translators (Carvalho 2007: 58-64) and dictionaries (Carvalho 2006: 316) tend to translate each and every element of a binomial literally. Consequently, in many cases, they fail to attain the *intended legal effect* of the communicative event and they produce unidiomatic translations.

6. Compiling a comparable corpus

In order to study binomials in English and determine their translation equivalents, I have compiled and explored a bilingual comparable corpus made up of authentic *agreements* and *contratos*, totalling, approximately, one million words. Exploring such a corpus greatly depended on the principles of Corpus Linguistics and the software used was Scott's *WordSmith Tools* (1996).

Corpus Linguistics is the study of language based on examples of real life language use (Tognini-Bonelli 2001: 54). It is based on empirical analyses of a large and principled collection of natural texts, known as a "corpus". It makes extensive use of computers for analysis and depends on both quantitative and qualitative analytical techniques. The table below provides the essential information on the bilingual corpus.

Table 1. Corpus information

Genre	**Agreements (English)**	**Contratos (Brazilian Portuguese)**
Corpus size (280 texts) (28 x 5 = 140)	705 744 words	289 984 words
Types	10 233	11 413
Type/Token ratio	1.58	4.08

The corpus is made up of 280 texts: 140 in English and 140 in Brazilian Portuguese. There are 5 samples of 28[1] different kinds of agreements in each language. Therefore, our corpus is termed *comparable*. A comparable corpus

[1] The *contratos* included in the corpus were: Shareholder's Agreements, Powers of Attorney, Banking Services Agreements, Credit Card Agreements, Articles of Incorporation, Sale and Purchase Agreements, Transaction Agreements, Promise to Purchase Agreements, Donation Agreements, Assignment Agreements, Escrow Agreements, Supply Agreement, Software License Agreement, Loan Agreements, Franchise Agreements, Personal Warranty Agreements, Product Warranty Agreements, Lease Agreement, Car Rental Agreements, Healthcare Agreements, Consulting Agreements, Professional Services Agreements, Translation Agreements, Publishing Agreements, Agency Agreements, Health Insurance Agreements, Confidentiality Agreements, and Employment Agreements.

consists of texts in two or more languages originally written in the language they represent and compiled according to similar criteria (Tognini-Bonelli 2001: 6-7).

The most time-consuming and difficult part of this study was compiling the corpus and balancing it. Being able to come up with the same number of kinds of agreements in both languages was not an easy task. In fact, it was not possible to compile 5 samples of all the *contratos* found. Kwok (2000: 2) states the reason for the difficulty in finding legal agreements is because they are signed between private entities and, therefore, are not readily accessible to the public when compared to laws and regulations, for instance.

In our case, I believe the setbacks in compiling and balancing a comparable corpus have two main reasons. First, there are many more documents available in English on the internet. Second, there were two legal systems involved and, therefore, the types of agreements used in each one vary.

The first reason is clearly because English predominates on the Internet. However, in addition to this, I also believe that it is also due to the much more dynamic and intense legal and trade relations in the English-speaking countries. Regulatory requirements in the U.S. have been promoting a never-experienced level of transparency, and, consequently, an unprecedented wealth of information on the web.

The second reason concerns the different legal traditions: Civil Law and Common Law, which lead to certain agreements being quite common in one legal system, but sometimes non-existent in the other (e.g. trust agreements in Brazil, *parceria rural* in the U.S.).

7. Tagging and exploring the Corpus

Corpus linguistics was used as a methodology because it enables the analysis of large data by means of computational tools such as word lists, concordance lines, clusters, among others, by which the researcher can identify the occurrence of repeated events, and promptly access the immediate context involving the search item.

After compiling and balancing the corpus, the CLAWS 7 tagset (Constituent Likelihood Automatic Word-tagging System) developed at the Unit for Computer Research on the English Language (UCREL) at the University of Lancaster[2] was employed in order to optimize retrieval of the binomial expressions. Each word (token) in the corpus received a tag indicating its grammatical category. The figures below show two versions of the same text: untagged and tagged.

[2] http://www.comp.lancs.ac.uk/ucrel/claws/

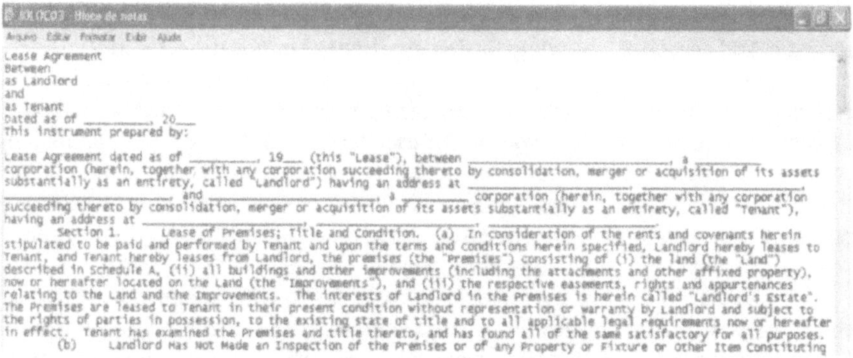
Lease Agreement
Between
as Landlord
and
as Tenant
Dated as of ________, 20__
This instrument prepared by:

Lease Agreement dated as of ________, 19__ (this "Lease"), between ________________, a ________ corporation (herein, together with any corporation succeeding thereto by consolidation, merger or acquisition of its assets substantially as an entirety, called "Landlord") having an address at ________________, and ________________, a ________ corporation (herein, together with any corporation succeeding thereto by consolidation, merger or acquisition of its assets substantially as an entirety, called "Tenant"), having an address at ________________.

Section 1. Lease of Premises; Title and Condition. (a) In consideration of the rents and covenants herein stipulated to be paid and performed by Tenant and upon the terms and conditions herein specified, Landlord hereby leases to Tenant, and Tenant hereby leases from Landlord, the premises (the "Premises") consisting of (i) the land (the "Land") described in Schedule A, (ii) all buildings and other improvements (including the attachments and other affixed property), now or hereafter located on the Land (the "Improvements"), and (iii) the respective easements, rights and appurtenances relating to the Land and the Improvements. The interests of Landlord in the Premises is herein called "Landlord's Estate". The Premises are leased to Tenant in their present condition without representation or warranty by Landlord and subject to the rights of parties in possession, to the existing state of title and to all applicable legal requirements now or hereafter in effect. Tenant has examined the Premises and title thereto, and has found all of the same satisfactory for all purposes.

(b) Landlord Has Not Made an Inspection of the Premises or of any Property or Fixture or Other Item Constituting

Figure 1. Untagged text (fragment)

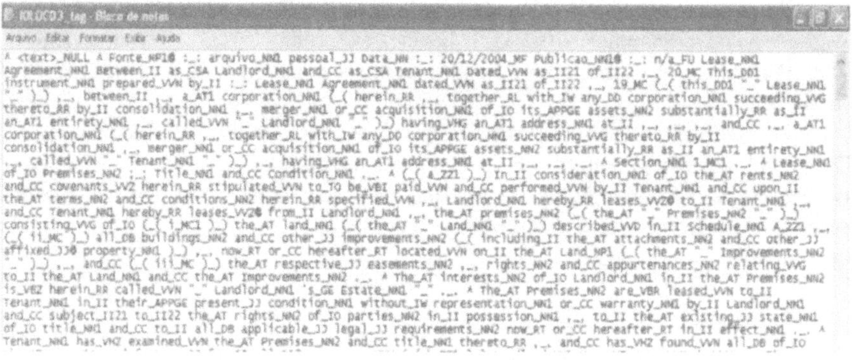

Figure 2. Tagged text (fragment)

After tagging the entire English corpus, the binomials were retrieved according to the definition adopted in this research, that is, *two words belonging to the same grammatical category joined by* and *or* or.

The CLAWS 7 tagset comprises over 130 different part-of-speech tags. To streamline identifying the binomial expressions using WordSmith Tools, I grouped all CLAWS 7 tags into 9 search strings representing 8 grammatical categories:

1) Articles - *_AT* *CC *_AT*
2) Determiners - *_D* *CC *_D*
3) Prepositions - *_I* *CC *_I*
4) Adjectives - *_J* *CC *_J*

5) Nouns - *_N* *CC *_N*
6) Pronouns - *_P* *CC *_P* and - *_APPGE* *CC *_APPGE*
7) Verbs - *_V* *CC *_V*
8) Adverbs - *_R* *CC *_R*

By using the tags to retrieve binomial units, I examined the concordance lines and clusters for each search strings. Here, I shall illustrate the findings for binomials formed by adverbs.

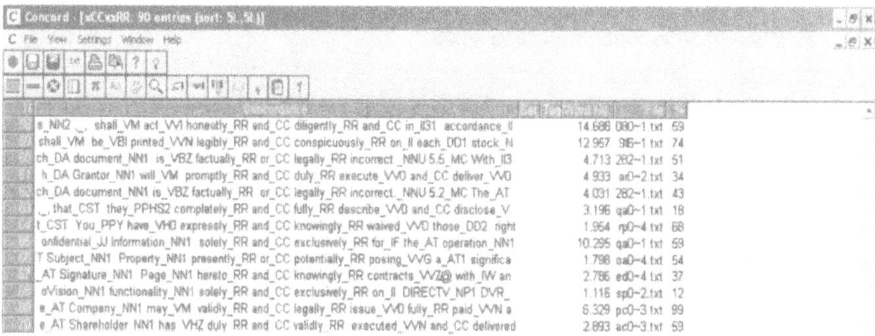

Figure 3. Concordance lines (fragment) for adverb query

After examining the concordance lines, I needed to find which binomials occurred repeatedly in the corpus. For the sake of this study, a binomial had to occur at least 3 times in the corpus in at least 2 different texts. To draw the binomials from the concordance lines, I used the Clusters tool, which rendered the following results for binomials formed by adverbs:

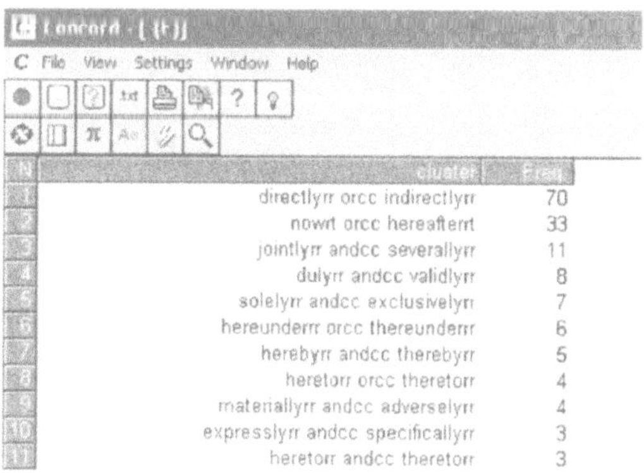

Figure 4. Clusters (fragment) for adverb query

From the word clusters above and the figures showing their frequency in the corpus, the binomial expressions formed by adverbs in the corpus were: *duly and validly*, *now or hereafter*, *jointly and severally*, *duly and validly*, *solely and exclusively*, *hereunder or thereunder*, *hereby and thereby*, *hereto or thereto*, *hereof or thereof*, *materially and adversely*, *expressly and specifically*, *hereto and thereto*, *irrevocably and unconditionally*, *wholly or partially*, and *thereof or otherwise*. To identify all the binomial expressions in the corpus, similar queries were carried out for all the remaining word classes.

8. Finding translation equivalents

The next steps depended on whether or not I was able to provide a *prima facie* translation for the binomial corresponding to the translation equivalent. In this paper, I shall exemplify with the first situation[3]. Therefore, the following steps were: providing a *prima facie* translation, examining the greater context of the binomial and determining a translation equivalent. If, on the one hand, the first stage (extracting binomials) was largely dependent on computer tools, the second (assigning a *prima facie* translation) is entirely qualitative and intuitive. In other words, to provide a *prima facie* translation for a given binomial I relied on my expertise as a legal translator and trained lawyer. The third (examining concordance lines in English) and fourth (examining concordance lines in Portuguese) stages are also qualitative but are based on corpus data.

To illustrate stages 2, 3, and 4, I have chosen to examine *wear and tear*. The two following pictures show concordance lines for the binomial in English and the concordance lines for its equivalent in Brazilian Portuguese: *desgaste natural*.

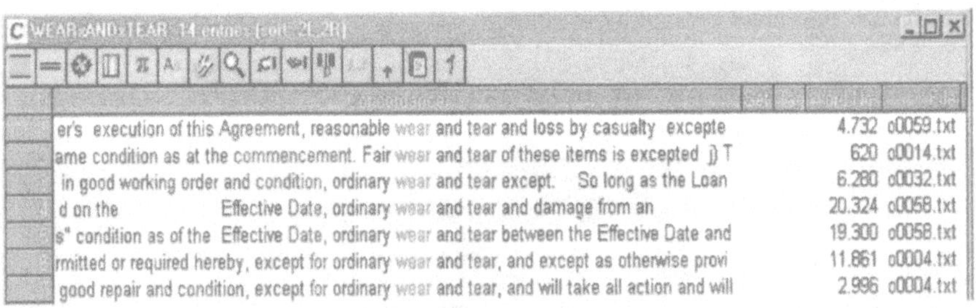

Figure 5. Concordance lines (fragment) for *wear and tear* (Stage 3)

[3] For the cases in which I was not able to come up with a *prima facie* translation for the binomial, I attributed a *prima facie* translation to the collocates.

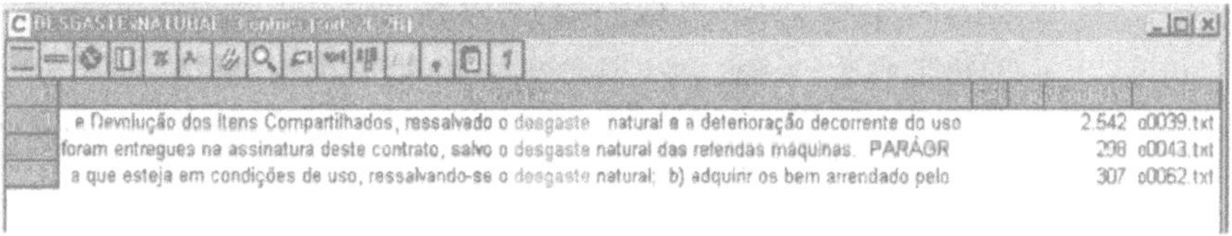

Figure 6. Concordance lines (fragment) for *desgaste natural* (Stage 4)

After examining the concordance lines, I sought to identify language patterns for the binomial under analysis. By looking at the concordance lines you can see that *wear and tear* is always preceded by an adjective: *fair*, *natural*, *ordinary*, *reasonable*; and that it is employed in phrases such as: *except for ordinary wear and tear* and *ordinary wear and tear excepted.*

Next, to determine the translation equivalent, the same procedure was applied to *desgaste natural*. The patterns found were the phrases *salvo o desgaste natural* and *ressalvado o desgaste natural*. These phrases are considered idiomatic translations for the binomial at issue in perfect naturally occurring Portuguese, thus enabling the translator to attain the same legal effect in the target language. For each of the 816 binomials resulting from our findings, the linguistic information, including language patterns, equivalents and cultural remarks, were displayed in a table such as the one below:

Table 2. Organization of terminological information

	wear and tear (24[4])	desgaste natural (3[5])
Terminological info	**Patterns** • [in good repair and condition] except for *ordinary/reasonable/fair/normal/ customary* wear and tear • [in good repair and condition] *ordinary/reasonable/fair/normal/ customary* wear and tear [only] excepted **Example** *[...] Lessee shall return the Equipment, freight prepaid, to Lessor in good*	 • salvo o desgaste natural • ressalvado [apenas] o desgaste natural **Example** *São obrigações do LOCATÁRIO: [...] b) conservar os BENS locados na*

[4] Corpus frequency.
[5] Corpus frequency.

	repair, condition and working order, ordinary ***wear and tear*** *resulting from proper use thereof only excepted, in a manner and to a location reasonably designated by Lessor.*	*forma como os recebeu, ressalvado apenas* ***desgaste natural*** *decorrente de uso regular, sendo expressamente vedado ao LOCATÁRIO realizar qualquer modificação ou adaptação nos BENS;*
Notes (legal/ lang. info)	The binomial in English is always preceded by one of the collocations. There are 4 occurrences of the pattern: *wear and tear and NN1*, that it, *wear and tear and loss* (1), *wear and tear and damage* (3).	Contrary to regulatory texts and legal dictionary entries, in legal agreements *desgaste natural* is not followed by the expression *da coisa*. It only occurs in LOMs[6].

9. Findings

By exploring the corpus, I was able to retrieve 816 binomials in English. Because of space limitations, it is not possible to display all of the results. However, the table below shows frequency values for the top ten binomials in the corpus.

Table 3. Top 10 binomials and corpus frequency

Binomial	Corpus frequency
terms and conditions	276
any and all	252
directly or indirectly	104
successors and assigns	92
his or her	85
costs and expenses	82
representations and warranties	81
force and effect	74
due and payable	65
in and to	58
all or any	56

[6] Each of the 28 types of *contratos* were identified with by 3 letters (e.g. LOM – Car Rental Agreement).

It is interesting to analyse the correspondence between binominals and grammatical category:

Table 4. Number of binomials found according to grammatical category

Grammatical category	# Binomials
Articles	0
determiners	5
prepositions	54
Adjectives	102
Nouns	489
Pronouns	11
Adverbs	15
Verbs	140
TOTAL	**816**

The table indicates that the highest number corresponds to binomials formed by nouns. This is evidence of the wide usage of nominalization in legal language. Another finding, which corroborates the well-known wordiness of legal language, is the high amount of binomials formed by prepositions (e.g. by and with, in and to, etc.)[7].

I have attempted to show that to attain the intended legal effect in the target language the translator must treat binomial expressions as units and, therefore, must not necessarily translate each one of their elements separately. To this end, I have sought to stress the advantages of using naturally occurring language in the search of translation equivalents and of using carefully compiled quantitative data in language studies.

Lastly, my findings on each binomial have been displayed in charts which do not *prescribe* a translation in Brazilian Portuguese, but rather provide naturally occurring language patterns and contexts for the legal translator to draw his own conclusions; thus, being able to attain the "intended legal effect" (Šarčević 2000: 12).

References

Barleben, D. (2003). "Legal Language, Early Modern English and their Relationships." *Early and Later Modern English Language and Culture: an Online Encyclopedia*. Toronto: University of Toronto.

[7] For additional findings please refer to http://tinyurl.com/2mmofg.

Bhatia, V. K. (1993). *Analysing Genre. Language Use in Professional Settings.* London: Longman.

Crystal, D. and D. Davy (1969). *Investigating English Style.* Bloomington: Indiana University Press.

Carvalho, L. (2006). "Os Dicionários Jurídicos Bilíngües e o Tradutor: dois binômios em direito contratual". *Tradterm* 12. São Paulo: Humanitas, 309-347.

Carvalho, L. (2007). *A tradução de binômios nos contratos de common law à luz da lingüística de corpus.* Master's thesis. São Paulo: Universidade de São Paulo.

Diniz, M. H. (1999). *Tratado Teórico e Prático dos Contratos.* Vol. 1. São Paulo: Saraiva.

de Groot, G. R. (1998). "Language and law." *Netherlands Reports to the Fifteenth International Congress on Comparative Law.* In: E. H. Hondius (ed.), Antwerpen/Groningen: Intersentia Rechtswetenschappen, 21-32.

Gustafsson, M. (1975). "Some Syntactic Properties of English Law Language". *Publication No. 4.* Turku, Finland: University of Turku, Department of English.

Kwok, W. H. (2000). *Some Linguistic Devices in Legal English that Cause Problems to the Translation of Legislative Texts from English to Chinese.* Master's thesis. MacArthur: University of Western Sydney.

Malkiel, Y. (1959). "Studies in irreversible binomials". *Lingua* 8, 113-160.

Mellinkoff, D. (1963) *The Language of the Law.* Boston: Little, Brown and Company.

Nevalainen, T. (1999). "Early modern English Lexis and Semantics". In: R. Lass (ed.), *The Cambridge History of the English Language*, vol. III. Cambridge: Cambridge University Press, 332-458.

Mayoral Asensio, R. (2003). *Translating Official Documents.* Manchester and Northampton: St. Jerome.

Parr, A. C. (1998). "Practical Issues on Legal Translation." *Antipodean* 1, 17-25.

Rossini, A. (2005). *A linguagem dos contratos bancários internacionais em inglês: um estudo descritivo baseado em lingüística de corpus.* Master's thesis. São Paulo: Pontifícia Universidade Católica de São Paulo.

Šarčević, S. (2000). *New Approach to Legal Translation.* The Hague/London/Boston: Kluwer Law International.

Scott, M. (1996). *WordSmith Tools*, version 3. Oxford: Oxford University Press.

Tagnin, S. E. O. (1989). *Expressões idiomáticas e convencionais.* São Paulo: Ática.

Tagnin, S. E. O. (2005). *O jeito que a gente diz.* São Paulo: Disal.

Tognini-Bonelli, E. (2001). *Corpus Linguistics at Work.* Amsterdam/Philadelphia: John Benjamins.

Vystrcilová, R. (2000). *Legal Language. Characteristic Properties, Features and Peculiarities of Written Legal Texts. Main difficulties of Legal Translation.* Doctoral thesis. Olomouc, Czech Republic: Univerzita Palackého.

Ruth Morris
Bar-Ilan University
Israel

MONOGLOTS AND POLYGLOTS, OR PRINCIPLES AND APPLICATION: DEALING WITH LINGUISTIC DIVERSITY IN ENGLISH-SPEAKING LEGAL SYSTEMS

1. Introduction

This article compares and contrasts prevailing attitudes to linguistic diversity in the English legal system with other situations in former times and elsewhere. Many of the world's legal systems have evolved from English law, which in the eighteenth century changed from an overtly multilingual system to one which became resolutely monoglot. The switch from multilingualism to monolingualism was neither abrupt nor smooth, and on the numerous occasions on which legislative efforts were made to achieve it, it was always controversial. The early multilingualism and the subsequent switch to monolingualism were both highly emotive. The legacy of this historical emotiveness about multilingual issues in the law is frequently maintained and reflected in the contemporary confusion in respect of the entitlement to and provision of language-mediation services for those who do not fall within the monolingual culture of the law: the deaf, the hard of hearing, and those whose preferred language is other than that of the legal proceedings. There are two opposing judicial schools of thought about entitlement to an interlingual interpreter: the pragmatic approach, which agrees to provide an interpreter only if perceived as being necessary in order to ensure the smooth operation of the legal process, and that of natural justice. The resultant judicial confusion in attitudes to entitlement to linguistic mediation services often spills over to arrangements for the provision of interlingual interpreters, in turn further affecting attitudes to entitlement because of the negative impact of often inadequate interpreting on the operation of the legal process.

2. "Practical and fair" interlingual interpretation arrangements

The use of different languages in a single legal system is, of course, far from unknown. Mellinkoff (1963: 35) notes the "countless collateral relatives as well as a polyglot parentage" of the common law of England and the language of that law. Although objective reasons may have led to the evolution of such situations, other factors are often responsible for their perpetuation. The specific language used by the legal system may be far from a negligible quantity. Pollock and Maitland (1911: 87) write that one of the "most momentous and permanent effects" of the Norman Conquest was its effect on the language of English lawyers, "for language is no mere instrument which we can control at will; it controls us". Regardless of whether factors such as inertia, self-interest or bad translation are responsible for a particular language being used in a given setting or for language being used in a particular way, the result is that the actors in a certain legal system in which a given linguistic pattern or order prevails are not linguistically and psychologically free. Moreover, attitudes towards those who come into contact with the system but do not conform with established behavioural (including linguistic) codes may be coloured by prejudices, including linguistic ones. In addition, outsiders may resent the fact that they are excluded by linguistic codes from even understanding, let alone participating in, the legal system.

Twentieth-century discussions of language issues with special reference to the practice of law in former British colonies regularly echo the same kind of objections to switching to the vernacular as those voiced historically in England. They derive from linguistic, technical and attitudinal issues – the absence of textbooks and terminology in the vernacular, the existence and drawing up of law reports in a foreign language, the problems of inaccuracies arising from mistranslation, the need to quote certain material verbatim, and the belief that only English can serve as the language of the law. The latter is ironic, given the fact that in England in earlier times, it was Latin and law French which filled the role now occupied by English in the legal systems of a number of former British colonies. Interestingly, an eighteenth-century commentator observed that "the law is scarce expressible properly in English".[1]

The historical background of complex attitudes to foreign languages in English law can sometimes shed light on the legal grounds for a decision to provide an individual with interpreting services (Morris 1995 and 1996). The relevant view of contemporary accusatory criminal procedure is that the very principle of defendants being present at their own trial requires not only physical but also mental presence. In other words, defendants must understand both the nature of the proceedings and specific testimony against them. There is a concomitant need to plead with an understanding mind (Polack and Corsellis 1990). Such understanding cannot exist without comprehension of both the words and – to some extent – the processes taking place in court. Where the defendant is represented, there is also a need to be able to communicate with counsel. For these reasons, legal "competence" requires the specific ability to communicate, which is normally understood as oral communication. The communication must be two-way, i.e. the ability to both understand and make people understand (Morris 1999).

[1] *Per* Roger North, quoted by Goodrich (1987: 437), who calls the sentiment a "curious view".

In the discussion in the late-nineteenth-century English case of *Berry*, a deaf man tried and found guilty of theft, Judge Kelly drew what he considered to be a parallel with the situation of a foreign-language speaker with no knowledge of English: "I remember once trying a foreigner who knew no word of English, and, there being a doubt as to the efficiency of the interpreter, and whether the prisoner could understand every word of the proceedings, I ordered the jury to be discharged."[2] This comment is remarkable not only for its clear assumption of a foreign-speaker's entitlement to interpretation, but also for its insistence that the interpreter must be highly competent so as to ensure that the prisoner will have a complete understanding of the proceedings. Other similarly trenchant comments on entitlement to interpreting services have, however, been criticised by various criminal courts fearful of the consequences for the judicial system of recognising a genuine right to such services. These would involve the recognition of a duty for the courts to provide accurate interlingual interpretation in a range of languages, thereby imposing on the system financial costs and the burden of administrative arrangements which it is unwilling to bear. The traditional solution is for arrangements for interpreting services to be considered as resting with the parties to criminal proceedings, thereby relieving the courts of any responsibility for provision. However, the court's ultimate responsibility for quality control cannot be evaded in the same fashion. Thus in the modern English case of *Jalika Begum* it was held: "If it were self-evident that the interpreter had not been capable of communicating in English, no doubt the court would interfere."[3] Across the border in Scotland, however, *Mikhailichenko* has shown this to be far from the case. In civil cases, on the whole it is accepted that the state has no obligation to provide interpreting services, although both judicial comment and the literature argue that interpreting can be just as important for the protection of civil liberties in civil proceedings as in criminal ones (Groisser 1981). In England, employment tribunals and immigration appeal tribunals are two major areas in which interpretation services are frequently provided by the authorities.

Even before today's global village, linguistic diversity was frequently present in the legal system. Judicial arrangements show a considerable range of variation in pragmatic or institutionalised solutions to such situations. A review of judicial comment in predominantly English-speaking jurisdictions shows that the question of entitlement to language mediation services, provided orally by an interlingual interpreter, is considered from one of two alternative viewpoints. One is that only when the handicap is so major as to interfere with the smooth running of legal proceedings should an interpreter be provided. The other is that considerations of natural justice require that non-English-speaking-background

[2] *Per* Kelly C.B. *in R. v. Berry* (1876) 1 Q.B. 447 at 451.

[3] *R. v. Mayor and Burgesses of the London Borough of Tower Hamlets ex parte Jalika Begum* [1991] Imm AR 86 .

(NESB) individuals be enabled to speak and to follow a complete version of English-language proceedings in their preferred language, in order to make their presence at the proceedings meaningful. These two contrasting views are linked by the idea that any view of entitlement to interpreting services is frequently inextricably linked with the practical (and not infrequently problematic) arrangements for the provision of such services, with the result that the language of rights is supplanted by pragmatic arguments of varying degrees of soundness (Morris 2007).

The consequence of the interpretation-as-the-last-resort viewpoint is that even judicial recognition of a defendant's complete inability to hear, understand or speak the language of the court is not necessarily tantamount to an acknowledgment of that particular individual's entitlement to the services of a competent intralingual interpreter who will provide the defendant with a complete and accurate version in their preferred language of everything said in court. Instead, the court, while acknowledging the linguistic handicap, may consider that other solutions are acceptable. Such solutions, which are frequently applied to this day, may include the provision of counsel, whether or not able to speak the defendant's language, and/or of frequent or occasional summaries, written or oral, of testimony. Often the question of any right to interpreting services is ignored altogether, and supplanted by the issue of need. Since the precise degree of need is normally assessed by monolingual speakers of the language of the court, who view the question in terms of perceived negative impact of any solution adopted on the proceedings, the threshold for triggering interpretation provision is often set extremely high. When testifying, defendants or witnesses may be required to try to manage without any linguistic mediation in order to demonstrate their need for it. In so doing, they may give a negative impression of their credibility, and the quality of their testimony is likely to suffer. A further problematic aspect involves the question of whose need: that of the court, or alternatively of the defendant or witness? Occasionally, a judge may go to the logical extreme, as in the 2007 ruling of a Maryland court in the case of Mahamu Kanneh, where child molestation and rape charges against a man who had waited for trial were dismissed on the grounds that his right to a speedy trial had been violated. In the three years since he had been charged, he had neither been in custody nor on trial, inter alia because of the prosecution's difficulties in finding an interpreter for his mother tongue, Vai, spoken by 100,000 speakers, primarily in Sierra Leone and Liberia. Ironically, on the day that the judge gave her ruling, an interpreter was in court.

The foregoing discussion of attitudes both to the use of different languages in various legal systems and to the specific situation of individuals who do not speak or for various reasons cannot understand the language of legal proceedings has sought to show how much individual or societal attitudes vary in determining reactions to and treatment of such individuals, particularly when the court uses its discretion to determine an NESB individual's entitlement to the services of an interpreter. It is contended that the same variation is seen in the factors which tend to be cited in considering the provision of specific solutions to the language-handicap situations under consideration here. These factors are – or are perceived to be – bound up in the arrangements for and impact of providing interpreting services. They are defined variously as "practical" or "reasonable". At times factors such as "judicial economy" may be cited. Commenting on a bilingual legal hearing, a Canadian court has observed that although ideally, reasons should be delivered in the language of the litigants, "courts are not committed to ideal situations but rather to practical and fair dispositions".[4] We will now examine judicial views of what comprise practical and fair interpreting arrangements.

Two major considerations should dominate: the availability of interpreters for particular languages, and the quality of the interpretation provided. Ideally, there would be a register of competent individuals available at short notice to interpret all languages in any legal (and other) situation at any time in any location in a given country. In practical terms, this is clearly not going to be feasible. The question is where compromise is acceptable, and where the authorities are open to criticism for failing to achieve a situation closer to the ideal than the often haphazard arrangements that characterize many jurisdictions.

In addition to availability and quality, other important factors relating to provision include responsibility, payment, mode, extent and bias. The first two factors need to be settled as an organisational matter on a national basis; the last three must be dealt with on a case-by-case basis. An individual interpreter should be questioned to ensure that no reason exists for doubting impartiality in a particular set of circumstances.

Judicial comment frequently justifies the use of a less than adequate interpreter by the fact that no better individual was available at the time, an attitude that has been roundly rejected by more than one court of appeal, as in *R. v. Walker and Chinley*: "The test is not one of availability but of competency".[5] The same reasoning was applied in the 1993 drink-driving case of *Mikhailitchenko* by the Scottish High Court, which found that there had been unfairness and declared proceedings in the sheriff court void.[6] The grounds were that for the proceedings to continue with the same interpreter after the prosecution had agreed with the defence that the official interpreter was not competent necessarily meant that the defendant's "mere physical presence"[7] was not sufficient to ensure that he had "the fullest opportunity of understanding the proceedings [...] taking place before

[4] *Robin v. College de St-Boniface* (1984) 15 D.L.R. (4th) 198 at 208.

[5] *R. v. Walker and Chinley*, (1910) 15 B.C.R. 100.

[6] *Mikhailitchenko v. Normand* 1993 S.C.C.R. 56.

[7] *H.M. Advocate v. Olsson* 1941 J.C. 63 at pp.63-64; 1941 S.L.T. 402.

him".[8] In other words, although – exceptionally for a court in the United Kingdom, and commendably – a separate defence interpreter was present in addition to the "official" court interpreter, the court's arrangements were such that the proceedings, for linguistic reasons, could not be fully understood by the defendant. The "requirements of justice"[9] were not thus satisfied. The provision of any number of interpreters cannot necessarily guarantee communication. Where the court, as in *Mikhailitchenko*, is insensitive to communications (including interpreting) issues, justice is less likely to be done. When in *Mikhailitchenko* the sheriff refused permission for the defence interpreter to correct the official interpreter's errors, he was obstructing a vital quality-assurance or monitoring process which should, ideally, be part of all situations where there is interpreting.

The emphasis that is placed on interpreter competence in *Walker* or *Mikhailitchenko* is rare in case reports, where compromise over interpretation quality appears to be the norm. Yet the quality of the interpreting provided will inevitably affect the value of any entitlement to interpreting services that has been recognized. As Steele points out (1992), in a Canadian context, gaining the right to an interpreter, whether through the common law, statute or the Constitution, is a hollow victory unless the applicant can be assured that the interpretation will be of a high enough standard to ensure that justice is done. In arguing that the traditional deference of the appellate courts to lower court judges' actions in respect of interlingual interpretation is misplaced, Steele further observes that the solutions adopted by trial judges have more to do with judicial economy than with a true test of need: "The result is that the right to an interpreter can, in practice, be a mirage." (1992: 226)

The assumption that trial judges refuse to adjourn proceedings or to require suitable interpreting arrangements to be made for reasons of cost-effectiveness is doubtless true in part; but in the light of historical and attitudinal issues, it may also be argued that more contentious and less cost-related aspects also play a role. If legal practitioners and the bench on the whole have little understanding of and little or no empathy with the situation of the NESB defendant or witness, as well as very little grasp of the complexities of the translation and, especially, interpretation processes, it is hardly surprising that they find it difficult to perceive the importance of ensuring "the highest standards" of interpretation (Royal Commission on Criminal Justice Report 130). It would appear obvious that what has been identified as the "inconsistent quality of interpreters" is the result of the makeshift or patchy arrangements that prevail in many judicial systems (Morris 1999).

Confusion over responsibility for providing interpreters in the court system further complicates any attempt to achieve efficient, high-quality provision. The

---

[8] *Mikhailitchenko* at 63.

[9] *Olsson* at 63-64.

question is whether the provision of interpreting is the responsibility of the state, and whether the courts or another body or bodies should be required to make the relevant arrangements. If the state has the responsibility to provide *competent* interpreting services, then logically it can be argued that there is a resultant obligation to ensure the availability of trained, competent, certified interpreters as well as to deal with related problems. Unless a completely different attitude to NESB individuals is adopted by the administrative offices of the court, the bench, lawyers and ancillary staff alike, even undivided responsibility on the part of the courts for providing interpreting services will not improve standards.

As the European Court of Human Rights ruled in the 1989 case of *Kamasinski*, the obligation of the competent authorities is not limited to the appointment of an interpreter: if they are "put on notice", it may extend to a control over the "adequacy" of the interpretation.[10] The point argued by Steele (1992) – that any right to interpretation services is meaningless unless a competent interpreter is provided – is thereby reinforced, albeit in a somewhat muted form, on the European level. Logically, it may be argued that ultimately the legal authorities must *always* be responsible for the quality of interlingual interpretation provided in their judicial system, and must act accordingly.

A historical review of attitudes to the provision of interpreting services as reflected in case reports, particularly from England and the United States, fails to demonstrate steady progress towards an efficient system of providing quality interpretation on request for all individuals with a determined (by whom?) degree of language handicap. In Canada, the situation as far as interpreting between the two official languages is concerned appears to have improved in recent years. Since the late twentieth century, the resulting enhanced awareness of the importance of accurate interlingual interpretation in legal settings has started to spread gradually to Canadian native languages also (Roberts 1989, Roy-Nicklen 1989, Roy-Nicklen and Phillips 1990). The main factor to emerge from a historical review of case reports is the major impact that an individual attitude – whether on the part of a lawyer, an interpreter or, occasionally, a judge – can have on interpreting standards and awareness. Here, the impact of a major constitutional change, specifically the 1982 *Canadian Charter of Rights and Freedoms*, has been considerable. The first appellate case considered by Canada's Supreme Court following the Charter was the seminal case of *R. v. Tran* (1994). Here, as indicated by Chief Justice Lamer, the reasons for judgment were somewhat longer than would normally be warranted because this was the first time that the Court had considered Section 14 of the Charter, guaranteeing the right to the assistance of an interpreter. In *Tran* the Supreme Court observed:

---

[10] *Kamasinski v. Austria*, (1989) 13 E.H.R.R. 36 at 74.

> The elevation of the right to interpreter assistance to the level of a constitutional norm is a significant step requiring, at a minimum, that the rules and principles governing interpreters which have been developed under the common law and under various statutes be reconsidered and, where necessary, adapted to fit with the dictates of the new Charter era.[11]

What *Tran* does specifically and saliently, is to address the issue of adequacy of interpretation, i.e. the area of quality, rather than the field of entitlement which was the focus of appellate discussion throughout much of the twentieth century:

> Where an interpreter was appointed and it is the *quality* of the interpretation provided that is being challenged, it is necessary to determine whether there has been a *departure or deviation* from what is considered *adequate interpretation*. While the interpretation provided need not be perfect, it must be *continuous, precise, impartial, competent and contemporaneous*. (952 and Morris, *Missing Stitches*)

With the exception of such major constitutional developments and subsequent appellate scrutiny of issues relating to quality issues in court interpreting, the only major difference between contemporary practice and the historical situation is the availability of technical devices, such as wired and unwired amplification and transmission aids, telephone interpreting and computer-aided transcription (CAT) systems. For example, although rarely used in the courts for literate hearing-impaired individuals, CAT systems can provide a quasi-instantaneous transcript on a screen. Had such a system been available, it would have obviated the court's dilemma in the 1978 American case of *Ferrell v. Estelle*, where it considered that to grant the deaf defendant's request that it provide stenographers who could "simultaneously transcribe words spoken during trial" might disrupt the public's right to an orderly trial.[12] The appellant had lost his hearing in the incident for which he was put on trial, and had not yet acquired any alternative form of communication such as lip-reading or sign language. The court justified its stance by arguing that a defendant's constitutional rights to understand legal proceedings are "practical, reasonable rights rather than ideal concepts of communication", and that even these pragmatic rights may not be exercised without limit. The question that arises is where and by whom the limit is set. In the case of a deaf defendant conversant with sign language, the *Ferrell* court would have provided a sign language interpreter, who could have worked without disrupting the proceedings. It offered to grant frequent recesses. Was it reasonable to refuse some form of written communication with the defendant?

In connection with the issue of interpreting mode, Bankowski and Mungham's observations on unsatisfactory technical aspects of the Swansea

---

[11] *R. v. Tran* (1994) 2 S.C.R. at 961.
[12] *Ferrell v. Estelle* 568 F.2d 1128 (1978) at 1131.

Welsh-language trial highlight some of the potential problems relating to the provision of interpreting: "The business of translating caused great confusion at certain points; for instance when a policeman quoted in English a statement made originally in Welsh, which had then to be translated back into Welsh for the accused, who gave an answer in Welsh, which then had to be turned into English."[13] This example of deficient practice illustrates the vital importance of treating original-language (L1) material as such. A further issue concerns the impact of using the consecutive technique in legal proceedings where the interlingual interpreter is unable to achieve "legal equivalence" not merely semantically but also rhetorically, as was the case at a Welsh-language trial: "the use of translations made the presentation of any sustained or effective oratory or argument impossible. In the words of one observer of the trial, 'beautiful spasms of Welsh were followed by the interpreter's precise, though sometimes stumbling, English'" (Bankowski and Mungham 1980: 68).

In Canadian courts, where bilingual judges tend to be the norm and greater sophistication generally prevails in respect of interpreting, the drawbacks of consecutive interpretation have even been the subject of judicial comment.[14] The advantage of the consecutive mode – that it is provided out loud and can therefore be readily monitored – has as its antithesis the fact that for listeners who can understand the original material, concentration is made difficult, since it is impossible to prevent a good part of their attention from focusing on the quality of the interpretation itself.[15] It also requires more time, a factor which can become frustrating. For this reason, in the American case of *Negron* it was stated explicitly that simultaneous interpretation (doubtless *chuchotage*, a whispered version) should have been arranged, and that an interpreted version of everything uttered in court should be provided for the defendant.[16]

Moreover, providing mediation through an interlingual interpreter is not necessarily the best or only approach. Even if the system remains officially monolingual, pragmatic bilingual adaptation may be necessary to bridge the language gap in certain situations, particularly the pre-trial phase. For example, a U.S. court has noted that "some mechanism, whether it be the use of written

---

[13] Bankowski and Mungham (1980: 68), citing (erroneously) Fishlock (1972: 100) as the source of this information.

[14] See *Robin* as discussed in Morris, *Missing Stitches*. Judge Monnin suggests that, pending the recruitment of more Manitoba judges capable of using French without assistance, arrangements should be made for simultaneously provided interpretation (i.e. the arrangement used in conference interpreting situations today, using electronic equipment) as well as audio-taping arrangements. He argues that such measures would both preserve the original-language testimony, needed for subsequent review, and also enable proceedings to flow smoothly, particularly on the vital level of cross-examination.

[15] *Cormier v. Fournier* (1986) 29 D.L.R. (4th) 675 at 678.

[16] *United States of America ex rel. Negron v. the State of New York* 310 F.Supp. 1304 (1970).

Spanish consent forms, training of police officers in a second language, or some other creative device, must be adopted to ensure that police do not abridge the constitutional rights of these individuals simply because they do not speak English".[17]

3. *The Chicken and the Egg*

In the predominantly English-speaking jurisdictions studied, it may be deduced from case reports that, when dealing with an NESB individual, courts do not generally determine their practice in respect of the provision of interpreting services in terms of any right arising under considerations of natural justice. Instead, the main consideration is the particular set of circumstances perceived as being present and their presumed impact on the proceedings, rather than any objective assessment of the NESB individual's linguistic ability and recognition of any resultant right to equal participation through linguistic mediation.

In a critical evaluation of the situation, it may be argued that judicial participants' attitudes to language-switching generally are influenced by a lack of information and awareness of issues relevant to interlingual interpretation, and are further influenced at times by prejudice, misapprehension, confusion or inefficient administrative arrangements. Such factors govern specific attitudes to the provision of interpreting services to individual NESB defendants and witnesses, not infrequently outweighing or even precluding any consideration of rights. An alternative reading is that the right of the NESB individual is viewed as conflicting with and subordinate to that of the English-speaking participants, particularly lawyers and jurors. A third way of viewing the situation is to identify the legal system as entirely denying any specific, inherent right on the part of an NESB individual to use any language other than that of the proceedings.

On the whole, perceived or actual difficulties related to providing specific interpreting services affect judicial perception of entitlement and the palliation of any acknowledged linguistic handicap. In other words, if it is known or feared that obtaining a competent interpreter will be a problem, and if negative prior experiences have occurred, judges and lawyers are less likely to insist on interpretation for an NESB participant. The question of entitlement normally does not arise. NESB individuals are often in no position to insist on receiving interpreting services, let alone competent ones. Without an interpreter, they are

[17] *United States v. Gaviria*, 775 F. Supp. 495 (1991) at 502, cited in *State of North Carolina v. Antonio Ramirez Penalosa, NO. COA05-1553*. See also Ohio's Summit-Lorain Project, which develops "Model policies and procedures for law enforcement officers to serve and protect limited-English proficient persons", see http://www.co.summit.oh.us/sheriff/LEP.pdf.

even more unlikely to indicate an inability to follow proceedings, yet will be even more distant from due process.

Essentially, I would argue, the legal system sees entitlement to interpretation not as a right but as a problem because of the difficulties of arranging for provision – i.e., the implementation of the right. Even in countries where it is the norm to hold trials through the medium of interpretation, it is frequently accepted that the standard of court interpreting is low, particularly in the lower courts, although the logical legal consequences are not always drawn.[18]

Since failure to provide competent interpreting can in turn pose a problem in legal proceedings, the situation can easily become nightmarish. In organisational terms, cases involving NESB participants, particularly witnesses, require more careful planning than monolingual legal events. A judge's discretion to authorize the provision of interpreting services can further complicate scheduling and arrangements, since in a particular case the court's perception and assessment of linguistic need and resultant entitlement may differ from that of the lawyer or psychologist.[19]

A further aspect of entitlement to language-switching services relates to the way in which both NESB individuals and interpreters are perceived by and interact with the legal system. In a critical look at a draft report on access to interpreters in the Australian legal system, Laster (1990: 228) argues that the proposed reform measures are "cost-based" rather than "rights-led". Following this approach, unless both individual legal practitioners and the system address a multitude of issues such as access to legal advice, differences in discourse patterns and body language, and different perceptions of the legal system, no number of competent interpreters readily available through any legal interpreter scheme, however efficiently organised, will be able to redress the inequalities of a multicultural society. In this vein, presenting an Australian research project designed to identify the major sources of difficulty in cross-cultural communication between lawyers and clients, D'Argaville (1991) lists a series of cultural barriers (not all exclusive to NESB individuals) to lawyer-client communication. Although not new, the study's tentative finding that lawyers on the whole seem to be insufficiently sensitive to possible non-communication would bear out the indications of the case reports surveyed for this study. Where judges have discretionary and, sometimes, ultimate power[20] to order or exclude the provision of interpreting services, any such insensitivity will militate against the likelihood of palliating a language handicap.

[18] *Meghi Naya v. R.* (1952) 19 E.A.C.A. 247; *Mohamed Farah Musa v. R.* (1956) 23 E.A.C.A. 469. See also Jones 1990 (1983): 65-67.

[19] *Filios v. Morland* [1963] S.R. (N.S.W.) 331 at 332.

[20] *Filios v. Morland* ([1963] S.R. (N.S.W.) 331.

The legal system's tendency to approve the provision of interpreting services only where the court considers that the smooth operation of the system would otherwise be impossible has been noted in the literature and shown by case reports. Writing in the mid-1970s in the United States, Cronheim and Schwartz (1976) note that courts tend to appoint interpreters for the benefit of the court rather than for the welfare of the defendant. The tension between absolute judicial control of events in the courtroom and interlingual interpreters' opposing views of their duties vis-à-vis NESB individuals has similarly been identified on appeal, with at least one ruling from Australia to the effect that interpreters' professional duties to their clients outweigh judges' control over proceedings in their court. In the civil case of *Gradidge* the appellate court ruled that the interpreter did indeed have a duty to keep her deaf client abreast of what is happening in court, because of the litigant's need for and right to interpreting services:

> The difficulties (...) arose because of the opinion which the interpreter formed, and expressed, about her duty to interpret exchanges between the court and the barristers, and to do so despite an instruction by his Honour, with the acquiescence of counsel then appearing for the appellant (...) Many witnesses will have a smattering of the English language. At least they may have enough to comprehend the general drift of the proceedings, even if their knowledge is insufficient to communicate and understand sufficiently to give evidence. But a deaf person, save for lip-reading, will be in a silent world where the mysteries of the court's process will inevitably be enlarged. The need is accordingly greater to ensure that such a person has as full an understanding as possible of what is occurring in the case.[21]

There are fewer references in case reports to the situation of witnesses, although arguably this is an area which may have even greater potential impact on proceedings than the provision of interpreting services to defendants.[22] In particular, in the absence of competent interpreting services NESB witnesses are unlikely to be prepared to testify, although this is difficult to document from case reports. On the whole, failure to provide any or adequate interpreting services during pre-trial phases is not considered to justify the exclusion of statements made under those circumstances. However, where the judge hearing an appeal is prepared to entertain the notion that linguistic difficulties may create procedural problems, police failure to provide any or competent interpreting services may

---

[21] *Gradidge v. Grace Bros. Pty. Ltd.* (1988) 93 FLR 414 at 422-423.

[22] *R. v. Ram* [1989] Crim.L.R. 457. A potentially vital defence witness gave testimony in such bad English as to be incomprehensible. "At one point the judge told the jury he would translate, even though he did not speak Bengali." See http://tinyurl.com/2jhs3x, retrieved July 2007.

lead to the exclusion of pre-trial statements.[23] It may also provide a defendant with a "reasonable excuse" for having, for example, failed to comply with a requirement to provide a specimen in the case of drink-driving charges.[24]

On appeal, the provision of an incompetent or biased interpreter in the court below may be held sufficient grounds for ruling that the trial was unfair or a nullity.[25] The appellate court's judgment may take account of considerations of natural justice or of pragmatic circumstances.[26] However, the normal appellate view is that in the absence of any showing of prejudice (something normally impossible in the absence of recordings of both language versions), no specific disadvantage can be identified as having occurred and the appeal is therefore refused. When an appeal is considered by several courts in succession, major differences will not infrequently be present in the degree to which opinions differ and passions are stirred on the issue of entitlement to interpreting services.[27]

In systems which make a distinction between felonies and misdemeanours, the absence of interpretation for an unrepresented NESB individual in the latter instance has been considered insignificant. An echo of such attitudes is to be found in contemporary English reports which indicate that on the whole, greater efforts are made to provide interpreting services in serious cases (Morris 1993a). The provision of counsel who also speaks the defendant's language has frequently been held to be a satisfactory substitute for the services of a interpreter, although some legal commentators – rightly, in the view of the present author – hold this practice to be unsatisfactory (Piatt 1990).

Case reports extending over a number of centuries and a variety of jurisdictions reflect a range of attitudes towards interpreting provision (Morris 1999, 1995). These include not merely whether interpretation is to be provided, but for whom, by whom, and of what part of the proceedings. For example, in a seventeenth-century English murder trial, the court demonstrated overtly contrasting attitudes towards providing interpreting services for the various NESB defendants, differing on the basis of class, not on the basis of severity of language handicap.[28] Even in contemporary cases where the court has authorised the

[23] See *R. v. Bassil and Mouffareg* (1990) *Legal Action*, December 1990 at 23, *R. v. Van Axel and Wezer* (1991) *Legal Action* September 1991 at 12, both heard by Sich J. See also *United States v. Gaviria* 775 F. Supp. 495 (1991), *United States v. Fawaz Yunis* 681 F. Supp. 909 (1988) and *United States v. Fawaz Yunis* 859 F.2d 953 (1989).

[24] *Beck v. Sager* [1979] RTR 475.

[25] *H.M. Advocate v. Olsson* 1941 J.C. 63; *Liszewski v. Thomson* [1942] J.C. 55; *Mikhailitchenko v. Normand* 1993 S.C.C.R. 56; *Iqbal Begum* (1991) 93 Cr.App.R. 96.

[26] See *R. v. Mayor and Burgesses of the London Borough of Tower Hamlets ex parte Jalika Begum*, [1991] Imm AR 86.

[27] *United States ex rel. Negron v. the State of New York* 310 F.Supp. 1304 (1970); *United States ex rel. Negron v. the State of New York* 434 F.2d 386 (1970).

[28] *Borosky alias Boratzi and Ors* (1682) 9 Howell's State Trials 1.

provision of interpretation for the defendant throughout the proceedings, instructions have been given for interpreting to be interrupted during the judge's charge to the jury in order to avoid the possibility of distraction.[29] Similarly, in an Australian civil case involving a deaf plaintiff, the interpreter was instructed to refrain from rendering a particular passage for her client into sign-language.[30] In multidefendant trials, interpreting has sometimes been provided by one of the defendants for another, a practice which on appeal has been ruled to be unacceptable.[31] In certain jurisdictions, regulations require each NESB defendant to have a personal interpreter providing a version of the proceedings out loud, a situation that has resulted in a cacophony which is rightly criticised by the judicial participants.[32] Only if the parties concerned agree to waive their personal interpreters can use be made of simultaneous interpretation provided via infrared transmission by a single interpreter.[33] Judicial comment on entitlement may specify the mode in which linguistic mediation is to be provided and, concomitantly, its extent or scope.[34] Such comment may also refer to the perceived relative merits or disadvantages of different modes of interpretation.[35]

On the whole, appellate comment on the issue of entitlement and provision of interpretation has reflected the natural justice view, while accepting that perfection cannot be achieved and that pragmatic considerations must be allowed to have their effect. In the lower courts, perceived practical considerations appear to prevail over principle. Thus in practice, "ear-to-ear" contact may not take place because of failure to provide interpreting services or because of the inadequacy of such services (Piatt 1990). Similarly, the obvious inadequacies of a particular interpreter's performance may not lead to the proceedings being interrupted or that interpreter being substituted. Yet again, an incompetent interpreter may, although his or her services have been dispensed with, subsequently be re-engaged, even re-appearing before the same judge (Morris 1993b).

Lastly, in jurisdictions in which political factors have led to regulation of the language in which legal proceedings are to be carried out, these may be cited as limiting a court's discretion to hear a case in a particular language and concomitantly mandating a particular party's use of an interpreter, even where the

---

[29] *R. v. Reale* (1974) 58 D.L.R. (3d) 560.

[30] *Gradidge v. Grace Bros. Pty. Ltd.* (1988) 93 FLR 414.

[31] *Liszewski v. Thomson* [1942] J.C. 55.

[32] California: August 17, 1992 letter from Frank M. Almeida, Director, Court Interpreter Services, United States District Court, Central District of California.

[33] Almeida, ibid.; *People v. Resendes* 210 Cal.Rptr.609 (Cal.App.5 Dist. 1985).

[34] *United States of America ex rel. Negron v. the State of New York* 310 F.Supp. 1304 (1970).

[35] *Cormier v. Fournier* (1986) 29 D.L.R. (4th) 675, 69 N.B.R. (2d) 155 (Q.B.), aff'd on other grounds 78 N.B.R. (2d) 406 (C.A.).

court has the linguistic skills to communicate directly with the party and the litigant in question has no funds to engage an interpreter.[36]

A survey of case reports indicates that judicial figures seldom acknowledge that coping with the linguistic aspects of legal proceedings in English can be genuinely difficult for non-native speakers who can manage most other situations in that language.[37] This is a rule that appears to be proved by an exceptionally enlightened statement such as that in *State v. Inich* that "it is often the case that a person who understands and speaks with reasonable ease the language of the street, or of ordinary business, encounters difficulty and embarrassment when subjected to examination as a witness during proceedings in court".[38] Clearly this was the view held by the court-appointed psychiatrist in the 2007 case of the Vai speaker in Maryland.[39]

Writing in the late 1960s, Callejo (1968: 52-53) presents an emotive picture of the Spanish-speaking defendant's experience of "due process" in the English-speaking justice system in the United States. His argument – that interpreting services are not a satisfactory substitute for an "on-going, continuous awareness of what is happening because it is happening in the Spanish language" – is one that is accepted to this day in parts of officially bilingual countries such as Canada or Belgium. It is one which would be wholeheartedly espoused by Welsh-language campaigners. However, despite the ever growing size of the Hispanic population (both legal and illegal) in the United States, the system is still, officially, monoglot and English-speaking, and in the light of pressure from English Only movements will probably stay that way. Nevertheless, as Bryant and Riche (1993: 95) point out, "in many ways the majority population will have to assimilate to this increasingly large minority". The question is whether one way of adaptation will, eventually, be the introduction of court proceedings in Spanish, as Callejo so passionately advocates. Suffice it to say that it is vital to remember how emotive an issue language may be, as demonstrated forcefully inter alia by *Lau v. Nicholls*,[40] the highly publicised landmark case in the areas of bilingualism and biculturalism in the United States, and the post-First World War Anglo-Saxon backlash that led to state laws prohibiting German language instruction in private schools which were subsequently ruled unconstitutional in *Meyer v. Nebraska*.[41] Even reasonable sounding approaches may conceal far more irrational attitudes:

[36] *In the estate of (deceased) Hartley and Another v. Fuld and Others* [1965] 2 All E.R. 652; In *re Trepca Mines Ltd.*,[1960] 1 W.L.R. 24.

[37] For more on judicial and other insights, or lack thereof, into the plight of the non-native speaker facing criminal charges, see Morris, *Pragmatism*, pp. 271-274.

[38] *State v. Inich* (1918) 55 Mont. 1, 173 P. 230, cited in Macy at 931.

[39] "'Justice,' Montgomery County-style", *Washington Times*, editorial, http://tinyurl.com/3b6hlb, last accessed July 2007.

[40] *Lau v. Nichols* 414 U.S. 563 (1974).

[41] *Meyer v. Nebraska* 262 U.S. 390, 67 L. Ed. 1042 (1923).

> By its own account, the "official English" movement seeks to stimulate debate on the sensitive issue of language and to promote social unity through a common tongue. In fact, however, the movement makes language the rallying point for simmering intolerance, frustration, fear, and distrust.[42]

It should by now be obvious how small a distance separates eighteenth-century England and twentieth-century America. The issue of language use can be an emotive one at any time. The feelings of frustration, resentment and disempowerment resulting from inability to understand and hence participate meaningfully in judicial proceedings are illustrated by the language and sentiments of England's Courts of Justice Act in 1731 just as vividly as they are by Callejo's picture of the Spanish-speaker's situation in the Californian justice system nearly 250 years later (Morris 1995).

4. Conclusion

This article has sought to show that in English-language legal systems, an NESB individual's entitlement to interpreting services is not on the whole an issue which is evaluated and addressed on the basis of objective criteria by qualified experts. The determination of any right to use a language other than that of the proceedings is predicated on an assumption that there must be a demonstrated need, generally defined narrowly as the court's (or sometimes a party's) inability to communicate with and control the NESB individual in its own language. Furthermore, this need is likewise assessed not in an objective fashion but in the light of ideological criteria. Those criteria are arguably the linguicist or imperialist ones of a monoglot legal system, which looks with varying degrees of mistrust on those from different linguistic and cultural backgrounds. In certain times and places, on the other hand, the pendulum may swing the other way, so that at times an over-liberal system or individual may bend over backwards in an attempt to accommodate a presumed language handicap, and if the system cannot meet other legal constraints such as the right to a speedy trial, the upshot of failure to provide an interpreter may be that the public is denied the chance to see justice done for reasons which may have less to do with the obscurity of the language and more to do with failure to contact the appropriate sources.[43]

---

[42] Note (1987) "'Official English': Federal Limits on Efforts to Curtail Bilingual Services in the States." *Harvard Law Review* 100:1345-1363.

[43] "Although the defendant speaks an obscure language, finding a qualified interpreter, especially in a large, ethnically diverse area like Washington, DC, would be quite easy if the court had contacted the ALC or any of our members for assistance. Our trade association has numerous members in the Washington metropolitan area, one practically across the street from the Montgomery County courthouse. The court failed to contact any of these firms."

The present author would argue that the only solution to this situation is, firstly, for an automatic right to be granted to NESB individuals to speak their preferred language, with no need to demonstrate linguistic handicap; and secondly, for suitable arrangements to be made for the proper provision of interpreting services. In today's global village, on the whole a solution can always be found, even if it involves additional resources. This would circumvent the judicial citing of unavailable or inadequate language intermediaries as justification for rejecting claims of entitlement. A number of legal systems have long had to grapple with solutions to the situation of the non-native speaker. By acknowledging a formal right to interpreting services, and giving substance to that right by properly organising the provision of language-switching services, an enlightened system shows that its claim to administer justice is more than an empty slogan in the ears of non-native speakers. On evidence, Lord Widgery has said, "Quality is what matters in the end".[44] It is suggested that the same dictum holds equally true for the quality of interlingual interpretation at all stages in judicial proceedings.

On the whole, the judicial system sees problems as being necessarily created by the use of interlingual interpreters. In reaction, there tends to be a belief that to a large extent these difficulties can be avoided by refusing to grant the right to interpretation as a whole, or to authorise the provision of interpreting services for a particular individual. Such approaches ignore the attested major communicative and psychological difficulties that can result for a non-native speaker if forced to try to function effectively in a second language in formal situations, including legal settings. Apparent financial savings made by not providing an interlingual interpreter or by using a cheaper and probably less competent individual are likely to be more than offset by the additional time required in the lower court because of faulty communication and any subsequent appeal lodged on the basis of linguistic inadequacies and resultant legal complications.

The case reports and other literature surveyed for the various (predominantly English-speaking) jurisdictions covered by this paper relate to a considerable range of situations over time and space, and yet show that, on the whole, the issue of entitlement to interpretation is considered a problem by all systems, whether for practical reasons (having to provide and, potentially, bear the cost of the interpreter) or for more ideological ones (such as unwillingness to recognise the justification for an intermediary, or the system's reluctance to accept a loss of linguistic, and perhaps other, control over certain individuals, and, potentially, whole groups within the society administered by the legal apparatus). Like many other aspects of interlingual interpretation, entitlement is not the apparently

[44] *R. v. Turnbull* [1977] Q.B. 224 at 231-A.

objective issue it might at first appear to be, and hence the nitty-gritty of provision is far from a level playing field.[45]

References

Bankowski, Z. and G. Mungham (1980). "Political Trials in Contemporary Wales: Cases, Causes and Methods". In: Bankowski, Z. and G. Mungham (eds.), *Essays in Law and Society*. London, Boston and Henley: Routledge Direct Editions, 53-70.

Bryant, B. E. and M. F. Riche (1993). "Hispanics in the United States: A Different Kind of Immigrant?". *LPLP* (originally in *Cosmos* 2/1, 1992), 17(1), 95.

Callejo, R. A. 1968. "The Case for the Spanish Speaking", *Trial*, Oct/Nov. 1968, 52-53.

Cronheim, A. J. and A. H. Schwartz (1976). "Non-English-Speaking Persons in the Criminal Justice System: Current State of the Law". *Cornell Law Review* 61, 289-311.

D'Argaville, M. (1991). "Serving a Multicultural Clientele: Communication Between Lawyers and Non-English-speaking Background Clients". In: G. Bird (ed.), *Law in a Multicultural Australia*. National Centre for Crosscultural Studies in Law. Melbourne: University of Melbourne/Monash University, 83-91.

Fishlock, T. (1972). *Wales and the Welsh*. London: Cassell.

Goodrich, P. (1987). *Legal Discourse*. Macmillan.

Groisser, D. S. (1981). "A Right to Translation Assistance in Administrative Proceedings". *Columbia Journal of Law and Social Problems* 16(4), 469-520.

Jones, A. (1990). *Jury Service: A Practical Guide*. London: Robert Hale.

Laster, K. (1990). "Access to Interpreters". *Legal Service Bulletin* 15(5), 227-228.

Laster, K. and V. L. Taylor (1994), *Interpreters and the Legal System*. Sydney: Federation Press.

---

[45] See http://najit.org/Advocacy/NAJITATAStatementFinal_07302007.pdf, retrieved July 2007. "The courts, the defense, the prosecutors' offices, and law enforcement agencies all need to establish language assistance processes that work accurately and effectively. Only when the justice system taps into existing networks of language professionals to seek out potential interpreters, will shocking situations such as the Mahamu Kanneth case be avoided. 'There is nothing easy about any trial where liberty is at stake and a victim is at loss. It is even less so when there are multiple languages involved. However, fundamental due process requires a level playing field, and that all persons answering to the law of the land be given a similar opportunity to answer. A Movant is entitled to such fairness regardless of his ability to speak and comprehend English. Perfect understanding is not required to mete fairness, but a reasonable understanding is.' (*Santos Adonay Pagoada vs. Commonwealth of Kentucky* No. 97CR-1002 (2001)). NAJIT has prepared a position paper entitled "Preparing Interpreters in Rare Languages", which bears upon the current situation: [http://tinyurl.com/2qq2ve]."

Macy, J. E. (1947). "Annotation – Use of Interpreter in Trial". A.L.R. 172, 923-952.

Mellinkoff D. (1963). *The Language of the Law*. Little, Brown and Company, Boston and Toronto.

Morris, R. (1993a). "Nobs And Yobs – the Provision of Interpreters for Legal Proceedings involving High-status Foreigners and Others". In: C. Picken (ed.), *Proceedings, XIIIth World Congress of FIT (International Translators' Federation)*. Institute of Translation and Interpreting, 356-366.

Morris, R. (1993b). "United Kingdom Report on Court Interpreting Services", given at Workshop on the Inadequacies of Court Interpreting Services, World Conference on Human Rights, Vienna. Available at http://tinyurl.com/ysqgxu

Morris, R. (1995). "Pragmatism, Precept, and Passions: The Attitude of English-Language Legal Systems to Non-English Speakers", In: M. Morris (ed.), *Translation and the Law*, American Translators Association Scholarly Monograph Series, Vol. VIII. Amsterdam and Philadelphia: John Benjamins, 263-279.

Morris, R., (1996). "Great Mischiefs – An Historical Look at Language Legislation in Great Britain". In: D. A. Kibbee (ed.), *Language Legislation and Linguistic Rights.* Amsterdam and Philadelphia: John Benjamins, 32-54.

Morris, R. (1999). "The Face of Justice: Historical Aspects of Court Interpreting". *Interpreting: International journal of research and practice in interpreting* 4(1), 97-123.

Morris, R. (2007). "Dies, Attard or Lockerbie? Enlightened and unenlightened judicial views of interpreters in English-speaking legal systems". In: F. Pöchhacker, A. L. Jakobsen and I. M. Mees (eds.), Copenhagen Studies in Language 35, *Interpreting Studies and Beyond: A Tribute to Miriam Shlesinger*. Samfundslitteratur Press (forthcoming).

Morris, R. (2007). "Missing Stitches: An overview of judicial attitudes to interlingual interpreting in the criminal justice systems of Canada and Israel". *Interpreting: International journal of research and practice in interpreting* 9 (2) (forthcoming).

Piatt, B. (1990). "Attorney as Interpreter: A Return to Babble". *New Mexico Law Review* 20(1), 1-16.

Polack, K. and A. Corsellis (1990). "Non-English speakers and the criminal justice system". *New Law Journal*, Part 1, 23.11.90, 1634-36, Part 2, 1676-77.

Pollock, F. and F. W. Maitland (1911). *The History of English Law Before the Time of Edward I.* Cambridge: Cambridge University Press

Roberts R. P. (1989). "Translating and Interpreting in Canada's Far North: A True Intercultural Challenge". *Bulletin of the CAAL/Bulletin de l'ACLA* 11(2), 97-108.

Royal Commission on Criminal Justice, Report (1993). (Cm.2263, HMSO, London).

Roy-Nicklen, L. (1989). "Legal Interpretation – Canada's Northwest Territories". In: D. L Hammond (ed.), *ATA, Proceedings of the 29th Annual Conference*. Medford: Learned Information, Inc., 429-435.

Roy-Nicklen, L. and M. Phillips (1990). "Legal Interpreting in Canada's Far North". In A. Aguirre (ed.), *Proceedings of the Northeast Conference on Legal Interpretation and Translation*. Jersey City, New Jersey: The Consortium of Educators in Legal Interpretation and Translation, 83-88.

Steele, G. J. (1992). "Court Interpreters in Canadian Criminal Law". *Criminal Law Quarterly*, February, 218-251.

Part III

LEGAL AND COURTROOM DISCOURSE

Chris Heffer
Cardiff University
Wales

JUDGEMENT IN COURT: EVALUATING PARTICIPANTS IN COURTROOM DISCOURSE

Attorney:	Thou art the most vile and execrable Traitor that ever lived.
Raleigh:	You speak indiscreetly, barbarously and uncivilly.
Attorney:	I want Words sufficient to express thy viperous Treasons.
Raleigh:	I think you want Words indeed, for you have spoken one thing half a dozen times.
Attorney:	Thou art an odious Fellow, thy Name is hateful to all the Realm of England for thy Pride.

(From the trial of Sir Walter Raleigh. c. 1603)

1. Introduction

In 21st-century common law criminal trials, witness examinations are meant rationally to present the disputed "facts" of the case before the judge or jury. These "fact-finders" then deliberate on that evidence to reach a verdict. Only if and when the defendant is found guilty will the judge pass legal and moral judgement. Until then, explicit expression of ethical judgement is meant to be suspended. Yet the above exchange reminds us both that this was not always the case, and that we are dealing with interested parties who are already likely to hold strong opinions about other participants in the trial. Rules of evidence notwithstanding, there is a strong interest on the part of the advocates to convey their judgement of other participants' behaviour and character to the judge and/or jury who will decide the case. Trial lawyers thus face a strategic tension between the need to conform to the evidentiary rules which prevent explicit construal of judgement and the desire to persuade a jury who might be influenced by such construals. This is part of a broader tension in legal-lay courtroom interaction between a "paradigmatic" mode of reasoning and discourse construction based on objective logical principles, rules and definitions, and a "narrative" mode based on the subjective reconstruction of personal experience (Heffer 2005). In the above passage, Raleigh and the Attorney follow their narrative-mode instincts and make no attempt to ground their accusatory judgements in "objective" facts. In contrast, much of the modern jury trial process – from the presentation of "Opening Facts" (in England and Wales) to the focus on "facts in issue" (facts to be determined by the "fact-finder" or "fact-trier") and "material facts" (facts that are relevant to the legal charges) – is ostensibly designed to do just that.[1]

This paper explores the relation between factual evidence and subjective judgement in three interrelated ways. At its core is a corpus-based analytical overview of the linguistic construal of judgement by legal professionals in court. Surrounding that core analysis is a reflection on methodology: I present a limiting case of the use of corpus methodologies and a systematic analytical framework to provide empirical grounding for the apparently ephemeral and elusive field of evaluation. Beyond that reflection on methodology, I shall consider more generally the relationship between evidence and the judgement of participants in research on courtroom discourse.

I shall begin with this more general stocktaking aim by reappraising how some of the key texts in the area of courtroom discourse have explored the nexus between testimonial fact and subjective opinion and have, at the same time, judged the behaviour of participants in courtroom discourse. I next introduce two methodological tools which promise a more rigorously empirical take on the linguistic realisation of evaluation in court: the systemic-functional lexical-semantic appraisal framework of judgement (Martin 2000; Martin and White 2005) and a large, representative corpus of official court transcripts (Heffer 2005). With these tools, I attempt an empirically-grounded analysis of judgement in court, beginning with a quantitative overview of the realisation of judgement in the various trial genres and moving on to a more specific analysis of the judgement of lying in cross-examination. This leads to a putative model of evaluative keys (or positionings) assumed by participants in courtroom discourse. Finally, I return to reflect on the relationship between evidence and evaluation in the observation of courtroom discourse.

2. Fact and opinion in courtroom discourse and its observation

The relationship between testimonial evidence and subjective judgements of the witnesses producing that testimony has always been central to social scientific

[1] As social constructionists (Berger and Luckmann 1967) have pointed out, facts can be made and not found. Having noted that "fact" does not always assume some pre-existing objective state of affairs, I shall desist from the annoying habit of using scare quotes around the word "fact".

studies of the courtroom. In the thirty or so years since language and law studies began to come to the fore, considerable evidence has been adduced in this area, but the methods used to uncover that evidence and the overt or covert judgements made of the courtroom participants have shifted to some extent. Rather than attempting anything resembling a balanced overview of this now extensive area, I shall take a "sampling" approach based on snapshots of two influential texts published in each of the equidistant years 1979, 1990 and 2001, representing early, middle and relatively recent periods in the history of language and law research. In doing so, I shall try to show what these texts tell us about the types of judgements that are made by, and of, the participants in courtroom discourse.

2.1. Cognitive deficiencies

Two of the key language and law texts of 1979 (Loftus 1979; Lind and O'Barr 1979) both addressed the question of how the evidentiary facts are distorted in the minds of the lay participants processing the incoming data. Loftus (1979) applied the already extensive psychological literature on memory to the specific context of eyewitness accounts and found that numerous cognitive factors could affect the accuracy of those accounts. Through a number of experimental studies, she found weaknesses in eyewitnesses' capacity to acquire and initially store information at the scene, to retain that information in memory over periods of time, and finally to retrieve it when recounting the scene. Often these incapacities were related to linguistic influences. For example, after viewing a film of a car crash, subjects asked how fast the cars were going when they *smashed* into each other gave a higher speed than those asked the same question using the verb *hit*. When asked a week later whether they had seen any broken glass, those who had been given the *smashed* question were more than twice as likely to say "yes", even though there was in fact no broken glass. The presupposition in *smashed* clearly affected both retention and retrieval of memories. Loftus also showed that the problem caused by the inability of eyewitnesses to recount their experiences accurately is exacerbated by the jury's tendency to give undue weight to those accounts. Jurors judged eyewitnesses as more credible than other types of witness, whereas in fact they were less accurate.

Jurors' evaluations of witness testimony were also the key focus of the highly influential Duke University Law and Language Project, the findings of which were reported in Lind and O'Barr (1979). The Duke research team found not only that mock jurors were heavily influenced by their social psychological judgements of witnesses but also that these judgements were significantly affected by the speech style of these witnesses. In a series of "matched guise" experiments, mock jurors listened to recordings of the same actors reading out versions of testimony which were substantively the same but stylistically different. In each case, certain linguistic features had been altered to produce "powerful" and "powerless" styles of speaking. The powerless style included such features as hedging, hesitation and deferential terms, while the powerful style lacked these features, was louder and had a greater pitch range. Lind and O'Barr concluded that:

> For both the male and female witnesses, the power speech testimony produced perceptions that the witness was more competent, attractive, trustworthy, dynamic, and convincing than did the powerless testimony. (1979: 72)

Thus testimony which was propositionally alike led to markedly different judgements of the witness on stylistic grounds. The study therefore appeared to show a serious incapacity of jurors to assess testimony fairly and accurately.

These two key studies from 1979 were essentially negative judgements of the cognitive capacity of lay participants in the judicial process to fulfil their assigned tasks in a legally acceptable manner. Eyewitnesses appeared incapable of providing accurate accounts of what they had seen and powerless witnesses failed to come across as credible irrespective of the truth value of their evidence. Meanwhile, jurors gave undue credibility to the inaccurate accounts of eyewitnesses and they judged witnesses according to the way they spoke as well as what they said. Both studies were empirically grounded in experimental methods and, in the case of Lind and O'Barr, extensive discourse analysis of 150 hours of recordings of criminal trials in North Carolina. One might infer from the findings, then, that the legal system should not be relying on lay people to judge witnesses. That inference would be wrong since we now have ample evidence to show that "experts" such as judges and investigators fare no better than lay people when it comes to psychological biases (Fitzmaurice and Pease 1986; Wagenaar *et al.* 1993; Wise and Safer 2004; Kassin *et al.* 2005), but Loftus, Lind and O'Barr were writing at a time when the jury system was seriously under attack (Findlay and Duff 1988).

2.2. Representational discrepancies

The sample texts from 1990 (Conley and O'Barr 1990; Berk-Seligson 1990) focus on discrepancies in the representation of the disputed facts and their witnesses. In *Rules versus Relationships*, Conley and O'Barr (1990) studied the way litigants in small claims courts narrated the disputed events that had brought them to court. They found that while some litigants produced narratives which linked real-world events to the legal framework, thus easing the judge's decision-making task, many others recounted stories of social injustice, soured relationships and the need for personal and social remedies. While judges preferred the "rule-oriented" accounts to the "relation-oriented" ones, such rule-based accounts are quite alien to normal storytelling practices:

> ... lay litigants have theories of evidence, proof, causation, blame, and responsibility which differ markedly from the official legal versions. The law's preference for information that is acquired visually rather than aurally, its insistence that a story be told from a consistent perspective, and its effort to draw a sharp line between fact and opinion all run contrary to the conventions of everyday storytelling. (Conley and O'Barr 1990: 176-77)

In other words, legal professionals make no concessions for the fact that storytelling is usually undertaken in a narrative mode rather than in a paradigmatic mode.

The other key text from 1990 shows how the testimony itself can be represented erroneously by court interpreters. Berk-Seligson (1990 and 2002) details the numerous ways in which court interpreters impose their subjective interpretations on the ongoing testimony. For example, she shows that interpreters tend to render witness testimony in a more "powerless" fashion (in Lind and O'Barr's terms) than the original and, in general, that "the interpreter has the powerful capability of changing the intent of what a non-English-speaking witness wishes to say in the way that he or she would like to say it" (Berk-Seligson 2002: 196-97). The English-speaking juror in this context is not in a position to distinguish the intent of the witness from the representation of the interpreter, with the result that the juror is judging not the witness herself but an already-interpreted version of that witness.

In this work on discrepancies in representation, the authors are not so much making judgements about the capacity of the participants to undertake their tasks in general, but about the abnormality of the institutional context which requires extra-special abilities beyond those required in "normal" contexts. So, the problem with "relational" litigants is not that they are unable to narrate the disputed events (they can do that in ways which would seem perfectly normal in everyday contexts) but that they are unable to narrate in the "abnormal" legal fashion expected by judges. Similarly, the problem with court interpreters is not their capacity to interpret from the other language and to convey the informational content accurately but their lack of awareness that even subtle changes in style (such as the introduction of, or non-translation of, discourse markers) can have effects on the way a witness is judged by the jury. These institutionally-specific problems are different from the general incapacities revealed in the texts from 1979: eyewitnesses are likely to be inaccurate in whatever context of telling and people are almost always influenced by their social psychological judgements of interlocutors. On the contrary, it is the court specialists who need to develop special skills. Judges in small claims courts need to develop the ability to "read" relational accounts, while court interpreters need special training:

> If the research findings presented in this book and others in this field demonstrate that there are routine discrepancies between what speakers say in the courtroom and the way in which interpreters render what is said, this by no means intimates that interpreters should be removed from the judicial process. ... If anything, the research demonstrates that interpreting in its various forms is a highly intellectually demanding task, and those who prove themselves to be skilled interpreters should be held in the highest regard. (Berk-Seligson 2002: 236-37)

2.3. Interactional violence

The two texts I have sampled from 2001 (Matoesian 2001 and Ehrlich 2001) are both monographic studies of individual rape cases which draw heavily on social and feminist theory. Matoesian (2001) is a detailed conversation-analytic study of the 1991 Kennedy-Smith rape trial. In an earlier study of rape trials, Matoesian (1993) had identified a number of strategies used by defence cross-examiners to challenge the credibility of rape complainants. These included the manipulation of question form and the embedding of evaluative comments to turn eliciting dialogue into self-serving judgemental monologue; close management of the topic through repetition, reformulation and elaboration; the strategic use of silence to comment on the witness's response (or lack of it); and direct challenges to the witness's source of knowledge, which act as "epistemological filters" (1993: 184) to her testimony. However, as Conley and O'Barr (1998) point out, these judgement strategies are common to cross-examination of witnesses in any type of criminal case. So Matoesian (1993), along with other work on the language of cross-examination (see for example Drew 1990), revealed a certain deceptiveness on the part of cross-examiners. However, in his later book, Matoesian (2001) goes one judgemental step further and claims that cross-examiners are effectively enacting "rape of the second kind":

> ... whereas the rape trial indeed employs generic impeachment strategies, like other criminal trials, it also activates, through those same strategies, a covert interaction with the patriarchal logic of sexual rationality in crucial moments to fashion the penetrating thrust of blame attributions against the victim. (Matoesian 2001: 234)

The "patriarchal logic of sexual rationality" is the term Matoesian gives to the mechanism that relates male-dominated expectations of sexuality to the "microculture of language use" (2001: 40) and much of the book is concerned with explicating stylistic devices which create "rhythms of domination" which lead to the "penetrating thrust of blame attributions against the victim". Rather than merely badgering the complainant, as claimed by Drew (1990), the cross-examiner is figuratively raping the "victim".

Ehrlich (2001) is a detailed discourse analysis of the proceedings (in a university tribunal and criminal trial) against a male student accused of sexual assault. Like Matoesian, Ehrlich draws on a pre-existing social theoretical framework (in her case feminist critiques of the law), which she applies to "the nitty-gritty linguistic details of actual verbal interaction" (Ehrlich 2001: 1-2). However, where Matoesian focuses on the power of trial talk to revictimise the victim, Ehrlich is more concerned with the role of talk in "defining and delimiting" the range of meaning options available to the different trial participants. Like Matoesian (1993 and 2001), Ehrlich identifies some of the interactional strategies used by cross-examiners to achieve discursive (and thus evaluative) control, such as strategic questioning, presupposition and selective reformulation. However, she goes on to show how these presuppositions and pseudo-assertions construct an ideological frame which severely constrains the way in which evidence may be evaluated. Accordingly, the complainants are seen to have had "numerous" and "unlimited" options for resisting the sexual aggression, so that their own responses to that aggression come to be construed as "ineffectual and passive", while the explanation that they were gripped by "paralysing fear" is discounted as a motivation for their inaction (Ehrlich 2001: 91-2). The complainants and their witness are thus not afforded the same "latitude and range of gendered subject positions" as the defendant:

> ... their identities as "ineffectual agents" are thrust upon them by a dominant discourse that constrained their possibilities for representing their strategic agency. Indeed, the gendered subject positions made available (in the case of Matt) and thwarted (in the case of the complainants and their witness) within these institutional settings all worked in the service of the same goal: protecting a range of sexual prerogatives for Matt at the expense of the complainants' sexual autonomy. (Ehrlich 2001: 150)

Ehrlich (2001) and Matoesian (2001) are representative of a shift towards focussing on the behaviour of legal professionals in court rather than the capacity of lay participants or the special skills demanded by the institutional context. Cross-examiners use numerous strategies to deceive the witness and thus convey negative judgements of that witness to the jury, but they go beyond that to revictimise the victim. However, in neither book are the legal professionals judged so overtly as that. In both the authors' conclusions, the "accused" are abstract institutional entities. For Matoesian, it is "the rape trial" which "employs ... strategies" and "activates ... a covert interaction" that fashions "the penetrating thrust of blame attributions". And for Ehrlich, the ineffectuality of the complainant's identity and the thwarting of her subject positions are "thrust upon" her not by the cross-examiner but by "a dominant discourse".

Methodologically, Matoesian and Ehrlich are indicative of a tendency in more recent years to move away from attempts to provide representative samples of data (a paradigmatic approach) and towards studies with narrative coherence. Both Conley and O'Barr (1990) and Berk-Seligson (1990) took an ethnographic approach involving participant observation of the courtroom over several weeks or months. They also attempted to collect a representative sample of texts. Conley and O'Barr (1990: 32) recorded 466 small claims cases and transcribed and studied 156 of these, while Berk-Seligson (2002: 43) recorded 114 hours of judicial proceedings over a period of seven months, including a wide variety of courtroom genres (e.g. hearings, pleas, trials, sentencings). Matoesian and Ehrlich, on the other hand, both approach courtroom discourse from a social theoretical standpoint. Unlike most social theory, their work is highly empirical since it deals with the "fine-grained" (Matoesian 2001: 38) or "nitty-gritty" (Ehrlich 2001: 1) details of socially situated verbal interaction. Nevertheless, it is difficult to generalise their findings since they study individual cases rather than representative samples and thus base their analyses on the language of very few legal professionals and witnesses in just one specific context.

3. An empirical framework

In the above survey of the literature on the relation between court testimony and the judgement of witnesses, I claimed to have adopted a sampling method. However, the account is clearly a partial one and the "sampling" was primarily a rhetorical ruse. In other words, the account was motivated more by narrative than scientific concerns. In Heffer (2005), I argue for the need to find a middle way (both in the linguistic practice of jury trials and in their study) between narrative and logico-scientific (paradigmatic) approaches. In what follows, though, I present a limiting case of empirical grounding in an area – the discourse analysis of subjective judgement – which would not appear at first sight particularly amenable to a scientific approach. The object is to see to what extent we can separate out the linguistic evidence from our own subjective evaluations of that evidence. I shall firstly define the scope of judgement we shall be working with, and introduce a systematic framework for analysing judgement within the scope of that definition. Then I shall define a data set which is broadly representative of the investigative domain.

3.1. The semantic system of JUDGEMENT

The term "judgement" can be used to refer to someone's powers of discernment, their considered opinions on any topic, or a judge's authoritative opinion on rights and obligations. However, I have already *de facto* limited the scope in this paper to the evaluation of human behaviour, and specifically to the evaluation of witnesses and defendants by trial lawyers and judges. I shall now further restrict the scope to the linguistic construal of judgement through lexis. This is a crucial restriction since evaluation of someone's behaviour, as can be seen in the work of Matoesian and Ehrlich, can be conveyed in many other ways: prosodically (e.g. surprise intonation), paralinguistically (e.g. loudness, silence), pragmatically (e.g. presupposition), interactionally (e.g. turntaking), and non-verbally (e.g. gaze, gesture, facial expression). This limitation is necessary partly due to the nature of the data set (official court transcripts) and partly due to the nature of the linguistic framework I shall be applying (a lexical-semantic one).

This delimitation of judgement is in line with the systemic-functional view of JUDGEMENT[2] as a semantic resource "construing our attitudes to people and the way they behave – their character (how they measure up)" (Martin and White 2005: 52). Within the appraisal framework (Martin 2000; White 1998; Martin and White 2005), JUDGEMENT is one of three "systems" used to construe a speaker's attitude to things, the others being AFFECT (emotional response) and APPRECIATION (aesthetic response). Attitudinal feelings towards entities tend to be positive (+ve) or negative (–ve), and contrast with opinions about propositions, which tend to be epistemic and involve degrees of certainty.[3] JUDGEMENT can be further divided into attitudes that concern someone's social esteem –

normality how unusual they are (*lucky, peculiar, predictable*)
capacity how capable they are (*mature, stupid, witty*)
tenacity how resolute or reliable they are (*brave, reckless, loyal*)

– and those where negative judgement might result in social sanction –

veracity how honest they are (*candid, dishonest, devious*)
propriety how ethical they are (*good, corrupt, cruel*)

At the most basic level, the framework provides a convenient metalanguage for talking about people's judgements of others in general. For example, we can use the framework in this elementary form to roughly summarise the shifts in the judgement of courtroom participants in the literature surveyed in the previous section. The texts from 1979 (Loftus, and Lind and O'Barr) focussed primarily on the **incapacity** of witnesses and jurors to cope with the specific legal tasks –

[2] In appraisal theory, small capitals are usually used to indicate the lexical-semantic systems available to the speaker. Thus, the semantic system (JUDGEMENT) is distinguished from the speaker's judgemental faculty or opinions in general (judgement). Martin and White (2005) use bold instead. I shall use the small capitals convention, but only when explicitly referring to the SFL appraisal framework.

[3] See Thompson and Hunston (2000) for an introduction to the slippery terminology involved in linguistic discussions of evaluation/stance/attitude/viewpoint.

particularly the separation of testimonial fact from social judgements – assigned to them in the courtroom. Those in 1990 (Conley and O'Barr, Berk-Seligson) were more concerned with the **normality** and **tenacity** of their litigants and interpreters. In both cases, the participants behaved in a "normal" fashion for narrators and interpreters but this lacked the special skills demanded by the specialised context of the trial. Furthermore, the reliability of the interpreters in re-presenting the testimony was held to account. Finally, in the texts from 2001 (Matoesian, Ehrlich) we see at least a covert judgement of the **veracity** and **propriety** of the trial lawyers. The cross-examiners, in particular, use deceptive techniques, but they go beyond dishonesty to the impropriety of revictimising the rape complainants. More importantly, the very institutional structure of the law, and of society at large, is effectively held to be improper.

When we turn, though, to the "nitty-gritty linguistic detail" of analysing discourse using this system, the situation becomes more complex. On the one hand, an outburst from the Lord Chief Justice in the early modern trial of Lady Lisle (from the Helsinki corpus of historical texts) provides, in 1), exceptional support for this framework:

1) LCJ: Thou art a strange, prevaricating, shuffling, snivelling, lying rascal.

We might analyse this outburst as 2), where we see that the noun phrase moves from evaluations of social esteem to evaluations of social sanction:

2) Thou art a **strange** [–ve normality], **prevaricating** [–ve tenacity], **shuffling** [–ve tenacity], **snivelling** [–ve capacity], **lying** [–ve veracity] **rascal** [–ve propriety].

On the other hand, the semantic categories proposed by Martin and White are far from watertight, as might be expected of such a slippery field as evaluation: capacity slips into tenacity, veracity into propriety, and so on. Often context clarifies, but not always: *reasonable* behaviour in most contexts shows a capacity for reason, but also suggests that the person is reliable, normal and beyond reproach; a *dishonest* witness not only lies, but can also be both unreliable and morally reprehensible (as we shall see).

Martin and White (2005: 61-8) make a crucial distinction between judgement which is effectively written into the text (**inscribed**) and judgement which is called upon from the reader (**invoked**). Judgement is inscribed through the use of attitudinal lexis, particularly adjectival epithets (*normal, capable, reliable*), but also through attitudinal nouns (*liar, thief, saint*) and verbs (*lie, steal*). Judgement is invoked, on the other hand, by appealing to cultural scripts and background knowledge. For example, in 3), from the data described below, the cross-examiner is ostensibly eliciting information about the usuality of an event.

3) Does he normally leave his door wide open or unlocked? [CR69]

However, drawing on our cultural scripts, we might see this as an invitation to evaluate the supposed behaviour as stupid. And the jury, drawing on their accumulated knowledge of the defendant by that point in the trial (he is not stupid but lives in a rough area), might construe this as an invitation to evaluate the defendant's testimonial behaviour as deceitful. Similarly, while Matoesian (2001) uses the label "victim" to inscribe innocence (+ve propriety) to the rape complainant (and thus exclude the ethical alternative of false allegation), he invokes, or even provokes, a judgement of negative propriety (linguistic rape) through the metaphorical "*penetrating thrust* of blame attributions". Martin and White describe any such invoked instance as a **token** (t,) of judgement. As we move towards this more reader-oriented invoked judgement, though, objective analysis merges into increasingly subjective interpretation.

3.2. A corpus of legal-professional trial talk

Armed with a systematic analytical framework, we want to be able to apply this to a data set broadly representative of the domain of legal-professional trial talk. A suitable set of corpora of official court transcripts was designed and compiled for Heffer (2005). The texts in the key corpora of witness examinations and judicial summings-up (2005: 221-25) were selected via a quota sampling procedure to ensure representativeness with respect to the variables accounted for in the transcripts: location of court (various Crown Courts in England); type of offence (theft, GBH, rape etc.); party (prosecution, defence); type of witness (lay, expert, police etc.); type of judge (circuit, high court etc.); and sex of barrister, witness and judge. The corpora include speech by 103 barristers and 72 judges, thus avoiding to some extent the skewing caused by idiolect (2005: 58-63). The transcripts are from 150 ordinary trials, thus avoiding the skewing created by celebrity lawyers on celebrity cases. In addition, smaller corpora of opening and closing speeches and the judge's sentencing remarks were compiled on similar principles. Since we are interested here only in legal-professional judgements of lay witnesses, a LEGAL-LAY[4] corpus was constructed (Table 1) consisting solely in the language addressed by counsel and judges to witnesses, the defendant and the jury. Apart from the monologic genres of counsel's opening and closing

[4] Sub-corpora are referred to in SMALL CAPITALS to distinguish them from the trial genres themselves.

speeches (OPENING, CLOSING), the judge's summing-up (divided into jury DIRECTIONS and the REVIEW of evidence) and the judge's act of SENTENCING, this included all and only counsel's turns addressing witnesses (c-w turns) during examination-in-chief (CHIEF) and cross-examination (CROSS).[5]

Table 1. The LEGAL–LAY corpus

Component	No. of texts	Size in words
Counsel		
OPENING	16	57,500
CHIEF (c-w turns)	100	223,600
CROSS (c-w turns)	127	407,800
CLOSING	10	37,400
Judge		
DIRECTIONS	100	323,000
REVIEW	100	648,500
SENTENCING	100	66,300
Totals	**553**	**1,764,100**

While this corpus is strong in representativeness, it is weak in terms of its representation of the communicational context since it relies on official court transcripts (Heffer 2005: 52-8). Conversation analysts from Atkinson and Drew (1979) to Matoesian (2001) have provided rich transcripts encoding as many as possible of the prosodic, paralinguistic and non-verbal features in the interaction between counsel, witness and judge. Court reporters (official transcribers), on the other hand, mostly ignore these features and have also been known to "tidy up" the grammar of counsel and judges (Walker 1990). However, it is a given in language and law work that data will be defective in some respect: the key is to make the most of the data you manage to obtain. Furthermore, it is a well-known methodological axiom in language research in general that "[b]readth and depth generally operate in inverse proportion to each other" (Milroy and Gordon 2003: 72). Court reporters are legally bound to produce a "verbatim" transcript, which is generally understood as one containing all the "words" of the original, so while rich ethnographic analysis is not possible, there should be no problem studying the frequency and distribution of lexical items, and given the representativeness of the corpus, the findings can be generalised beyond the specific context.

[5] Annotation of the texts meant that it was very easy to link any one barrister turn with its interactional context in the "mother" corpus. The trial corpora in Heffer (2005) include 54 very short re-examinations, which have been left out of the LEGAL-LAY corpus for practical reasons.

4. An empirical analysis of judgement in court

Given a systematic framework for coding lexical items conveying judgement and a corpus that is as representative as possible of the domain under investigation, what can we learn about the way legal professionals in general explicitly convey their judgement of lay participants in the trial process? Following the general approach adopted in Heffer (2005), I shall begin with a broad-brush quantitative survey of JUDGEMENT items in the data and then move some way towards more fine-grained qualitative analysis.

4.1. A corpus-based methodology

The initial aim was to sketch a quantitative picture of how the various trial genres linguistically construe judgement. This takes us far from the conversation analytic concern with the linguistic minutiae of social interaction and towards the computational linguistic concern with automatic categorisations of enormous corpora of texts. At the computational extreme of attitudinal analysis of texts is the rapidly growing field of sentiment analysis. The primary aim of sentiment analysis is to develop computational systems for automatically classifying target texts as evaluatively positive or negative, which has significant commercial applications in such areas as market research, and data and web mining. Most of the studies work with a testbed of 1000 positive and 1000 negative movie reviews (Pang and Lee 2004) and tend to rely either on a "bag of words" approach, which compares the frequencies of words in the "positive" and "negative" documents, or on a "semantic orientation" approach which identifies each word in the document as "positive" or "negative" and then compares the totals. However, both these methods are semantically and contextually crude and neither approach has managed to achieve 90% accuracy. The appraisal framework has recently been introduced to this area precisely because it enables "more fine-grained analysis of the expressions of sentiment in a document" (Whitelaw *et al.* 2005: 630). Here we see that "fine-grained analysis" is very much a relative notion since we are still dealing with large-scale automatic analysis.

My own study is a little further down the qualitative end of the continuum to the extent that I was interested in the distributions of each of the JUDGEMENT categories in each of the trial genres represented in the LEGAL-LAY corpus, rather than simply the overall orientation of the texts. However, the initial methods were similar to those used by Whitelaw et al. (2005). First a lexicon of "candidate" judgement items was constructed for each of the JUDGEMENT categories (normality, capacity, tenacity, veracity, propriety). Then the items were retrieved automatically from each of the subcorpora in the form of concordances. And finally the concordance lines were manually checked for judgemental relevance.

Clearly, invoked judgement is impossible to retrieve in a corpus without first qualitatively analysing all the texts (a task well beyond the scope of this study). On the other hand, restricting the selection of items to adjectival epithets would be too restrictive for an institutional site where explicit construal of judgement is for the most part proscribed. The selection was thus restricted to judgement inscribed through attitudinal lexis, but extended from adjectives to other lexical word classes (nouns, verbs, adverbs) and from single words to phrases. For example, *fraud*, *exaggerate* and *economical with the truth* were all selected for Veracity, and *on the ball* was selected for Capacity. The conceptual organisation of *Roget's Thesaurus* (Kirkpatrick 2000) provided a rich source of lexical items and these were amply supplemented by entries in the *New Oxford Thesaurus* (Hanks 2000). The resulting lexicons consisted of between 500 and 800 forms for each JUDGEMENT category.[6]

The next stage involved retrieving the items from the trial corpora. Concordances of items in each lexicon were retrieved using WordSmith Tools (Scott 1996). The lines were then manually analysed to weed out items such as the "position" sense of *lie* and other non-judgemental senses.[7] On the other hand, judgements which were mediated through attribution to another source (*He said she was dishonest*), or were conditional (*That would be dishonest*) were retained. Similarly, items such as *innocent* and *indecent* which were used meta-judgementally in contexts such as the judge's directions on the law and review of evidence (*He does not have to prove he is innocent*) were retained in the analysis.

A sample of judgement lexis retrieved from the data can be seen in Table 2, with frequently occurring items indicated in italics.

Table 2. Inscribed JUDGEMENT in court (adapted from Martin 2000: 156)

Social Esteem	Positive (admire)	Negative (criticise)
normality (fate)	*normal*, regular, usual…	*unusual*, rare, odd…
"Is he or she special?"	ordinary, *reasonable*…	strange, curious, funny…
	special, fortunate, lucky…	unfortunate, tragic, pitiful…
capacity	*able*, capable, competent…	unable, incapable,
"Is he or she capable?"	*aware*, sensitive…	stupid…
	careful, prudent…	silly, depressed…
		careless, hysterical…

[6] The use of wildcards in the search phase to cover morphological variation means it was not possible to know precisely how many word forms were in each lexicon.

[7] Given that over 12,000 lines were retrieved, this phase was extremely labour-intensive and so could not involve close and careful contextual analysis; alternative readings were largely ignored and preference went to the category most closely associated with the particular lexical item.

tenacity "Is he or she dependable?"	*responsible*, sensible... *reliable*, trustworthy... determined, conscientious...	*confused*, reckless, foolish... unreliable, forgetful, unsure... worried, nervous, troubled...
Social Sanction	Positive (praise)	Negative (condemn)
veracity (truth) "Is he or she honest?"	*tell the truth...* honest, truthful... frank...	*lie*, mislead, trick, cheat... *dishonest*, liar, deceitful... fraudulent, corrupt, sham...
propriety (ethics) "Is he or she beyond reproach?"	*innocent*, lawful, remorse... good, right-minded, moral... decent, caring, kindly...	*guilty*, *criminal*, unlawful... *bad*, terrible, appalling... *indecent*, *abuse*, offensive...

4.2. JUDGEMENT and the trial stages

The method outlined in the previous section enables us to provide a quantitative overview of judgement in the LEGAL-LAY corpus (Tables 3 and 4). It is important to note that the figures in the tables represent the accumulated frequencies (per 100,000 words) of 500-800 terms in each case, so the figures on the whole are comparatively low, as would be expected of genres where explicit construal of judgement is proscribed.

Table 3 indicates the results for the categories concerned with social esteem. Both one- and multi-word items counted as single occurrences of JUDGEMENT.

While Normality showed no significant variation across the genres, there was a notable difference in the inscription of Capacity and Tenacity between counsel's turns in examination-in-chief and cross-examination. Cross-examiners judged Capacity and Tenacity over twice as frequently as examiners. The Capacity category was dominated by just two words – *able* and *aware* – which accounted for 75% of Capacity in CHIEF and 56% in CROSS. However, the words are used very differently in the two types of examination. Over half of the occurrences in CHIEF are questions of the form *Are/were you able...?*. Apart from the knotty question of whether *able* is a lexical item (and thus part of appraisal) or a grammatical item (and thus part of modality), these uses were evaluatively neutral.

Table 3. Lexical inscription of social esteem in LEGAL-LAY corpus (items per 100,000 words)

SPEAKER and Trial Stage	SOCIAL ESTEEM			
	Normality	Capacity	Tenacity	TOTAL
COUNSEL				
OPENING	57	110	26	193
CHIEF (c-w)	65	85	17	167
CROSS (c-w)	74	191	38	303
CLOSING	61	241	59	361
JUDGE				
DIRECTIONS	54	185	82	321
REVIEW	60	154	63	277
SENTENCING	54	222	66	342

In contrast, only 9% of the occurrences of *able* and *aware* in CROSS are in this interrogative form, while the others can be found in pseudo-declaratives, such as tag questions, in which the barrister is clearly evaluating the witness, as in 4):

4) Q. Yes, but you were **able** to do it, were you not? [CR33][8]

The differences between the JUDGEMENT categories were far more marked with regard to Veracity and Propriety (Table 4). The table includes both the figure for lexical judgements of Propriety and for the metalinguistic mention of Propriety (indicated as "Propriety"), while the *Total* figure excludes the metalinguistic citations.

[8] Cross-examination no. 33. CH = CHIEF, CR = CROSS, SU = SUMMING-UP, SE = SENTENCING.

Table 4. Lexical inscription of social sanction in LEGAL-LAY corpus (items per 100,000 words)

SPEAKER and Trial Stage	SOCIAL SANCTION			
	Veracity	Propriety	"Propriety"	*Total* (V+P)
COUNSEL				
OPENING	92	27	"118"	119
CHIEF (c-w)	30	25	"13"	55
CROSS (c-w)	142	97	"1"	239
CLOSING	251	190	"24"	441
JUDGE				
DIRECTIONS	65	98	"713"	163
REVIEW	95	98	"26"	193
SENTENCING	86	759	"30"	845

The table tends to confirm suggestions made in Heffer (2005) about the structure and function of the various trial stages. Firstly, though based on a relatively small sample, there appears to be a net distinction between the inscription of Veracity and Propriety in the opening speeches (119 per 100,000 words) and the closing speeches (441). Unlike in most US jurisdictions, in England and Wales the defence do not usually reply to the prosecution's opening speech, which is often referred to as their "Opening Facts", so it is meant to be a "neutral" statement of their case. Indeed, we see a relatively high frequency of metalinguistic references to Propriety, as in the judge's legal directions, since the Prosecutor explains the indictment to the jury. These openings are in reality quite evaluative (Heffer 2005: 75-7), but the evaluation tends to be invoked rather than inscribed. On the other hand, the closing "Arguments" of prosecution and defence are intended to be adversarial and are flagged up to the jury by the judge as "opinion" and are thus more overtly evaluative.

Secondly, we see an even more marked distinction between the two main types of examination. With respect to examination-in-chief, the cross-examiner inscribes Veracity roughly 5 times more frequently (30 v 142 per 100,000), and Propriety roughly 4 times more frequently (25 v 97 per 100,000). These figures lend support to the view that counsel is essentially concerned with eliciting the story in examination-in-chief but discrediting its narrators in cross-examination. Examination in general appears to have grown less evaluative with regard to Propriety as the law of evidence has grown tighter. The Propriety figure for examination in my small Early Modern corpus of trials (extracted from the Helsinki historical corpus) is 324 per 100,000 words, over three times as frequent as modern cross-examination and almost nine times as frequent as examination-in-chief.

Finally, we see a very strong focus on Propriety in the adjudicatory phase of the trial. Firstly there is a high density of metalinguistic "Propriety" items (713 per 100,000) in the legal directions section of the summing-up. The function of directions is, to a great extent, to provide the jury with the law's own classification system for judgement and the key task required of the jury consists in choosing from the binary Propriety options of *guilty* (the predominant key term in the directions) or *not guilty*. Secondly, Propriety is construed lexically in sentencing (759 per 100,000 words) almost eight times more frequently than in cross-examination (97) and over thirty times more frequently than in examination-in-chief (25). It is also inscribed almost nine times more frequently than Veracity is in sentencing. The reason for this preponderance of Propriety items is that sentencing is no longer concerned with testimonial truth but with punishing the convicted defendant, and it is the "relative moral wickedness" of a crime which partly determines the severity of punishment (Hart 1962: 37).

4.3. Judgemental intensity and sentencing

The above analysis focussed on the distribution of JUDGEMENT categories across the trial genres and the lexical density of judgement items in any one genre. This does not say anything, though, about the intensity of the judgements being conveyed. In selecting candidate items, I took a fairly liberal approach to lexical inscription. This is because, outside sentencing, there was very little use of clear attitudinal epithets. For example, the most frequent adjectival epithet construing negative Veracity in cross-examination is *dishonest*, but this occurs only 5 times per 100,000 words, in comparison to 71 per 100,000 words for the lemma *LIE*, which construes the negative Veracity more indirectly. Table 5 indicates the most distinctive or "key" lexical items realising judgement in each of the genres. The "keyness" of each word was calculated, using the KeyWords tool of Wordsmith Tools (Scott 1996), by comparing its frequency in the wordlist for the trial-genres sub-corpus (e.g. CLOSING, SENTENCING) with the frequency of the same word in a reference wordlist for the entire LEGAL-LAY corpus. A word which is positively "key" here occurs more often than would be expected by chance in comparison with the LEGAL-LAY corpus as a whole. The words indicated in the table are those items realising JUDGEMENT which ranked highest in the keyword lists. The figures indicate the statistical strength of the "keyness" (a log-likelihood test), while gaps in cells indicate that there were no statistically significant keywords for that combination.

Table 5. Evaluative distinctiveness in the LEGAL-LAY corpus (k=keyness)

SPEAKER and Trial Stage	SOCIAL ESTEEM			SOCIAL SANCTION	
	Normality	Capacity	Tenacity	Veracity	Propriety
COUNSEL					
OPENING					*abuse* k=45
CHIEF (c-w)			*confirm* k=28		
CROSS (c-w)		*understand* k=65		*truth* k=52	
CLOSING			*in doubt* k=28	*fraudulent* k=52	
JUDGE					
DIRECTIONS	*reasonable* k=245		*reliable* k=95	*lies* k=155	*guilty* k=867
REVIEW				*denied* k=48	
SENTENCING				*trust* k=19	*appalling* k=93

Statistically, the strongest keywords (apart from *lies*) are all adjectival epithets (*guilty*, *reasonable*, *reliable*, *appalling*), but the first three of these are being used meta-judgementally in the legal directions. Indeed, the only two adjectival epithets in the grid which actually judge the behaviour of the witness or defendant are *fraudulent* used in closing speeches and *appalling* used in sentencing. Beyond these top keywords, though, SENTENCING reveals a range of other keywords which, though not all adjectival epithets, convey a particularly strong sense of negative propriety: *convicted, aggravating, gravity, no remorse, wicked, suffered* (victim), *evil, unprovoked, dreadful, frightening, cruelty* and *caused misery*.

The intensity of the inscription of judgement in sentencing does appear (apparently following Hart) to be calibrated with the severity of the crime. Thus, a man convicted of unlawful use of a metal detector, receiving a fine of £100, is told by the Assistant Recorder (a part-time judge):

5) It is **not appropriate** for people to go around those lands, passing on other people's land searching for potentially valuable items that there may be buried beneath the surface of the ground and removing them **without any say so** from the owner. [SE16]

A man convicted of stealing over £1000 from an elderly resident in his care, is told by the Circuit Judge:

6) I accept Mr S. made out the appropriate authorities and cheques in your favour, but that having been done, for you then to use the monies for your own purposes was *downright* **dishonest** and was **taking advantage of an elderly man**, and of course it was an **abuse of trust**, a *serious* **abuse of trust** having regard to your respective positions. [SE23]

Finally, a serial sex offender is handed down the following judgement:

7) Your record as far as sexual offences are concerned is *quite* **appalling**. Indeed, in this case on the last occasion when you appeared in front of me I said, and I still think and believe, that your conduct was verging on the **satanic**. In relation to counts 8, 9 and 10, the rape, buggery and false imprisonment, you behaved *quite* **atrociously**. You are an **evil** man and you are a **wicked** man. [SE30]

Perhaps only the sentencing of the notorious serial-killer doctor Harold Shipman could have produced more intense judgement:

8) The time has now come for me to pass sentence upon you for these **wicked, wicked crimes**. Each of **your victims** was your patient. You **murdered** *each and every one of* **your victims** by a *calculated* and **cold blooded perversion** of your medical skills. For your own **evil** and **wicked** purposes you **took advantage of** and *grossly* **abused the trust** that each of **your victims** reposed in you. ... The *sheer* **wickedness** of what you have done *defies description* and is *shocking beyond belief.* (http://www.the-shipman-inquiry.org.uk/trialday.asp?Day=58)

A couple of observations are of note here. Firstly, in Bakhtinian terms, the texts are mostly monoglossic; that is, they consist primarily in categorical assertions which do not overtly recognise other voices. In truth, the judge generally does take into account the mitigating circumstances of the defendant, as in "I accept Mr S." in (7), but the main thrust of sentencing is an authoritative proclamation of guilt. Discourse during the trial itself is ostensibly heteroglossic, as the parties fight out their cause, while sentencing is seen as the moment for a unitary voice of condemnation. The second observation is that the intensity or force of the judgement is heightened through intensification (*downright, serious, quite, grossly, sheer, shocking beyond belief*) and quantification (*each and every one of*). These two factors – the positioning of the appraiser and the amplification of the judgement – are likely to have a considerable effect on the uptake of the judgement by the jury during the trial stages.

5. Judgement and lying in cross-examination

While we have seen that the lexical inscription of Propriety is more or less *prescribed* in judicial sentencing as a public justification for the sincerity of the sentence, such inscription is *proscribed* in cross-examination. Cross-examination is fundamentally concerned with judging the witness, and thus invites lexical inscription, but during a "fact-finding" stage of the trial process in which opinions are not meant to be explicitly expressed. As we saw above, despite the clear focus on the veracity of the witness, the explicit epithet *dishonest* is comparatively rare. Cross-examination is thus a useful site for investigating more subtle construals of judgement. In particular I shall consider how the ascription of lying to the witness becomes transformed into a judgement of Propriety. First, I shall outline the general context of lying in cross-examination. Then I shall analyse the cotexts of the most frequent item realising JUDGEMENT in cross-examination – the lemma *LIE* {*lie, lies, lied, lying*} – and shall show how they work to position the appraiser and amplify the judgement. Finally, I shall briefly analyse the opening of a single cross-examination.

5.1. Lying and cross-examination

According to the law of evidence, there are several legal means of cross-examining to discredit the witness (Keane 1996; Tapper 1999). These come together to build up a picture of the witness as a narrator who is unreliable, since she is deficient in:

> **Capacity** – she is incapable of telling the truth owing to the quality of her memory or powers of perception, her incomplete knowledge of the facts, or a general mental incapacity;
>
> **Veracity** – she is dishonest, as indicated by her inconsistent statements, mistakes and omissions in evidence, and any other matters showing a general reputation for untruthfulness;
>
> **Propriety** – she is reprehensible, as shown by previous misconduct and convictions.
>
> (Heffer 2005: 133)

The predominance of the lemma *LIE* is indicative of a preoccupation in cross-examination with the technique of "impeachment", or "[t]he act of discrediting a witness, as by catching the witness in a lie" (Garner 1999: 756). This is most commonly achieved by showing inconsistencies between the witness's testimony in court and her previous statements in police interview and under examination. However, showing inconsistency is not sufficient for demonstrating that the witness has been lying. Coleman and Kay (1981: 28) point out that a prototypical lie consists in three key elements:

1) The proposition is false;
2) The speaker believes the proposition to be false;
3) In uttering the proposition, the speaker intends to deceive the addressee.

A lie must have at its core a false statement, but there can be very good reasons (memory lapse, performance slips, police coercion) why an account narrated on two very different occasions, often months apart, can appear inconsistent (Coulthard 2000), even if the speaker believes they are telling the truth. And we now know that genuine eyewitness accounts are very often inaccurate (Loftus 1979). Even if knowledge of these psychological realities is not common among lay people, mere inconsistency is generally not sufficient to make people believe someone is lying. Such inconsistencies in themselves affect judgements of the Capacity of the witness, but not necessarily their Veracity. The witness, then, must believe the statement to be false. But even here we allow for speakers to tell falsehoods without considering them liars. Coleman and Kay note metaphors (*He's a pig*), sarcasm (*That's clever!*) and hyperbole (*I'm dying of hunger*) as such examples where the speaker is telling a falsehood with no intention of deception. Thirdly, then, a speaker must intend to deceive the addressee. At this point we become concerned with the Veracity of the witness, but there are various degrees of lying associated with different levels of moral approbation. So-called "white lies" are generally shrugged off as morally insignificant and, in court, jurors are directed by judges that not all lies are relevant in deciding guilt. For example, lies told out of shame, or to cover disgraceful behaviour, or to bolster a just cause are not considered legally relevant. So the law of evidence effectively adds another element for a lie to be considered relevant to the decision-making process:

4) The speaker has a guilty motivation in uttering the lie.

At this point, judgement of lying arguably moves from a question of Veracity to a question of Propriety, and this explains the cross-examiner's concern with establishing the impropriety of a witness's lying.

5.2. The ENGAGEMENT and GRADUATION of *LIE*

The cross-examiner thus faces two tasks in suggesting to the jury that the witness is dishonest. Firstly, she must claim that the witness is, in fact, lying. Secondly, she must indicate that the witness has a guilty motivation in uttering the lie or lies. Two attendant resources in the construal of appraisal – ENGAGEMENT and GRADUATION – assist in achieving these two tasks (Martin and White 2005: 92-160). ENGAGEMENT (described above as subject positioning) is concerned with:

> ... the ways in which resources such as projection, modality, polarity, concession and various comment adverbials position the speaker/writer with respect to the value position being advanced and with respect to potential responses to that value position – by quoting or reporting, acknowledging a possibility, denying, countering, affirming and so on. (2005: 36)

GRADUATION (described above as amplification but also including diminution) is concerned with gradability and, since attitude resources like JUDGEMENT are inherently gradable, "graduation has to do with adjusting the degree of an evaluation – how strong or weak the feeling is" (2005: 37). We can see the importance of these resources in the analysis of judgement in cross-examination by considering more closely the cotexts of the 283 concordances of *LIE* retrieved from the CROSS corpus.

The resources of ENGAGEMENT are particularly useful in helping establish the claim that the witness is lying. In 19 (6.7%) of the concordance lines, the proposition on credibility is explicitly pronounced through the subjective projectors *I SUGGEST* and *I PUT to you*.

9) You see, **I suggest to you** that you are lying when you say that... [CR76]
10) That **I put to you** officer is a blatant lie. [CR34]
11) What **I am suggesting to you** was that that was a lie... [CR15]

Martin and White (2005: 129) note that such formulations:

> ... involve authorial interpolations and emphases which are directed against some assumed or directly referenced counter position. Such formulations are dialogistic in that they acknowledge the presence of this counter view in the current communicative setting and are contractive in that they challenge, confront or resist this particular dialogistic alternative.

In other words, the cross-examiner does not hide the fact that the witness will maintain that they are telling the truth but will try to contract the possibilities for advancing this alternative reality. One way of severely contracting the dialogic potential is by coercing concurrence from the witness, and one of the most coercive forms of elicitation is the negative question tag, which occurs in 18 cases (6.4%) immediately after *LIE*:

12) So that is a lie, **is it not?** [CR41]
13) It is you that is lying, **is it not?** [CR81]
14) That was a lie, **was it not?** [CR53]

In trying to meet the other challenge – that of suggesting a guilty motivation – cross-examiners make ample use of the resources of GRADUATION. Simple quantifiers (*another*, *many*, *more*, *all*) are used in 16 cases (5.7%) to help suggest that the lies are habitual, which in turn suggests that the witness is a "liar" rather than simply someone who has told one or two lies.

15) Is that **another** lie? [CR05]
16) So, **all** lies and **more** lies to the police. Correct? [CR54]
17) Or is it that there are **so many** lies and inconsistencies in what you have said... [CR33]

Then there are 18 cases (6.4%) of quantification through figurative collective nouns, which add metaphorical force to the graduation:

18) You told **a pack of** lies did you not? [CR58]
19) This interview is **a litany of** lies, is it not? [CR65]
20) ...your evidence...has been **a catalogue of** lies from start to finish... [CR80]

Repetition (9 cases; 3.2%) is an important intensifying device:

21) Well, you told **lie after lie after lie**, did you not? [CR54]
22) ...what you have done is to **tell a lie, get caught out, tell another lie, get caught out**. [CR21]

Adverbs such as *again* (8) also contribute to the effect of the lying being persistent:

23) ...even at that stage you were lying **again**, setting up **again** a self-defence lie? [CR65]

In 25 cases (8.8%), the force of the lie or lying itself is raised:

24) That is a **complete and utter** lie by yourself. [CR35]
25) You were lying **through your teeth** to them, were you not? [CR32]

Often the graduation realises other JUDGEMENT categories at the same time as intensifying negative veracity. Most frequently (16 cases; 5.7%), modifiers both intensify the lying itself and inscribe negative propriety to the act of lying.

26) I suggest that it is a **wicked** lie to say that... [CR39]
27) Were you telling the officer a **filthy** lie there? [CR05]
28) Why did you tell us that a month ago if it was a **wretched** lie? [CR06]

In some cases barristers focus on the witness's capacity for lying:

29) You do **not have any difficulty in** lying when you are under oath, do you? [CR66]
30) You are **prepared to** lie **to anybody** about what was happening... [CR96]
31) ...those lies in interview demonstrate your **capability of** lying very easily. [CR60]

In other examples, they stress the normality of the witness's lying:

32) Did you **use to tell** lies to other people at school? [CR91]
33) You just tell lies **as and when it suits you to do so**? [CR54]
34) **One of your little lying times**, is it not, this? [CR65]

This brief analysis of the cotext of *LIE* in cross-examination shows how ENGAGEMENT and GRADUATION are used by counsel effectively to narrativise the act of lying, to flesh out the bare bones fact of an untruth into the normal, conscious and criminally-motivated behaviour of a person of bad character.

5.3. From lying to fraudulent intent

In a final move towards the qualitative end of the methodological continuum, I would like to focus in on the opening of a very ordinary cross-examination to consider further complicating factors in our analysis of judgement. The defendant is accused of benefit fraud but in the preceding examination-in-chief the defence have attempted to portray him as a rather inadequate individual who has been duped by his wife, who filled in the Department of Social Security (DSS) benefit forms for him. The cross-examination begins abruptly with the prosecutor immediately putting his case to the defendant. (In the following passages, inscribed judgement is indicated in **bold**, engagement and graduation in *italics*, and invoked judgement underlined.)

1 Q. Let us understand each other from the outset, *my general suggestion to you is that* [pronounce] between 27th August of 1993 and 26th August 1997 you, assisted by your wife, were **running a** *thoroughly* **dishonest racket** [–ve propriety] to obtain money that you were not entitled to from the DSS. What do you say to that?
2 A. No, we were not.
3 Q. Whether you filled in the forms yourself or not *I suggest to you that* [pronounce] you knew exactly what was going on [t, –ve veracity], and that you were living very well on the proceeds [t, –ve propriety] of that **dishonesty** [–ve veracity]. What do you say to that?
4 A. I did not know what was going on. [CR80]

From the start, the prosecutor is categorising the defendant's putative activity not simply as "dishonestly filling in forms" (a matter of veracity) but as "running a thoroughly dishonest racket" (a matter of propriety). While lying is often construed as a venial sin (particularly post-Clinton), a *racket* is "an illegal enterprise carried on for profit, such as extortion, fraud, prostitution, drug peddling etc." (CED 1991: 1227), all clearly "mortal" sins. The judgement is explicitly inscribed in both turns (**dishonest**; **running a racket**; **dishonestly**), intensified (*thoroughly* dishonest), and projected through explicit subjective pronouncements (*my general suggestion to you is that*; *I suggest to you that*). But there are also attempts to invoke the judgement:

you knew exactly what was going on [t, –ve veracity]
you were living very well on the proceeds [t, –ve propriety]

The legal requirement in England and Wales for the cross-examiner to put his case to the witness is an institutional recognition of the dialogic nature of the trial, and the repeated questions "What do you say to that?" are an extremely formal acceptance of that dialogic nature. But the pronouncements themselves are designed to restrict that heteroglossic space as far as possible.

The prosecutor then begins attacking the acknowledged weakness in the defence case, the fact that the defendant lied in interview. In five of his following six turns, he repeats *you lied* and the defendant agrees twice. So the question of veracity is almost beyond dispute. The real question is the motivation behind the lying. The prosecutor thus investigates some possible "innocent" motivations for lying (which might be claimed by the defence or entertained by the jury). Firstly he considers the possibility of compulsion, or negative normality:

> 19 Q. My point is you do not have a medical problem whereby you lie without realising it [t, +ve normality]. You **lie** [–ve veracity] for a reason, do you not?

Here the prosecutor is focussing on construing positive normality: the defendant is a normal person without a medical problem who lies in the way a normal person lies, i.e. for a reason. This is important because judicial condemnation is legitimated by the physical and mental normality of the accused. Then the prosecutor considers the possibility of impulsiveness, or negative capacity.

> 23 Q. You are **not stupid** [neg –ve capacity], *are you*, when it comes to answering questions?
> 24 A. Not really, no.
> 25 Q. You **can** [+capacity] think through the way the questions are going and decide whether you are going to tell the truth or decide whether you are going to lie [t, –ve veracity]. You are **able** [+ve capacity] to do that, *are you not?*
> 26 A. Yes.
> 27 Q. The fact that you are **illiterate** [–ve capacity] and *perhaps* **ill-educated** [–ve capacity] does not create a problem [t, +ve capacity], *does it?* It does not create a problem when it comes to deciding whether to tell the truth or not [t, –ve veracity].
> 28 A. No, not really.

Arguably, the main thrust of the judgement here is conveyed not by the lexical inscriptions of capacity but by the subtle tokens of negative veracity. Some jurors might already construe turn 23 as ironic understatement (not stupid = cunning), but this line becomes more clearly invoked in turn 25: "think through the way the questions are going" imputes strategic acumen to the defendant, while "decide whether you are going to tell the truth or decide whether you are going to lie" suggests that the defendant considers the possibility of lying each time he answers a question, which in turn suggests that he is a habitual (though not compulsive or impulsive) liar. Ironically, by answering "yes" to the prosecutor's question "You are **able** to do that, *are you not?*", the defendant appears both to be admitting to such strategising and yet be incapable of actually carrying out such strategic thinking.

By this stage the prosecutor has ruled out two possible excuses for the defendant's lying – that it is compulsive (–ve normality) or that it is impulsive (–

ve capacity) – and has managed to suggest that the lying is calculated, and that therefore the defendant is a calculating liar (–ve propriety). Two more excuses for the lying are ruled out in turn 27: that it is due to illiteracy or ill-education. At the same time, these two negative judgements of the defendant's capacity are nevertheless presupposed by being projected from *the fact that*. Within 27 turns, then, the prosecutor appears to have established that the defendant is at once illiterate, ill-educated and a calculating liar – a picture which might fit some jurors' stereotype of the lower-class criminal.

6. Evaluative key

The short qualitative analysis above reveals both the strength and weakness of the appraisal framework for analysing judgement. The great weakness is that, as the analysis becomes more situated, the framework begins to look clumsy and the analysis becomes increasingly subjective. In the rich communicative context of courtroom interaction (which, as noted above, is only partly represented through the official court transcript), applying *a priori* semantic categories to units of text of varying length is not optimal for producing truly fine-grained and contextually aware qualitative analysis. And while raters might agree to a considerable extent on assigning categories to attitudinal lexis (Whitelaw *et al.* 2005), the identification of tokens of judgement is much more subjective. One of the major problems in analysing evaluation is that it tends to be prosodic rather than particulate in nature. Evaluated things are sensed, as Pike (1982: 13) puts it, "as somehow flowing together as ripples on the tide, merging into one another in the form of a hierarchy of little waves of experience on still bigger waves". It is exceptionally difficult to convey those prosodies or waves through the analysis of particulate words.

At the same time, the great strength of this framework is precisely that it enables finer-grained *quantitative* analysis than simply word counts or collocational analysis. This makes it ideal for helping to characterise types of discourse. One of the most promising outcomes of previous work using the JUDGEMENT framework has been the identification of evaluative "keys" that operate in specific types of discourse. Hymes' notion of "key" as the "tone, manner or spirit of the speech act" (Hymes 1974: 57) is extended to encompass different patternings of appraisal features across texts. Martin and White (2005: 164) define "key" as:

> [S]ituational variants or sub-selections of the global evaluative meaning making potential – typically reconfiguration of the probabilities for the occurrence of particular evaluative meaning-making options or for the co-occurrence of options.

More simply, we can define an evaluative key (in a somewhat shorter noun phrase) as a set of normative constraints on the appraisal options available to the speaker. With regard to JUDGEMENT, the key variables appear to be whether:

1) The judgement is inscribed or invoked;
2) The judgement is of social esteem (normality, capacity, tenacity) or social sanction (veracity and propriety);
3) The judgement is sourced in the speaker/author (unmediated) or is mediated through attribution to another participant.

White (1998) distinguished between the keys of **reporter voice**, in which the news is presented as a series of neutral facts and in which no authorially-sourced inscribed judgement could be found, and **writer voice**, in which such unmediated inscribed judgement could be found. Writer voice is then subdivided into **correspondent voice**, in which unmediated inscribed social esteem is common but unmediated inscribed social sanction is rare, and **commentator voice**, in which there are no obvious constraints on judgement options and inscribed social sanction is common. Coffin (2003) reveals similar distinctions in school history textbooks and student history essays. **Recorder** key presents history as an unproblematic factual account and, while it invokes judgement, it does not inscribe it in an unmediated way. In contrast to this are two **appraiser** keys correlating with White's writer's voice: **interpreter** key, in which inscribed social esteem is likely but inscribed social sanction unlikely, and **adjudicator** key in which there are no constraints on the judgement options available.[9]

Although a systematic analysis of evaluative keys in the LEGAL-LAY corpus would require very careful manual coding well beyond the scope of the present study, the evidence adduced here and in Heffer (2005) does suggest that we might find a similar set of keys to those found by White (1998) and Coffin (2003). I have set out a putative set of keys and the JUDGEMENT options they might entail in Figure 1. As with White and Coffin, I begin with the basic distinction between adopting an overtly neutral or overtly evaluative stance with respect to the evidence adduced. My rough equivalent to the **reporter** or **recorder** keys is the **fact-finder** key. This label reflects the ostensible role of the legal professional in helping the jury to "find", and thus also evaluate, the "facts" for themselves. Since the facts are meant to be brought before the jury without prior evaluation, in this key there should be no, or minimal, unmediated inscribed judgement. Within this fact-finder key, though, I distinguish between an **examiner** key and an **arbitrator** key. The examiner is a figure who is authorised to "take testimony" (Garner 1999) and thus facilitates the presentation of evidence by the witness rather than

[9] Coffin also draws a little on the appraisal system of APPRECIATION in her classification.

presenting her own evidence or evaluating that of the witness. Examination-in-chief is prototypically delivered in **examiner** key, which explains the low levels of inscription of social esteem in CHIEF (Table 3) and the very low levels of inscription of social sanction (Table 4). The arbitrator, on the other hand, is '[a] neutral person who resolves disputes between parties' (Garner 1999). The meaning we are interested in here is not the resolving of the dispute but the neutral handling of the two cases. Thus, while the examiner neutrally elicits the case of one party, the arbitrator neutrally presents the cases of both parties. English judges work in an **arbitrator** key when reviewing the evidence of both sides in the summing-up. Here they report the 'he said, she said' details of the trial testimony; indeed, *he, said* and *she* are the top three keywords in the REVIEW sub-corpus (Heffer 2005: 196). Consequently, although judges should not directly inscribe their judgement of the participants, in reporting the testimony of the two sides they often present invoked judgement (and sometimes inscribed judgement) mediated through attributions to the various participants.

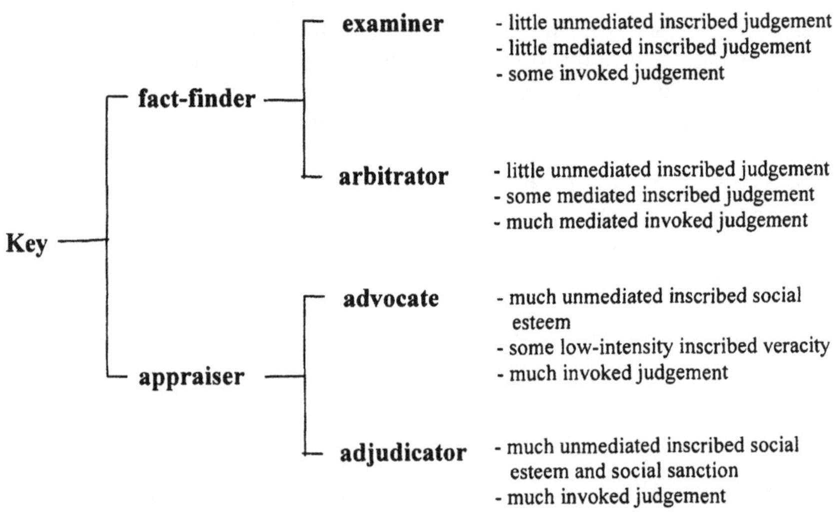

Figure 1. Possible keys of legal-lay discourse (options for construing judgement)

The adoption of a "neutral" **fact-finder** key does not mean the barrister or judge is not appraising the witness, but simply that he or she is doing so more covertly. Examiners will carefully construct both their individual questions and their line of questioning to present their witness in the best possible light: as competent, reliable, truthful, upstanding citizens. They will simply not inscribe those judgements overtly. Similarly, judges in summing-up frequently convey their view of a witness, but they will make sure that it is heavily mediated and modalized so that it accords with an arbitrator key (Heffer 2005: 188-205). For example, in a case which hinges almost entirely on the reliability of a police officer in identifying the defendant in an adjacent car, the judge's crucial evaluation of the Tenacity of that witness (*reliable*) is both heavily modalized and mediated through attribution and disclamation:

> 35) ... one should take into account the fact that this was not a chance meeting between people who did not expect to meet each other. He was wholly interested in that car. That is, as I say, the only reason why he was there. So, it is a matter for you, but you may think that that is something that may cause his identification to be the more reliable. However, as I say, that is entirely a matter for you to assess. [SU62]

The **appraiser** keys, on the other hand, are more overtly evaluative. The **advocate** key, prototypically followed in cross-examination, falls somewhere between the examiner and the adjudicator. The advocate does not simply take testimony but pleads a case and so has a strong interest in conveying her evaluation of participants to the jury. At the same time, in witness examination, the advocate is also always an examiner. Consequently, in **advocate** key we find a considerable amount of unmediated inscribed social esteem (CROSS in Table 3) and a fair amount of low intensity inscribed social sanction, but primarily in relation to veracity (CROSS in Table 4).[10] We saw how cross-examiners have to draw extensively on the resources of ENGAGEMENT and GRADUATION to transform permissible judgements of veracity into circumscribed but invoked judgements of propriety. Finally, the **adjudicator** key, prototypically realised in the judge's sentencing remarks, makes no constraints on the appraisal options available and frequently inscribes negative propriety.

7. Conclusion

This paper set out to explore the relation between factual evidence and subjective judgement in courtroom discourse. By applying a systematic semantic framework to a large, representative corpus of legal-professional discourse, I was able to provide a broad overview of the linguistic construal of judgement by legal professionals in court. This quantitative picture for the most part confirms findings in Heffer (2005) regarding the nature of legal-lay discourse: that it

[10] This is an approximation – I have not systematically coded mediated and unmediated occurrences.

involves a tension between rational, legally-framed fact-finding and subjectively evaluative narrative construction. Additionally, though, I have suggested here that a number of different evaluative keys might be available during the various phases of the trial. This can account for variation in evaluation both across the trial genres and through history: the examiner-in-chief speaks in **examiner** key, the cross-examiner principally in **advocate** key and the Attorney in the opening quote is speaking in **adjudicator** key.

This research can be taken in a number of directions. The analysis of evaluative keys could be made much more robust through manual coding of part, or all, of the corpus. Direct analysis of court recordings, or even videotaped recordings,[11] might reveal to what extent an appraisal analysis can be integrated with analysis of pragmatic phenomena. It would also be extremely useful to carry out the type of experimental work conducted by Lind, O'Barr et al. in the 1970s to attempt to find answers to such questions as: whether inscribing or invoking judgement in cross-examination has a differential effect on mock jurors; to what extent judgement mediated through attribution (as in the English judge's review of the evidence) is interpreted as the speaker's own judgement; and to what extent invoked judgement meets a consensual response in the jury. These are not easy questions, but they would take the research beyond description to possible application.

This paper has also been a methodological exploration of the relation between factual evidence and subjective judgement in the analysis of discourse. Evaluation remains an ephemeral and elusive field but I believe there is a place for both "thin" and "thick" description (Geertz 1973), for superficial analyses of large representative corpora to help map out the discourse territory and for fine-grained qualitative analyses of partial data which can provide invaluable theoretical insights. One criticism that can easily be made of the research reported here is that it works with "already interpreted" data. The complex courtroom interaction has already been interpreted by the court reporter, but also the semantic universe comes "already interpreted" by the appraisal theorists who produced the JUDGEMENT categories. In Heffer (2005) I deliberately avoided applying a unitary framework to avoid the dangers of "narrative smoothing" in data analysis, or only "hearing" what fits your preconceived narrative (Spence 1986: 223). There is a distinct danger of selective hearing in the systemic-functional framework as a whole since it tries to provide a complete and coherent "narrative" of language. In particular, SFL practitioners often appear deaf both to the pragmatic real-time complexities of situated discourse and the entire cognitive dimension of communication. The appraisal framework does provide a rich metalanguage for describing evaluative phenomena at a textual level and seems

---

[11] Unfortunately, research recordings are currently not permitted in English and Welsh courts, but this option is available in some US jurisdictions.

particularly useful in illuminating macrolinguistic patterns of evaluation across text. The problems come when it ceases to be a useful heuristic and starts to become an uncomfortable straitjacket, when the focus goes on the labelling rather than on the explication. In Martin and White's own terms, the discourse then moves from dialogic engagement to monologic contraction.

Finally, I set out in this paper to consider more generally the relationship between evidence and the judgement of participants in research on courtroom discourse. In the initial survey we saw how research into language and law has moved to some extent from an attempt to conform to a Popperian value-neutral social science, with an emphasis on data sampling and experimental methods (Loftus 1979, and Lind and O'Barr 1979), to one in which commitment to just causes is considered more legitimate (Matoesian 2001 and Ehrlich 2001). As we move towards greater social commitment, though, we need to be extremely careful once again not to listen too selectively. Matoesian and Ehrlich provide extremely insightful and illuminating accounts of discourse in the rape trial, but they entirely suppress the voice of the defendant. With conviction rates for reported rape falling to around 5% in the UK (Berlins 2007), there is understandably great concern that not enough rapists are being convicted but, at the same time, 26% of appealed rape cases which are referred to the FBI lead to exoneration on the basis of DNA evidence (Connors et al. 1996). We should always remain open to such counter-evidence and the implications it might have for our analysis of discourse. At the same time, though, we would do well to remember that the activities of academics are in many ways similar to those of lawyers in court: we couch our investigations in the language of factual description, yet while we would not go so far as to judge another as "the most vile and execrable Traitor that ever lived", we are often ultimately advocating a particular judgement of individuals and institutions.

References

Atkinson, J. and P. Drew (1979). *Order in Court: The Organisation of Verbal Interaction in Judicial Settings*. London: MacMillan.

Berger, P.L. and T. Luckmann (1967). *The Social Construction of Reality: A Treatise in the Sociology of Knowledge*. New York: Anchor.

Berk-Seligson, S. (1990). *The Bilingual Courtroom*. Chicago: Chicago University Press.

Berk-Seligson, S. (2002). *The Bilingual Courtroom*. 2nd ed. Chicago: Chicago University Press.

Berlins, M. (2007). "Conviction rates for rape have plummeted since the 1970s. Is there anything we can do to change that?". *The Guardian*, 24 January 2007.

CED (1991) *Collins English Dictionary.* Glasgow: HarperCollins.
Coffin, C. (2003). "Reconstruals of the past - settlement or invasion? The role of JUDGEMENT analysis". In: J. R. Martin and R. Wodak (eds.), *Re/reading the Past: Critical and Functional Perspectives on Discourses of History.* Amsterdam: John Benjamins, 219-46.
Coleman, L. and P. Kay (1981). "Prototype semantics". *Language* 57, 26-44.
Conley, J. M. and W. M. O'Barr (1990). *Rules versus Relationships: The Ethnography of Legal Discourse.* Chicago: University of Chicago Press.
Conley, J. M. and W. M. O'Barr (1998). *Just Words: Law, Language and Power.* Chicago: Chicago University Press.
Connors, E., Lundregan, T., Miller, N. and T. McEwen (1996). *Convicted by Juries, Exonerated by Science: Case Studies in the Use of DNA Evidence to Establish Innocence after Trial.* Department of Justice, Office of Justice Programs: National Institute of Justice, US.
Coulthard, M. (2000). "Whose text is it? On the linguistic investigation of authorship". In: S. Sarangi and M. Coulthard (eds.), *Discourse and Social Life.* London: Pearson, 271-87.
Drew, P. (1990). "Strategies in the contest between lawyer and witness in cross-examination". In: J. N. Levi and A. G. Walker (eds.), *Language in the Judicial Process.* New York: Plenum Press, 39-64.
Ehrlich, S. (2001). *Representing Rape: Language and Sexual Consent.* London: Routledge.
Findlay, M. and P. Duff (1988). *The Jury Under Attack.* London: Butterworths.
Fitzmaurice, C. and K. Pease (1986). *The Psychology of Judicial Sentencing.* Manchester: Manchester University Press.
Garner, B. (ed.) (1999) *Black's Law Dictionary.* St. Paul, Minn.: West Publishing Co.
Geertz, C. (1973) *Interpretation of Cultures.* New York: Basic Books.
Hanks, P. (ed.) (2000). *The New Oxford Thesaurus of English.* Oxford: Oxford University Press.
Hart, H. L. A. (1962). *Law, Liberty and Morality.* Oxford: Oxford University Press.
Heffer, C. (2005). *The Language of Jury Trial: A Corpus-aided Analysis of Legal-Lay Discourse.* Basingstoke: Palgrave Macmillan.
Hymes, D. (1974). *Foundations in Sociolinguistics: An Ethnographic Approach.* Philadelphia: University of Pennsylvania Press.
Kassin, S. M., Meissner, C. A. and R.J. Norwick (2005) "'I'd know a false confession if I saw one': A comparative study of college students and police investigators". *Law and Human Behavior* 29, 211-27.
Keane, A. (1996). *The Modern Law of Evidence.* 4th ed. London: Butterworths.
Kirkpatrick, B. (ed.) (2000). *Roget's Thesaurus of English Words and Phrases.* London: Penguin.

Lind, E. A. and W. M. O'Barr (1979). "The social significance of speech in the courtroom". In: H. Giles and R. N. St. Clair (eds.), Oxford: Blackwell, 66-87.
Loftus, E. (1979). *Eyewitness Testimony*. London: Harvard University Press.
Martin, J. R. (2000). "Beyond exchange: Appraisal systems in English". In: S. Hunston and G. Thompson (eds.), *Evaluation in Text: Authorial Stance and the Construction of Discourse*. Oxford: Oxford University Press, 142-75.
Martin, J. R. and P. R. R. White (2005). *The Language of Evaluation*. Basingstoke and New York: Palgrave.
Matoesian, G. (1993). *Reproducing Rape: Domination through Talk in the Courtroom*. Cambridge: Polity Press.
Matoesian, G. (2001). *Law and the Language of Identity: Discourse in the William Kennedy Smith Rape Trial*. Oxford: Oxford University Press.
Milroy, L. and M. Gordon (2003). *Sociolinguistics: Method and Interpretation*. Oxford: Blackwell.
Pang, B. and L. Lee (2004). "A sentimental education: Sentiment analysis using subjectivity summarization based on minimum cuts". *Proceedings of the 42nd Annual Meeting of the Association for Computational Linguistics*. Barcelona: ACL.
Pike, K. L. (1982). *Linguistic Concepts: An Introduction to Tagmemics*. Lincoln, NE: University of Nebraska Press.
Scott, M. (1996). *WordSmith Tools*. Oxford University Press.
Spence, D. (1986). "Narrative smoothing and clinical wisdom". In: T. R. Sarbin (ed.), *Narrative Psychology: The Storied Nature of Human Conduct*. Westport, CT: Praeger, 211-32.
Tapper, C. (1999). *Cross and Tapper on Evidence*. 9th ed. London: Butterworths.
Thompson, G. and S. Hunston (2000). "Evaluation: An introduction". In: S. Hunston and G. Thompson (eds.), *Evaluation in Text: Authorial Stance and the Construction of Discourse*. Oxford: Oxford University Press, 1-27.
Wagenaar, W. A., van Koppen, P. J. and H. F. M. Crombag (1993). *Anchored Narratives: The Psychology of Criminal Evidence*. Hemel Hempstead: Harvester Wheatsheaf.
Walker, A. G. (1990). "Language at work in the law: The customs, conventions, and appellate consequences of court reporting". In" J. N. Levi and A. G. Walker (eds.), *Language in the Judicial Process*. New York: Plenum Press, 203-44.
White, P. (1998). *Telling Media Tales: The News Story as Rhetoric*. Doctoral thesis. Sydney: University of Sydney.
Whitelaw, C., Garg, N. and S. Argomon (2005). "Using appraisal groups for sentiment analysis". *Proceedings of the 14th ACM International Conference on Information and Knowledge Management*. New York: ACM Press, 625-31.
Wise, R.A. and M. A. Safer (2004). "What U.S. judges know and believe about eyewitness testimony". *Applied Cognitive Psychology* 18, 427-43.

Iwona Witczak-Plisiecka
University of Łódź
Poland

LINGUISTIC ASPECTS OF DEONTIC *SHALL* IN THE LEGAL CONTEXT

1. Introduction

The present paper addresses the problem of deonticity in the legal context with special emphasis on the function of the English modal verb *shall* found in normative texts, i.e. statutes, conventions, contracts, wills etc. It is argued that the deontic *shall*, which in the legal domain is used mainly to impose obligation or confer legal rights, can be approached as a vehicle for deontic speech acts, i.e. indirect speech acts where the verb *shall* carries the illocutionary directive force. Such acts are core examples of deontic expressions present in legal texts drafted in English, but are rare outside the legal domain, which further adds to their relative incomprehensibility and opaqueness among lay audiences. The semantic aspects of *shall* revive the question of the autonomy of language and linguistic analysis, thus introducing a wider methodological context. It further raises important questions concerning the very nature of meaning and the nature of modality in general. The aim of the present study is to present the "legal" use of *shall* and point to the linguistic theoretical problems which arise from the analysis of its distribution.

2. The autonomy of legal language.

Much of linguistic research is carried out with the background assumption that language at large constitutes a self-contained entity which can be analysed (at least to a limited degree) out of (particularised) context[1]. The notion of such (in theory) objective study and the multiple difficulties associated with the analysis conceived in this way have resulted over the years in constant movement away from what can be seen as typically semantic analysis towards more pragmatic

[1] For a contrary view see e.g. integrational linguistics (Harris 1998, Harris and Wolf 1998, Harris 1996).

approaches[2]. The field known as pragmatics, although closely related to the philosophy of language, from which it emerged, has established itself as an area of research whose aim is to incorporate contextual data and explain meaning in context. It is evident that in order to theorise about language and explain how language works one has to admit a level of generalisation even though such generalisation can never be perfect. In this perspective, the semantics of *shall* can serve as an illustration of the illusionary division between semantics and pragmatics. It is also evident that the very notion of legal language as a type of LSP conveys and is an instance of encoded pragmatic information. Thus, although legal language analysis is typically placed within the area of applied linguistic studies, it also offers interesting insights into language in theory.

It is accepted as common sense knowledge that legal language constitutes a consistent subdomain of natural language. One very prominent characteristic feature of legal language is that it is typically a language of action. Conferring rights or imposing obligations can successfully be analysed in terms of speech acts in the tradition of Austin (1962) and Searle (1969) (cf. e.g. Kurzon 1986 for application in the legal domain)[3]. Irrespective of a particular language, e.g. English, Polish, German etc., there is an implicit belief that despite the diversity of situations found in the legal context (cf. e.g. Danet 1980), there are characteristics stable enough to be recognised as determinants of legal language understood as a semantically restricted variation (cf. e.g. Kittridge and Lehrberger 1982, Sager et al. 1980, Danet 1985, Mellinkoff 1963, or Wilkoń 2002 and Żydek-Bednarczuk 2005 on Polish data). These characteristics include features such as: high level of formality, syntactic complexity (e.g. long sentences, high level of nominalisation), self-referentiality, restricted semantics ("secured" technical meanings of lexical items or phrases). With reference to the English legal language a very prominent characteristic is the use of modal verbs and expressions found within the legal domain, especially in normative texts. It has been shown in numerous both intra- and inter-linguistic studies that deontic *shall* shows very high frequency in the legal context. Biber et al. (1999, p.486) report that it is the least frequent modal verb in the LSWE corpus with its frequency being below 250 per million words (where *will* has been identified as the most frequent one with 3 500 occurrences per million). The next section summarises

---

[2] It is evident that the semantics–pragmatics distinction is only a useful generalisation which emphasizes the relevant differences in focus of linguistic research; while semantic studies concentrate on lexical, dictionary-like maximally decontextual meaning, pragmatic research favours the contextual element, aims and effects of linguistic action, typically perceived in terms of speech acts or events. However, the differences reside mainly in the bias accepted by particular researchers.

[3] For a discussion of speech acts in the legal context with relevant literature see Witczak-Plisiecka 2001.

how *shall* is accounted for vis-à-vis other modal verbs of the English language with respect to its function.

3. Modality, deonticity and modal verbs[4]

The notion of modality has been discussed from many divergent perspectives in logic, philosophy and linguistics. It constitutes a very complex field which in linguistics focuses on grammaticalised forms of speaker's attitudes to their utterance content. In the English language it can be conveyed in many different forms, typically via mood or the use of modal verbs, which show scalar meanings decipherable (or inferred) in context. A number of definitions of modality available in relevant literature concentrate on a variety of aspects. Palmer (1990) defines it as a semantic-grammatical category and suggests that "modality is concerned with the status of the proposition that describes the event" (Palmer 2001: 1) while Downing and Locke (2002: 382) propose that "modality is to be understood as a semantic category which covers such notions as possibility, probability, necessity, volition, obligation, and permission". "A Comprehensive Grammar of the English Language" edited by Quirk et al. claims that modality includes concepts such as volition, probability, and obligation (Quirk et al. 1992: 120) and "at its most general [sense, it] may be defined as the manner in which the meaning of a clause is qualified so as to reflect the speaker's judgement of the likelihood of the proposition it expresses being true" (Quirk et al. 1992: 219). In much the same manner, Huddleston et al. (2002) claim that modality is centrally concerned with the speaker's attitude towards the factuality or actualisation of the situation expressed by the rest of the clause. It is noteworthy that there are theories within which modality is solely approached through meanings ascribed to modal verbs and some of these do not recognise the deontic use of *shall* at all (e.g. Palmer 1965).

It is significant that all the above-mentioned definitions, although well-established and widely accepted, are not only very broad and vague, but also reflective of the diversity of opinions and the present understanding of the notion of modality in grammar. In short, it is accepted that modality interacts with other modules, such as e.g. tense, aspect, mood, and that it does not map systematically across languages, as cross-linguistic data show that it can be marked morphologically or by separate free-standing words. Furthermore, it has been shown that the inventory of modal meanings can be different across languages. Modality manifests itself as a complex, many-faceted phenomenon and as such it may not lend itself to a unified approach both across meanings and languages.

---

[4] This section includes selected data discussed in Witczak-Plisiecka (in press a).

As Palmer concluded in 1986, "modality … does not relate semantically to the verb alone or primarily, but to the whole sentence" (Palmer 1986/2001: 2)[5].

There are two main perspectives on the meaning of modal auxiliaries in linguistics. Within one, modal verbs are each ascribed a number of distinct semantic meanings which may produce ambiguity due to the multiple reference involved. In the other, it is claimed that instead of being polysemous, a modal verb as a lexeme may be vague. Common criteria for description of modal verbs include e.g.: a) indeterminacy (Huddleston et al. 2002); b) subjectivity (Palmer 2001, Quirk et al. 1992); and c) strength, kind, and degree (Huddleston et al. 2002).

From the logical point of view (e.g. Rescher 1968), the most often quoted categories of modality include: *alethic*, the basic category based on the distinction between truth and falsity, as well as *deontic*, which relates to duties; *epistemic*, which relates to belief and knowledge; *temporal*, which relates to time, *boulomaic,* which relates to desire; *evaluative*, which relates to opinion; *causal*, which relates to the cause-and-effect situation. Many researchers recognise just two categories: *epistemic* and *deontic*, and claim that each modal verb can have two types of meaning: intrinsic and extrinsic, which also correspond to the notion of deonticity and epistemic modality respectively (e.g. Biber et al. 1999). In order to illustrate the diversity of linguistic approaches to *shall* and the closely related *will* an overview of selected classifications with reference to modality has been provided below.

Reflecting back in the history of linguistic thought, a relative difficulty in classifying English modal uses and English modal verbs can already be seen in Jespersen's (1963) atomised account of modality[6]. Jespersen (1963: 320) by his own admission accepted his list "as a tentative scheme of the purely notional ideas expressed more or less vaguely by the verbal moods and auxiliaries of various languages" and acknowledged that categories frequently overlap, and some of the terms are not quite unobjectionable. The notional moods identified by him, evidently in search of all-inclusiveness, are as follows (Jespersen [1924] 1963: 320-321):

Table 1. Notional moods according to Jespersen (1963) [7]

1. Containing an element of will:	**2. Containing no element of will:**
Jussive: go (command)	Apodictive: twice two must be (is
? Compulsive: he has to go	necessarily) four.
Obligative: he ought to go/we should go.	Necessitative: he must be rich (or he

[5] Among other researchers Quirk et al. (1992: 219) also emphasize "an imperfect match" between types of modality and modal verbs.

[6] For critical evaluation of Jespersen's typology see e.g. Lyons 1977 and Palmer 1986.

[7] Emphasis and question marks are mine.

? Advisory: you should go.	could not spend so much).
? Precative: go, please.	Assertive: he is rich.
? Hortative: let us go.	Presumptive: he is probably rich; he would (will) know.
Permissive: you may go if you like.	Dubitative: he may be (is perhaps) rich.
Promissive: I will go/it shall be done.	Potential: he can speak.
Optative (realizable): may he be still alive!	Conditional: if he is rich.
Desirative (unrealizable): would he were still alive!	Hypothetical: if he were rich.
Intentional: in order that he may go.	Concessional: though he is rich.

The categories which are clearly deontic have been underlined, those on the verge of deonticity are indicated by a question mark.

Quirk et al. (1992) suggest another classification and claim that each of the major modals have both an intrinsic ("human control involved") and extrinsic ("human control not involved") meanings, which in reality represent a continuum, cf. Table 2 below.

Table 2: Meanings of the Modals adapted from Quirk et al. (1992: 221)

MEANINGS OF THE MODALS	
Modal verbs	***The intrinsic to extrinsic continuum***
Can / could ↔ may / might	*permission ↔ possibility/ability*
Must, have (got) to, need (non-assertive) ↔ should, ought to	*obligation ↔ necessity*
will / would ↔ shall <rare and restricted>	*volition ↔ prediction (future)*

It is noteworthy in the context that the table presents both *shall* and *will* as typically non-deontic although Quirk does mention the deontic use of *shall*, but only in the footnote and defines it as a very restricted use which always coincides with a third-person subject in legal or quasi-legal discourse. It is also suggested that such a *shall* is close in meaning to *must* (Quirk 1992: 230).

Huddleston (1984 and 2002) identifies two major modal categories: epistemic and deontic. In his opinion, modality can be further analysed in that the statement in a sentence with epistemic modality is a true or false proposition, while a statement in a sentence with deontic modality represents an action. Consequently, the time of the statement in a sentence with epistemic modality is generally present or past, while deontic modality is generally found in future sentences. Other characteristics include the fact that the epistemic and deontic modalities interact differently with negation and tense, and that both epistemic and deontic modalities can express possibility and necessity, as shown in the table below. In Huddleston's approach deontic uses are considered as more basic, with the epistemic ones arising by extension (see Table 3 below).

Table 3. Classification of MOD according to Huddleston et al. (2002: 166) (an extract, emphasis added)

	Possibility	Necessity
Epistemic	i. *He may have been delayed.*	iii. *He must have been delayed.*
Deontic	ii. *You may stay if you wish.*	iv. *You must pull your socks up.*
Ambiguous	v. *He may sleep downstairs.*	vi. *You must be very tactful.*

Like Quirk et al. (1992), Huddleston et al. (2002: 194) provide a note on three deontic uses of *shall*, which is dubbed as "peripheral and rare". These are: 1) constitutive/regulative uses (e.g. *The committee shall meet...*); 2) speaker's linguistically expressed guarantee (e.g. *You shall have your money back tomorrow*); and 3) direction-seeking uses (e.g. *Shall I close the window?*).

Another, less known, classification has been suggested by Werner (2003) on the basis of his research into modality and temporality in the English language (cf. Table 4 below).

Table 4: A comparison of modals according to Werner (2003: 128) (emphasis added)

		1	2	3	4
Modal base		Epistemic	Totally realistic up to time		
Ordering source		Stereotypical	Stereotypical	**Deontic**	Potential
	Existential	MAY/MIGHT/CAN	MAY/MIGHT	**MAY**	CAN
	Universal	WILL/MUST	WILL	**MUST**	MUST

Werner entirely excludes *shall* and *will* from deontic modals. In fact, he does not mention the possibility of a deontic use of either *shall* or *will* all throughout his dissertation.

One more example of a typology of modalities in English comes from Paul Larreya (2004) and is reproduced in Figure 1 below.

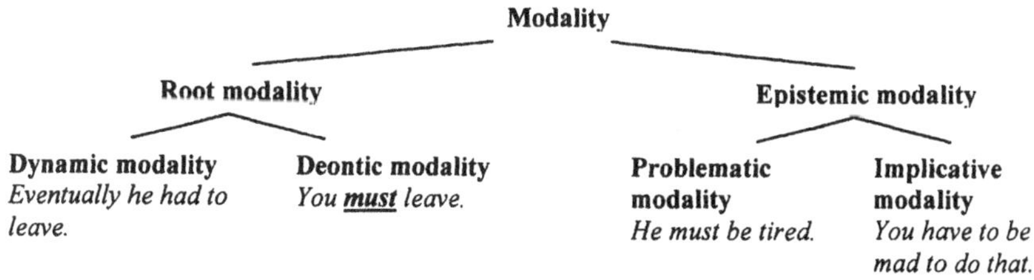

Figure 1. Types of modality (Larreya 2004)

In his thesis Larreya (2004) proposes a primary distinction between *a priori* as opposed to *a posteriori* modalities. It seems that, influenced by Sweetser (1990), Larreya first suggests the division into root and epistemic modality. He further identifies deontic modality as a kind of root modality associated with moral potentiality, where the dynamic/deontic distinction parallels the allegedly natural distinction between the domain of "affect and/or action" and the domain of "knowledge". The only example of deontic use provided by the author in this context is that of *must.*

All the above-mentioned examples of typologies, whether concentrating on abstract modal categories or modal verbs of the English language, serve to show that deontic *shall* receives very little attention in overall studies of the English grammar. Their uses are seen as peripheral, almost non-existent, or explicitly not worth attention. This treatment is in conflict with the legal understanding of the verb *shall* (as well as *will*) as within the semantically restricted domain of legal language, as shown in further sections of the paper, their deontic distribution constitutes the most frequent use.

4. Modality, deonticity and tense

The relationship between modality and tense is also a complex one. For example, it is often indicated that there is no separate tense to express the imperative, which can be recognised as a very basic type of modality. What is especially interesting with respect to *shall* (but also *will*) in the legal context is its relation to the notions of futurity and deonticity as apparently language users lack means to delineate the two senses in a systematic way. It is often emphasized, e.g. in descriptive grammars of the English language, that the verbs are markers of modality rather than tense due to the fact that they belong to a clearly defined system of modal verbs. Palmer (1986) claims that "SHALL and WILL (and especially WILL, which is widely used where normative grammars recommend SHALL) seldom refer simply to future tense" (Palmer 1986: 216). It is noteworthy in the context that deonticity itself has been presented as convergent with the use of the future tense (or rather future reference), cf. Huddleston as discussed in the previous section.

In summary, there are three main solutions to the problem of the tense/modality relation:

a) all tense is modality;
b) future tense and modality are distinct (where e.g. *will* and *shall* form periphrastic future tense parallel to morphological future expressions present in other languages);
c) there is ambiguity between modality and tense.

There is amply discussed evidence and a number of assumptions concerning all these proposals. For many researchers futurity of *will* is a consequence of its interpretation as a modal of prediction and hence adopting such an approach *will* can unambiguously be taken to be a modal (cf. Enç 1996, Palmer 1990 and 2001, Huddleston et al. 2002). Biber et al. (1999: 495) note that *shall* "'is noteworthy' in that it marks volition more often than prediction, although it is generally rare in both functions" and almost non-existent in American English. Considering cross-linguistic data (evidence from both Indo-European and non-Indo-European languages) the notion of future tense is often presented as a second class function, derived from or being on the surface of more rudimentary ones (Comrie 1985, Fleischman 1982). This holds true irrespective of the form in which modality is expressed, i.e. whether it is expressed in a periphrastic way or via morphological markers. This fact supports the view that futurity is a result of the ongoing process of grammaticalisation, where lexical meaning of a particular form is gradually weakened and eventually replaced or accompanied by a new conventional meaning (cf. Lehmann 2002 and 1995). Etymologically, both *shall* and *will* first involved the notion of willingness and duty and thus their semantic aspect of "futurity" is seen as idiomaticized and relatively new a reading. It has already been noted above that since the future is necessarily less certain, future time reference is very different from present and past reference, as a result inevitably modal (Lyons 1977, Palmer 1990 and 2001). Jaszczołt (2003 and 2004), while working to further develop Discourse Representation Theory, proposes one level of semantic representation for a modal verb, the interpretation being a matter of the degree of intentionality on the part of the speaker. With reference to *will*, she suggests that modality subsumes all its other senses. Her idea seems to be another voice in favour of preserving the ambiguity (or rather inherent vagueness, as there is no clear ambiguity of reference either) of the meaning of *shall*. Clearly, in many cases it is not possible to decide whether the use is future or directive, due to pragmatic factors which cannot be recovered out of context and on many occasions are not readily accessible even in (relatively defined) contexts. The emerging continuum reading seems to confirm Werner's (2003) point in his suggestion that there are entailment relations between *must-will-should-can* modalities respectively, which may appear another methodological solution to the problem given the future-oriented interpretation of these modals[8]. Still, this approach, while introducing some clarity, does not offer the means to distinguish between the two uses either.

It is evident that modality cannot be formalised in a theoretically sound way without either a fine degree of generality or violation of its complexity. On a semantic level the most frequent senses of a modal verb may be enumerated and explained in a dictionary-like manner; however, on a pragmatic level the recognition of these senses is by no means simple and shows the limitations of formal theories which do not allow fuzzy edges and vague categories. The next section presents data gathered within the legal domain.

4. Distribution of *shall* in legal English texts

Distribution of *shall* in English legal language has been researched both on the basis of contemporary and historical texts. Gotti (2001), having analysed the uses of *shall* and *will* in Middle English and Early Modern English statutes included in the Helsinki corpus, indicates that the deontic aspect is the most frequent use of the legal *shall* of those times; it constitutes 130 out of 246 uses (Gotti 2001: 101). However, it should also be noted that it is not significantly high vis-à-vis the dynamic modal use of *shall* (130 vis-à-vis 116 uses). In conclusion, the author emphasises the fact that although *shall*-forms are widespread and as such their presence is an important characteristic of legal texts analysed in the study, the modal is not very frequent in general and comprises three main semantic meanings, primarily that of obligation, but also ones related to permission and prediction.

Evidence from contemporary legal language shows that there are relatively few examples of *shall* used as a marker of futurity within the field. Example (1) in Table 5 below includes one instance of *shall* with future reading (cited in bold), while examples (2) to (8) are problematic, starting from (2), which is apparently a constitutive rule in that it offers description of a desired situation.

[8] However, Werner's point can only be defended if we accept that his *must-will-should-can* entailment chain in fact represents the most typical, core meanings of the four modals cited.

Table 5: Extracts from legal texts including modal verbs[9]

1)	The Tenant will- (a) Pay the Rent at the times and in the manner specified (b) Pay for all gas and electric light and power which **shall** be consumed or supplied on or to the Property during the tenancy ...
2)	the marriage of any such person solemnized before the expiration of six months from the date of the granting of judgement of divorce **shall** be void
3)	I appoint (...) to be my Executor and direct that all my debts **shall** be paid as soon as convenient after my death
4)	The annual fee **shall** be paid at the time of ...
5)	If the child support payment is a fixed sum, it **shall** be adjusted annually ...
6)	This Agreement **shall** take effect subject to the provisions of section 11 of the Landlord and Tenant Act
7)	The returning officer **shall** send the documents containing the oaths of the returning officer and assistant returning officer without delay to the Chief Electoral Officer.
8)	There **shall** be a Chief Electoral Officer who **shall** be appointed by resolution of the House of Commons to hold office during good behaviour. He or she may be removed for cause by the Governor General on address of the Senate and House of Commons.
9)	The fee shall be doubled each succeeding year in which the annual fee remains unpaid, but the total annual fee **shall not** exceed ...
10)	The directors, administrators and employees of bodies involved in an adoption **shall not** receive remuneration which is unreasonably high in relation to services rendered.
11)	No person **shall** act as an election officer knowing that they do not meet the requirements for an election officer set out in this section.

Although most of the examples above appear to be a mixture of futurity and deonticity, as they describe a desired state of affairs and demand that it come true in the future, legal professionals are reluctant to accept any level of indeterminacy. Deontic *shall* is recognised as standard and recommended for use, as can be seen in the quotation below cited from a handbook by Robinson (1973: 39), teaching law students how legal documents should be drafted:

> the use of '*shall*' indicates that the legal subject is under obligation to act in accordance with the terms of the provision (...) it does not indicate something in relation to the future.

[9] The data included in the table come from the author's corpus of legal texts.

Such uses of *shall* are sometimes regarded as restricted and perceived as typically British. Both in European contexts and in the United States they have met with strong criticism along with suggestions that they be replaced with *must* in order to avoid possible ambiguity between future and deontic readings especially among lay audiences, addressees of legal documents not trained in the law. Generally, within what is now recognised as the Plain Language Movement, the use of *shall* has been deemed obsolete, "dead", undesirable, and adding to incomprehensibility of legal texts[10]. The importance and relative difficulty in understanding the function of modal auxiliaries used in legal documents may be further illustrated by the fact that there have been instances when the courts decided to interpret modal auxiliaries separately or seek advice from an expert linguist to decide on the type of modality they introduced (cf. Klinge 1992: 52), even though it is apparent that the level of subjectivity while using modal expressions in legal texts is much lower than in everyday situations. However, the *must*-for-*shall* replacement, even if it was to be accepted, does not offer a satisfactory solution either, as there are problematic examples, especially with regard to negative expressions. Although *shall not* can be successfully replaced with *must not* in uses such as 9) in Table 5 above, it is questionable if the replacement could be applied in 10) to 12), especially in 11) and 12) where *shall* collocates with the negative *No person* and *no one*.

In summary, it seems especially relevant to acknowledge the omnipresence of deontic *shall* in English legal language. Its distribution is further illustrated in the concordances from a legal corpus, presented in the Appendix. It is clearly visible that nearly all of the instances of *shall* quoted are deontic in nature. Although reliable conclusions would require further research, both quantitative and qualitative, even on the basis of this preliminary study and in the light of other research findings it can be concluded that *shall* in legal language is by no means "rare and peripheral" but constitutes a core modal. It is clearly a characteristic feature of legal normative discourse.

Further evidence that the reading of *shall* and, as a result, understanding of the modal system of English is characterised by inherent vagueness, but focuses on the deontic value, comes from legal translation and cross-linguistic studies. For example, the deontic force in Polish is typically conveyed via present tense expressions; cf. examples in Table 6 below:

---

[10] Cf. Richard Lauchman's (2005: 47) explicit demand verbalized in a section title: "Eliminate "shall" from your writing" and his advice to drafters: "Shun the ambiguous *shall*. The word is used vaguely in five distinct ways, and it requires interpretation. (…) It is a "dead" word never heard in everyday conversation. (…) [Y]our reader encounters it only in contracts, rules, regulations, and so on. (…) *Shall* has been interpreted in various ways by various judges; some say it means "must," but others insist it's just a recommendation, and means "should." Never *suggest* legal obligation. *State* it." Other voices of criticism on the legal *shall* include Mowat (1999), Asprey (2003) and Trosborg (1991).

Table 6. Deontic *shall* and its Polish counterparts in the legal context

Rokiem obrotowym spółki **jest** [is] rok kalendarzowy	The calendar year **shall be** the financial year of the company
Otwarcie likwidacji **powoduje** [results in] wygaśnięcie prokury	The opening of liquidation **shall result** in the expiry of the power of the commercial power of attorney
W sprawach określonych (...) **stosuje się** [are applied] przepisy Kodeksu Cywilnego	The matters defined (...) **shall be governed** by the provisions of the Civil Code

This use is parallel to modern drafting practice in English, as well as intralingual recommendations within the above-mentioned Plain Language Movement, where it is often suggested that the mandatory *shall* could, and often should, be replaced with the use of the present tense. Thus, the typically British deontic *shall*, or rather its English English use, finds present tense counterparts in other legal cultures – cf. Williams's (2005: 89) example of parallel expressions in Table 7 below[11]:

Table 7. Deontic *shall* vis-a-vis the indicative present tense in the legal context

The national flag of the Republic *is* black, gold, green, white, red and blue, as described in Schedule 1. (Section 5 of the South African Constitution 1997)	The national flag of the Republic *shall be* the flag the design of which is determined by the President by Proclamation in the Gazette (Section 2(1) of the Interim South African Constitution 1994)

The examples quoted above show that legal sentences are characterised by continuing effects, i.e. they project into the future. As such, as has been mentioned in the section on modality and tense, deonticity can be conveyed via the modal verb, most typically *shall*, but also others, or can be introduced via the indicative present tense, which extends into the future by describing a required state of affairs.

[11] On the basis of the "World-Data" corpus of thirty six English-language legal documents culled from various countries, Williams (2005) presents statistical data concerning the distribution of *shall* across legal cultures. He also provides statistics on "*shall*-free data" and although the analysis is based on rather limited materials, the discussion is well worth reading and supportive of the view that the deontic function can be rendered in various ways in the legal context.

5. Conclusions

It is apparent that the boundary between deontic modality and futurity in English legal language is fuzzy or may even be non-existent. The general feeling about modality in the legal context is consistent with that expressed by Enç (1996) with reference to language at large, i.e. that such modality "dictates" that what is demanded is that some situation hold in the future. However, although future tense sentences seem to share more properties with modal statements than with other tenses (as acknowledged in Enç (1996)), equating futurity with modality hurts language users' intuitions about meaning and can be viewed as harmful oversimplification. Thus, modal verbs seem to be best discussed in terms of prototypes, radial categories or scalar domains which are inevitably characterised by a degree of vagueness. Relevant methodological tools for the analysis of the legal *shall* and its semantic properties can only be found in pragmatic, or most probably pragmatic-cognitive theories of meaning. Drawing on pragmatic models which define speech acts as "primary units of meaning" (e.g. Searle and Vanderveken 1985, Vanderveken 1990 and 1991, Barker 2004), deontic *shall*, an auxiliary of command, can be viewed as a vehicle for a deontic speech act. Within explicitly cognitive approaches, the future interpretation of deontic *shall* may be explained via e.g. the process of subjectification (Langacker 1990 and 1999) or invited inference (cf. Traugott et al. 2002). In construction grammar, a quasi-cognitive approach where meaning is the result of integrating the meanings of lexical items into the meaning of constructions, the legal structure with the use of *shall* must be recognised as a grammatical unit being a conventional association of syntactic, semantic, pragmatic and phonological information (cf. Goldberg 1995 and 2003, Kay 2002, Croft and Cruse 2003). It can also be claimed that deontic *shall* forms a cognitive blend in the understanding of Fauconnier and Turner (Fauconnier 1985, Fauconnier and Turner 1996), where the notions of futurity and deonticity have been amalgamated and eventually constitute one entity (cf. Witczak-Plisiecka in press (b)). It must be accepted, however, that in all these approaches the meaning of *shall* remains inherently vague.

In search of solutions to the semantics of modality on supra-lexical level, it has also been suggested that speech-act modality should be recognised as a separate grammar category. Sweetser (1990) claimed that speech act-modality should be included in the grammar system next to root and epistemic modality types, which together offer a better description of the notion. This option further emphasizes the salience of function, and its dominance over form. As other cognitive and semi-cognitive approaches it offers a limited level of formality at the expense of being non-contradictory and unified an account.

In summary, it is certain that evidence from applied and theoretical research and a comparative study of classifications of modality and modal verbs together with the distribution of the deontic *shall*, all prove the uniqueness of English legal language and strengthen the premise that it constitutes a consistent, highly specialised and idiomaticised sub-domain of general English. The semantics of *shall* also makes it evident that language is inherently dynamic and not readily formalisable; that the deontic function (and function in general) can be associated with various linguistic forms and the relationship between form and meaning can only be discussed in terms of expectations. The deonticity of the modal verb *shall* can only be recovered in the context from which it derives its pragmatic force.

References:

Asprey, M. M. (2003). *Plain Language for Lawyers.* Sydney: The Federation Press.

Austin, J. L. (1962). *How to Do Things with Words*. Oxford: Clarendon Press.

Barker, S. J. (2004) *Renewing Meaning. A Speech-Act Theoretic Approach.* Oxford: Clarendon Press.

Biber, D., Johansson, S., Leech, G., Conrad, S. and E. Finegan (1999). *Longman Grammar of Spoken and Written English.* Harlow: Longman.

Comrie, B. (1985). *Tense*. Cambridge: Cambridge University Press.

Croft, W. and A. D. Cruse (2003). *Cognitive Linguistics*. Cambridge: Cambridge University Press

Danet, B. (1980). "Language in the Legal Process". *Law and Society Review* 14(3), 445-564.

Danet, B. (1985) "Legal Discourse". In: T. van Dijk (ed.), *Handbook of Discourse Analysis*. New York: Academic Press, 273-91.

Downing, A. and P. Locke (2002). *A University Course in English Grammar*. London and New York: Routledge.

Enç, M. (1996). "Tense and Modality". In: S. Lappin (ed.), *The Handbook of Contemporary Semantic Theory*. Oxford: Blackwell, 345-358.

Fleischman, S. (1982). *The future in thought and language. Diachronic evidence from Romance*. Cambridge: Cambridge University Press.

Fauconnier, G. (1985) *Mental Spaces: Aspects of Meaning Construction in Natural Language*. Cambridge, Mass.: The MIT Press.

Fauconnier, G. and M. Turner (1996). "Blending as a Central Process of Grammar". In: A. Goldberg (ed.), *Conceptual Structure, Discourse and Language*. Stanford: CSLI, 113-130.

Goldberg, A. E. (2003). "Constructions: a new theoretical approach to language". *Trends in Cognitive Sciences* 7 (5), 219-224.

Goldberg, A. E. (1995). *Constructions: A Construction Grammar Approach to Argument Structure*. Chicago and London: Chicago University Press.

Gotti, M. (2001). "Semantic and Pragmatic Values of *Shall* and *Will* in Early Modern English Statutes". In: M. Gotti and M. Dossena (eds.), 89-111.

Gotti, M. and Marina Dossena (eds.) (2001). *Modality in Specialised Texts: selected papers of the 1st CERLIS Conference*. Bern: Peter Lang.

Harris, R. (1996). *The Language Connection. Philosophy and Linguistics.* Bristol: Thoemmes Press.

Harris, R. (1998). *Introduction to Integrational Linguistics*. Oxford: Pergamon.

Harris, R. and G. Wolf (eds.) (1998). *Integrational Linguistics: A First Reader.* Oxford: Pergamon.

Huddleston, R. (1984) *Introduction to the grammar of English.* Cambridge: Cambridge Textbooks in Linguistics: CUP.

Huddleston, R. and G. K. Pullum (2002) *The Cambridge Grammar of the English Language*. Cambridge: Cambridge University Press.

Jaszczołt, K. (2004). "Futurity in Default Semantics", http://www.cus.cam.ac.uk/~kmj21/Futurity.rev.CRiSPI.Aug04.pdf (accessed April 2005)

Jaszczołt, K. (2003). "The modality of the future". In: P. Dekker and R. van Rooy (eds.), *Proceedings of the 14th Amsterdam Colloquium*, ILLC, University of Amsterdam, 43-48.

Jespersen, O. (1963 [1924]). *The Philosophy of Grammar.* London: George Allen and Unwin Ltd.

Kay, P. (2002). "An Informal Sketch of a Formal Architecture for Construction Grammar". *Grammars* 5, 1-19.

Kittridge, R. and J. Lehrberger (eds.) (1982). *Sublanguage. Studies of Language in Restricted Semantic Domains*. Berlin and New York: Walter de Gruyter.

Klinge, A. (1992). *Legal Discourse and Modality.* Copenhagen: Copenhagen Business School.

Kurzon, D. (1986). *It is Hereby Performed ... Explorations in legal speech acts.* Amsterdam and Philadelphia: John Benjamins.

Langacker, R. W. (1999). "Losing control: Grammaticization, subjectification, and transparency". In: A. Blank and P. Koch (eds.), *Historical Semantics and Cognition*. Berlin and New York: Mouton de Gruyter, 147-175.

Langacker, R. W. (1990). "Subjectification". *Cognitive Linguistics* 1, 5-38.

Lauchman, R. (2001-2005). *Plain Language. A handbook for writers in the U.S. Government.* http://www.lauchmangroup.com/PDFfiles/PLHandbook.PDF (accessed May 2005).

Larreya P. (2004). "Types of modality and types of modalisation". Paper presented at the Second International Conference on Modality in English. Pau, 2-4 September 2004. http://www.univ-pau.fr/ANGLAIS/ modality/posters/larreya.pdf. (accessed March 2005)

Lehmann, C. (1995). *Thoughts on Grammaticalization.* München and Newcastle: Lincom Europa.

Lehmann, C. (2002). "New reflections on grammaticalization and lexicalization".

In: I. Wischer and G. Diewald (eds.), *New Reflections on Grammaticalization*. Amsterdam and Philadelphia: John Benjamins, 1-18.

Lyons, J. (1977). *Semantics* ,vol. 1 and 2. Cambridge: Cambridge University Press.

Mellinkoff, D. (1963). *The Language of the Law*. Boston: Little, Brown and Company.

Mowat, C. (1999). *A Plain Language Handbook for Legal Writers*. Scarborough, ON: Carssell.

Palmer, F. R. (1965). *A Linguistic Study of the English Verb*. London: Longmans.

Palmer, F. R. (1990). *Modality and the English Modals* (2nd ed.). London and New York: Longman.

Palmer, F. R. (1986/2001). *Mood and Modality*. Cambridge: CUP.

Quirk, R., Greenbaum, S., Leech, G. and J. Svartvik (1992). *A Comprehensive Grammar of the English Language*. London and New York: Longman.

Rescher, N. (1968). *Topics in Philosophical Logic*. Dordrecht: Reibel.

Robinson, S. (1973). *Drafting: Its application to conveyancing and commercial documents*. London: Butterworths.

Sager, J.C., Dungworth, D. and P. F. McDonald (1980). *English Special Languages*. Wiesbaden: Oscar Brandstetter Verlag.

Searle, J. R. (1969). *Speech Acts. An Essay in the Philosophy of Language*. Cambridge: Cambridge University Press.

Searle J. R. and D. Vanderveken (1985). *Foundations of Illocutionary Logic*. Cambridge: Cambridge University Press.

Sweetser, E. (1990). *From Etymology to Pragmatics. Metaphorical and cultural aspects of semantic structure*. Cambridge and New York: Cambridge University Press.

Traugott, E. C. and R. B. Dasher (2002). *Regularity in Semantic Change*. Cambridge and New York: Cambridge University Press.

Trosborg, A. (1991). "An Analysis of Legal Speech Acts in English Contract Law". *Hermes Journal of Linguistics* 6, 65-90.

Vanderveken D. (1990). *Meaning and Speech Acts. Volume I: Principles of language use*. Cambridge: Cambridge University Press.

Vanderveken D. (1991). *Meaning and Speech Acts. Volume II: Formal semantics of success and satisfaction*. Cambridge: Cambridge University Press.

Werner, T. A., (2003). *Deducing the Future and Distinguishing the Past: Temporal Interpretation in Modal Sentences in English*. Doctoral thesis. New Brunswick: The State University of New Jersey. http://ling.rutgers.edu/papers/WernerThesis.pdf. (accessed July 2007)

Williams, C. (2005). *Tradition and Change In Legal English. Verbal Constructions in Prescriptive Texts*. Bern: Peter Lang.

Wilkoń, A. (2002). *Spójność i struktura tekstu*. Kraków: Universitas.

Witczak-Plisiecka, I. (2001). *Semantic and Pragmatic Aspects of English Legal Texts*. Doctoral thesis. Łódź: University of Łódź.

Witczak-Plisiecka, I. (in press a). "Deontic '*shall*' and futurity in English legal texts". In: P. Stalmaszczyk (ed.), *PASE Studies in Linguistics*. Łódź: WUŁ.

Witczak-Plisiecka, I. (in press b). "Teoria aktów mowy w aspekcie kognitywnym na przykładzie deontycznego użycia angielskiego czasownika *shall* w kontekście prawa". In: G. Habrajska (ed.), *Pragmatyczne aspekty kognitywizmu*. Łódź: WUŁ.

Żydek-Bednarczuk, U. (2005). *Wprowadzenie do lingwistycznej analizy tekstu*. Kraków: Universitas.

Appendix[12]

Concordances with *shall* in the legal context.

N	Concordance	Set
2681	, the original document	**shall** be deemed not to
2682	rs occurs, the company	**shall** send to the registra
2683	tances, section 13(9)	**shall** have effect as if th
2684	the original document	**shall** be deemed not to
2685	-three of this Act" there	**shall** be substituted "sent
2686	ee. 10. Dáil Éireann	**shall** be summoned and
2687	times and places as he	**shall** determine. Article
2688	at case, subsection (5)	**shall** have effect as if fo
2689	as "a shadow director")	**shall** be treated for the
2690	h paragraph (a) relates	**shall** not be deemed rea
2691	section 21(3)(a) above	**shall** ensure that records
2692	ubsection (5), a person	**shall** not act as auditor
2693	om this section applies	**shall** also be qualified fo
2694	ceive and the company	**shall** permit him to be h
2695	comply with this section	**shall** be liable to a fine
2696	the arrangement relates	**shall**, if it was entered I
2697	muneration. 19.—(1) It	**shall** be a term of the c
2698	(5) to (7) of section 78	**shall** apply as they apply
2699	ich this section applies	**shall** not be passed at a
2700	ng to be heard, and (c)	**shall** issue a decision in
2701	d to in subsection (1), it	**shall** be the duty of the
2702	(2) to (7) of section 213	**shall** apply to such contr
2703	isqualification order, he	**shall** be deemed to be s
2704	to be such a certificate	**shall** be received in evid
2705	conclusion, information	**shall** be neither sought n

Concordances with *shall not* in the legal context.

N	Concordance	Set
1	) above, the Post Office	**shall not** approve an ele
2	n (1). (3) The Bank	**shall not** authorise an inv
3	ion (1). (4) A court	**shall not** deal with an of
4	The same Dáil Éireann	**shall not** continue for a l
5	07. (3) A company	**shall not** purchase any o
6	an 240. (4) A court	**shall not** make a commu
7	an investment company	**shall not** constitute a war
8	6 of this Constitution, it	**shall not** be obligatory o
9	276 of the Principal Act	**shall not** be exercised, e
10	gender equality clause	**shall not** operate in relati
11	32 to 3737, a company	**shall not**— (a) make
12	39, sections 32 and 37	**shall not** apply to any c

[12] The data come from the author's corpus of English-language legal documents.

13	ubsections (1) and (3)	**shall not** affect the rights
14	60 of the Principal Act	**shall not** apply to any
15	(7) and (8), a company	**shall not** enter into an a
16	. (4) Subsection (2)	**shall not** apply in relation
17	50. (5) This section	**shall not** apply to a wind
18	inatory equality clause	**shall not** operate in relati
19	rson under this section	**shall not**, in itself, be pr
20	contract of employment	**shall not** override any su
21	se of vocational training	**shall not**, in respect of
22	n under subsection (4)	**shall not** affect the conti
23	rovider of agency work	**shall not** discriminate ag
24	sentence or other order	**shall not** be varied or re

Ioana Costache
University of Bucharest and Oxford University
Romania and England

NINETEENTH-CENTURY ROMANIAN CONTRACTS FOR WORKS: A CASE STUDY

1. Introduction

The aim of the present paper is to provide an analysis of a particular text-type by comparing two groups of Romanian legal texts, a contemporary one and one from the early 19th century, in order to trace the diachronic development of specific structural and pragmatic features. The first part of the paper is a description of the two groups, and the second is a discussion of the main structural differences and of aspects such as shared characteristics, text-internal versus extralinguistic points of reference and the achievement of textual coherence (in the classic framework of Halliday and Hasan 1976, with subsequent amendments by Vestergaard and Schrøder 1985).

The corpus consists of two sets of contracts. The emergent structure of each set will be presented in turn, each clause being illustrated with a number of relevant examples given in Romanian (diacritics omitted for convenience) and in English translation. The first set is made up of five contracts for works concluded in 1819 by Costandie, bishop of Buzau, with various contractors employed for the construction of a new church. There are four main contractors (Iosef Weltz, the builder; Hristea, who is to provide and carry the sand; Anastase the carpenter, and three painters) and six distinct contracts (two with the builder, one with the sand provider, the carpenter and the painters, respectively, and an anonymous, unsigned contract for the carving of windows). The second group of texts is made up of two templates[1] for contracts for civil engineering construction, provided by two Romanian government bodies (the National Housing Agency and the Ministry for Small and Medium Enterprises and Cooperation).

2. Nineteenth-century contracts for works: macrostructure

The six contracts differ in length and detail; however, a shared macrostructure emerges, as presented below.

[1] Available online at www.anl.ro/ro/model-contract2.pdf and www.mimmc.ro/consultanta/art_991.

a) An introductory formula whereby the contractor acknowledges that he is giving the contract to the beneficiary (speaking both in his name and on behalf of his employees and subcontractors, as will be shown later):

1) Incredintez cu acest zapis al mieu la prea cinstita mina prea sfintii sale parintelui episcopul (Potra 1961: 725)
I entrust this contract to his grace the bishop

2) Incredintez cu acest adevarat zapis al mieu la prea cinstita mina prea sfintii parintelui episcopul Buzau, chir Costandie (Potra 1961: 729)
I entrust this true contract of mine to his grace the bishop of Buzau, father Costandie

3) Adica noi zugrafi care mai jos ne vom iscali, incredintam cu zapisul nostru la blagoslovitoarea dreapta prea sfintii sale parintelui mitropolitul (Potra 1961: 737).
We the undersigned painters entrust our contract to the Metropolitan (sic!)

b) A statement of publicity, similar in format to the "let it be known that..." formula found in powers of attorney:

4) precum sa sa stie ca... (Potra 1961: 725, 729, 731, 734, 737)
for it to be known that...

c) The object of the contract, presented first in a general, synthetic clause introduced by the complementizer "ca" (*that*) in example (4) above, then described in detail.
General description:

5) [ca] m-am tocmit la prea sfintia sa ca să lucrez unsprezece ferestre de pietrarie la biserica cea noua a prea sfintii sale (Potra 1961: 725)
[that] I was hired by his grace to do the stonework for the windows of his grace's new church

6) [ca] pentru zidirea bisericii noaă a Sfintului Dimitrie, am luat tot lucrul si mestesugul zidarii asupra mea din temelie si pana se va ispravi biserica de tot, cu toti mesterii zidari si salahorii miei (Potra 1961: 729)
[that] for the building of the new church dedicated to Saint Demetrios I undertook to do all the building work, together with all my master masons and my workers

7) [ca] m-am tocmit la prea sfintiia sa ca sa car nasip, cu carale mele si nasipul mieu, in curtea prea sfintii sale (Potra 1961: 731)
[that] I was hired by his grace to carry sand with my own carts and deliver it to his yard

8) [ca] m-am tocmit la prea sfintiia ca sa fac trei cruci mari de fier pentru ca sa sa pue deasupra bisericii cei noaă (Potra 1961: 734)
[that] I was hired by his grace to make three big iron crosses to be placed on top of the new church

The detailed description varies from one contract to another, according to the complexity of the works involved; the shortest description is actually a reiteration of the object of the contract, with the additional specification of a unit of measure:

9) voiu cara nasip cu carale mele in curtea prea sfintii sale din destul (Potra 1961: 731)
I will carry enough sand with my carts to his grace's yard to make sure it suffices

where the quantity is to be measured by the bucket provided by the chief architect.[2] The more detailed descriptions (of building and carpentry works) exhibit a marked tendency towards exhaustiveness, which manifests itself in two ways: a lengthy enumeration of the structural elements to be built / goods to be provided, and an all-inclusive, general clause stating that the contractor will provide anything else that may be required, without asking for extra payment:

10) Si in scurt orice trebuinta va avea biserica pina in sfirsit de mestesugul zidarii, sa fiu dator a-l face eu cu mesterii si salahorii miei (Potra 1961: 730)
Briefly, I take it upon myself to carry out, together with my master masons and workers, any work of masonry that the church may need until it's completed

11) Cu un cuvint orice lucru va trebui bisericii, in launtru, pa dinafara, sus si jos, de mestesugul dulgherii si al timplarii, [...] sa fiu dator neaparat a le face in plata banilor ce mai sus zic, fara a mai face prea sf. sale cerere macar de un ban peste tocmeala care de buna voia mea am facut (Potra 1961: 733)
In one word, no matter what carpentry or joinery work needs to be done for the church, inside and out, up and down [...] I will be bound to do it and consider it paid by the said amount, and I will not ask his grace for any extra money apart from the sum that I agreed to of my own free will

d) The duties and obligations of the beneficiary: to provide the necessary material for the works. This is specified in detail for each contract, according to the nature of the works, and the terminology requires expert knowledge:

12) Eu adica cu tot mestesugul, iar prea sf. sa sa-mi dea toata materia cea trebuincioasa, adica scinduri, stilpi, grinzi, scinduri de brad, podini, capriori,

---

[2] In the six contracts, the chief architect is referred to either as "meimar (meemer, meimer)-basha" or as "arhitecton", reflecting the Turkish or Greek lexical influence on specialized terminology, respectively.

piroane mari si mici si cu un cuvint orice materie va fi trebuincioasa la dulgherie si tamplarie (Potra 1961: 732).
I will provide the work, and his grace will give me all the necessary material, that is timber, poles, beams, fir boards, floorboards, scaffolding, nails big and small, in one word any material that will be needed for carpentry and joinery.

e) Terms of payment: the amount due and the manner of payment, either as a lump sum or in instalments (the preferred method), as well as the due dates for the payment of instalments.

13) Iar prea sfintiia sa episcopul sa-mi plateasca de fiescare fereastra cite taleri patruzeci, tocmai (Potra 1961: 726)
And his grace the bishop is to pay me forty silver coins per window

14) acesti bani sa mi-i dea sfintiia sa in patru castiuri, adeca acum inainte taleri trei mie; apoi dupa ce voiu ridica zidurile de doi stanjeni de la ferestre in sus sa-mi mai dea inca taleri doua mii cinci sute (Potra 1961: 730)
his grace is to give this money to me in four instalments, with an advance payment of three thousand silver coins now; then after I have built the walls four meters high from the windows upwards he is to give me another two thousand five hundred.

15) prea sfintiia sa sa-mi plateasca banii cistiuri, cistiuri, carind si luind (Potra 1961: 731)
his grace is to give me the money in instalments as I carry the sand

16) sa urmeze si prea sf. sa cu darea banilor rinduri rinduri, lucrind si luind, ca pina sa va ispravi tot lucrul desavirsit, sa se istoveasca si suma banilor (Potra 1961: 733).
his grace is to pay accordingly, as the work progresses, so by the time our work is complete, the money will have been all paid up

Acknowledgement of receipt is to be made on the back of the contract:

17) trecindu-se toate cistiurile in dosul acestui zapis (Potra 1961: 733)
all the payments are to be recorded on the back of this contract

18) si cati bani voi primi, sa-i trec in dosul acestui zapis (Potra 1961: 731)
and all the money I receive I will write down on the back of this contract

f) A warranty clause whereby the contractor undertakes not to cause delays, to comply with requests, to provide quality work and, failing that, or in case the beneficiary is simply not satisfied, to start again:

19) Iar cind (fereasca dumnezeu) din pricina nemaestrii mele, ori din pricina ca nu voiu lucra zidurile si boltile cu lucrare temeinica si se va intimpla ori

darimare, ori a sa crapa zidurile, atunci sa fiu dator a raspunde orice paguba sa va intimpla. Si mai inainte de toate sa fiu dator a fi napristan la lucru ca sa nu se faca vreun cusur. Si orice lucrare proasta voiu face, neprimita placerii prea sf., sa fiu dator a strica si a face dupa placere si bine (Potra 1961: 730)
And (god forbid) should it be that the walls and vaults collapse because of my lack of skill, or because I have not built them strong, or should the walls crack, then I am to be held accountable for any damage that may occur. And above all I bind myself to be the first on site, and prevent any damage from happening. I take it upon myself to tear down any bad piece of work that his grace disapproves of, and to build it again properly and as required.

20) iar cind inprotiva voi urma, ori adeca nu va fi lucrul bun,ori poleiala mincinoasa, atunci sa fiu pagubas de toata cheltuiala (Potra 1961: 735).
and should I do otherwise, that is if the workmanship be faulty or the gold foil counterfeit, then I am to cover all the expenses

In some cases, the warranty clause and the settlement of disputes are collapsed:

21) Si cind impotriva voiu urma, ori nu va fi nasipul bun, ori voi face precurmare si din pricina mea vor sta mesterii [...] atunci prea sfintia sa in puterea acestui zapis sa ma traga la judecata si judecata sa ma indatoreze sa platesc orice paguba si pierdere de vreme se va pricinui din pricina mea (Potra 1961: 731)
And should I do otherwise, or if the sand is not good, or if I stop and cause delays in the masons' work [...] by virtue of this contract, his grace can bring me to justice, and I shall be liable to pay for any damages and [compensate for any] waste of time that I may have caused

g) A final formula whereby the contractor states that he has signed the contract in the presence of witnesses. Iosef Weltz's contract contains an additional element resembling today's informed consent, i.e. one of the witnesses confirms that the contract has been read out in detail to the contractor, who has agreed to its contents:

22) cetindu-i acest zapis din pont in pont in auzul mesterului si multamit fiind, precum l-au iscalit chiar cu condeiul sau, sunt martor (Potra 1961: 730).
I testify that this contract was read out item by item to the master mason, who agreed to it and signed it in his own hand

3. Contemporary contracts for works: macrostructure

Contemporary contracts for works are structured as follows:

a) A thorough identification of the parties, including details such as the form of organisation of the legal entity, its registered office and representatives.

b) The object of the contract.
c) The value of the works.
d) The duration of works, with provision for delays due to adverse weather conditions.
e) List of all the technical documents annexed to the contract.
f) Conditions for subcontracting.
g) Warranty clause.
h) Conditions applying to the contractor's employees.
i) Terms of payment.
j) *Force majeure*.
k) Settlement of disputes.
l) Termination of contract.
m) Miscellaneous (terms and definitions; date and number of copies; signatures).

4. Discussion

There are few structural differences between the two groups of contracts, confirming that "the period between 1780 and 1865 saw an important evolution towards the modernisation and unification of (normative) legal language, so that we may say that by the mid-19th century this functional style has achieved its modern form" (Stoichitoiu-Ichim 2002[3]). The recitals are obviously different, and in 19th-century contracts there are no specific clauses regulating *force majeure* or the termination of contract. Failure to comply with requirements seems to be understood simply as due to the contractor's inability to do proper work; therefore, the contractors explicitly undertake to redo everything that may be rejected either for technical or for aesthetic reasons, and to compensate for the waste of time and building material:

23) Si orice lucrare proasta voi face, neprimita placerii prea sfintii, sa fiu dator a strica si a face dupa placere si bine (Potra 1961: 730)
And I bind myself to undo any bad piece of work that I may have done or [any piece of work] that his grace is not satisfied with, and to do it again properly and as required

24) Iar cand voi face precurmare lucrului, ori nu voiu pune mesteri de ajuns ca sa sa savarseasca biserica [...] ori voiu face lucru mincinos si netemeinic, ori neprimit placerii prea sf. si dreptului cuvant, atunci sa fiu osandit ca sa platesc toata paguba cherestelii si a celorlalte materii cum si pierderea de vreme (Potra 1961: 733)
And if I stop working, or if I fail to provide enough men to finish the building [...] or should my work be faulty and weak, or should it not be as agreed and

[3] http://www.unibuc.ro/eBooks/filologie/discurs/Capitolul%202.htm. Translation mine.

to his grace's liking, I shall be liable to pay for all the wasted timber and the other materials, as well as for the waste of time

One of the crucial differences between the two groups of texts arises in the clause describing the object of the contract and the technical documentation annexed. In modern contracts, the object of the contract is specified strictly in text-internal terms (where "text" is to be interpreted loosely as including not only the contract in itself, but also the annexed graphs, plans, surveys etc), whereas 19th-century contracts rely on text-external reference to an extent that might make them appear surprisingly ambiguous, given their legal nature. There is a pragmatic solution to their apparent inconsistency: all the parties involved, not only the beneficiary in relation to contractors X, Y, Z taken individually, but also the contractors in relation to one another, rely on shared knowledge of two types, both extralinguistic and text-internal. On the one hand, reference is made to extralinguistic terms of comparison:

25) sa fac doaă coloane in biserica din caramida (ca la Sarban Voda) (Potra 1961: 729)
to build two brick columns in the church (like the ones at Sarban Voda [Church])

26) toate jeturile de la strani [...] sa le fac din nou intocmai ca cele de la manastirea Sfantului Ion cel Mare (Potra 1961: 732)
to make all the pews exactly like the ones at S. John's monastery

Samples are also accepted as terms of comparison:

27) noi sa fim datori a lucra lucrul curat dupa pruba ce este la Mitropolie (Potra 1961: 737, the painters' contract)
we bind ourselves to work exactly as we did for the sample found at the Metropolitan Cathedral

Other factors are architectural plans and *ad-hoc* expert supervision:

28) sa fac coloanele pa dinafara bisericii [...] intocmai dupa planul ce am dat prea sf. sale iscalit de mine (Potra 1961: 729)
to build the outdoor columns [...] following the plan that I gave to his grace, signed by myself

29) dupa cum se vede la plan (Potra 1961: 730)
as shown in the plan

30) legaturi prin zid de jur imprejur pa unde va fi cu cuviinta si mi se va arata de meemer-basa si de neamt (Potra 1961: 732)

reinforcements in the walls, wherever necessary and wherever the chief architect and the German will show me

31) Turnul sa-l fac inalt dupa masura ce mi sa va da de meemer-basa si sa-l savarsesc cu toate cele trebuincioase dupa placerea prea sf. si povata lui meemer-basa (Potra 1961: 732)
I will build the spire as tall as the chief architect tells me and I will do all the necessary work, as his grace requires and the chief architect advises

32) asemenea si legaturile strasinii sa am a le face dupa povata neamtului (Potra 1961: 732)
I am to make the eaves according to the German's advice

"The German" is Iosef Weltz, the master builder, and the use of the definite description in the carpenter's contract to refer to him is just another reference-assigning shortcut that contributes to the coherence of the whole set of contracts. Reference is assigned not only at the level of individual contracts, but at the macro-textual level of the entire set, which makes such texts particularly suitable for investigation in the framework put forth by Vestergaard and Schrøder 1985, which extends Halliday and Hassan's notion of coherence so as to cover not only relations between textual units, but also relations between texts. Intertextuality, understood as "the factors which make the utilization of one text dependent upon knowledge of one or more previously encountered texts" (Beaugrande and Dressler, 1981: 10) is a common feature of both sets of contracts, but contemporary contracts restrict it to the relation between the main document and the annexes, whereas in 19th-century contracts its scope was wider.

Unlike modern specifications, 19th-century contracts could be surprisingly flexible as far as crucial technical aspects were concerned:

33) Iar inaltimea bisericii sa fie cit va cere simetria si placerea sf. sale (Potra 1961: 730)
And the height of the church is to be dictated by symmetry and by his grace's liking

However, this is not to be taken as a sign of poor workmanship or looseness in the drafting of the contract, but rather as another manifestation of the parties' reliance on text-external points of reference and an increased assumption of common ground, compared to nowadays. This supports Paltridge's assertion to the effect that "the genre analyst needs to move away from the physical aspects of language and how they reflect reality to how the text, as a whole, is conditioned by external considerations" (Paltridge 1994: 295).

5. Conclusion

Despite sceptical considerations such as those expressed in Bertucelli-Papi (2000) with regard to the adequacy of (speech act theory and other) pragmatic notions to the diachronic investigation of texts, the theoretical equipment of pragmatics and discourse analysis lends itself to this kind of research; moreover, such investigations are likely to shed new light on the development of particular genres, text-types, and varieties of specialised language, such as for example legal language.

References

Bertuccelli Papi, M. (2000). "Is a diachronic speech act theory possible?". *Journal of Historical Pragmatics* 1(1), 57–66.

Beaugrande, R. de and W. Dressler (1981). *Introduction to text linguistics*. London: Longman.

Bhatia, V.K. (1996). *Analysing Genre: Language Use in Professional Settings*. London: Longman.

Halliday, M. A. K., and R. Hasan (1976). *Cohesion in English*. London: Longman.

Paltridge, B. (1994). "Genre analysis and the identification of textual boundaries". *Applied Linguistics* 15, 288–299.

Potra, G. (1961). *Documente privitoare la istoria oraşului Bucureşti 1594 – 1821*. Bucuresti: Editura Academiei Republicii Populare Române.

Stoichitoiu-Ichim, A. (2002). *Semiotica discursului juridic*. Bucharest: University of Bucharest Press.

Vestergaard, T. and K. Schrøder (1985). *The Language of Advertising*. Oxford: Blackwell.

Jan Chovanec
Masaryk University in Brno
Czech Republic

THE SAME THOUGH DIFFERENT: TOBACCO HEALTH WARNINGS IN EUROPEAN COMMUNITY MEMBER STATES

1. Introduction

Health warnings on tobacco products represent a text type which, though limited in size, obtains wide exposure and has remained unchanged for an extensive period of time. Referring to the text of Directive 2001/37/EC of the European Parliament and of the Council of 5 June 2001 on "the approximation of the laws, regulations and administrative provisions of the member states concerning the manufacture, presentation and sale of tobacco products" – which represents a recent attempt on the part of the EU to unify health warnings on tobacco products in its member states – this article focuses on the translation of the warnings into several national languages published in the Official Journal of the EU. It outlines the development of tobacco health warnings as a specific text type and notes some of the structural possibilities for the linguistic realization of such warnings. By comparing the wording of the mandated tobacco health warnings in several European countries, the article points out the existence of subtle differences between the various language versions. These differences are classified into several types – some motivated by different structural requirements of the respective languages and others by different choices in the process of translation. Most importantly, in several instances the differences result in a reduced degree of equivalence; consequently, consumers in various countries may be warned of the same fact in a significantly different manner.

2. Tobacco health warnings – a historical perspective

A historical overview indicates that the development of the "tobacco health warning" text type was a gradual one, in which the interests of various stakeholders – ranging from health authorities and anti-smoking public groups to tobacco industry representatives – have played a significant role. Most countries have seen several "generations" of warning labels introduced by legislators over the decades, reflecting the growing evidence of the link between smoking and health hazards as well as the requirements of consumer protection laws.

The first health warning appeared in 1966 in the United States and had the following form: *Caution – cigarette smoking may be hazardous to your health* (Chapman and Carter 2001). This was replaced in 1970 by the text *Warning – the US Surgeon General has determined that cigarette smoking is dangerous to your health.*

The two warnings clearly show the gradually increasing strength of the warning message. While the former uses the mild word "caution" (cf. Mahood 2005: 10 on the insufficiency of such signal or "marker words"), the latter explicitly specifies the illocutionary force of the utterance. There is also a marked shift in modality: the 1966 warning identifies the possible link between smoking and damage to health as a modally-hedged proposition, i.e. a mere possibility rather than a factual statement, while the 1970 warning makes the link factual, though hedging it by means of a reference to an authority responsible for such a link. In neither case, however, is the nature of the hazard or danger specified. Such general warnings are in stark contrast to the modern practice of providing highly specific information, sometimes further strengthened by the use of photographs and visual representations (see below).

The use of attribution in the texts of warnings, as in the 1970 example, has been interpreted as favourable to the tobacco industry. For this reason, the pattern "attribution + warning message" may be avoided in some countries, e.g. in Canada because "this ordering of the language forms a word block and allows the dissonant smoker to ignore the rest of the warning" (Mahood 2005: 10). As a result, too wordy a message may lose its impact.

The attribution, which can serve as the rhetorical move of an appeal to authority, can be included in the warning in alternative ways. In Canada, for instance, the current warning labels include the line *Health Canada* at the bottom of a structured text superimposed on a picture. Similarly, the warning texts in Brazil identify the attribution (*O Ministério da Saúde adverte*) in smaller print so that it would not disrupt the text of the warning itself (for links to the visuals, see References).

3. Types of warnings

Tobacco health warnings can be classified in numerous ways. Broadly speaking, they can be textual, as in the majority of cases, or textual and pictorial, as is currently the practice in Canada, Brazil and Australia. The trend is towards combining text with graphic visuals; the Directive 2001/37/EC gives the power to individual member states to use visuals on tobacco products. The visuals are to be chosen from a set of 42 pictures, stipulated by Decision 2003/641/EC and accessible from a library of pre-tested source materials (see Figure 1).

Figure 1. One of the 42 mixed-mode tobacco health warnings to be potentially used in EU member states, © European Communities, 2005.

Textual warning labels may consist of a single sentence, as the warnings mandated by the Directive 2001/37/EC and implemented in EU member states (see below), or several sentences or sentence fragments making up a more extensive text, as is common, for instance, in Canada and Australia.

Extensively textual warnings have, for instance, been in effect in Australia since the adoption of the Trade Practices (Consumer Product Information Standards) (Tobacco) Regulations 1994. Under the regulations, tobacco products must include one of six warnings (called "warning messages") printed on the front page of the package, namely: *Smoking causes lung cancer; Smoking is addictive; Smoking kills; Smoking causes heart disease; Smoking when pregnant harms your baby*; and *Your smoking can harm others*. These sentences are accompanied by the attribution *Health Authority Warning*, specifying the source of the text (i.e. the voice speaking to the consumer belongs to the state bureaucracy rather than the tobacco producers) as well as its precise illocutionary force. The reverse side of tobacco product packets includes the same text with more detailed information. Thus, for instance, in the case of the warning *Smoking is addictive* (which was not included in the 1985 generation of Australian warnings as a result of successful lobbying by pro-tobacco interest groups; cf. Chapman and Carter 2001: 9), the expanded text, written in a personal style and accessible colloquial language, runs as follows:

> SMOKING IS ADDICTIVE
> Nicotine, a drug in tobacco, makes smokers feel they need to smoke. The more you smoke, the more your body will depend on getting nicotine and you may find yourself hooked. It may be difficult to give up smoking once you are hooked on nicotine. For more information, call 13 2190.
> Government Health Warning
> (source: Schedule 1 to Trade Practices (Consumer Product Information Standards) (Tobacco) Regulations 1994 No. 83)

Most of these extended health warnings (officially referred to as "explanatory messages") follow a similar textual structure which could be summarized as a sequence of the following five components:

1. a factual statement (expanded or reformulated in the first sentence),
2. a reference to the consumer's behaviour (direct or implied, posed as a conditional),
3. a possible result of the conditional behaviour of the smoker (with a modal force),
4. an appeal for the consumer to act,
5. attribution – appeal to authority.

Linguistically, warnings can be described in terms of informational vs. imperative style (cf. Tiersma 2002 and Vanderveken 1990) and the mixture of the two. Informational warnings provide some facts about the danger of a particular activity and the illocutionary force of the utterance has to be derived by the reader (e.g. *Smoking causes fatal lung cancer*). Imperative warnings, on the other hand, caution the reader either to engage or refrain from engaging in some activity; the reasons for such recommended action have to be worked out by the reader (e.g. *Protect children: don't make them breathe your smoke*). Out of the sixteen health warnings mandated for use in the EU, thirteen are informational statements and only two are imperatives. In one case, the warning is both informative and imperative.

A mixed warning with both an informational and an imperative component would, according to Tiersma (2002: 64), be ideal. However, Directive 2001/37/EC provides only for one warning message in such a combined form: *Smoking is highly addictive, don't start*. Tiersma explains that "[m]any governments will balk at the imperative element [...] given the tax revenues that derive from smoking". It may, however, be anticipated that the explicitness of such messages might actually be counterproductive: imperatives might provoke resistance on the part of smokers to "being told how to behave". Informational warnings, on the other hand, rely on many presuppositions and may thus be more effective in triggering the smokers' inferencing processes, ultimately leading them to decide to change their behaviour. Moreover, the underlying meta-imperative – "Don't smoke" –

does not then have to be tediously repeated in each warning message; in the EU warnings, such explicitness is avoided – the imperative warnings merely caution *don't start, protect children: don't make them breathe your smoke* and *get help to stop smoking.*

The degree of directness thus provides another perspective when approaching tobacco warnings. Many of the warnings in the form of informative statements do, in fact, have an underlying conditional structure with an implied imperative: If you want/don't want X, then do/don't do Y. This is the case, for instance, in the following EU warnings: *Smoking when pregnant harms your baby* and *Your doctor or your pharmacist can help you stop smoking.*

The avoidance of the meta-imperative "Don't smoke" is also apparent in the new Australian regulations in effect from 2006. They stipulate that the explanatory message should contain the following appeal: *You CAN quit smoking. Call Quitline 131 848, talk to your doctor or pharmacist, or visit www.quitnow.info.au.* The dialogic structure, evidenced by the emphatic modal verb indicating that the sentence may operate as an answer to a smoker's potential objection "I'm unable to stop smoking", is supported by three direct imperatives asking the smoker to seek institutional help. The persuasiveness of the first sentence and the structural repetition in the next sentence add urgency to the overall message.

Informational warnings may also communicate indirectly by capitalizing on the relationship between the text and the accompanying picture, as well as the presence of word play or allusion (cf. the Canadian warning labels *Idle but deadly*, *Cigarettes are a heart breaker,* or *Where there's smoke there's hydrogen cyanide* possibly alluding to the proverb "Where there's a will there's a way").

A useful perspective on the nature of warnings is also provided by the degree of facticity of the communicated proposition. Tobacco health warnings may then be divided into factive vs. non-factive propositions (typically when a causal link between smoking and particular illnesses is predicated with varying degrees of possibility and probability expressed by means of modals, cf. *Smoking kills* vs. *Smoking can kill*).

An investigation of the link between the form of the warning labels and their effectiveness, i.e. their perlocutionary effect, is beyond the scope of a linguistically-oriented study. Some information on this issue may be found in the literature; e.g. in Strahan et al. (2002).

4. Tobacco Health Warnings in the EU

Directive 2001/37/EC provided for the implementation of sixteen warnings into the laws of EU member states (cf. Joossens 2005 on the preparatory process). This concerned two general health warnings, printed on the front of tobacco product packages, and fourteen additional health warnings, printed on the reverse side of packages. The warnings (see Figure 2) are rotated in such a way as to ensure uniform exposure of the individual texts.

General health warnings

1. Smoking kills/Smoking can kill.
2. Smoking seriously harms you and others around you.

Additional health warnings

1. Smokers die younger.
2. Smoking clogs the arteries and causes heart attacks and strokes.
3. Smoking causes fatal lung cancer.
4. Smoking when pregnant harms your baby.
5. Protect children: don't make them breathe your smoke.
6. Your doctor or your pharmacist can help you stop smoking.
7. Smoking is highly addictive, don't start.
8. Stopping smoking reduces the risk of fatal heart and lung diseases.
9. Smoking can cause a slow and painful death.
10. Get help to stop smoking: (telephone/postal address/ internet address/consult your doctor/pharmacist).
11. Smoking may reduce the blood flow and causes impotence.
12. Smoking causes ageing of the skin.
13. Smoking can damage the sperm and decreases fertility.
14. Smoke contains benzene, nitrosamines, formaldehyde and hydrogen cyanide.

Figure 2. General and additional health warnings listed in Directive 2001/37/EC

The individual member states of the EU were responsible for implementing the provisions of the Directive within their own countries, i.e. introducing the warning messages in their official languages. The usual practice is that all instruments of the EU are first translated into the languages of the member states and published by the EU. Then, the translated EU instruments are used to modify domestic legislation. In other words, the implementation of the Directive under discussion was a two-step process involving first its translation and second its actual implementation. In the subsequent examples, we focus on the first stage, i.e. translation of the source text into the various languages. The actual wordings of the tobacco health warnings in the official translations in the Journal may occasionally differ from those in the national legislations on account of stylistic modifications or misprints, for example.

The translations are made available in the Official Journal of the EU. When the actual translations are placed side by side, they may be related to the original English text of the Directive as in the example of the seventh additional warning in Figure 3.

7.	SMOKING IS HIGHLY ADDICTIVE, DON'T START
CZ	Kouření je vysoce návykové, nezačínejte s ním
D	Rauchen macht sehr schnell abhängig: Fangen Sie gar nicht erst an!
DK	Rygning er stærkt vanedannende: lad være med at begynde
EST	Suitsetamine tekitab kergesti sõltuvust, ära alusta
F	Fumer crée une forte dépendance, ne commencez pas
FIN	Tupakointi aiheuttaa voimakasta riippuvuutta. Älä aloita
GR	Το κάπνισμα είναι εξαιρετικά εθιστικό, μην το αρχίσετε
HU	A dohányzás súlyos függőséghez vezet. Ne kezdje el.
I	Il fumo crea un'elevata dipendenza, non iniziare
LT	Rūkymas sukelia priklausomybę - nepradėk.
LV	Smēķēšana ir ļoti kaitīgs ieradums, nesāc!
NL	Roken werkt zeer verslavend; begin er niet mee
P	Fumar causa elevada dependęncia. Não comece a fumar
PL	Palenie szybko uzależnia nie zaczynaj palić
SK	Fajčenie je vysoko návykové, nezačínajte
SL	Kajenje povzroča hudo zasvojenost, zato ne začnite kaditi
SP	El tabaco es muy adictivo: no empiece a fumar
SW	Rökning är mycket beroendeframkallande, börja inte röka

Figure 3. The wording of additional health warning No. 7 in the individual national languages of the EU (source: The Official Journal of the EU; Maltese version not available).

It is clear that there are some minor differences between the individual language versions. In the case of the seventh additional health warning, the underlining identifies some differences from the original English text. Most of these concern the addition of "to smoke" to the imperative "don't start", thus making the warning more specific and explicit, as in Portuguese, Polish, Slovenian, Spanish and Swedish (cf. also the phrase "with it" in Czech). In German, the particles *gar erst* are added, being the approximate equivalent of: "don't even start in the first place". French, Italian, Portuguese and Slovenian choose a different syntactic structure: instead of the copula + adjective, they use a full verb + a noun: "creates/causes ... a dependency". In Spanish, the expression "tobacco" replaces "smoking" as the subject of the sentence.

Such differences are also observable in the wordings of the other warnings. While it is not the purpose of this paper to document all such changes, there are certain affinities between them which allow them to be grouped into several distinct categories. Some of the differences have no serious implications concerning the conceptual meaning communicated by the warnings, but some of them result in non-equivalence.

Five basic differences can be observed in the analysed material. The first four either expand the source warning by adding some information, or modify it by selecting an alternative way of expressing it, while the last one changes the content of the message.

Expansion of syntactic structure

This change occurs when a simple sentence or a complex sentence with a non-finite clause expressed by an infinitive or a participle is expanded by adding another finite verb form. This accounts for the differences in sentence structure in the following examples (AW = additional warning, GW = general warning):

Example 1

AW8 *STOPPING SMOKING REDUCES THE RISK OF FATAL HEART AND LUNG DISEASES*

D *Wer das Rauchen aufgibt, verringert das Risiko tödlicher Herz- und Lungenerkrankungen* [Whoever gives up smoking reduces ...]

FIN *Lopettamalla tupakoinnin vähennät vaaraa sairastua kuolemaan johtaviin sydän- ja keuhkosairauksiin.* [If you stop smoking, you will reduce ...]

SK *Keď prestanete fajčiť, znížite riziko smrteľných srdcových a pľúcnych chorôb* [When you stop smoking, you will reduce ...]

Change of syntactic structure

In several instances, the translations change the syntactic structure of the original. In the next example, for instance, a finite clause is changed into a nominal phrase. As a result, one of the two imperatives is removed, and the responsibility of the smoker for exposing children to smoke is diminished:

Example 2

AW5 *PROTECT CHILDREN: DON'T MAKE THEM BREATHE YOUR SMOKE*

SL *Varujte otroke pred vdihavanjem vašega cigaretnega dima* [Protect children from breathing in your cigarette smoke]

There is also the contrary situation: finite sentence structures in the original text are changed into non-finite sentence fragments, as in Example 3:

Example 3
AW10 *GET HELP TO STOP SMOKING: (...)*
P *Para o ajudar a deixar de fumar: (...)* [To help to stop smoking ...]
I *Per aiutarvi a smettere di fumare: (...)* [To help you to stop smoking ...]

There are also instances when sentence constituents change their grammatical roles, as in the following Finnish example where the replacement of the original verb "help" with "get" leads to a change in the subject of the sentences, the original subject being expressed by a genitive in the translated version:

Example 4
AW6 *YOUR DOCTOR OR YOUR PHARMACIST CAN HELP YOU STOP SMOKING*
FIN *Lääkäriltä tai apteekista saat apua tupakoinnin lopettamiseen* [(From) doctor or pharmacist you will get help ...]

Change in the personal vs. impersonal manner of presentation
This is a relatively frequent change, already documented with two instances in Example 1 above. Often, though not always, it overlaps with the expansion of syntactic structure – the expression of originally non-finite clauses by means of finite structures requiring the use of grammatical subjects in the form of personal pronouns. Other instances when an impersonal construction in the source text is changed into a personal one in the translated versions, include, for instance:

Example 5
AW4 *SMOKING WHEN PREGNANT HARMS YOUR BABY*
P *Se está grávida: Fumar prejudica a saúde de seu filho* [If you are pregnant ...]
DK *Hvis du er gravid, skader rygning dit barns sundhed* [When you are pregnant ...]

There are also instances of the contrary process: an originally personal manner of presentation is changed into an impersonal one. This change is significant because it may diminish the impact of the warning message on the reader:

Example 6

AW4 *SMOKING WHEN PREGNANT HARMS YOUR BABY*

I *Fumare in gravidanza fa male al bambino* [Smoking in pregnancy harms the baby]

Addition of information

This change is the result of a specification of a more general original warning. Most typically, this concerns the inclusion of the attributes "tobacco" or "cigarette" to modify other nouns, such as "smoking" or "smoke", as in the following examples:

Example 7

AW6 *PROTECT CHILDREN: DON'T MAKE THEM BREATHE YOUR SMOKE*

PL *Chroń dzieci: nie każ im wdychać dymu z twojego papierosa* [Protect children: don't make them breathe in the smoke from your cigarette]

D *Schützen Sie Kinder - Lassen Sie sie nicht Ihren Tabakrauch einatmen!* [Protect children: don't let them breathe in your tobacco smoke]

In several instances, various languages modify the object of the verb "to harm", which is used in the fourth additional warning and the second general warning, by adding the word "health":

Example 8

AW4 *SMOKING WHEN PREGNANT HARMS YOUR BABY*

CZ *Kouření v těhotenství škodí zdraví Vašeho dítěte* [Smoking in pregnancy harms the health of your baby]

F *Fumer pendant la grossesse nuit à la santé de votre enfant* [Smoking during pregnancy harms the health of your baby]

In this case, the translation option of specifying the general predicate "to harm" may increase the strength of the warning. In the case of the general warning in Example 9, however, the specification may actually work in the opposite direction. The relatively vague predication "smoking harms you" may be interpreted by smokers as ambiguous, meaning either "it harms you physically" (i.e. your health) or "it harms you socially" (i.e. the way an individual is perceived by others). While in the case of unborn children (as in Example 8 above), the specification of the former interpretation may be beneficial because the latter is actually not applicable, in the case of adult smokers, the removal of the ambiguity may be counterproductive with respect to the effect of the message. It makes the warning more specific but, at the same time, more limited – in the process of "overtranslation", one aspect of meaning is gained while another is lost: the focus shifts from social and physical harm to physical damage only.

Example 9

GW2 *SMOKING SERIOUSLY HARMS YOU AND OTHERS AROUND YOU*

F *Fumer nuit gravement à votre santé et à celle de votre entourage* [Smoking seriously harms your health and that of those around you]

SP *Fumar perjudica gravemente su salud y la de los que están a su alrededor* [Smoking seriously harms your health and that of those who are in your surroundings]

Change of information – alteration of propositional content

Unlike the previous examples, which documented differences in grammatical structure and the amount of information provided, there are also several instances when the translation process has resulted in a significant shift of meaning, rendering the translations of the warning labels semantically different from the original.

The most serious example is shown in Example 10, where "impotence" in the original text is translated as "infertility" in the Czech version. This is a clear mistranslation which was not corrected in the subsequent editing and got as far as the relevant Czech regulations. As a result, this translation mistake has been circulating on all tobacco packages bearing this warning in the Czech market. Though the translator could (and should) have used "impotence", a loanword in Czech to describe the particular condition (this is used in the translations into all other EU languages except the French version, which uses its domestic equivalent *l'impuissance*), he or she opted for a domestic expression with a completely different meaning and effect. The text of this warning addresses men by directly appealing to their manhood, which is under threat. The mistranslated version entirely misses the intended effect of the original.

Example 10

AW11 *SMOKING MAY REDUCE THE BLOOD FLOW AND CAUSES IMPOTENCE*

CZ *Kouření může snižovat krevní oběh a způsobuje neplodnost* [Smoking may reduce the blood flow and causes infertility]

Moreover, not only does the mistranslation weaken the strength of the warning but it also duplicates the information provided in another additional warning (No. 13) – *Smoking can damage the sperm and decreases fertility*. As a result, Czech consumers receive a somewhat restricted warning about the dangers of smoking (*Smoking ... causes *infertility* vs. *Smoking ... decreases fertility*).

It would seem that thanks to the fact that the text of the Directive is written in English, the warnings should not undergo any changes in those EU countries where English is the official language. Although a mere transcription should not lead to the kinds of changes which occur in translation, the adoption of ready text is still subject to incidental change. Thus, for instance, the Irish version of the additional warning No. 11, as provided for in the European Communities (Manufacture, Presentation and Sale of Tobacco Products) Regulations 2003, runs as follows: *Smoking may reduce the blood flow and cause impotence*. This wording omits, most likely by overlooking, the third person singular suffix on the verb.

The misprint, however, has significant consequences for the status of the predication: the factive proposition in the present tense, conveying the modality of certainty, is changed into a non-factive proposition expressing a mere possibility on account of the modal auxiliary "may", which, due to the loss of the finite verb marker, extends its scope to the second verb as well. Such a grammatical re-categorization resulting in the weakening of the proposition has been documented in two other instances: once in Slovak (the same mistake, though concerning the text of the additional warning No. 13: *Fajčenie môže poškodiť semeno a zhoršiť plodnosť* ["Smoking can damage the sperm and *decrease fertility"] – instead of "decreases") and once in Polish (exactly the same mistake as in Ireland, though not in the translation but in its transcription into the respective regulation).

It should be added that the actual warning messages encountered by consumers in the member states of the EU may differ from the translations published in the Official Journal of the EU (used in this article). Some changes may have been introduced by legislators as stylistic modifications, others as choices of more fitting expressions and still others as typos. For instance there were, as opposed to the officially published translations, three such changes in the Czech regulations and ten in the Slovak.

5. Conclusion

Tobacco health warnings represent a text type which reflects changes in consumer protection legislation and changing attitudes towards smoking. The presence and form of the warnings indicate differences in their use in developed and developing countries (cf. Aftab et al. 1999). Great attention to the form of warning messages has traditionally been paid in Canada, where warnings have a combination of textual and pictorial content, in Australia, which is introducing new warning messages and strongly graphic images from 2006, and in the

European Union, which recently unified the health warnings on tobacco products in its member states.

Directive 2001/37/EC provided a list of sixteen warnings to be translated into the official languages of the individual member states and implemented through their laws and other legal instruments. The warnings are mostly informational statements rather than imperatives alerting consumers to preferred forms of behaviour. The illocutionary force of the warning messages is not explicit and has to be inferred by consumers.

An analysis of the translations published in the Official Journal of the EU reveals that the texts of the warning messages in the official languages of the EU are occasionally different from the English source text. Frequent deviations can be found in syntax, where non-finite English structures such as infinities and participles are expanded into full clausal structures with finite verb forms. Several languages have also adopted alternative syntactic structures. There are also frequent shifts in the manner of presentation – from impersonal to personal and vice versa, which has an impact on the effect of the warning messages. In a number of cases, additional information is supplied, making the translations more specific and concrete. There are, however, also several differences which do not arise from different translation solutions or requirements of the different language systems. Such differences result in non-equivalence between the source texts and the translations and can be traced to either translation errors or mistakes in the transcription of translated and untranslated texts.

References

Aftab, M., Kolben, D. and P. Lurie (1999). "International cigarette labelling practices", *Tobacco Control* 8: 368-372, http://tc.bmjjournals.com

Cavalcante, T. M. (2005). "Labelling and Packaging in Brazil" World Health Organization, http://www.who.int.

Chapman, S. and T. Carter (2001). "A Critical History of Warning Labels on Australian Cigarette Packs", http://www.vctc.org.au/industry/aust-pack-warnings.pdf.

Evaluation of the Health Warnings and Explanatory Health Messages on Tobacco Products – Executive Summary, http://www.health.gov.au.

Joossens, L. (2005). "European Community Directive on packaging and labelling of tobacco products" World Health Organization, http://www.who.int

Leech, G. (1983). *Principles of Pragmatics*. London: Longman.

Mahood, G. (2005). *Canada's Tobacco Package Label or Warning System: "Telling the Truth" about Tobacco Product Risks.* World Health Organization, http://www.who.int.

Review of Health Warnings on Tobacco Products in Australia. Discussion Paper, April 2001. Canberra: Commonwealth Department of Health and Aged Care, http://www.health.gov.au.

Strahan, E. J., White, K., Fong, G. T., Fabrigar, L. R., Zanna, M. P. and R. Cameron (2002). "Enhancing the effectiveness of tobacco package warning labels: a social psychological perspective" *Tobacco Control* 11, 183-190, http:\\tc.bmjjournals.com.

Šarčević, S. (1997). *New Approach to Legal Translation.* Dordrecht: Kluwer Law International.

Tiersma, P. M. (2002). "The Language and Law of Product Warnings". In: J. Cotterill (ed.), *Language in the Legal Process.* Basingstoke: Palgrave Macmillan, 54-71.

Vanderveken, D. (1990). *Meaning and Speech Acts, Volume 1: Principles of Language Use.* Cambridge: Cambridge University Press.

Sources

EC source texts

Directive 2001/37/EC of the European Parliament and of the Council of 5 June 2001 on "the approximation of the laws, regulations and administrative provisions of the member states concerning the manufacture, presentation and sale of tobacco products", http://europe.eu.int/eur-lex/

Translations of Directive 2001/37/EC into the languages of EU member states. In *Official Journal of the EU*, http://europe.eu.int/eur-lex/

Commission Decision of 26/V/2005 on the library of selected source documents containing colour photographs or other illustrations for each of the additional warnings listed in annex 1 to Directive 2001/37/EC of the European Parliament and of the Council, http://europa.eu.int/comm/health/ph_determinants/life_style/Tobacco/Documents/com_1452_en.pdf

Australian regulations

Trade Practices (Consumer Product Information Standards) (Tobacco) Regulations 1994 No. 83, http://frli.law.gov.au/

Trade Practices (Consumer Product Information Standards) (Tobacco) Regulations 2004, http://scaleplus.law.gov.au/html/pastereg/3/1855/pdf/2004No264.pdf

Brazilian warning labels
http://tobacco.health.usyd.edu.au/site/supersite/resources/docs/gallery_packwarnings.htm
http://www.anvisa.gov.br/divulga/noticias/2003/221003_2.htm

Canadian warning labels
www.hc-sc.gc.ca/english/media/photos/tobacco_labelling/

Czech regulations
Vyhláška ze dne 30. září 2003, kterou se stanoví požadavky na tabákové výrobky, č. 344/2003 Sb. [Regulations No. 344/2003 Sb. of 30 September 2003 setting the requirements on tobacco products]

Irish regulations
European Communities (Manufacture, Presentation and Sale of Tobacco Products) Regulations 2003, S.I. No. 425 of 2003.

Slovak legislation
Zákon č. 377/2004 Z.z. o ochrane nefajčiarov [Act No. 377/2004 on the protection of non-smokers]

Víctor M. González Ruiz
Universidad de Las Palmas de Gran Canaria
Spain

CHANGING THE LAW ON MARRIAGE: THE SEMANTICS OF TOLERANCE

1. Introduction

On 1 July 2005, the Spanish Parliament passed an Act which allows homosexual couples to marry. This piece of legislation represents a U-turn for the way in which marriage has traditionally been defined and is still defined in almost every country in the world, i.e. a legally recognised union between a man and a woman[1]. The new Act, which was presented by the Spanish Government as a Bill on 12 January 2005, also gives same-sex partners the right to adopt and enjoy the same pension and inheritance rights as heterosexual couples.

Given the strength and the extent of this legislative move in social policy, one could expect the new Act to be a comprehensive piece of legislation on family and marriage with a detailed list of the new rights which homosexuals will be able to enjoy from now on. The new Act, however, is a short and simple reforming statute[2] (*ley modificativa*), which succinctly lays down seventeen modifications to be made to the Civil Code (*Código Civil*), the basic legislation in Spain governing the relationship between citizens.

2. The new Act as a reforming statute

Reforming statutes are the main resource at the disposal of the Parliament to update the law[3]. Their purpose is to modify rules which are outdated, useless or simply wrong. This means that this type of Act contains references only to those elements of previous legislation that have to be changed and how they have to be changed. In most cases, Parliamentary drafters use reforming Acts to rewrite parts

[1] Before Spain, only Belgium, the Netherlands and Canada had fully recognised the right of homosexuals to marry.

[2] In this paper, the words *Act* and *statute* are used as synonyms.

[3] Parliament may also update the law by enacting completely new Acts. Apart from legislation, Castiñeira Palou (1989: 175-176) points out other legal and non-legal resources to update the law, e.g. improvement of public and judicial services, as well as educational and economic campaigns.

of old statutes, add and replace words or paragraphs, repeal existing law and postpone the date of termination of enacted rules[4]. In this case, the Act allowing homosexuals to marry adds a new paragraph to a section of the Spanish Civil Code and gives a new draft to sixteen other provisions of the same set of civil rules.

Starting with the title, the Act makes its reforming nature very explicit. In an explanatory fashion, the piece of law under study is given the name *LEY 13/2005, de 1 de julio, por la que se modifica el Código Civil en materia de derecho a contraer matrimonio* ("Act No. 13/2005, passed on 1 July 2005, modifying the Civil Code with regard to the right to marry"). The style of the other provisions in the Act, except for the preamble, is as neutral, concise and direct as the title and follows the traditional format of reforming statutes, where legislators are supposed to write according to the principles of clarity and precision.

In terms of form, the Act consists of three main elements: the preamble, divided into two parts[5]; the central body of provisions, which contains only one section composed of seventeen paragraphs; and four schedules. Apart from these, it also includes the title of the Act as a heading and two formulae which are centuries old: an initial one, announcing the enactment of the statute[6]; and a concluding one, where the Head of State (the King of Spain) orders all Spanish nationals to comply with the new rule[7]. The formal structure of the new marriage Act is as follows:

Title of the Act → Enacting formula → Preamble → Main body of provisions → Schedules → Closing formula

The most important part of this reforming Act is the set of seventeen paragraphs contained in the main body of the statute. Here, drafters have employed the basic unit of Spanish legislation: the *artículo* (the section); and, subsequently, they have made a further division into paragraphs. These paragraphs, headed by Arabic numerals, each describe a change in a different section of the Spanish Civil Code.

When describing the modifications to the previous law, legislators have been concise and clear and have used graphic elements in order to help the reader to distinguish the two main types of content in each paragraph: first, the part

[4] For a full discussion on the form and contents of Spanish and Catalan reforming statutes (*leyes modificativas*), see Castiñeira Palou (1986, 1989).

[5] Reforming statutes do not always include a preamble. However, when they provide a dramatic change to existing legislation, as in this case, a preamble is included in order to explain the reasons behind the reform.

[6] *JUAN CARLOS I REY DE ESPAÑA A todos los que la presente vieren y entendieren. Sabed: Que las Cortes Generales han aprobado y Yo vengo en sancionar la siguiente ley.*

[7] *Por tanto, Mando a todos los españoles, particulares y autoridades, que guarden y hagan guardar esta ley. Valencia, 1 de julio de 2005. JUAN CARLOS R.*

which is being modified (*texto marco*/frame text[8]) and, second, how it is modified (*texto de regulación*/regulatory text[9]). As an example, they have used inverted commas for the latter (i.e. the new text replacing the old provision), indenting it further to the right, and laying it out as a separate piece of text.

Although the changes contained in the new Act are mainly of a terminological nature (i.e. they have basically replaced a few words with others in some provisions of the Civil Code), legislators have used the so-called *estilo de regulación* (regulatory style), by which the old law is given a new draft. As a consequence, provisions are entirely rewritten in the reforming statute, even though only a word or two have been changed. The reasons underlying this decision not just to include a general stipulation establishing that some terms are to be replaced with others in some particular provisions could be summarised as follows: on the one hand, because legislators normally prefer to redraft old provisions in order to make the alterations clearer and easier to comprehend; and, on the other hand, because the replacements to be applied here are not straightforward "one-for-one" changes, but "two-for-one" substitutions together with subtle reformulations of the old law.

3. The changes to the old law

It has been said that the new Act reforms seventeen provisions of the Civil Code concerning the areas of marriage and family[10]. And it does so in a surprisingly simple manner, since most of the changes have to do merely with the need to use terms which do not refer expressly to the sex of the married person. However, in a few provisions, the linguistic reform goes slightly further with the addition or omission of a sentence in order to extend the right to marry and its corresponding benefits to homosexual citizens. This is the case in sections 44 and 178[11]. In the former (see 1 below), which is the first provision in the Civil Code relating to the requirements to marry, the new sentence establishes, in a general way, that marriage is to be understood independently of the gender of the partners ("Marriage shall have the same requirements and effects when the spouses-to-be are of different sex and when both are of the same sex"). In fact, this is the only

[8] An introduction to each paragraph indicating the type of change which is being carried out.
[9] The text containing the modification.
[10] In its first two schedules, it also extends the new rights of homosexuals to all related legislation. In the first one (*Disposición adicional primera*), it provides that all Spanish legislation regarding marriage is to be construed independently of the sex of the married individuals. In the second one (*Disposición adicional segunda*), the Act expressly modifies some parts of the *Ley de 8 de junio de 1957, sobre Registro Civil* (Spanish Civil Register Act 1957).
[11] A sentence is also added in section 175. But, in this case, the provision is not specifically addressed to homosexual couples.

explicitly positive stipulation to be found in the main body of the statute: it expressly confers rights to a group of citizens who could not enjoy them in the past.

In the other provisions, by contrast, the job of legislators has been to neutralise language in order to make the law accessible to heterosexuals and homosexuals alike. In section 178 (see 8 below), for example, they have deleted a sentence which provided that, in a given situation, the person adopting a child and the child's single legal parent had to be of different sexes. By omitting this express requirement, the right to adopt under the circumstances described in this section is made universal.

Likewise, the intention of legislators behind the semantic changes specified in the other fourteen provisions has been to do away with every direct reference to sex or gender in the Civil Code as far as marriage and family are concerned. As a result, they have replaced the expressions *el marido y la mujer* (the husband and the wife) and *el padre y la madre* (the father and the mother) with the collective nouns *cónyuges* (spouses) (see 2, 3, 9, 10, 11, 12, 13, 14, 15, 16 and 17 below) and *progenitores* (parents) (see 4, 5 and 8 below), respectively. In section 164, *el padre y la madre* (the father and the mother) has been converted into *los que ejerzan la patria potestad* (those enjoying the custody of a child) (see 6 below).

The changes specified in the main body of the reforming statute are given below[12]:

1) A sentence is added to section 44 of the Civil Code:
Art. 44. El hombre y la mujer tienen derecho a contraer matrimonio conforme a las disposiciones de este Código.

Art. 44. *El hombre y la mujer tienen derecho a contraer matrimonio conforme a las disposiciones de este Código. El matrimonio tendrá los mismos requisitos y efectos cuando ambos contrayentes sean del mismo o de diferente sexo.*

2) Section 66 of the Civil Code is redrafted:
Art. 66. El marido y la mujer son iguales en derechos y deberes.

Art. 66. *Los cónyuges son iguales en derechos y deberes.*

3) Section 67 of the Civil Code is redrafted:
Art. 67. El marido y la mujer deben respetarse y ayudarse mutuamente y actuar en interés de la familia.

[12] The new draft of the Civil Code provisions is given in italics. The changes relevant to this study are underlined.

Art. 67. *Los cónyuges deben respetarse y ayudarse mutuamente y actuar en interés de la familia.*

4) The first sentence of section 154 of the Civil Code is redrafted:
Art. 154. Los hijos no emancipados están bajo la potestad del padre y de la madre.

Art. 154. *Los hijos no emancipados están bajo la potestad de sus progenitores.*

5) The first sentence of section 160 of the Civil Code is redrafted:
Art. 160. El padre y la madre, aunque no ejerzan la patria potestad, tienen el derecho de relacionarse con sus hijos menores, excepto con los adoptados por otro o conforme a lo dispuesto en resolución judicial.

Art. 160. *Los progenitores, aunque no ejerzan la patria potestad, tienen el derecho de relacionarse con sus hijos menores, excepto con los adoptados por otro o conforme a lo dispuesto en resolución judicial.*

6) Paragraph 2 of section 164 of the Civil Code is redrafted:
2.° Los adquiridos por sucesión en que el padre, la madre o ambos hubieran sido justamente desheredados o no hubieran podido heredar por causa de indignidad, que serán administrados por la persona designada por el causante y, en su defecto y sucesivamente, por el otro progenitor o por un Administrador Judicial especialmente nombrado.

2.° Los adquiridos por sucesión en que uno o ambos de los que ejerzan la patria potestad hubieran sido justamente desheredados o no hubieran podido heredar por causa de indignidad, que serán administrados por la persona designada por el causante y, en su defecto y sucesivamente, por el otro progenitor o por un administrador judicial especialmente nombrado.

7) Subsection 4 of section 175 of the Civil Code is redrafted:
4. Fuera de la adopción por ambos cónyuges, nadie puede ser adoptado por más de una persona. En caso de muerte del adoptante, o cuando el adoptante sufra la exclusión prevista en el artículo 179, es posible una nueva adopción del adoptado.

4. Nadie puede ser adoptado por más de una persona, salvo que la adopción se realice conjunta o sucesivamente por ambos cónyuges. El matrimonio celebrado con posterioridad a la adopción permite al cónyuge la adopción de los hijos de su consorte. En caso de muerte del adoptante, o cuando el adoptante sufra la exclusión prevista en el artículo 179, es posible una nueva adopción del adoptado.

8) Subsection 2 of section 178 of the Civil Code is redrafted:
2. Por excepción subsistirán los vínculos jurídicos con la familia paterna o materna, según el caso:

1.° Cuando el adoptado sea hijo del cónyuge del adoptante, aunque el consorte hubiere fallecido.

2.° Cuando sólo uno de los progenitores haya sido legalmente determinado y el adoptante sea persona de distinto sexo al de dicho progenitor, siempre que tal efecto hubiere sido solicitado por el adoptante, el adoptado mayor de doce años y el padre o madre cuyo vínculo haya de persistir.

2. Por excepción subsistirán los vínculos jurídicos con la familia del progenitor que, según el caso, corresponda:

1.° Cuando el adoptado sea hijo del cónyuge del adoptante, aunque el consorte hubiere fallecido.

2.° Cuando sólo uno de los progenitores haya sido legalmente determinado, siempre que tal efecto hubiere sido solicitado por el adoptante, el adoptado mayor de doce años y el progenitor cuyo vínculo haya de persistir.

9) The second sentence of section 637 of the Civil Code is redrafted:
Art. 637. [...] Se exceptúan de esta disposición las donaciones hechas conjuntamente a marido y mujer, entre los cuales tendrá lugar aquel derecho, si el donante no hubiese dispuesto lo contrario.

***Art. 637.** [...] Se exceptúan de esta disposición las donaciones hechas conjuntamente a ambos cónyuges, entre los cuales tendrá lugar aquel derecho, si el donante no hubiese dispuesto lo contrario.*

10) Section 1323 of the Civil Code is redrafted:
Art. 1323. El marido y la mujer podrán transmitirse por cualquier título bienes y derechos y celebrar entre sí toda clase de contratos.

***Art. 1323.** Los cónyuges podrán transmitirse por cualquier título bienes y derechos y celebrar entre sí toda clase de contratos.*

11) Section 1344 of the Civil Code is redrafted:
Art. 1344. Mediante la sociedad de gananciales se hacen comunes para el marido y la mujer las ganancias o beneficios obtenidos indistintamente por cualquiera de ellos, que les serán atribuidos por mitad al disolverse aquélla.

Art. 1344. Mediante la sociedad de gananciales se hacen comunes para los cónyuges las ganancias o beneficios obtenidos indistintamente por cualquiera de ellos, que les serán atribuidos por mitad al disolverse aquella.

12) Section 1348 of the Civil Code is redrafted:
Art. 1348. Siempre que pertenezca privativamente a uno de los cónyuges una cantidad o crédito pagadero en cierto número de años, no serán gananciales las sumas que se cobren en los plazos vencidos durante el matrimonio, sino que se estimarán capital del marido o de la mujer, según a quien pertenezca el crédito.

Art. 1348. Siempre que pertenezca privativamente a uno de los cónyuges una cantidad o crédito pagadero en cierto número de años, no serán gananciales las sumas que se cobren en los plazos vencidos durante el matrimonio, sino que se estimarán capital de uno u otro cónyuge, según a quien pertenezca el crédito.

13) Section 1351 of the Civil Code is redrafted:
Art. 1351. Las ganancias obtenidas por el marido o la mujer en el juego o las procedentes de otras causas que eximan de la restitución, pertenecerán a la sociedad de gananciales.

Art. 1351. Las ganancias obtenidas por cualquiera de los cónyuges en el juego o las procedentes de otras causas que eximan de la restitución pertenecerán a la sociedad de gananciales.

14) Section 1361 of the Civil Code is redrafted:
Art. 1361. Se presumen gananciales los bienes existentes en el matrimonio mientras no se pruebe que pertenecen privativamente al marido o la mujer.

Art. 1361. Se presumen gananciales los bienes existentes en el matrimonio mientras no se pruebe que pertenecen privativamente a uno de los dos cónyuges.

15) Paragraph 2 of section 1365 of the Civil Code is redrafted:
2.° En el ejercicio ordinario de la profesión, arte u oficio o en la administración ordinaria de los bienes propios. Si el marido o la mujer fueren comerciantes, se estará a lo dispuesto en el Código de Comercio.

2.° En el ejercicio ordinario de la profesión, arte u oficio o en la administración ordinaria de los propios bienes. Si uno de los cónyuges fuera comerciante, se estará a lo dispuesto en el Código de Comercio.

16) Section 1404 of the Civil Code is redrafted:
Art. 1404. Hechas las deducciones en el caudal inventariado que prefijan los artículos anteriores, el remanente constituirá el haber de la sociedad de gananciales, que se dividirá por mitad entre marido y mujer o sus respectivos herederos.

Art. 1404. *Hechas las deducciones en el caudal inventariado que prefijan los artículos anteriores, el remanente constituirá el haber de la sociedad de gananciales, que se dividirá por mitad entre los cónyuges o sus respectivos herederos.*

17) Section 1458 of the Civil Code is redrafted:
Art. 1458. El marido y la mujer podrán venderse bienes recíprocamente.

Art. 1458. *Los cónyuges podrán venderse bienes recíprocamente.*

As the paragraphs above show, the limited extent of the changes on the surface does not mirror the far-reaching consequences of the reform in marriage legislation.

4. A matter of social policy: an analysis of the preamble

The new Act on marriage introduces such a dramatic change in the law that legislators have been obliged to include a preamble in order to explain the reasons behind the reform. This introduction to the new piece of legislation is written in a style which is rhetorical as well as slightly archaic, and consists of two parts. In the first one, the authors refer to marriage as a fundamental right which is contained in the Constitution and which should be protected and treated carefully by legislators. This is followed by a historical description of the changes in society towards the acceptance of homosexual relationships and families. Finally, emphasis is given to the need for the law to recognise same-sex unions and act accordingly by enacting this Act which, moreover, is consistent with current moves in EU legislation.

In the second part of the preamble, alluding again to the protection of some of the basic rights provided by the Constitution (e.g. all Spanish citizens will be equal before the law independently of their sex, opinion or any other personal or social circumstance), drafters justify the new Act as the means to end a history of discrimination towards homosexuals. They recognise the essential role of gay-rights campaigners in the enactment of the reforming statute and, before concluding, briefly describe the effects and the changes brought about by the new Act.

The elaborate style of the preamble resembles other texts introducing new legal rules, where cross-references to other pieces of legislation and a tendency to verbosity are usual. Its purpose is to offer a reasoned argument in favour of the change in the law. On this occasion, the authors, stating the Government's case for same-sex unions, allude to the need to protect the fundamental rights of all members of society, as well as the obligation of lawmakers to adapt legislation to the ethos of contemporary times. They do so by exposing their ideas in a progressive, calm way. But, as far as the preamble is concerned, whether the grounds given to support the law are convincing enough or not, will depend more on the expectations of the particular reader than on the efficiency of the discourse.

5. Conclusions: social, legislative and linguistic reforms

Changes in the law are not always welcome. And this is the case of the new Act on marriage, which has been poorly received by conservative and religious groups as well as by a large number of citizens in Spain. Many of those against the reform claim that giving legal recognition to same-sex unions and calling them *marriage* mean going against the laws of tradition and custom, which have so far restricted this right to opposite-sex couples. Even some of the citizens who have welcomed the reforming statute may have difficulty in acknowledging from now on that homosexual partners will use the word *marry* to refer to their public commitment as a couple. It seems clear that the new law demolishes some deeply rooted "background assumptions" about marriage which we may have as members of a community. The idea of marriage exclusively linked to a man and a woman is still too strong to persuade most people brought up in a Catholic society like Spain that it is normal for two men or two women to go through the social process of getting married.

As the preamble itself states, "for the last two centuries, the Civil Code has reflected the dominant ideology, and it has not been necessary to ban, nor even refer to, same-sex marriage, since it was considered that the relationship between same-sex partners could not possibly develop into a legal marital relationship". As a consequence, the Civil Code did not expressly forbid same-sex partners to marry before the reform. There were even two sections devoted to the instances in which marriage was prohibited by law, and homosexual unions were not among these possibilities[13]. In fact, the Civil Code banned same-sex marriage by not mentioning it.

As I have already explained, in the fundamental provision of the Code regarding marriage (i.e. section 44), a paragraph has been added in order to indicate the extension of rights to include everyone regardless of their sex. But, before the enactment of the new Act, this section read as follows: *El hombre y la mujer tienen derecho a contraer matrimonio conforme a las disposiciones de este Código* ("Men and women are entitled to get married according to the provisions in this Code"). Thus, restricting the application of this provision to opposite-sex couples seems to confirm that the law was interpreted following the rule of statutory construction *expressio unius est exclusio alterius*, which is used in English law and establishes that expressing something means excluding what has not been mentioned[14]. In a similar manner, the rights contained in the other modified provisions were addressed in the past to pairs of citizens with a particular combination of sexes (i.e. a man and a woman), so that, as a consequence, those who were not mentioned were intrinsically prevented from enjoying these rights.

The Government's purpose behind the new Act is to do away with this discrimination because it considers that Spanish society has evolved into a different model of community, where same-sex couples exist and are generally respected by fellow citizens. Thus, as a result of a change in the behaviour and attitude of most Spaniards, legislators have redefined the social and legal meaning of the word *marriage*; and they have done so by neutralising all references to sex or gender in the new marriage provisions of the Civil Code. As a likely consequence of this legal reform, the whole concept of *marriage* will be progressively redefined in the future and will probably come to represent a reality far from the traditional idea of family and opposite-sex lifelong unions.

At this point, one could question whether the law has been modified because society behaves differently nowadays; or whether the way in which society comprehends the fact of marriage will be changed by the reforming legislation. From my point of view, both ideas are correct, since, as many authors have pointed out, "language does not just provide words for already existing concepts; it crystallizes and stabilizes ideas" (Fowler 1986:18). In this respect, the enactment of the new statute reflects a certain social reality and, at the same time,

[13] These are sections 46 and 47 of the Civil Code, which remain unaltered after the reform.

[14] Strasser (1997) offers an in-depth reasoned examination of US legislation and its recognition of same-sex unions, and describes situations where there is no express prohibition of homosexual marriage in the law.

reinforces a new definition of marriage and family where the sex of their components will no longer be a requirement.

By altering the linguistic expression of the old rule, the authors of the reforming statute have acted consistently with the idea that language is inevitably linked to social behaviour and change. Now it remains to be seen how long it will take for the new definition of *marriage* to become an intrinsic part of the community's "ideology" in the sense given by Fairclough (1989: 2): a "common-sense" assumption "implicit in the conventions according to which people interact linguistically, and of which people are generally not consciously aware".

References

BOE (Boletín Oficial del Estado) (2005). "Ley 13/2005, de 1 de julio, por la que se modifica el Código Civil en materia del derecho a contraer matrimonio." *BOE* 157 (2/7/2005): 23632-23634, http://www.boe.es

Castiñeira Palou, M. T. (1989). "Las leyes modificativas." In: GRETEL (Grupo de Estudios de Técnica Legislativa). *Curso de técnica legislativa*. Madrid: Centro de Estudios Constitucionales, 173-199.

Erdozain López, J. C. (ed.) (2004). *Código Civil*. 23rd ed. Madrid: Tecnos.

Fairclough, N. (1989). *Language and power*. Harlow: Longman.

Fowler, R. (1986). *Linguistic criticism*. Oxford: Oxford University Press.

GRETEL (1989). "Borrador de directrices sobre la forma y estructura de las leyes." In: GRETEL (Grupo de Estudios de Técnica Legislativa). *Curso de técnica legislativa*. Madrid: Centro de Estudios Constitucionales, 305-323.

Navarro-Valls, R. (1995). *Matrimonio y derecho*. Madrid: Tecnos.

Strasser, M. (1997). *Legally wed. Same-sex marriage and the Constitution*. Ithaca/London: Cornell University Press.

Part IV

STATUTORY INTERPRETATION

Anne Wagner
Université du Littoral Côte d'Opale
France

MAPPING LEGAL KNOWLEDGE

> "C'est cesser de montrer la langue comme un édifice construit d'un seul bloc, mais substituer à cette image celle d'un étal offrant des types linguistiques parmi lesquels on ne saurait choisir au hasard. C'est montrer comment ces variétés se répartissent selon les niveaux économiques, sociaux et culturels, comment elles peuvent ou non être adéquates à une situation donnée, comment elles jouent dans le mécanisme de la distinction" (Klinkenberg 2001: 43-44).

1. Introduction

Law is, by definition, the codification of modes of expression in a given society. However, its use is distinctive owing to the ways in which users apply or modify it. The shift in meaning between the product and its expression can be analysed not only within its content but also by means of the communication employed. The influence of spheres from the government and the legal profession is one of the main issues to explore.

Consequently, understanding the respective parts of legal discourse implies a deep analysis of three kinds of interference in the work under examination:

1) The linguistic method used: The semantic production, the articulation of its elements as well as the formation and meaning of its terms.
2) The method of legal conceptualisation: the analysis of the means employed to assure that the idea conforms to the implementation of the legal system under examination, and
3) The method of socialisation: its adequacy between the intention of the production and its application.

The jurist, being naturally a linguist, uses the subtleties of everyday language. Its flexibility in meaning allows him/her to specialise his/her discourse:

> There exists a real world understood in common as such by all members of the family, each of whom is capable of employing a shared discourse within a common interpretive framework of values, protocols and procedures. (Scott 1992: 176)

2. Anchorage of legal knowledge

Validating the meaning of an apparently obscure production is accompanied by an interpretive process. The interpreter will reveal his/her creative capacity when he/she masters this process. But there is no perfect example of readability. It is, then, the job of the user of interpretive rules to construct a coherent discourse, in symbiosis with the ideas of the source production. He/she will have to use the linguistic tools to clarify vague discourse and so adapt the meaning of terms to render legal texts more readable and clearer to all communities. As such, clarity is not a synonym for readability in a specific case. Only the interpretative capacity of the jurist permits him/her to uncover the meaning intended by the author (see Wagner and Cacciaguidi-Fahy 2006, Raymondis and LeGuern 1976).

As such, indeterminacy constitutes a relevant part of legal communication. It is like a dynamic game which aims to find a balance between social reality and law (Wagner 2005). For instance, for the purposes of arbitration or adjudication, the judge can make a choice among the available possibilities of meaning – i.e. plurality – that are advantageous for his/her legal reasoning. Consequently, he/she can determine the balance to be struck, since the possibility of more messages implies a larger set to select from.

Even when a decision is reached in a specific space and time, there is a high likelihood that other actors in some other space and time will try to re-negotiate this "equilibrium" (Wagner 2005: 175-178). Legal discourse is subject to plurality. However, legal predictability creates a strict framework for the conditions of its applications. The comprehension of thoughts is thereby facilitated; abusive comparisons, which interfere with the clarity of the law, are avoided and so cannot be considered as a means of oppression, or a menace:

> Les incertitudes du droit finissent à ce que le droit n'apparaît plus comme un moyen de protection mais comme un moyen d'oppression, comme une menace... (Hocreitère 2003: 143).

Bentham notes that the rules of law are not definitive and adapt themselves to the evolutions of society. He goes further in his analysis when stating that "Law is a kind of personification as if the Law were a living creature" (in Burn and Hart 1977). Plurality can, thus, become an instrument for shifts in meaning. A word with multiple senses is thus either a source of progress in the interpretation and application of the law, or a source of dissipation of sense with, as a corollary, diminishing legal predictability (Wagner 2004).

2.1. The social and contextual interpretation of data

Legal interpretation is a captivating activity for the jurist who can conceive hypotheses. The reader is seduced by the sophisticated repartee which is established between the law and the means of expression: language. It offers him/her the opportunity to enter the world of legal communication by his/her active participation in the comprehension of the law. As such, the debate over dynamism in legal discourse can be permanent. Some analyses have shown that interpretation is controlled by the evolution of systems of norm production; an evolution to which opportunist interpretative models are applied.

Two possibilities of transaction underlie any legal production. They are the consequence of the descriptive intention of the legislator: 1) what degree of flexibility is given to the user/interpreter of the rule?, and/or 2) what degree of rigidity will be imposed on him in the application?, will he/she have the capacity to "speak" or interpret the law? This ambiguity is perceivable in the formulation of Acts in France. Several years after their promulgation, some of them are still unenforceable as there is no decree of application. This subtle game of legal administration and its consequences is noticeable in numerous countries.

Research into the intention of the legislator gives the interpreter space within the confines of the text to produce a dynamic application of the law. In his/her search for meaning, he/she essentially uses semantic or syntactic tools and takes the consequences of the application of the law into account.

This contextual method, whose main focus is law, is recognised as being the modern method of interpretation, where dynamism and pragmatism show the intentional interventionism within interpretation. This modern method of interpretation is defined by Driedger (1983: 196), as follows:

> The words of an Act are to be read in their entire context and in their grammatical and ordinary sense harmoniously with the scheme of the Act, the object of the Act, and the intention of the Parliament.

This implies that the sense of the law in a general context is already determined. Its application must take into account the explicit elements to which are added the subjective parts coming from the user's comprehension of the intention of the legislator. The "free" parts include several foreseeable adjustments: what are the influences of the prescriptions on the appropriateness of the rule to its objective, the methods of investigation on the applicability as well as the results of external interventions? Sullivan (1994: 115) reminds us that:

> Courts are obliged to determine the meaning of legislation in its total context, having regard for the purpose of the legislation, the consequences of the proposed interpretations, the presumptions and special rules of interpretation as well as admissible external aids [...]. An appropriate interpretation is one that can be

> justified in terms of a) its plausibility, that is, its compliance with the legislative text; b) its efficacy, that is, its promotion of the legislative purpose; and (c) its acceptability, that is, the outcome is reasonable and just.

This notion of vagueness, subject to interpretation by the interpreter, is reviewed by Gendreau (2006: 108) when she asserts that the final product is only stable if:

> Ce flou engendre un espace spongieux capable d'absorber les changements extérieurs (le contexte) et de les intégrer dans l'environnement juridique et l'organisme administrative. Ce contexte constitué de faits et de valeurs affecte directement la signification du champ des possibilités des règles de compétences.

Perelman (1978: 37) goes further in explaining that:

> C'est la dialectique du législative et du judiciaire, de la doctrine et de l'autorité, du pouvoir et de l'opinion publique, qui fait la vie du droit et lui permet de concilier la stabilité et le changement.

Kalinowski (1978: 41-42) completes this definition when he states that:

> L'interprétation juridique est une interprétation pratique. Celui qui interprète un texte législatif (au sens large) veut arriver à savoir [...] comment il doit se comporter ou comment doit se comporter celui qu'il enseigne (cas du professeur de droit) ou conseille (cas de l'avocat par exemple). [...] Le législateur (au sens large) promulgue un certain nombre de textes posant des règles d'action, pouvant, voire devant guider ceux qui ont à agir. Aussi veut-on les connaître. Mais si elles se révèlent quelquefois ne pas être les règles qu'on cherche, on leur fait dire ce qu'on juge désirable.

Brink's (1989: 190) idea in relation to legal indeterminacy sheds some more light over the game of interpretation from a linguistic perspective when he states:

> Legal indeterminacy does not follow from semantic indeterminacy of legal provisions. This is because (a) the interpretation of a legal provision must also be guided by an appeal to its underlying purpose (abstract intent), and (b) what the law requires in a particular case is the decision that coheres best with the total body of legal standards, and not just what the correct interpretation of the closest legal provision, considered by itself, dictates. These two aspects of legal interpretation imply that a (fuzzy) case involving a provision that is semantically indeterminate may nonetheless be interpretively determinate.

2.2. A difficult choice: obscurity or clarity?

Côté (1999: 24) recalls in his treaty that the interpretation of law is a "creation subjected to constraints". This observation can be verified with legal professionals when they are construing meanings. They are compelled to use methods of interpretation that are recognized in order to modify semes, i.e. shifts in meaning (Vatvedt Fjeld 2005: 157-172).

Statutory law cannot provide a legal edifice with definitive certainty. Conveying a single and non-changeable degree of truth through a communicative process is impossible. While statutes are supposed to be implemented by the legislature as a consistent and binding statutory scheme, fuzziness in words within acts is presumed to reflect differences in the intended meaning and effect. Therefore, legislators have reworked the model of communication into one enabling interpretation of texts. LeBel (2001: 7) adds that "fringes" in vagueness have to be diminished to avoid implicitness as much as possible in the construing process:

> ne consiste-t-il pas à réduire autant que faire se peut, la marge de l'incertitude dans le contenu et les effets des engagements ? [...] On essaie aussi d'exclure le "non-dit" ou la part de l'implicite dans l'espoir de réduire le contrat à sa forme et à sa lettre, comme d'éviter les aléas des interprétations judiciaires.

White (1994: 34) notes that

> Each of us loads any expression with significances that derive from our prior experience of language and life... And it is not only words that mean differently to people, but the sentences and/or other utterances in which they appear, the cultural background against which they acquire their meaning, the silence into which they are intrusions.

In other words, indeterminacy is a medium of communication permitting the non-determination of the constituent words. But it is a "création encadrée de sens ". It can be an overtly "promoted" indeterminacy (Wagner 2005: 178-179). This new creation can have an influence over the drafters of law if they are conscious of the strategies of interpretation. They have the capacity to orientate the textual logic by using specific wording. These means can be increased or decreased depending on political, functional and linguistic orientations. The resulting drafting can also shift the source meaning. Mackaay (1999: xii) confirms this hypothesis when he writes:

> tout se passe comme si, implicitement, la tâche était de minimiser la somme des coûts de l'incertitude, de l'inadaptation et de la formulation du contrat. [...] L'incertitude provient ici de l'inopportunité de demander une plus grande précision à l'instrument juridique employé.

This construction confirms the creative capacity of the interpreter. However, this capacity highlights the weakness of the transmission of meaning. Indeed, the subjective influence of the author can lead to a complete change in meaning. Each rule has an indeterminate outer edge. As such, it can be compared to the "open texture" referred to by Hart (1976: 167-168) where:

> la texture ouverte de la règle de droit signifie qu'il existe, en effet, des domaines de conduite pour lesquels on laisse aux tribunaux ou à l'administration le soin de développer de nombreux points, en établissant une balance, à la lumière des circonstances, entre des intérêts concurrents dont les poids varient d'une espèce à l'autre [...] que ce soit à la frange des règles ou dans les domaines laissés ouverts par la théorie des précédents, les tribunaux remplissent une fonction de création de règles que les organes administratifs exercent principalement dans l'élaboration de directives variables.

In other words, the words used by drafters have enough potential meaning and variability and people cannot be certain of the intended meaning from drafters. There is rather a possibility of vagueness with possible shifts in meaning in space and time: socio-linguistic fuzziness (Wagner 2004). We are then more oriented towards a Peircean vision of interpretation, "a mirror of a society" (Wagner 2002: 243-293). As a consequence, "predicting everything is a pure fiction" (Portalis 1844-1992: 1).

From a semiotic viewpoint, the interpretation process means decoding at the same time the language and the context, but also the cultural constraints. The matrix of interpretation can vary from one culture to another; for, the meaning of a word, of a rule of law in an act reflects cultural norms, sociological systems and the legal culture of a state (Wagner et al 2005).

3. Strategy of legal communication

The interpreter of law integrates in his/her data collection new formulations which are combined with specific cognitive content. Consequently, saying that words have definably specific, bounded meanings is not that simple in law, since if this were the case, laws would be too rigid and only one single meaning would exist and fit only specific circumstances. The interpreter may take a fresh look at the meaning of a word, distinctive from that originally envisaged:

> A défaut alors d'avoir pu découvrir le sens d'un texte, l'interprète sera réduit à lui attribuer un sens (Côté P.A. 1999).

Indeterminacy can thus contaminate all words and only the ability of lawyers or judges may give them specific meanings. As such, the interpreter of law has to master completely the linguistic process – the discourse basis – and the capacity for assimilation of conceptualized terms. The method can work as follows:

1) To analyze terms that are not considered "concepts" in common language,
2) To determine the specific value from the legal community of a common language word, and
3) To carry out an expert analysis of the source language structure whose organization may shift the common meaning of a specific term.

Gérard Cornu (2000: 320) reminds us that:

> Le combat contre le vocabulaire courant est en porte-à-faux lorsqu'il vise des termes de ce vocabulaire qui sont chargés d'un sens technique de précision au regard du droit. Quant au rêve de les éliminer pour ne plus désigner les notions juridiques que par des termes d'appartenance exclusive, c'est une utopie dangereuse et une cause perdue.

Lenoble-Pinson (2005) also points to the various forms of shifts in meanings in the French language; for instance, the social reassignment of words. Consequently, the way to interpret these "motion pictures" (Malloy 1990: 211-215), or symbolic vehicles, depends upon the confrontation of their usual meaning against the use the state wants them to convey.

This unpredictability is highly visible in the administration of law, because content can become very specialized and so have to be deciphered by specific organizations concerned with finding coherence within legal discourses (Suspene 2006: 391-413). They try to meet the expectations of political authorities, who wish to have acts comprehensible by all citizens:

> Nos concitoyens veulent des lois claires, simples, stables – des lois qui disent sans équivoque ce qui est permis et ce qui ne l'est pas, qui soient écrites dans leur langage, le langage de notre temps (27 May 1975).

Consequently, behind each term we will not only find a specialized meaning but also a statute and/or a precedent. Gridel (1994) notices that legal language is a language of foolery which is within the reach of the initiated and not within the reach of laymen. Dupret (1998: 316) makes it clear that:

> what distinguishes, even more, the layman from the professional depends upon the context of their respective ability, of their belonging to different "communities" involved in different "pragmatics".

It is then necessary to know the cultural aspects within time and space, so that we may understand the social institutions of the country. Their written statements result from their "forms of life", and the "play on language" (Wittgenstein 1958: 146), which vary according to the "institutional practices of the interpreting community" (Fish 1980: 116). These intrusions lead to a sub-set varying according to time, space and social structure. This kind of organization modifies the content and the mode of reflection, which can only be understood by the study of interrelationships. Arnaud (1993: 231) draws out the importance of such a way of investigation, which cannot be conceived:

> sans faire appel aussi bien à l'ensemble des disciplines visant à décrire, analyser et expliquer l'apparition, le fonctionnement et les mécanismes de conversations d'un système social qu'aux nécessités logiques et techniques propres à un système juridique cohérent.

Plurality in meaning is thus an impediment to univocal knowledge. It is the root of the complexity of the message.

3.1. Plurality in meaning

Interpretation of meaning is therefore the result of historical phenomena which have their roots in the conception of discourses stamped with a common law tradition. This oral tradition has conferred on the rule of law both flexibility and rigidity when dealing with its interpretation. This problem of legibility is real. Indeed, in 1975 the English political authorities set up a parliamentary committee led by Lord Renton, whose aim was to analyze difficulties of comprehension and find solutions to them. The findings show that linguistic unpredictability can cause difficulties in legal textual interpretation:

> Une insécurité linguistique "contrôlée", pour être difficile, a l'avantage de favoriser un espace de remise en question continuelle, espace essentiel à l'ouverture aux autres et à la langue des autres. (Harvey and MacDonell 1997).

Discourses and the words used are tools that regulate rules, acts or any decision from public authorities. As such, the interpretation of law is currently made in light of its principal sources, which are statutory law and judicial precedents. Written words are of supreme authority, but are integrated in the logic of interpretive reasoning. This flexibility is proof that the capacity of the legislative discourse, which is situated, by Act, outside of time and space, can become a living reality. Butler (1997) defines its sense when she affirms that the language "remains alive when it refuses to 'encapsulate' or 'capture' the events and lives it describes." This doctrine is aimed at and authorizes the interpretation of discourse. The two elements that shape decisions are the power of deformation of concepts, and of a shift in meaning associated with vague outlines in discourse. Their use by the legislator is not accidental: it is the culmination of a voluntary act whose purpose is to simplify the formulation of written law. Indeterminacy is characteristic of the application of judicial precedent. In the domain of bioethics, for example, this process of simplifying, rationalizing and unifying discourse is expressed as follows:

> Devenant mondiale, l'institutionnalisation du langage de la bioéthique apparaît aussi plus ambiguë ou, plus exactement, les contradictions y sont fortes entre, d'un côté, la globalisation culturelle qui manifeste plutôt une tendance à l'uniformisation de type hégémonique et, d'un autre côté, l'universalisme des droits de l'homme qui se heurte, à l'inverse, au risque de fragmentation (Byk 2000: 27).

Legal discourse uses terms that have "lexical potentialities" as explained:

> Dans la charge juridique d'un terme, c'est-à-dire dans l'ensemble de son contenu intellectuel juridiquement relevant, la valeur est l'élément d'appoint qui exalte le sens, le sel du signifié [...] Elle est toujours destinée à épicer un texte. C'est une "*potentialité lexicale*" (Cornu 2000: 117).

The semantic content specializes the language according to the users' centres of interest. Thus trade jargon, technical uses or slang arise; each of them having specified criteria of use. This capacity of distortion creates a legal language; for law can give a peculiar meaning to some terms; what Cornu (2000: 117) refers to as "lexical potentiality". This potentiality consists in matching the meaning of a word to the present day context. The creation of "spaces in meaning" (Fish 1989: 129) confers on the rule of law, modified in its enforcement, a stability on which the rule of precedent can take roots: continuity is ensured between theory and practice. Fish also writes that:

> Les mots sont intelligible seulement si l'on admet l'hypothèse d'un contexte de production de l'intention, d'une pré-décision déjà en place de la part de la personne qui est en train de parler ou d'écrire ... Les sens ne sont pas enfouis dans les mots mais surgissent et deviennent clairs à la lumière des conditions de fond et d'intelligibilité qui les entourent. (Fish 1989: 150).

However, we must not mistake appearance(s) where interpretation can hide various thoughts (Pont 1884: 6). Indeed, in law terminological margins are difficult to find. Only some legal genres have been able to set up semantic borders. Statutory discourse is one of them. This discourse can determine terminological definitions of words that may be difficult to comprehend. Consequently, having legal determination of words can ease the understanding process for all communities. But it does not mean that semantic indeterminacy is once and for all avoided. Indeterminacy will only cease when one momentary experience (i.e. a case in court) is considered. It will then turn into a contextualized determinacy:

> Because the meaning of language is inherently contextual, we have declined to deem a statute "ambiguous", for purposes of lenity merely because it was possible to articulate a construction more narrow than that urged by the Government (Solan 2004: 859).

In other words, indeterminacy is a mode of communication permitting the non-determination of constituent words. Words in law lack effective referents. They are idle, they are not connected with a "living reality" but with statutes, and their determination will be provided only when exemplified. Even the simplest words ("person" and "night" in this case) can have an abundance of meanings in the light of distinctive Acts. In the 1828 Statute of Frauds Amendment Act, for example, it is provided that *person* includes a *corporation*. Under the 1978 Interpretation Act, *person* includes a body of persons corporate or unincorporated. Finally, in the 1845 Railway Clauses Consolidation Act, *person* includes a limited company. As a consequence, statutory wording is not a closed system but has an open texture where relative indeterminacy is used to interpret statutes (Wagner 2005):

> Parliament often uses general words intentionally in the belief that judges are the most adept in filling in the details (Freeman 1994).

> Il apporte ces nuances, ces gradations, ces ménagements qui sont indispensables à toute bonne politique (Lenain 1992: 11).

This evasive criterion, "fuyance" (Gény 1922: 173), can be also analysed through the example of *night*, having different meanings within the ambit of three English Acts:

> What time shall be considered night: provided always that for the purposes of this Act the night shall be considered and is hereby declared to commence at the expiration of the first hour of sunset, and to conclude at the beginning of the last hour before sunrise (Night Poaching Act 1828, s.12)

> "night" means the period between 11 p.m. and 5 a.m. (Customs and Excise Management Act 1979, s. 1)

> … means the time between half an hour after sunset and half an hour before sunrise (Highways Act 1980, s. 329(1)).

Cornu (2000: 89) highlights the influence of statutory law over polysemy when he writes:

> de la loi ne peut venir aucune action d'ensemble contre la polysémie. Mais cette réserve une place à des interventions déterminées sur le postulat qu'il est de bonne politique, quand cela est possible, de tempérer les inconvénients de la polysémie. Ainsi le législateur peut-il entreprendre certaines actions régulatrices correspondant à

> une sorte d'auto-limitation de l'usage de la polysémie, ou même à prendre des initiatives destinées à prévenir la formation de la polysémie.

As such, neutrality in legal discourse does not exist. Interpretation plays a crucial role in law. But it is often subject to controversy as to the potential semantic interpretation (Wagner 2005). Lenain (1992: 96) also gives some new insights into the consequences of indeterminacy within the sphere of politics and the importance of reasoning in an "unsteady environment".

3.2. Thoughts on "unsteady environment" in legal discourse

Delpérée (2006: 481-493) shows the difficulties of associating the concept "neutrality" with an unsteady environment in the long term. He emphasizes the fact that legal drafting imposes a global approach without neglecting possible interferences when deciphering other documents, parliamentary reports and discourses from the executive (Delpérée 2006: 484-485). As a "faiseur de loi", he (2006: 486-487) demonstrates how difficult it is to combine, in the process of legal drafting, stylistics, legal content and general political discourse:

> Un impératif, en particulier, est souvent perdu de vue. C'est celui de la cohérence, celui de la logique interne du corpus législatif. Mes collègues sont prêts à accepter une réforme législative dès l'instant où elle répond à leurs préoccupations. Ils ne se demandent jamais "après" quelle disposition et "avant" quelle autre disposition le nouveau texte va s'insérer. Ils ne se demandent pas si le nouveau texte préserve l'unité du vocabulaire, de style et, plus fondamentalement encore, de préoccupations. Ils ne s'interrogent pas sur ce que l'on appelait naguère "l'économie générale de la loi".

Neutrality is a legal fiction. Indeterminacy still remains necessary for the comprehension, for instance, of European multilingualism. Obscurity is vital so as to translate the meaning of legal texts in different languages, but causes some difficulties in the current management of law. As such, the transfers of legal data as to their source legal meaning are subject to interferences from the multiple translations carried out (see e.g Doczekalska, Gotti or Šarčević, this volume).

Among the difficulties of understanding normative text (Bergeal 2004), we can find semes specific to legal discourse (Pendleton 1992). Indeed, the user is not only confronted with the meaning of law and its interpretation but also with its possible shifts in space and time. He/she will use – consciously or not – a process of deconstruction. His/her first step will be to deconstruct the primary meaning to better understand the use of simple elements, which may be vital for use, i.e. pronouns, articles, modals (Wagner 1999). And his/her last step will be to position his/her interpretation within space and time and perhaps to adapt it to the evolution of society. The English Interpretation Act 1978 is a good example, as it provides that:

> words importing the masculine gender include the feminine;
> words importing the feminine gender include the masculine, and
> words in the singular include the plural and words in the plural include the singular.

Proponents of a better understanding of law – either specialists or lay people – seem to adhere to specific actions, i.e. the symbolization, codification, normalization or standardization of legal language. The prime goal is to avoid conflicts in communication and to aim at a better discourse coherence. This idea is not new, in fact. Berriat-Saint-Prix (1835) tried to demonstrate that a good style depended on correctly employed expressions. He listed ten potential mistakes (Berriat-Saint Prix: 43), but most of them are still committed nowadays (Adler M. 2006):

> **Première**: termes et expressions barbares;
> **Deuxième**: termes et expressions qui ont vieilli;
> **Troisième**: inversions forcées et inutiles;
> **Quatrième**: tournures extraordinaires ou obscures, constructions vicieuses;
> **Cinquième**: accumulations superflues de termes synonymes pour exprimer la même idée;
> **Sixième**: régime des verbes mis à des cas différents de ceux que ces verbes exigent;
> **Septième**: temps des verbes employés hors des relations qu'ils expriment;
> **Huitième**: emploi d'un trop grand nombre de termes latins ou techniques;
> **Neuvième**: suppression de mots qui sont des parties nécessaires de certaines expressions composées; et
> **Dixième**: phrases longues outre mesure, et où l'on exprime plusieurs idées, ou raconte plusieurs faits qui exigeraient des phrases séparées.

4. Case study: Analyzing "parity" in French legal discourse

In June 1998, Mr. Lionel Jospin, the French Prime Minister, brought to the desk of the parliamentary assemblies a constitutional bill dealing with equal opportunities between women and men. The lawyers wondered about including it in the hierarchy of French legal norms. How can one situate equality between women and men, given that it is clearly stated in the preamble to the Constitution of 4 October 1958?

The constitutional council remained very cautious and invalidated the parity in the new electoral rules elaborated by the Parliament in January 1999. The French government urged legislators to persevere in the elaboration of positive discriminations/affirmative actions.

4.1. An outfit for equality or an instrument to "make" equality?

The constitutional bill dated 19 April 1946 showed in its preamble and "declaration of human rights" its willingness to recognize equality of both sexes in the enjoyment of liberties and in social and economic rights. Within the scope of Article 1, after the definition of freedom and equality, subsection 2 gives women the same rights as those of men before the law and in all fields. Articles 24, 28 and 38 reinforce the enjoyment of these rights by the assertion of women's prerogatives to accede to social and professional life in accordance with the dignity recognized to all citizens. These elements are partially repeated in the Constitution of the Fourth Republic of 27 October 1946, where the preamble underlines the equality of rights between women and men in all fields.

The Constitution of the Fifth Republic of 4 October 1958 sums up these rights by repeating in its preamble the French people's attachment to national sovereignty as defined by the Declaration of the Rights of Man and of the Citizen of 1789, confirmed and completed by the preamble to the Constitution of 1946.

Parliamentary discourse rests on these constitutional foundations to affirm the specialization of specific rights to women whose discriminative function is to ensure equality before the law of all citizens, without distinction of origin, race or religion. The French members of Parliament legitimate their interventions with contributions aiming at integrating, explicitly, equality within the scope of the constitutional Bill. Numerous questions over the judiciousness of the forthcoming legal tools were raised when contemplating this difficult and theoretical specification, because of its discriminatory trend and its concrete use.

The integration of equality for women and men in the Constitution does underline the foundations of the democratic and republic system. The suggested reform has no direct legal effect, but a supposed intention, even an inflamed obligation with its inscription into legal norms. This legal logic is used in order to implement means of action over a fact which has not been, until now, part of its sphere of possible action. Therefore, the link of causation has not yet been validated by the constitutional judge. We can notice that the reform was aimed at correcting a fact; the access for women to parity of elective positions.

Consequently, the legislator is not satisfied with the principles drafted by the Declarations of the Rights of Man and of the Citizens of 26 August 1789, which only uses the term "man" to specify rights and duties. The legislator wanted to clarify the generic definition:

> all citizens, being equal in the eyes of the law, are equally eligible to all dignities and to all public positions and occupations, according to their abilities, and without distinction except that of their virtues and talents.

The drafters of the bill reckoned that the abilities, virtues and talents had to be completed by the specification of women's equality to accede to mandates and positions. Mr Didier, a French Deputy, confirmed on 15 December 1998 at the National Assembly that "a criterion has not yet been listed within the republican virtues: the female sexual gender".

However, the willingness to draft favourable conditions for the access of women to mandates and positions led to an institutionalization of the differences between sexes. To admit that women could have a right of way over men and could be elected just because of their sexual gender raised two issues: the existence of a procedure which is not explicitly stated: parity; and the temptation of discrimination against women exacerbated by the implementation of relevant measures.

The Constitution recalls in Title I that national sovereignty belongs to the people, who exercise it through their representatives and by way of referendum. The link between the governed and the governing is the voting system whose criteria are laid down in the Constitution and in the electoral code. Article 3 specifies that the right to vote is enjoyed by all French nationals of either sex. Therefore, the French legislators do not have to affirm the concept of "equality", but do have to determine how law can become more flexible, so that the concept may integrate the notion of parity in the arbitration of the voting.

In his political speech of 19 June 1997, the Prime Minister made it clear that a constitutional bill could "enable female French citizens to have an active part, openly, public life". The members' contributions to the debate on the bill were relevant to the issues of parity and equality.

At the National Assembly, on 15 December 1998, Mr Bacquet reminded the House that

> behavioural scientists have reckoned that at the rate registered since 50 years, it might take at least 500 years to accede to parity.

His intervention reinforces the idea that the solution results far more from a change in mentalities than from legal normalization. On the very same day, Mr Paul stressed the fact that

> the critics of our institutions take into consideration the disparity between law and facts, between proclaimed rights and the real rights enjoyed.

Mrs Bachelot-Narquin used a metaphor to insist upon the importance of the constitutional Bill as follows:

> the key we are going to turn together so as to open political power to women who have been excluded from it for such a long time (Bachelot-Narquin 1998: 17).

Mrs Casanova pointed out in her intervention that

> humanity should be legitimately represented under its twofold form, either feminine or masculine, to avoid traps of an asexual abstraction of the citizen, which always declines itself in the masculine (Bachelot-Narquin 1998: 19).

This contribution to the debate is of real interest, for it positions the issue not on a semantic or legal basis but on the insidious monopoly of power. The restoring of an equilibrium, referred to as "parity" by some people, can only be conceived with the implementation of related means enabling women to take on the positions they were longing to obtain. The birth of the idea of *positive discrimination/affirmative action* seems to be one of the solutions which could meet the members' expectations. Under this term, one can contemplate a series of legislative and statutory measures facilitating the access of women to public positions by eliminating constraints women experience in their social, professional and family activities.

This discriminatory conception is in compliance with the Convention of the United Nations concerning the elimination of all forms of discrimination against women that France signed in July 1980 and ratified in December 1983. This convention authorizes the States Parties to take temporary special measures in order to fight against discriminations in public life.

4. 2. The problematic construction of the bill

The bill was introduced to the desks of Parliament by Jospin's government, whose main trends and sensitivities differ with respect to the valuation of equality/parity between women and men. The bill is seeking to create a legal anchorage basis for the production of temporary norms whose aim is the elimination of all discrimination against women, under the constitutional Council's supervision. The Council made public its view on 18 November 1982:

> Yet ... the quality of citizen opens the right to vote and to eligibility in similar conditions ... without drawing a distinction between voters and eligible persons because of their sexual gender.

How can we be precise about the jurisprudential meaning without thwarting the real spirit of the Constitution?

4.2.1. Modalities of the constitutional revision

Therefore, the main hurdle to be overcome is the foreseeable hostility of the constitutional Council to the system of quotas proposed in 1982. This hostility can be examined in relation to specific conditions for a constitutional reform in compliance with Article 89:

> The right to propose amendments to the Constitution belongs currently to the President of the Republic, on the proposal of the Prime Minister, and to members of Parliament. The amending project or proposal must be passed by the two assemblies in identical terms. The amendment becomes effective when it has been approved by referendum. However, the amending project is not submitted to a referendum when the President of the Republic decides to submit it to Parliament, meeting as Congress; in this case the amendment is accepted only if it obtains a majority of three-fifths of the votes cast. The Bureau of the Congress is that of the National Assembly. The amendment procedure may not be initiated or pursued when the integrity of the territory is under attack. The Republican form of government is not subject to revision.

Using the voting procedure after the agreement of the two assemblies (by the Congress with a 3/5 majority, or by way of referendum) lays the bill open to the constitutional judge's rejection. The referendum path is the best solution (Article 11), since the bill adopted by the people leads the Council to refuse to control its constitutionality. Indeed, this initiative belongs only to the President of the Republic. However, we can stress that in the French political news where the keynote is cohabitation, the President did not express his will to take that initiative; the revision being instituted by the Parliament in compliance with the procedure forecasted under the Article 89.

Thus, constitutional reform is being used so as to integrate positive discriminatory measures. The claim for equality (parity) is nurtured in discourses about the crisis of representation, especially the distortion in meanings between the electorate, as the real representation, and the people and the nation, as theoretical abstractions. Consequently, the specification of women's representation collides with constitutional texts favouring sovereignty instead of this discourse.

4.2.2. Semantic difficulties for the integration of the bill in Title I - Sovereignty

The bill was instituted in June 1998 in the form of a unique Article and was introduced for a first reading at the National Assembly:

> The following subsection is added to Article 3 of the Constitution of 4 October 1958: "law favours equal access for women and for men to mandates and positions".

This definition was very similar to the one suggested by Professor Debbash in September 1993 during an interview at Parité – Info. However, this drafting gave rise to a series of critiques and reflections about its terminological contents.

The term "parity" did not explicitly arise in the drafting, contrary to the will of the Observatory for Parity. In its report, it recommended modification of Article 3 of the Constitution by integrating into the drafting the term "parity" – it was then referred to as "equal access" (Halimi 1998: 6-7). For the Observatory, there was a lack of precision in its meaning. For members of the commission for constitutional laws that notion was too restrictive (Colcombet and Tosca 1998: 6-7). Indeed, parity refers to a mathematical determinism impossible to implement, whereas the notion of equal access does not impose an obligation but establishes an ability.

The use of the verb "favour" generated criticism over its lack of guarantees at the implementation stage. Some say that it could leave the door wide open to temporary measures but also to quotas (Bachelot-Narquin 1998: 17). For others, this verb could result in incentive measures which are said to be difficult to implement: it must either disappear or become more explicit.

Its use came from an agreement reached during the period of cohabitation. Its content of weak legal impact could enable, because of its fuzziness, the consolidation of constitutional jurisprudence; but it could also disarm the drafter when he wished to circumvent it (Colcombet and Tosca 1998: 3-4). It would be better to use more "active" or "participative" verbs such as *assure* or *determine*. Thus, the law-making process could be interrupted by the constitutional judge who would notice the dissimilarity between equality and parity.

The French members of Parliament considered that the generic terms "mandates" and "positions" lacked qualification. They were amended so as to avoid any submission and became "electoral mandates" and "elective positions". There was a final remark on the whole sentence ("[the law] favours equal access for women and for men to mandates and positions"). The fact of specifying women and men could leave the door wide open to either sex for constitutional actions. According to Mrs Aubert, a member who spoke at the Assembly on 15 December 1998, this sentence would go completely against the preamble to the Constitution, which guarantees equality. That is the reason why an amendment was proposed during the second reading at the National Assembly and was adopted in the definitive version of the unique Article:

> law determines conditions under which is organized equal access for women and for men to electoral mandates and to elective positions.

This new drafting asserted the role of the legislator, reinforced the willingness for real equality, excluded the possible risks of constitutional actions and brought a more important legal guarantee to this device. Nevertheless, the Senate – in its second reading – kept the initial formula, which seemed "to define in a less rigid way the exact line of the possible legislative provisions" (Cabanel 1998-1999: 7) and put forward the following version:

> Article 1
> Article 3 of the Constitution of 4 October 1958 is completed by the following subsection: law favours equal access for women and for men to electoral mandates and elective positions.

4.2.3. The choice of the location and the legal impact of the Article voted by Parliament in Title I

Most members of Parliament consider the final text as imperfect on the legal plane. Its content and impact do not add anything to the current constitutional prescriptions. Consequently, the legislative logic aiming at instituting – in reality – equal representation between women and men has to rely on the neutrality of the approved text, which is non-prescriptive. Any type of legislation to follow has to find part of its roots in this legal anchorage, which is already unsteady.

The article is designed to authorize the Parliament to pass discriminatory Acts which cannot be censured by the constitutional Council. This kind of reshuffle should entitle the emergence of effective women's representation in the formulation of rules of law.

The legal impact of this revision will only be effective when prescriptions are subject to application texts (issued from the legislature or from the executive). The Senate's fuzziness in writing, which would prefer the verb "favour" as the driving force for a change in the French Constitution, might be a brake upon forthcoming productions. This wording does not clearly show the initially-desired drafting of the National Assembly. The room to manoeuvre, which seems very broad, can generate shifts in the effective implementation of equality. We should also talk about the weak performative meaning in the semantics, which could turn the constitutional judge into a judge of opportunity. His opinion will be demanded for the adoption of an organic law and will lead him, for instance, to construe the enforcement of mixity or of parity - if any. So, the only solution could result from a domestic reshuffle of the Council, which some lawyers consider to be conservative. The alternative could be limiting the legislative reform to the Lower Chamber only, which would result in circumventing the control of constitutionality, whereas the Senate could use the same legislative logic to establish equality within its Chamber.

Two possibilities were proposed to the legislator: an amendment of Article 3 or of Article 4. Some members of Parliament preferred the latter. However, Mrs Guigou - the French Minister of Justice - said that this amendment could deprive users of a broader legal impact:

> Giving such a responsibility only to parties could mean leaving it to their discretion, when in fact, it is because of their inaction that the government has instituted the current constitutional reform (Guigou 1999: 6).

There has been a breach and a specialization in the republican system of the current national and popular representation since the declaration of 1789 (Millard and Ortiz 1998: 189-203) by the specialization of “humanity” (Roudy 1999: 2) in its irreducible mixity. The revision will both contribute to clearing the 1982 jurisprudence away and to instituting effectively “positive discrimination” in a French legal document.

This constitutional reform has, according to its drafters and academics, just a “display” effect. Its validity will only be justified when a legislative electoral production is instituted determining, for instance, the modalities of ballot. Contemplation of a reversal of the Council’s jurisprudence can be forecast. The Council has already reversed its jurisprudence about the rights of asylum seekers – an imperfect text on the legal plane, without any meaning and any impact, which added nothing to the Constitution – and decided to record formally that the Constitution had been reviewed so as to clear the obstacle away and to bow to it (Carcassonne 1998: 17). The instituted constitutional bases do have the potential to promote equality, but how will it be carried out within a society where more than 90 per cent of political positions are held by men? What kind of electoral devices will promote equality in candidates or elected people? (Aubert 1998).

4.3. The reason for a positive discrimination

With the ratification of the UNO Convention, France is undergoing an irreversible process which is to undertake the embodiment of the principle “discriminations against women must be suppressed” in its domestic laws. This convention reaffirms the establishment of different steps for the implementation of temporary special measures against discrimination in public life.

4.3.1. Regulation by imposed and appropriate measures

The establishment of quotas as an imposed measure was denied and declared unconstitutional by the constitutional Council on November 18, 1982. So, the legislator can only refer to the Convention ratified in December 14, 1983 whose policy aims at eliminating all forms of discrimination against women and at adopting appropriate positive discriminatory measures so as to accelerate the process.

During the first reading, the National Assembly denied the inscription of the reform within the ambit of Article 4, deciding that it would be more valuable to integrate it within the field of Article 3 whose aim is the guarantee of the sovereign system. But the Senate affirmed, during the first debates, that the Bill was connected to the modalities of political parties' exercises. The Lower Chamber put forward the possibility of sanctions against parties which did not implement women's modalities of access. In its second reading, the Senate estimated that:

> the conditions of establishing equal access to mandates and positions should abide by the constitutional principle of freedom of parties enshrined in the Article 4 of the Constitution. Thus, it seems necessary that this Article should be revised if one wishes to adjust the parties' financing under unquestionable legal conditions (Cabanel G., 1998-1999: 12).

Members of the Upper Chamber proposed the drafting of a second Article within the project of the revision whose role would be to specify the meaning of the modified Article 3. The Senate did not give up its first idea, i.e. the specification of parties' interference in polls. Its proposal met the members' contributions expressed during the debates, i.e. "political parties hold one of the main keys to accede to equality" (Assemblée Nationale, 10 March 1994: 4).

An Article 2 (new) in the project submitted by the Senate (Cabanel G., 1998-1999: 8) was accepted and integrated during the third reading at the National Assembly:

> Article 2 (new)
> Article 4 of the Constitution is completed by the following subsection: they (parties) contribute to the implementation of the expressed principle in the last subsection of the Article 3 in the conditions laid down in law.

4.3.2. Unremitting fight for equality

The discriminatory Act in its reductive use of inequalities of treatment must, so as not to remain a supposed Act, open the door to legislators' new reflections. Therefore, the state should clearly forecast political parity by Acts imposing and guaranteeing women's representation. It would not be sensible to be satisfied with the recommendations from either the Observatory or European bodies (Tavares da Silva 1998: 218-232). Millard (1998: 272-273) called to mind the technical modes of enforcement of parity in European, regional, and municipal elections through voting using the system of proportional representation.

The reflection upon the implementation of the voting, quoted above, is wide open when one contemplates constituencies where elections are held on a majority basis. For instance, the granting of a double vote in each constituency would lead to increasing the number of politically elected representatives. But is this not a reasonable price to pay - Millard underlined – to have an equal democracy?

The change in mentalities suggests that the political representation within French society should be based upon "political biodiversity" (Albertini 1998: 20). Inequality in the treatment of women in public life was partly generated by the constitutional Council's jurisprudence and by "a discrimination exercised by the political class whose mentality and behaviours are behind the general evolution of society". Today, we must build up a tangible reality where the alterity of Women-Men would be of importance. This bill, unanimously adopted in the third reading by the National Assembly, does not settle the issue of equality: it opens a new way.

5. Conclusion

Mapping legal knowledge aims at having a better understanding of legal texts by 1) highlighting all the key discursive elements conveying the message, and 2) showing the logical order that links phrases and paragraphs between them. Indeterminacy is then a necessary tool and involves rhetorical speculation, or sometimes rhetorical invention that resembles more "a doctrine akin to that of the 'free finding of law'" (Watson 1985: 86) and can lead to the creation of a new reality. Therefore, the question of reassigning meaning to words and playing with words will continue to be a core issue in legal adjudication, since any word can be subject to interpretation, as was also the case with "tomatoes" in 1893 (cf. Nix v. Hedden) where the US Supreme Court had to decide whether they were fruit or vegetables (cf. Solan 2004). Acts open avenues for interpretive struggle and only the interpretive processes from judges can give a solution, specific to a case and to a period of time.

References

Adler, M. (2006). *Clarity for Lawyers: Effective Legal Writing*. London: The Law Society.

Albertini, P. (1998). Compte-rendu n°14. *Commissions des lois constitutionnelles, de la législation et de l'administration générale de la République*.

Arnaud, A. J. (1993). *Dictionnaire encyclopédiques de théorie et de sociologie du droit*. Paris: LGDJ.

Assemblée Nationale (10 March 1994). Compte-rendu n°38. Commission des lois constitutionnelles, de la législation et de l'administration générale de la République.

Assemblée Nationale (2 December 1998). Compte-rendu n°28, Projet de loi constitutionnel relatif à l'égalité entre les femmes et les hommes.

Assemblée Nationale (15 December 1998). Compte-rendu analytique officiel.

Aubert, M. H. (1998). 3ème Séance: égalité Femmes-Hommes: exception d'irrecevabilité. *Assemblée Nationale*, Compte-rendu analytique officielle.

Bachelot-Narquin, R. (1998). Compte-rendu n°14. *Assemblée Nationale, Commissions des lois constitutionnelles, de la législation et de l'administration de la République.*

Berriat-Saint-Prix, J. (1835). "Discours sur les vices du langage judiciaire". In: *Journal des Avoués.*

Brink, D. O. (1989). "Semantics and Legal Interpretation". In: *Canadian Journal of Law and Jurisprudence* 2(2), 181-191.

Burn, J. H. and H. L. A. Hart (eds.) (1977). *Jeremy Bentham, A Comment on the Commentaries and A Fragment on Government*. London: Athlone Press.

Butler, J. (1997). *Excitable Speech: A Politics of the Performative*. London: Routledge.

Byk, C. (ed.) (2000). *La bioéthique: un langage pour mieux se comprendre*. Paris: Editions.

Cabanel, G. (1998-1999). Rapport 247. *Sénat*: projet de loi constitutionnel relatif à l'égalité entre les femmes et les hommes.

Carcassonne, G. (1998). Compte-rendu n°14. *Assemblée Nationale, Commission des lois constitutionnelles, de la législation et de l'administration de la République.*

Catherine Bergeal (2004). *Rédiger un texte normatif.* Paris: Berger Levrault.

Perelman (1978), "L'interprétation juridique". In: *Archives de Philosophie du droit*, Vol. XVII.

Colcombet, F. and C. Tosca (1998). Compte-rendu n°28. *Assemblée Nationale, Commission des lois constitutionnelles, de la legislation et de l'administration générale de la République.*

Cornu, G. (2000). *La Linguistique Juridique*. Paris: Montchrestien.

Côté, P. A. (1999). *Interprétation des Lois*. Québec: Thémis.

Delpérée, F. (2006). "Comme aurait dit Boileau…". In A. Wagner and S. Cacciaguidi-Fahy (eds.), *Legal Language and the Search for Clarity*. Bern: Peter Lang, 481-493.

Driedger, A. (1983). *The Construction of Statutes*. Toronto: Butterworths.

Dupret, B. (1998), "La typification des atteintes aux bonnes moeurs". In: *International Journal for the Semiotics of Law* 11(33), 316- 334.

Fish, S. (1980). *Is there a Text in This Class ?* Cambridge: Harvard University Press.

Fish, S. (1989). *Respecter le Sens Commun.* Paris: LGDJ.

Freeman, M. D. A. (1994). *Lloyd's introduction to jurisprudence*. London: Sweet and Maxwell.

Gendreau, Y. (ed.) (2006). *Le Lisible et l'Illisible / The Legible and the Illegible.* Montréal: Les Editions Thémis.

Gény, F. (1922). *Sciences et Techniques en Droit Privé Positif,* Vol.1. Paris: Recueil Sirey.

Gridel, J. P. (1994). *Introduction au droit et au droit français*. Paris: Dalloz.

Guigou, E. (1999). Rapport n°1377. *Assemblée Nationale.*

Halimi, G. (1998). Compte-rendu n°14. *Assemblée Nationale, Commission des lois constitutionnelles, de la législation et de l'administration générale de la République.*

Hart, H. L. A. (1976). *Le concept de droit.* Bruxelles: Facultés Universitaires Saint-Louis.

Harvey J. C. and A. MacDonell (1997) ."La Francophonie sur les marges". In : *Actes du XVI colloque, Centre d'études francophones canadien de l'Ouest,* Univ. De Winnipeg: 17-19 Oct. 1996. Winnipeg: Presses Universitaires St Boniface.

Hocreitère, P. (2003). "Sécurité et insécurité juridiques après la loi Solidarité et Renouvellement urbains". In: *Revue Française de Droit Administratif.* January - February, 141-153.

Kalinowski, G. (1978). "Philosophie et logique de l'interprétation en droit". In: *Archives de Philosophie du droit*, Vol. XVII.

LeBel, L. (2001). *Incertitudes contractuelles et incertitudes judiciaires*. Montréal: Les Editions Thémis.

Lenain, P. (1992). *Le flou politique*. Paris: Economica.

Mackaay, E. (ed.) (1999). *Les incertitudes du droit* Montréal: Editions Thémis.

Malloy, R. P. (1990). "A Sign of the Times – Law and Semiotics, Reviewing Roberta Kevelson". In: *Tulane Law Review* 65, 211-215.

Lenoble-Pinson, M. (2005). *Mettre au féminin.* Conseil Supérieur de la Langue Française.

Millard, E. and L. Ortiz (1998). "Les voies juridiques de la parité: débats". In : J. Martin (ed.), *La Parité enjeux et mise en œuvre.* Toulouse: Presses Universitaires du Mirail.

Pendleton, M. (1992). "Creating a Vocabulary and a Conceptual Ordering Device for Conferring Appropriate Rights in Information: The Challenge for Law". In: R. Kevelson (ed.), *Law and The Human Science*. New York: Peter Lang, 301-317.

Pont, P. (1884). *Commentaire – Traité des societies civiles et commerciales*, Vol. 1. Paris: Hachette.

Portalis, J.-E.-M. (1844-1992). “Discours préliminaire sur le projet du Code Civil”. In: *Discours et rapports sur le Code civil*. Coll. Bibliothèque de philosophie politique et juridique, Centre de Philosophie politique et juridique URA-CNRS, Université de Caen.

Raymondis, L. M. and M. Le Guern (1976). *Le langage de la Justice Pénale*. Paris: CNRS.

Roudy, Y. (1999). 2ème séance: Parité Hommes-Femmes. *Assemblée Nationale*.

Scott, W. T. (1992). “The Empire of Signs and the Information Revolution”. In: Kevelson, R. (ed.), *Law and The Human Science*. New York: Peter Lang.

Solan, L. (2004). “Pernicious Ambiguity in Contracts and Statutes”. In: *Chicago-Kent Law Review* 79, 859-877.

Sullivan, R. E. (1994). *Driedger, On the Construction of Statutes*. Toronto: Butterworths.

Suspene, A. (2006). “Clarification et simplification du langage administratif en France – L’expérience du COSLA : Un aspect de la réforme de l’Etat”. In: A. Wagner, and S. Cacciaguidi-Fahy (eds.), *Legal Language and the Search for Clarity*. Bern: Peter Lang, 391-413.

Tavares da Silva, M. R. (1998). “Politiques de la Communauté et du Conseil de l’Europe”. In: J. Martin (ed.), *La Parité enjeux et mise en œuvre*. Toulouse: Presses Universitaires du Mirail, 218-232.

The Preparation of Legislation, report of a committee appointed by the Lord President of the Council. Chairman: The Rt Hon Sir David Renton, Cmnd. 6053, May 1975.

Vatvedt Fjeld, R. (2005). “The Lexical Semantics of Vague Adjectives”. In: V. Bhatia, J. Engberg, M. Gotti and D. Heller (eds.), *Vagueness in Normative Texts*. Bern: Peter Lang, 157-172.

Wagner, A. (1999). “La validité de la normalisation législative anglaise”. In: *International Journal for the Semiotics of Law* 12(1), 3-26.

Wagner, A. (2002). *La Langue de la Common Law*. Paris: L’Harmattan.

Wagner, A. (2004). “Le diagnostic de la pluralité en droit médical anglais et ses implications”. *Semiotica* 151(1/4), 183-200.

Wagner, A., Summerfield, T. and F. S. Benavides Vanegas (2005). *Contemporary Issues of the Semiotics of Law*. London: Hart Publishing.

Wagner, A. (2005). “Semiotic Analysis of the Multistage Dynamic at the Core of Indeterminacy in Legal Language”. In: V. Bhatia, J. Engberg, M. Gotti and D. Heller (eds.), *Vagueness in Normative Texts*. Bern: Peter Lang.

Wagner, A. and S. Cacciaguidi-Fahy (eds.) (2006). *Legal Language and the Search for Clarity*.Bern: Peter Lang.

Watson, A. (1985). *Sources of Law, Legal Change and Ambiguity*. Philadelphia: University of Pennsylvania Press

White, J. B. (1994). *Justice as Translation.* Chicago/London: The University of Chicago Press.
Wittgenstein, L. (1958). *Philosophical Investigations.* Oxford: Basil Blackwell.

Jarosław Wyrembak
University of Warsaw
Poland

EXPLORING THE LIMITATIONS OF STATUTORY INTERPRETATION: SOME REMARKS ON POLISH SUPREME COURT'S APPROACH TO THE INTERPRETATION OF SELECTED CRIMINAL LAW PROVISIONS

1. Introduction

In contemporary theory and philosophy of law, the lexical level of binding provisions is ascribed a varying degree of significance. At some point, this textual level is treated with utmost importance. In the literature on legal theory, there is the assumption that the substance of a legal norm is determined solely by the textual elements of the text constituting binding provisions. Inevitably, such a position makes it possible to refer to extra-textual or extra-linguistic reasons only in the case of serious doubts related to an interpretation implied by the linguistic structure of a provision under consideration. Nevertheless, there is no general consensus as to the degree and type of interpretation that could be arrived at by going beyond the wording of a normative act. Moreover, the reasons not found in the wording of the regulations in force could in fact provide an extra interpretation of the textual level of a legal norm reconstructed on their basis.

The other position, based on the idea of *ius et lex*, i.e. seeking the "right" law being "morally", "ethically" and "justly" legitimate etc., rejects the position whereby a legal norm is reconstructed solely through textual means. Instead, other values come to the fore, especially when the linguistic structure of a legal text remains unequivocal. It is assumed that the shape of a legal norm may be determined – or perhaps enriched – at the extra-linguistic level of a legal text.

Textual determinants are particularly preferred in the case of legal norms, at least officially, in some legal disciplines, most notably in criminal law. It is within this discipline that the safeguarding function of the law is particularly emphasized. Its enforcement seems especially difficult in the case of interference in the process of proper communication taking place between the legislator acting as the sender of specific messages and the addressees of legal norms acting as receivers of the messages. Hence, it is difficult to accept that the practice of appealing to extra-textual reasons within the reconstruction of legal norms could be free from the danger of causing such interference.

Does the linguistic level of criminal law provisions have an absolute value, binding the interpreter of a legal text completely? The answer to this question needs to be sought in the light of the position of the Polish Supreme Court on this matter. The aim of this paper is to provide a fairly exhaustive analysis of this position. I will examine statements made by the Supreme Court on the significance of the linguistic level of the substantive criminal law provisions. However, statements which were made in order to interpret provisions directly by expressing the statutory hallmarks of crime will be excluded from further analysis.

The position of the Polish Supreme Court towards the interpretation of material penal law can be analyzed from two slightly different perspectives. First, the Court tends to formulate, through its opinions, statements directly expressing a certain vision of methodology of interpreting the law. Those statements form a model of interpretation which can be presumed to have been affirmed and approved by the Supreme Court. The inspiration for such a model of interpretation usually comes from theory, or even philosophy, of law, and is deeply rooted in the legal literature and readily adopted by the Supreme Court in its practice.

The focus of this study will be limited to the analysis of statements posing a number of fundamental issues with respect to the methodology of legal interpretation. As such, they are the evidence of the Supreme Court's approval for a particular concept, or "school" of interpretation. Although they are expressed in order to resolve specific legal issues, they are often indicative of consistent reasoning and reveal a particular vision of interpretation, based on a general, or universal value.

The other point of view reflects the way in which the Supreme Court translates specific methodological assumptions, presented as if on a theoretical level, onto concrete resolutions in the area of practical application of the law. On assuming this perspective, the focus is not on those parts of opinions which directly expound a particular vision of the methodology of interpretation, but on those which seek to find out how the adopted methodological assumptions impact the method of resolving specific legal issues.

2. The Supreme Court's position on statutory interpretation

In the case of the Polish Supreme Court's position on the problems of interpreting material penal law provisions, it should be stressed that it consistently accentuates the textual level. The evidence for this can be found in frequent and unequivocal affirmation of the role of linguistic interpretation in the methodology of legal interpretation. Seen from this perspective, reasoning behind the reasons for the October 18, 2001 Decision[1] appears abundantly clear. The Supreme Court argues that

> The priority and fundamental importance in the process of interpreting a legal text undoubtedly lies in the language method used with reference to the rules of meaning valid in general language. The assumption of legislator's rationality results in a rule stating that if a provision unambiguously formulates a standard procedure, the interpretation should be arrived at accordingly. If, in turn, the directives of language-based interpretation do not allow to interpret a particular legal text as an unambiguous standard, one of usually language-wise allowable meanings of the text must be chosen by referring to axiological rationality of the legislator and following systemic or functional rules of legal interpretation. [2]

The importance of the textual aspect of legal provisions is also stressed in the order[3] of February 8, 2000. It contains the following statement:

> In line with the hierarchy of interpretation directives, the starting point for discussing a meaning of a provision (...) of the law is the language-based interpretation.

In the decision[4] of December 21, 1999, the priority of linguistic interpretation in interpreting a legal standard is considered "indisputable". Similarly, in the order[5] of November 3, 2003, the Supreme Court stresses the "leading role of language-based interpretation in reading the content of legal regulations properly". In view of the present discussion, the statement expressed in the justification for the order[6] of November 21, 2001 is particularly important. The Supreme Court stressed that:

> unambiguous wording (...) of regulations prevents the need for their correction in the future by means of other interpretation rules, including purpose- or system-driven rules. Such procedures would, in fact, lead to the abolition of the binding force of the proclaimed law by interpretation

Essentially, the statements cited above, stand in sharp contrast to the view expressed in the decision[7] of June 7, 2002. When interpreting one of the provisions of the Code of Minor Offences, the Supreme Court decides that "the strength of arguments of historical and purpose-driven nature leads to the rejection of the semantic interpretation" of the provision. Nevertheless, when

---

[1] Ref. *I KZP 22/01*

[2] The Court made a reference here to Wróblewski 1972, Morawski 1997, and Redelbach et al. 1992.

[3] Ref. *I KZP 49/99*

[4] Ref. *I KZP 44/99*

[5] Ref. *IV KK 295/02*. The Court made a reference here to Opałek and Wróblewski 1969.

[6] Ref. *I KZP 27/01*

[7] Ref. *I KZP 15/02*

using the same opinion for resolving other legal issues, also related to the Code of Minor Offences, the Supreme Court returns to the semantic interpretation. It also states that the interpretation does not provide an unambiguous response to the question concerning the normative sense of the provision interpreted. It affirms that "depending (...) on the element made prominent in the process of interpreting, various results are possible". Therefore, according to the Court, "it becomes necessary (...) to have recourse to other rules of interpretation". It is also stressed that in the present situation "undoubtedly, the purpose-driven interpretation must be given priority".

The reasoning contained in the decision[8] of October 29, 2004 seems particularly important here. It may also serve as a classic example of direct statements made by the Supreme Court to express its preferences for a specific methodology of legal interpretation. As already mentioned, it is a methodology developed and applied in the context of decisions referring to very concrete legal issues, which, however, does not deprive it of its general and universal nature. In the above-quoted opinion on the terms used in the Penal Code, the Supreme Court argues:

> When embarking upon the interpretation of a term (...), the Supreme Court adopted the so-called objective theory of interpretation, which assumes that the correct reading of the meaning of a particular provision and a further decoding of legal standards contained therein is decided upon by its content, not the intentions or will of the legislator.[9].

In extreme simplification, the meaning is determined by what the legislator wrote in a legal text, not what he intended to write. Further, the Supreme Court considered the principle of the so-called 'rational legislator'. Only through the adoption of this idealized concept, the Supreme Court argues,

> it is possible to evaluate the provision under examination, and the entire legal context in which it functions as an element of a coherent system, subject to axiologically justified purposes, constructed according to language rules and legislative techniques.

It is clear, the Supreme Court further reasons,

> that the parties applying the law in practice are aware that the assumption does not always come true (...). Nevertheless, rejection of this presumption would lead to interpretational latitude, and the result of the interpretation would mainly depend on the axiological system and assumptions adopted by the interpreting party, not the »rational legislator«.

---

[8] Ref. *I KZP 24/04*

[9] The Court made a reference here to Ziembiński 1978.

In the theory of law, as the Supreme Court pointed out, the role of interpreting parties

> »...consists *inter alia* in the fact that the system of legal standards should be presented to the society and the civil servant as a coherent and consistent system in its every aspect, even though the concepts of actual participants in the legislating process were incoherent, unclear, and clearly incompatible with the imaginations of rationality«[10].

The third presumption made by the Supreme Court, as the Court further argues,

> was to interpret the term used in (...) the Penal Code (...) in a manner compatible with the most broadly adopted hierarchy of interpretation directives in the doctrine and practice, that is the language-driven interpretation, followed by the systemic interpretation, and finally the functional interpretation.[11]

The analysis of the judicial statements quoted above, enables one to assume that the Supreme Court officially expresses a strong commitment to the rather traditional school of legal interpretation, which is deeply rooted both in the literature (the legal doctrine), and the approach found within the broadly understood practical application of the law. The statement is premised on the firm principle of giving priority to semantic interpretation, and thus confirming the text of normative acts with respect to interpretation related to a reconstruction of legal standards. If the Supreme Court chooses to refer to the background – e.g. by assuming that "the strength of arguments of historical and purpose-driven nature justifies the rejection of the semantic interpretation" – this is merely an exception that in fact confirms the binding rule. These statements also prove that the Supreme Court considers the principle of *clara non sunt interpretanda* as highly important, regarding any exemptions as a threat to the competences of the legislator and creating the contents of legal standards in a manner independent of the legislator's intention. Thus, the Supreme Court clearly stresses that deviation from the semantic interpretation is permissible only when this method of interpretation does not lead to the final resolution of interpretative ambiguities.

The views and perspectives presented so far are compatible with the classic school of interpretation – they correspond to its basic characteristics. More importantly, the analysis of the statements quoted above seems to reveal significant methodological problems. In my opinion, one of them concerns the hierarchy of importance in choosing various rules of statutory interpretation. This issue has not been yet resolved either at the level of general theory of law, or in the broadly understood practical law application. Equally, if there is a consensus

---

[10] The Court made a reference here to Ziembiński 1980.

[11] The Court made a reference here to Morawski 2002.

that the language (grammatical) rule should indeed be given priority, the problem of how to deal with the other rules of interpretation could be resolved in various ways. The Supreme Court itself in its various judgments seems to be presenting slightly different opinions in this respect. When referring to axiological rationality of the legislator, systemic and functional rules for interpretation, arguments of historical or purpose-driven nature, the Court does not unequivocally determine the mutual hierarchic relations between these elements.

However, the position of the Supreme Court on the basic methodological tenets of legal interpretation, is fairly clear. It becomes more complex as soon as the Supreme Court starts to implement praxeologically the officially manifested ideas, translating them onto specific procedures and resolutions to legal issues in the practical application of the law. The praxeological dimension of the problem, provides a definite benefit for developing a methodology. For example, the Supreme Court, after first stressing the importance of semantic interpretation from the theoretical position, further states that during the semantic interpretation, the correct meaning of a legal regulation is determined upon considering punctuation[12]. Then, applying this statement in practice, it further argues that in reference to the issue in question, the regulation analyzed "is a complex sentence, divided into logical segments by commas". It further reasons that

> the part of the regulation separated by a comma (...), in line with the principles of grammar and logic, should be read together, and the thought expressed in this fragment of a sentence cannot be divided (...)

The excerpt cited above illustrates the logic of the operations carried out to translate the methodological assumptions into the resolution of specific legal issues. It seems that such operations are sometimes performed in a way which may raise doubts as to whether the Supreme Court indeed always resolves interpretative ambiguities, which occur in specific regulations after applying the official methodology.

2. A case in point. The interpretive evolution of "reveal".

This problem is well illustrated by the manner in which the provisions of Article 60 § 3 of the Penal Code were interpreted. The provision states that

> The court shall apply an extraordinary mitigation of the penalty or may even conditionally suspend the execution of the penalty, with respect to a perpetrator who, co-operating with others in the commission of an offence, reveals information

[12] Ref. *I KZP 49/99.*

> pertaining to the persons involved therein or essential circumstances thereof, to the agency responsible for its prosecution.

In the practical application of the law, from the very enactment of the Code, the quoted regulation raised serious doubts as to its interpretation, in particular concerning the method of understanding the term "reveals", as used therein.

In its decision[13] of February 25, 1999, the Supreme Court decided that the provision cited is to be applied regardless of the fact whether the information provided by the perpetrator is already known to the agency responsible for crime prosecution, or not. Therefore, the Court has decided that the perpetrator "reveals" the information also when he or she provides the prosecuting agency with information already known to the agency.

This rather surprising decision sparked off a number of controversies, both among legal professionals and in the academic circles. Correctness of the resolution was questioned in particular by one of the Courts of Appeal[14]. It claimed that:

> The meaning of the term »reveals« does not leave any doubt that – in line with common understanding – it means making known, and thus public, what was not known before. As a consequence, the condition for revealing is met when the perpetrator provides the prosecuting agency with information and circumstances that were not previously known to the agency. The conflicting position of the Supreme Court on this matter, expounded in the decision of February 25, 1999 (...), is controversial - in the opinion of the Court of Appeal - since the result of the semantic interpretation has the decisive importance for setting the scope of application of art. 60 § 3 of the Penal Code.

The situation became particularly complicated when the Supreme Court itself drastically changed its position, holding, in the judgment[15] of 27 May 2002, that "the use in art. 60 § 3 of the Penal Code of the term 'reveals' means the requirement for providing the prosecuting agency with information previously unknown to the agency".

Interestingly, the opinion accompanying the judgment contains a statement according to which: "one must question the reasoning that leads to minimizing, and thus depriving the term »reveals« of the meaning related to the term in the popular sense and practical usage thereof, and one should define the term allowing for a significant shift in its meaning".

The verdict did not, however, put an end to the raging disputes over the proper understanding of the provision. A new interpretation could be found in the

---

[13] Ref. *I KZP 38/98.*
[14] See Judgment of 27 May 2002 - Ref. *V KKN 188/00.*
[15] Ref. *V KKN 188/00.*

order[16] of the Supreme Court of February 20, 2003. There, the Supreme Court decided that

> the term 'revealing' used in respect of a perpetrator in the context of information imparted to the crime prosecution agency, as contained in Article 60 § 3 of the Penal Code, means provision of only such information which, according to the knowledge of the informer, was not previously known to the agency.

The opinion accompanying the order contains, *inter alia,* the following:

> (...) It is impossible to forget the primary importance of the semantics in the interpretation of a legal standard. The interpretation of the term "revealing information" – adopting as a starting point the knowledge of the perpetrator as to what is known to the prosecuting agency and what cannot be subject to revealing – still corresponds to the common understanding of the word, taking into account also the results of systemic and functional interpretation.

Discrepancies in the understanding of the term "reveals" finally led the First Chairperson[17] of the Supreme Court to have the issue resolved by seven judges of the Supreme Court. Subject to the decision[18] of October 29, 2004, the Supreme Court held that:

> The term "reveals", used in art. 60 § 3 of the Penal Code, means provision by the perpetrator to the crime prosecution agency, as specified by this provision, with information that has not been previously known to the agency or such information which – according to the knowledge of the perpetrator – is unknown to the agency.

The reasons for the decision become clearer if we look at the following excerpt, where the Supreme Court admits:

> (...) it is easy to prove that the term "reveals", contained in art. 60 § 3 of the Penal Code, covers with its meaning information and circumstances previously unknown to the prosecution agency (...). From the semantic perspective, there is no doubt that the word 'reveals' in its prima facie transparent meaning refers to the very provision to the recipient of information previously unknown to him.

Finally, the significance of the court's decision is recognized in the following paragraph:

> When resolving the legal issue contained in the decision, as presented by the First Chairman, the Supreme Court was aware that the interpretation of the term "reveals"

---

[16] Ref. *II KK 113/02.*

[17] The Polish Supreme Court Act provides that there are a number of chairpersons, and a "First Chairperson".

[18] Ref. *I KZP 24/04.*

> may in some circumstances raise probative difficulties. Nevertheless, the effects of application or non-application of Article 60 § 3 of the Penal Code are so important that even if the decisions in this respect require greater effort, this is in all respects justified.

This assertion might mean that Supreme Court is at times prepared to consider circumstances which do not have much to do with the interpretation of the law, and particularly with the textual dimension of legal provisions. Surprisingly, there have been attempts to "justify" such decisions by referring to the assertion mentioned above. It is difficult to perceive a rational relation between seeking for the meaning of an ambiguous provision and potential trial difficulties that may occur in the wake of its application, as a consequence of choosing a particular meaning.

3. Conclusion

The Supreme Court's method of seeking the correct understanding of the provision in question is evidenced in particular by the judgements cited above. The dramatic changes in the interpretation may be perceived as a result of enriching the discourse – present in the theory and practical application of the law – with new arguments leading to the expression of varying opinions and the rather dramatic change of positions within a relatively short period of time. In my opinion, however, this statement does not necessarily need to finally explain the inclination of the Supreme Court to adopt clearly different understandings of the provision discussed, as shown in subsequent judgements. I believe that the analysis of the various positions, resulting from the sometimes radically different contextual orientations, may also prove something else. It might also be perceived as an effect of the inconsistent realization of specific implications resulting from the approved methodological foundations for the interpretation of the law with respect to resolving specific legal issues. Also, this holds true when such issues refer to principal questions related to the position of a legal text in light of interpretative attempts.

To conclude, the interpretive evolution of the term "reveal" shows that even if the importance of methodological aspects is frequently stressed by the Supreme Court, on the basis of an approved model of interpretation of the law, they might not always be implemented when resolving specific interpretive ambiguities. Therefore, even though the position of the Supreme Court on methodological foundations of legal interpretation of the law may seem clear when presented as a certain theoretical vision contained in the substance of the judgements, this clarity is sometimes lost in operations attempting to translate this vision into the resolution of specific legal issues.

References

Morawski. L. (1997). *Wstęp do prawoznawstwa*. Toruń: TNOiK.
Opałek, K. and J. Wróblewski (1969). *Zagadnienia teorii prawa*. Warsaw: PWN.
Redelbach, A., Wronkowska, S. and Z. Ziembiński (1992). *Zarys teorii państwa i prawa*. Warsaw: PWN.
Wróblewski, J. (1988). *Sądowe stosowanie prawa*. Warsaw: PWN.
Ziembiński, Z. (1978). *Teoria prawa*. Warsaw/Poznań: PWN.
Ziembiński, Z. (1980). *Problemy podstawowe prawoznawstwa*. Warsaw: PWN.

Part V

POLICE INTERVIEWS

Georgina Heydon
Monash University
Australia

THE IMPORTANCE OF BEING (IN)FORMAL: DISCOURSE STRATEGIES IN POLICE INTERVIEWS WITH CHILDREN

1. Introduction

Like many of its counterparts around the world, the Victoria Police Service in Australia trains police officers to obtain statements from young witnesses and victims of violent crimes. The resulting video-taped interviews form the child's evidence for the prosecution in court and, as such, are often critical to the success of a police case against an alleged offender. Given the disparity in institutionally-granted power between a police officer and a young child, these interviews present the police institution with a major challenge – how to adequately respond to the needs of a vulnerable child whilst satisfying the complex legislative requirements, and still facilitate an accurate witness statement. In light of the extensive research findings regarding the language of police interviewing (Agnew, Powell and Snow 2006, Ainsworth 1993, Atkinson 1992, Auburn, Drake and Willig 1995, Cooke 1996, Eades 1994, Fisher and Todd 1986, Guadagno, Powell and Wright 2006, Haworth 2006, Heydon 1997 and 2005, Lakoff 1990, Powell 2000, Redlich et al. 2004, Shuy 1998, Thomas 1989), we might expect that the discourse produced in these interactions would represent an almost prototypical example of the asymmetrical institutional interview. Indeed, the data examined in this study reveal the presence of interactional phenomena which clearly indicate such asymmetry, including discoursal indicators (Thomas 1989) and asymmetrical naming rituals (Lakoff 1990), both of which can be used by dominant participants to control the contributions of subordinate participants. However, the presence of features associated with less formal interactions indicates that institutionality is not a fixed property defined by the setting or the backgrounds of the participants, but may be manipulated and reconstructed in the turn-by-turn production of the discourse. This paper describes in interactional terms the methods used, consciously or unconsciously, by police interviewers when they must negotiate the challenging discursive realm that is the pre-recorded child witness statement.

2. Institutional context of the discourse: the VATE project

As a part of the Video and Audio Taping of Evidence (VATE) project, which has been in operation in Victoria, Australia since 1993, officers are trained in the procedures for interviewing children according to the guidelines laid down by legislation which allows these video taped interviews to be used in place of a court appearance by a child. The main emphasis of the training course is the rehearsal of an interview technique which will elicit information in such a way that it can be used as reliable evidence in court. There are, therefore, certain constraints on both the type of responses that are to be elicited and the way in which requests for information can be made. It is of primary importance that the information elicited is given freely by the child and without leading questions or verbal threats and bribes. In the literature supplied with the training materials, leading questions are defined as those which "imply the presence of information not previously mentioned by the child" (Powell and Thomson 1994: 209). For instance, the interviewer may not ask if *the man went home* when the child has not yet mentioned the gender of the person under discussion.

The training materials used in the VATE project at the time of this study were developed with a strong emphasis on rapport building and understanding the difference between children and adults in the comprehension of questions and knowledge of the interview procedure. Explaining the interview procedure to the child carefully is very important and interviewees are instructed to tell their child subjects to say *I don't know* if s/he doesn't know the answer to a question. This latter strategy is designed to reduce the possibility of the child making up answers under pressure . However, it is noted that "studies with protocols that allow the child to say *I don't know* have not eliminated the fabrication of false reports" (Powell and Thomson 1994: 207-208).

The first part of the present analysis aims to align the discursive features of the VATE interview with the interview structure outlined in the VATE training course guidelines by identifying utterances which mark boundaries, or frame shifts. Having delineated the segments of the tri-partite interview, the Opening and the Closure of the interview will be analysed in terms of frames and participation frameworks (Goffman 1974) as indicators of institutionality. A further examination of the data in terms of discoursal indicators (Thomas 1989) and receipt markers (Atkinson 1992) aims to reveal patterns of formality in the interview discourse. Through this detailed analysis, it will be possible to further our understanding of the unique character of the VATE interview as an interactional construct and consider the implications of the findings for police practice and training.

3. The Tri-Partite Interview Technique

The interview guidelines described in the VATE training course literature as the Tri-Partite Interview Technique involve approaching the interaction as three successive and largely discreet segments: Opening, Information Gathering and Closure. Each section includes a number of objectives or instructions for interviewers and the whole structure is presented in Appendix II.

The first part, the "Opening" consists of Rapport Development and Developmental Assessment, where the interviewer aims to put the child at ease with some simple questions such as the child's full name and birthday and an explanation about the purpose and procedures of the interview. The following is an extract from INT3 which demonstrates how the Opening may proceed:

Extract 1 (INT3)

1. PO4 You ready to go?...OK..this is a video taped statement at the Victoria Police Centre on Sunday the twenty-fifth of May 1997 and my name is Senior Constable (FN. SN) and with me is (FN) who I'm gonna be speaking to. (FN) can you tell me your whole name?
2. CH5 (FN. MN. SMN. SN)?
3. PO4 And how old are you (FN)?
4. CH5 Eight and I'm turning nine in (month. date)
5. PO4 (month. date). OK ..right. now before I turned the camera on. did I show you the camera and the TV outside?
6. CH5 Mmm. Yes
7. PO4 Yes?. and what's on the TV
8. CH5 Um well there's chairs with us sitting on them?
9. PO4 OK. and who' s looking at the TV?
10. CH5 Julie and Jenny?
11. PO4 ..OK. um while I'm speaking to you (FN) I'm going to be writing down what you tell me and the reason why I'm doing that is so that at the end when we've finished speaking I can go over what you've told me?. OK so that I remember everything
12. CH5 Yep
13. PO4 Yep?. and if at any time you want to stop talking to me and you. you feel like you want to take a break? OK you might want to go to the toilet or you might need a drink or something like that?. I want you to tell me that you want to take a break and we'll stop the video and we'll go outside OK?. and it's also really important that I tell you that if if I ask you a question and you don't know the answer or you don't understand

the answer I want you to say oh (FN) I don't know the answer or I don't understand what your saying OK? and that's OK to say that. all right? OK. now do you know why you're here today?

14. CH5 Um. yep. be- because Julie's studying language about children talking to policemen?

15. PO4 Mm hm? All right so when I speak to you about that. I want you to remember every thing that you can about what we're going to speak about. even if you think it's not really important I want you to remember everything that you possibly can

16. CH5 Yes

17. PO4 OK all right. now can you tell me why we're here today?

18. CH5 Um. because...so Julie can um. learn about her university thing?

In Extract 1 above we can see that PO4 begins in turn 1 with an acknowledgment of CH5's presence - *You ready to go?...OK..* - and then proceeds to make a statement which describes the situation - *this is a video taped statement* etc. PO4 then gives her rank and name before introducing CH5 using her first name - *and with me is (FN) who I'm gonna be speaking to* - and finishes the statement by requesting CH5's full name, which CH5 gives in her first turn, turn 2. In turns 3 and 4, CH5's age is established and acknowledged by PO4 in turn 5, where PO4 repeats the date just given by CH5 in turn 4. The remainder of turn 5 and turns 6-10 contain a question/answer exchange through which PO4 establishes CH5's understanding that the interview is being video-taped. In turns 11 and 13, PO4 describes to CH5 the interview procedure and CH5's rights, such as her right to *take a break.* These are quite long turns and between them, CH5 only offers an agreement marker - *yep* - in turn 12. At the end of turn 13, PO4 asks CH5 if she knows *why you're here today* and CH5 responds with a mention of the researcher in turn 14. However, PO4's following turn does not relate to CH5's response in turn 14, but rather discusses CH5's responsibility to provide full and detailed descriptions of *what we're going to speak about* which CH5 acknowledges in turn 16. PO4 then repeats the request for CH5 to explain why she is participating in the interview. When responding a second time, CH5 is more general in her description, changing it from *because Julie's studying language about children talking to policemen* to *because...so Julie can um. learn about her university thing.* In the second version, CH5 pauses for a long time after *because* and then alters this word to *so* and before stalling again soon after in *Julie can um.*

In addition to exemplifying the Opening sequence, this extract provides an important illustration of the vulnerability of the child's responses to the pressures of institutional questioning techniques. Turns 13-18 clearly demonstrate that the repetition of a question can cause a child to modify her/his response in the belief that the first response must have been "incorrect" (Powell and Thomson 1994). This observation is particularly pertinent here as PO4 has just explained to CH5 the need for detailed information in turn 15 before she repeats the question about the reason for CH5's participation in the interview in turn 17. Even though CH5 has acknowledged the direction from PO4 in turn 15 to provide maximum detail, she actually provides less detail when responding to the repeated question made in turn 17, than when she responded to the original request made in turn 13, before PO4 had mentioned anything about providing details in descriptions.

The second and longest part of the interview is labelled Information Gathering and it is here that the interviewer elicits the bulk of the information being sought. An "anchor" is established to focus the child on the day and approximate time that the event occurred using questions like *Tell me about school on Tuesday morning* – where Tuesday is the date given for the event. This is followed by the elicitation of an "Open Ended Narrative", using phrases like *think back to* and *remember* to encourage the child to recall the day in question, and any resulting narrative is then probed using first "open" questions like *what happened next*? And then "closed" questions, where interviewers are instructed to use the child's own version of the event to elicit further details. The interviewer selects a part of the narrative which s/he feels is pertinent and asks the child for further information about that part using yes/no questions, or asking the child to select one of a set of possible alternatives. These questions should also start with cues for the child to remember, for instance: *Think back to when you said a man came in, did he come through the front door, or the back door, or the side door?*; or as a yes/no question: *When the man came in, do you remember if he told you his name?* The child is encouraged to add information at any time, especially at the end of this section and in this way the narrative is elaborated and details refined.

The third part of the Tri-Partite Interview technique is called the Closure and it is here that the interviewer makes sure that s/he has properly understood the child's version of the event and finishes the interview.

In subsection VIII of the Closure – the Review – the narrative is read back to the child from notes which the interviewer has been making throughout the interview. The child is encouraged to interrupt if s/he feels that any detail is incorrect and to add any other information should s/he think of it. In subsection IX at the end of the Closure, the child is thanked and the interview concluded. In terminating the interview the child should be left feeling that they have 'done the right thing' and that should they desire to, they may contact the interviewer at any time for further discussion.

3.1. Frame identification in the tri-partite interview

In order to discuss the linguistic implications of the tri-partite interview technique, we first need to be able to identify the three parts of the interview as they appear in the data. This means that we must be able to find a particular utterance or type of utterance which marks the transition from one part to the next. Coupland, Robinson and Coupland's (1994) study of frame negotiation provides an example of how a particular utterance can be identified which marks the transition from phatically designed talk to the medical "business at hand" in doctor-elderly patient consultations. In their study, an utterance of the type *How are you?* (HAY?) was said to initiate a shift in footing (in Goffman's (1981) sense) from the relational to the professional (in this case, medical).

If we are considering the interviews which comprise the data for this study in terms of their division into three parts (i.e. the tri-partite structure described above), then we might expect to find transitional markers at the boundaries of these parts which function in a similar way to the HAY? utterance in the Coupland et al. study. In other words, we might be able to identify the particular type of utterance which marks the point at which a shift in footing takes place between the Opening and the Information Gathering part of the interview, and between the Information Gathering and the Closure.

Recalling the different features found in the Opening and the Information Gathering parts of the interview which were described above, the beginning of the Information Gathering is marked by the establishment of the "Anchor". Up to this point in the interview, the child has not been asked any questions regarding the Event. The establishment of the Anchor is the preliminary step before any requests for information regarding the Event may be made by the police officers. We would therefore expect to find that an utterance which contains those pieces of information that comprise the Anchor – the time and place of the Event – would mark the transition from the Opening to the Information Gathering. Extracts 2 and 3 give examples of this type of utterance.

Extract 2 (INT2)

21.	PO3	All right now I believe that on Thursday night. just gone. which was the twenty second of May. you were at the ballet school? is that right?
22.	CH2	Yep
23.	PO3	and something happened there at about six o'clock in the night
24.	CH2	Mmm

Extract 3 (INT5)

43.	PO5	Not really?..do you remember anything that happened at ballet at all. last week?
44.	CH6	Ah.. well we danced... um. ah we learnt a um a new bit of our dance?

The extracts above show two different ways in which the Anchor can be established, but in both cases there is a mention of *ballet* and an indication of the time being referred to. The example given in Extract 3 is fairly non-specific but it still makes a time reference which the child is able to correctly interpret, *last week*. In the other five interviews, the Anchor is similarly established with varying degrees of detail being given in one or more turns and from the data in each interview transcription we can illustrate the features of each Anchor in a table such as Table 1 below.

We can see that while all of the utterances which marked the transition from the Opening to the Information Gathering contained a time and mention of the Event place, only four of the seven utterances contained a discourse marker (for example in INT2, turn 21: *All right now*), and three contained some mention of the police officer's intention, for example INT3, PO4; 19: *and I'm going to be speaking to you about something*. However, it should be noted that all of the police officers mentioned to the children at some time in the Opening that they would be asking questions during the interview. The use of discourse markers generally is mentioned by Coupland et al. (1994) as a common feature of frame transitional utterances, and we should note also that in the case of INT5, where there is a false start to the Information Gathering, *now* occurs in the second attempt.

Table 1. Features of the frame transitional utterance between the Opening and the Information Gathering

	Discourse marker	***Mention of intention***	***Mention of time/date***	***Mention of place***
INT1	YES	YES	YES	YES
INT2	YES	NO	YES	YES
INT3	NO	YES	YES	YES
INT4	YES	YES	YES	YES
INT5	NO	NO	YES	YES
INT6	YES	NO	YES	YES
INT7	NO	NO	YES	YES

The transition from the Information Gathering to the Closure is similarly overt in the interviews. Because the officers wish to keep the child informed of the progress of the interview, each officer explains to the child subject that the Information Gathering section is over, and that the information elicited will next be presented to the child for her confirmation or adjustment. Extract 4 demonstrates the form that this transitional statement can take:

Extract 4 (INT2)

81.PO3	OK. now. what we might do. I'll just go back through and we'll just. I'll quickly go through my [notes]
82.CH2	[yeah]
83.PO3	and we'll just. review what you've. told me. and um. just to see that I've got my notes down right
84.CH2	Yeah
85.PO3	and we've got the story right. if I make a mistake just say. let me know
86.CH2	Yeah

We can see that, like the shift between the Opening and the Information Gathering, the shift from the Information Gathering to the Closure is initiated by the police officer (see turn 81). The child adds agreement markers in turns 82, 84 and 86 and no challenge to the shift in frame is raised. The generalised structure of the frame transitional utterance is:

discourse marker + mention of intention

and these two features are found in the frame shift from Information Gathering to Closure in every interview.

By identifying the frame transitional utterances, we can see very clearly the effect of the Tri-Partite Interview Technique on structuring the discourse produced by the police participants. The following section will further investigate institutional structures underlying the discourse by focusing the analysis specifically on the Opening and the Closure of the interview.

3.2. Frames and participation frameworks in the Opening

In the Opening, the police officers combine several activities. There is an identification process in which they first identify themselves and their location and then introduce the child, who is then told about the interview procedure.

In their opening statements, the police officers seem to invoke a "police on-record interview" frame where a description of the situation is addressed to an absent third party who is viewing the video-taped recording at some future time. Features which mark this frame are utterances which are formulaic and seemingly redundant, such as *This is a video-taped statement.* This frame having been invoked, the interviewing officer then seems to make an effort to switch frames perhaps in recognition of the fact that a police on-record frame is unlikely to be within the experience of their child subject. They achieve this switch using the utterance *and with me is [FN]*, which has echoes of a television or radio host introducing a guest to their programme, and as such likely to be a familiar frame to most children. However, almost immediately the police on-record frame is reinvoked in order to deal with the identification process described above.

Another way of describing participants' alignments is by reference to Goffman's description of a participation role framework whereby stretches of the interaction can be categorised according to "speaker roles" (Goffman 1974: 517). Goffman's speaker roles refer to the way in which participants align themselves to utterances produced in an interaction, and is closely related to his perhaps better-known concept of "footing" (Goffman 1981: 128) Three roles are identified by Heydon (2005: 48) that are considered crucial to the analysis of confessional or informative talk in police interviews: the roles of *author* (the utterance was "written" by the participant); *principal* (the participant takes responsibility for the impact or effect of the utterance); and *animator* (the participant actually physically produces the utterance). A fourth role, *figure*, is also relevant to the present study and it indicates a person being referred to by the utterance.

In the police on-record interview frame, these roles are attributed to participants in an unusual way. In their opening statements, the police officers switch from speaking for themselves in the first utterance, e.g.

> INT3: 1: PO4 *You ready to go?...OK..this is a video taped statement at the Victoria Police Centre on Sunday the twenty-fifth of May 1997 and my name is Senior Constable (FN, SN)*

to speaking for another when they introduce the child e.g.

> INT3: 1: PO4 *and with me is (FN) who I'm gonna be speaking to.*

Thus, in the opening statement, the police officer is the *animator* of the identification process and by introducing the child at the end of the opening statement in the third person, the police officer assigns the role of *figure* to the child. The roles of *principal* and *author*, however, can be shown to belong to neither participant. In the case of the opening statements, it is possible to argue that in making their statements to camera, the police officers themselves are only *animators* of a scripted statement which has been written by a third party representing the police force as an institution. If we consider Extract 5 below, we can see that in the first line of turn 1, PO1 states that she is *going to be reading from something.*

Extract 5 (INT6)

1. PO1	Here we go..(sits) OK..now I'm going to be reading from something. all right? so um. just bear with me. all right this is a video taped statement at the ah Melbourne Community Policing Squad today's um Sunday the twenty-fifth of May?. 1997?. can you tell the time (FN)?. have you got a wa- oh very good can you tell me what the time is by your watch?
2. CH3	Um. one past eleven?
3. PO1	So is mine. that's good. all right the time is one past eleven. my name is Senior Constable (FN. SN) and I'm with (FN). (FN) could you tell me what your full name is?

This mention of *reading from something* clearly indicates that the statement made by PO1 is not speech created by her, but rather a scripted statement created by someone representing the police force as an institution. Thus PO1 is not the *author* of the statement and, as the statements made by the other police officers at the commencement of their interviews are almost identical to this one, it is reasonable to postulate that none of the police officers occupy the role of *author* of this statement.

As to the role of *principal* of the statement, we must consider whether or not the police officer, as an individual, can be "held responsible for having wilfully taken up the position to which the meaning of the utterance attests" (Goffman, 1974, p. 517). If we consider how a person could be held responsible for taking up the "position to which the meaning of an utterance attests" when that utterance is a quote (i.e. the *author* of the utterance is someone other than its *animator*), we find that, since the form of the utterance is prescribed by its *author*, the only aspects of the utterance available to the speaker for adjustment are the decision to use the quote and the decision as to where the quote is used in relation to the rest of the discourse in which the speaker is involved. Having already established that the opening statement made by the police officers has been written by another, and that the statement is a standard feature of each interview transcription, it seems reasonable to assume that making the statement at the beginning of the interview is a requirement of carrying out the interview. Therefore, the police officer is not responsible for deciding whether or not to make the statement nor when it should be made and therefore cannot be considered responsible for any of the decisions that would place her/him in the role of *principal* of the statement.

This analysis indicates that the participation framework of the police on-record interview frame is one in which the speaker, the police officer, is assigned the role of *animator* of the utterances while the roles of *principal* and *author* seem to be assigned to a third party which might be identified as the police institution, though it could incorporate the justice system more broadly. We find further evidence of this participation framework in the second part of the Opening where the police officer explains to the child her rights and obligations in the interview procedure.

Extract 6 (INT3)

13. PO4	Yep?. and if at any time you want to stop talking to me and you. you feel like you want to take a break? OK you might want to go to the toilet or you might need a drink or something like that?. I want you to tell me that you want to take a break and we'll stop the video and we'll go outside OK?. **and it's also really important that I tell you that** if if I ask you a question and you don't know the answer or you don't understand the answer I want you to say oh (FN) I don't know the answer or I don't understand what your saying OK? and that's OK to say that. all right? OK. now do you know why you're here today?

In this rather lengthy turn, PO4 makes reference to a guiding protocol in the highlighted utterance implying that responsibility for the decision to make the statements about the interview procedure is not attributable to PO4 herself as she is only following the necessary procedure. In other words, the highlighted utterance indicates that the role of *principal* is occupied by someone other than PO4. Each of the interviews include a similar statement and thus the role of *author* is also clearly assigned to this third party.

Further, in the Opening, the requests being made are largely requests for information which is already known to the police officer. In the identification process, for instance, it would be reasonable to assume that the police officers would know in advance the full name and age of the child they are interviewing and the request to the child to state these details "on-record" is a requisite police formality.

INT1 shows an interesting departure from the police on-record interview frame, with CH1 finishing PO2's turn for her and thus taking over as *animator*:

Extract 7 (INT1)

27. PO2	I might take some notes? All right? so don't be put off by that. ah. if you wanna stop. you can just [say]
28. CH1	[Just] say at any time.

29. PO2	Yep. we can break. we can come back in start again do whatever. all right
30. CH1	OK

The reversal of roles begun by CH1 in turn 28 is completed by PO2 in turn 29 with her agreement marker *Yep* supplying confirmation to her own statement appropriated by CH1. PO2 then goes on to regain the role of *animator* of the statement discussing the child's rights. Detailed examination of the interviews with CH1 indicates that this is typical of her behaviour, and yet, these disruptions to the police protocol are momentary and never threaten the underlying institutional structure of the interview (cf. Frankel 1990, Heydon 2005: 174).

As police interviewers are expected to develop rapport during the Opening of the interview, we would expect to find here some indication of a relational frame being invoked involving some use of "phatically designed talk" (Coupland et al. 1994). In fact, an examination of the Opening of each interview reveals that an attempt to invoke a relational frame is made by only two interviewers, PO1 and PO6, presented here in the following two extracts:

Extract 8 (INT6)

29.	PO1	OK. and how long have you been going to ballet
30.	CH3	Um..six years
31.	PO1	Since you were how old?
32.	CH3	Three
33.	PO1	You must be very good at ballet are you?. OK all right now when do you go to ballet. classes

Extract 9 (INT7)

43.	PO6	How often do you go to ballet
44.	CH7	Um. three times a week. and one of them is for private lessons
45.	PO6	What days do you go to ballet
46.	CH7	um. Thursday Friday and Saturday

In these two interviews the police officers are using the child's interest in ballet to engage in some phatically-designed talk and to attempt to establish rapport. We can therefore confirm that a relational frame is invoked in order to achieve these goals.

To summarise, the analysis of frames in the Opening part of the interview reveals a complex discursive structure, though one dominated by the police on-record interview frame. This features a statement made "to camera" by the police officer as well as various other statements, such as those regarding the child's rights in the interview, all of which are considered a part of the police interview protocol. The discourse frames are reflected in the participation frameworks used in the Opening: the rather unusual assignment of roles appears to be a feature of the police on-record interview frame where the dominant speaker (i.e. the police officer) is making utterances under instruction and cannot therefore be considered the *principal* of those utterances. Furthermore, as many of the utterances were found to be formulaic and similarly phrased across all the interviews, the interviewing officer could not truly be said to occupy the position of *author* either.

The next section will consider the discourse structures that are involved in the review of the child's narrative by the police officers in the Closure of the interviews.

3.3. Frames and participation frameworks in the Closure

We noted earlier that the transition from the Information Gathering to the Closure is marked by an utterance which mentions the police officer's intention of presenting to the child for her confirmation the narrative elicited in the Information Gathering part. One example of the frame transitional utterance was given in Extract 4 above and two further examples are given in Extracts 14 and 15 below.

Extract 10 (INT7)

149.	PO6	Right. OK. certainly sounds very interesting. we'll stop the ah the tape there. but um just so I make sure I've got this right. so last Thursday you went to ballet?
150.	CH7	Yeah

Extract 11 (INT4)

67.	PO7	OK. I'm just going to go through what you've told me about this man OK and um I'd like you to just to make sure that I've got it right and if there's anything you want to add to what I've said you can just. interrupt me and add
68.	CH4	Yep

69.	PO7	Or um if there's something that's wrong that I've said you can just tell me if I've got anything wrong..OK you said that at ballet school on Thursday at about six o'clock?
70.	CH4	Yeah

The two extracts above include the transition into the Closure of INT7 and INT4 respectively. From this we can see that the Closure, as noted previously, commences with a mention of the police officer's intention. In Extract 14, PO6 in turn 149 makes an utterance pertaining to his intention - *but um just so I make sure I've got this right* - but does not elucidate any further, leaving it up to CH7 to interpret the frame as one where she may challenge or confirm the police officer's assertions as appropriate. However in INT4, PO7 makes her intentions and the child's role in the Closure much more explicit (see Extract 15). In turn 67, she begins the transitional utterance by telling CH4 that she is *going to go through what you've told me about this man* and in this and her following turn (69) she instructs CH4 to *make sure I've got it right*, and to *just tell me if I've got anything wrong.*

Further differences between these two approaches become apparent when we examine the remainder of the Closure. In the transitional utterance of INT7, PO6 seemed to indicate that he had appropriated responsibility for CH7's narrative by saying *um just so I make sure I've got this right.* This position is supported by the fact that in his review of CH7's narrative, PO6 states the parts of the story without any qualification as to the source of his information. For instance, in turn 149, after mentioning his intention, he says *so last Thursday you went to ballet* which does not attribute any *authorship* of the narrative to CH7. The remainder of the Closure of INT7 is undertaken using the same approach by the interviewer. This approach (also used in INT2) can be contrasted with that of PO7 in INT4, who overtly recognises the child as the *principal* and *author* of the narrative being discussed both in the frame transitional utterance (e.g. *I'm just going to go through what you've told me...*) and in her review of the narrative which follows (e.g. *you said that...*). Detailed analysis found that in INT4, where PO7 made explicit the child's role in providing any necessary adjustments to the narrative, CH4 was more likely to make such contributions to the review process. In contrast, CH7 only responded with affirmations to PO6's version of the Event and did not offer any corrections, even when there were inaccuracies in the police officer's account. Thus, the analysis reveals that the use of this framework better enables the child to offer feedback and corrections to the police officer as they review the narrative together. This approach is used in all the remaining interviews and appears to be favoured by the VATE technique.

Clayman (1992) discusses shifts in footing used by media interviewers to maintain neutrality and shows how assertions are attributed to a source other than the interviewer as a means of distancing the speaker from such assertions. Thus, we could argue that PO7 in INT4 has maintained a neutral stance regarding the content of CH4's narrative by not taking personal responsibility for the utterances and only referring to them as things said by CH4. PO6, on the other hand, appears to align himself more strongly with the content of CH7's narrative by not attributing his assertions about the Event to CH7.

If we consider this arrangement of participant roles in relation to the framework identified in the Opening, it is possible to see conflicting structures emerging. Whereas in the Opening there was a clear effort by all police participants to avoid *principal-* and *authorship* roles in the police on-record interview frame, the Closure produces disparate practices. When the narrative elicited by the police officer in the previous part of the interview was presented to the child, some police officers maintained a neutral stance in relation to the narrative by assuming the role of *animator* of the child's utterances (e.g. INT1, INT3, INT4, INT5 and INT6), while others aligned themselves more strongly with the child's narrative by appropriating the child's utterances as their own (e.g. INT2 and INT7). We will return to this issue of neutrality and alignment later, however, in order to address the issues raised earlier concerning the conflicting police requirements of the VATE interviews, it is first necessary to consider the use of discoursal indicators (Thomas 1989) and receipt markers (Atkinson 1992) by the police officers as they negotiate the frame transition and the interview as a whole. In this way, we will develop the analysis of a range of discourse features found in the data which give these interactions their distinctive character of mixed (in)formality.

3.4. Frame negotiation and discourse control acts

Given the interest of this study in the apparently conflicting aims of the VATE interview, namely the establishing both of authority and rapport, it is useful to consider the devices used by these officers to guide the children's narratives. Thomas (1989) identified discourse control acts as tools commonly used by the police officers for the purpose of guiding or controlling the contributions of an interviewee. She distinguishes three types of speech events which she describes collectively as discourse control acts: discoursal indicators, metadiscoursal comments and interactional controllers. These devices are said to "offer insights into the way in which a dominant speaker may deliberately limit the discoursal options of a subordinate interlocutor" (1989: 135). Here we shall consider the use of discoursal indicators, which "define the purpose and boundaries of the discourse and are surface level markers of the speaker's discoursal intent" (1989: 136). An example can be found in Extract 16 below.

Extract 12 (INT3)

19.	PO4	That's right. and **I'm going to be speaking to you about something that happened at ballet school last Thursday?** Can you remember ballet school last Thursday?
20.	CH5	Yes

The highlighted utterance shows PO4 defining the nature of the discourse to follow by stating that she will be speaking to CH5, and that the discussion will be focussed on a particular Event, at a particular time. Thus, PO4 establishes herself as the dominant speaker in the encounter by using the discoursal indicators to "define the purpose and boundaries of the discourse". This will affect the speaker roles in the talk that follows because by defining the boundaries of the discourse, PO4 has already established herself as the judge of what is to be deemed relevant in the discussion and CH5's contributions are limited to those found relevant by PO4. Discoursal indicators similar to that exemplified in Extract 16 are found in all of the interviews, particularly in the Opening and the transitional utterances between the Opening and the Information Gathering.

We also noted earlier that in the transitional utterances between the Information Gathering and the Closure, the police officers all state their intention of reviewing the child's narrative. These mentions of intention by the police officers can now be redefined as discoursal indicators and an example is provided in Extract 19, below.

Extract 13 (INT1)

149.	PO2	**So what I'm gonna do is. I'm just gonna go through and tell you. um. go back over the things that you've already said?** All right?
150.	CH1	Hmm

In the above extract we can see that PO2 is defining the boundaries of the discussion to follow by saying that she is *gonna go through and tell you, um, go back over the things you've already said.* In this way, the transitional utterance exemplified here is also being used as a discoursal indicator.

3.5. Receipt markers in police responses

In his article examining the discourse of informal court proceedings, Atkinson (1992) notes that arbitrators in the London Small Claims Court regularly employ receipt markers as a way of acknowledging contributions made by the parties involved in the dispute. Receipt markers, which typically include such utterances as *certainly, right* or *OK* are made by the first speaker following the second speaker's response to a question asked by the first speaker. Many examples of this device can be found in the data for this study, such as those highlighted in Extract 20 below.

Extract 14 (INT5)

189.	PO5	..Mm..now I'll just go back to the camera. you said it was a. a snap shot camera. but that's not right. it was a movie camera. right?
190.	CH6	Yeah. it one of those one's you hold up and you tape yourself
191.	PO5	**Right**. like this one's doing now?
192.	CH6	Yeah
193.	PO5	**OK**. so what happened after Julie. ah took the movie?
194.	CH6	um. he packed up and left
195.	PO5	**OK**. did he say anything when he left?
196.	CH6	No

The highlighted utterances occurring in turns 191, 193 and 195 are examples of receipt markers. They are being used by PO5 to show acknowledgment of CH6's utterances, such as in turn 190, where CH6 confirms the description of the camera used in the Event (a point of confusion earlier in the interview), and this is acknowledged by PO5 by the receipt marker *Right* in turn 191. To illustrate the high number of receipt markers found in the data, the following table is provided, which shows the number of receipt markers per total number of police officer turns in each interview and the proportion of these turns which contained receipt markers as a percentage.

Table 2. Number of receipt markers used by police officers per total number of police officer turns (percentages in parentheses)

	INT1	*INT2*	*INT3*	*INT4*	*INT5*	*INT6*	*INT7*	*TOTAL*
Receipt Markers	46/88 (52.3)	19/69 (27.5)	48/66 (72.7)	14/55 (25.5)	57/128 (44.5)	62/90 (68.9)	23/80 (28.8)	269/576 (46.7)

From Table 2 above we can see that across all the interviews, there is a 46.7% occurrence of receipt markers in the police officer turns although rates for individual speakers do vary considerably – INT3 and INT6 have very high rate of receipt markers per police officer turn at 72.7% and 68.9% respectively, while INT2, INT4 and INT7 all have rates of receipt marker occurrence well below the mean, at 27.5%, 25.5% and 28.8% respectively. Nonetheless, the fact that at least one in four turns by the police officers in each interview is prefaced by a receipt marker indicates that it is a prominent feature in the data.

In the concluding discussion below, the range of discourse features identified in the data will be considered in relation to the institutional goals of the police participants and the intentions of the VATE training scheme.

3.6. Duality in the discourse of police VATE interviews

We have seen that the institutionalisation of these interviews is expressed in the form of frame transitional utterances and participation frameworks that seem to have the principal role of mitigating the responsibility of the individual interlocutor. That is, the Opening can be said primarily to involve a frame labelled a police on-record interview frame, where the police officers seem to take on the role of *animator* of utterances whose *principal* and *author* were attributed to a third party represented by the police force as an institution. In the interview Closure it is possible to identify two different approaches, exemplified by PO7 in INT4 and PO6 in INT7. It was noted that PO7 in INT4 maintained a neutral stance in respect of CH7's narrative by using a footing device which attributed responsibility for the account to CH7. PO6 on the other hand did not overtly attribute the narrative to CH4, but rather made his account in the role of *principal* and *author* as well as *animator*. The examination of the Closure of INT4 and INT7 seemed to indicate that when the police officer assumes the role of *animator* of the child's utterances, as in INT4, the child feels more able to offer contributions to the summary. By contrast, in not making the participation framework explicit, PO6 in INT7 appears to have appropriated the child's narrative and thus reduce the possibility of CH7 offering any corrections or contributions.

In considering the participation frameworks of both the Opening and the Closure in terms of police institutional discourse we need to take into account the relationship between the police officers as an individual producing utterances which may classed as police institutional discourse, and the institution represented by such discourse. It seems reasonable to assume that in their daily work, police officers are considered to be carrying out a duty and representing the police force as an institution, rather than representing themselves as individuals, and that this would be somehow incorporated as a feature of police institutional discourse.

We could therefore conclude that the distribution of roles in the participation framework of the Opening (i.e. the police officer as *animator* of utterances attributable to the police institution) and the neutralistic stance taken up by PO7 through the shift of footing which places her in the role of *animator* of CH4's utterances, both conform to a notion of the police officer as a functionary of the police institution. In this sense, the participation frameworks support the institutionality and formality of the discourse, as proposed above.

Discoursal indicators (Thomas 1990) were said to support the police officer's position as the dominant participant by defining the boundaries of the discourse and restricting the allowable contributions made by the subordinate participant, the child. The use of discoursal indicators by the police interviewers in VATE interviews further emphasises the formality of the interaction, nonetheless such guidance of the interview structure is a necessary feature of this type of interview (Powell and Thompson 1994). The children must have a clear idea of what it is they are being asked to do and the whole encounter is heavily circumscribed by legislative requirements.

However, the co-occurrence of frequent receipt markers with discoursal indicators mark the VATE interview as an unusual variant of police institutional discourse. While the findings of the frame analysis, the distribution of participant roles and the discoursal indicators all indicate that the institutionality of the Tri-Partite Interview Technique is entrenched in the discourse, the frequency of receipt markers indicates that some contradictory force is at work in the production of these interactions. In addition to the receipt markers, relational or phatically-designed talk appears to be used by at least two officers to offset the underlying institutionality of the interviews and the overall use of the officers' first names is quite striking in its informality. The relational talk and first name use are both linguistic expressions of "Rapport Development", identified in the training guidelines as one step in the Opening section of the Tri-Partite Interview. Through the use of such devices the police officers are able to maintain an atmosphere where the children feel able to contribute meaningfully to the interaction. That such devices are reasonably successful is supported by the fact that all of the children in the study showed their willingness to provide a narrative of the dance class and/or the Event in some form. It was also notable that they were willing to inform the police officer if they did not know the answer to a question.

4. Conclusions

In presenting an interpretation of these findings, it is important that we attempt in some way to address the concerns of VATE interview practitioners and the justice system more broadly. In this way, it is possible to demonstrate to a wider audience that discourse analysis has the power to usefully contribute to police training and courtroom practices. There are certain risks associated with the use of VATE interviews in court cases and for the prosecution to continue to rely on the program, these risks must be outweighed by the advantages of reducing the stress on a child who is quite likely to be already traumatised. For instance, some commentators believe that the VATE process may in fact be advantageous to the defence as the role of the trial prosecutor in leading the evidence is diminished and the case for the prosecution must be constructed from evidence gathered by a police officer who is not a trained lawyer (Meadows 1995). The risk that the VATE interview provides greater scope for the defence to deconstruct the child's evidence is supported by Magistrate Coate of Victoria who observes that "[under the old system] the defence just has the child's statement and it's a more difficult task in cross-examination to get behind it" (cited in Meadows 1995: 970). Nonetheless, the VATE procedure is seen by some to be worth these risks as it does appear to work in reducing the stress on the witness: "[b]eing tested [in cross-examination], even though it's traumatic, may be easier than having to get the story out in the first place" (S.C. Cotterill cited in Meadows 1995: 970). Thus, the VATE interviews may function as a valuable opportunity for the child to tell his/her story – often for the first time – in an environment less formal than a court hearing and then later rely on this narrative for support when being cross-examined.

The value of this opportunity and the way in which it is observed by practitioners interviewing child witnesses is borne out by the results of the discourse analysis. Were the interview to conform exactly to normal police procedure, the result would no doubt be just as confrontational and confusing to the child witness as the proceedings of the court. Instead, the VATE interview is designed to consolidate the child's trust in the police officer: the importance of the police officer's displays of personal interest in the child's story is a very real consideration though one not normally associated with police institutional behaviour. In fact, it is more usual for police officers as individuals to display a minimal amount of personal interest in an interview subject, as their personal interests are considered secondary to the interests of the institution they represent.

It is clear then that there is considerable pressure on police officers in this situation to balance the requirements of the courts with the needs of the child, and the result is a unique and at times innovative blend of formality and informality. Police power and institutionality are expressed through discoursal indicators and participation frameworks of neutrality, while respect for the child's vulnerability produces the reassurances of receipt markers, first names and phatic communication. This duality of discourses is so fundamental to the process that it has become deeply embedded in the language of the VATE interview, demonstrating at the level of the interaction that the success of the program relies on the acceptance of some level of discursive contradiction.

References

Agnew, S. A., Powell, M. B. and P. C. Snow (2006). "An examination of the questioning styles of police officers and caregivers when interviewing children with intellectual disabilities". *Legal and criminological psychology* 11(1), 35-53.

Ainsworth, J. (1993). "In a different register: the pragmatics of powerlessness in police interrogation". *Yale Law Journal* 103, 259-322.

Atkinson, J. M. (1992). "Displaying neutrality: formal aspects of court proceedings". In: P. Drew and J. Heritage (eds.), *Talk at Work*. Cambridge: Cambridge University Press, 199-211

Auburn, T., Drake, S. and C. Willig (1995). "'You punched him, didn't you?': Versions of violence in accusatory interviews". *Discourse and Society* 6(3), 353-386.

Cooke, M. (1996). "A different story: narrative versus 'question and answer' in Aboriginal evidence". *Forensic Linguistics: The International Journal of Speech, Language and the Law* 3(2), 273-288.

Coupland, J., Robinson, J. D. and N. Coupland (1994). "Frame negotiation in doctor-elderly patient consultations". *Discourse and Society* 5(1), 89-124.

Du Bois, J. (1991). "Transcription design principles for spoken discourse research". *Pragmatics,* 1(1), 71-105.

Eades, D. (1994). "A case of communicative clash: Aboriginal English and the legal system". In: J. Gibbons (ed.), *Language and the Law*. Harlow: Longman Group, 234-264

Fisher, S., and A. Todd (eds.) (1986). *Discourse and institutional authority: medicine, education and law* (Vol. XIX). Norwood, NJ: Ablex Publishing Corporation.

Frankel, R. (1990). "Talking in interviews: a dispreference for patient-initiated questions in physician-patient encounters". In: G. Psathas (ed.), *Interaction Competence*. Washington, DC: University Press of America, 231-262.

Goffman, E. (1974). *Frame Analysis*. New York: Harper and Row.

Goffman, E. (1981). *Forms of Talk*. Philadelphia: University of Pennsylvania Press.

Guadagno, B. L., Powell, M. B. and R. Wright (2006). "Police officers' and legal professionals' perceptions regarding how children are, and should be, questioned about repeated abuse". *Psychiatry, psychology and law* 13(2), 251-260.

Haworth, K. (2006). "The dynamics of power and resistance in police interview discourse". *Discourse and society* 17(6), 739-759.

Heydon, G. (1997). *Participation frameworks, discourse features and embedded requests in police V.A.T.E. interviews with children.* Unpublished Honours Thesis, Melbourne: Monash University.

Heydon, G. (2005). *The language of police interviewing: a critical analysis*. New York: Palgrave Macmillan.

Lakoff, R. (1990). *Talking power: the notion of language in an institutional setting*. New York: Basic Books.

Meadows, H. (1995). "Sex, evidence and videotape". *Law Institute Journal (Victoria)* 69(10), 966-969.

Powell, M. (2000). "PRIDE: The essential elements of a forensic interview with an Aboriginal person". *Australian psychologist* 35(3), 186-192.

Powell, M., and D. M. Thomson (1994). "Children's eyewitness-memory research: Implications for practice". *Families in Society: The Journal of Contemporary Human Services,* April 1994, 204-215.

Redlich, A. D., Silverman, M., Chen, J. and H. Steiner (2004). "The police interrogation of children and adolescents". In: G. D. Lassiter (ed.), *Interrogations, Confessions, and Entrapment*. New York: Kluwer Academic, 107-125.

Shuy, R. W. (1998). *The language of confession, interrogation, and deception.* Thousand Oaks: Sage.

Thomas, J. A. (1989). Discourse control in confrontational interaction. In: L. Hickey (ed.), *The Pragmatics of Style*. London: Routledge, 133-156.

Appendix I

Transcription Conventions

Adapted from DuBois (1991)

Units	
Turn	{*carriage return*}
Word	{*space*}
Truncated word	-
Speakers	
Speaker identity/turn start	:
Speech overlap	[ ]
Pause	
Long	...
Medium	..
Short	.
Pitch	
Rising terminal pitch	?
Transcriber's perspective	
Researcher's comment	( )
Codes used for confidentiality of participants	
Police Officer's code	PO#
Child code	CH#
First name	(FN)
Middle name	(MN)
Second middle name	(SMN)
Surname	(SN)
Name of month (in DOB)	(month)
Day of month (in DOB)	(date)

Appendix II

The VATE Tri-Partite Interview Structure

OPENING

I. Rapport Development;

II. Witness Focussing; and

III. Demographic Details for Anxious Older Witnesses.

INFORMATION GATHERING

IV. Establishing Anchor

V. Open-Ended Narrative

VI. Open Questions

VII. Closed Questions

CLOSURE

VIII. Review

IX. Terminating the interview

Appendix III

VATE training interview set-up

The VATE training course consists of theory and practical components and the interviewing skills of trainees are tested in a mock interview. In order to create the most realistic environment for these mock interviews, the VATE coordinators organise for groups of school children, aged about ten years, to attend interview sessions with the trainees. A few days prior to these interviews, the VATE coordinators arrange for the children's school day to be disrupted in some fashion. A typical example might be two police officers in plain clothes attending a classroom and pretending to conduct a survey of the children's afterschool activities. The disruption organised by the VATE coordinators is usually referred to as "the Event" and any information about the Event becomes the target for elicitation in the police-child interviews a few days later. VATE trainees are told only the time and date on which the Event occurred and perhaps the type of class that it disrupted (e.g. normal class, assembly, special assembly etc.). Each trainee engages in a fifteen minute interview with at least two different children during the training day. The object of the exercise is to use the skills taught in the training course to elicit as many details as possible from the interviewee about the Event, including descriptions of the people involved.

Seven such training interviews were conducted at the Melbourne Police Centre in May 1997, and the video-taped recordings of those interviews formed the basis for the data used in this study. The child participants were pupils at a rural ballet school and the Event occurred during one of their classes.

Lorna Fadden
Simon Fraser University
Canada

QUANTITATIVE AND QUALITATIVE ANALYSES OF POLICE INTERVIEWS WITH CANADIAN ABORIGINAL AND NON-ABORIGINAL SUSPECTS[1]

1. Introduction

At various stages of most police investigations, it is common practice for police officers to interview people who they believe to have been involved in an illegal act, assuming of course that the suspects do not invoke their constitutional right to remain silent. This study focuses on investigative interviews with suspects who are questioned for their alleged involvement in a crime. More specifically, I address key discourse differences between two cultural groups in Western Canada – Aboriginals and non-Aboriginals.

Police interviews belong to a conversational genre called institutional discourse. Other types of institutional discourse include classroom interaction, service or commercial exchanges, courtroom discourse, etc. To distinguish institutional discourse from casual conversation, Levinson (1992) identifies three properties of the former, each of which is helpful in describing features of police interviews. First, institutional discourse is goal oriented. In the case of police interviews, the goal of the investigating officer or officers is to uncover information about events from a suspect or witness. The goal of many suspects, quite contrarily, is to conceal as much information as possible about his or her involvement in the events in question. Second, the institutional context places constraints on the appropriate or allowable contributions that participants may make. In investigative interviews, the investigator performs the asking, asserting, and consequently, topic selection, whereas the suspect's appropriate contribution is expected to be relevant response. Third, inferential frameworks may be in place in institutional discourse, specific to the context at hand. In a police interview, investigators, bestowed with institutional power and suspects who have none,

[1] An earlier stage of this work presented at the 8th Biennial Conference of the International Association of Forensic Linguists in July 2007, in Seattle, Washington, USA. For that presentation and this paper, I gratefully acknowledge the cooperation of Sgt. L. Rankin and the Vancouver Police Department, and Sgt. D. Dickson and the New Westminster Police Service, for providing the data upon which this work is conducted. Thanks also go to Dean Mellow and Nancy Hedberg for discussion and comments. Any blunders are, of course, my own.

interpret each other's input accordingly. Suspects may produce turns that maintain or resist their powerless roles in this setting.

The notion of power asymmetry in police interviews alluded to above is well documented (Ainsworth 1993, Haworth 2006, Heydon 2004 and 2005, Newbury and Johnson 2006, Thornborrow 2002). The investigator holds the power, both institutionally, and conversationally, and the suspect, little or none. The power imbalance in this context, as in many institutional contexts, grants the interviewing officer license to select the topics and steer the suspect's input with questions, thereby leaving the suspect in a position of responding. While the suspect may resist questioning through various means (see especially Haworth 2006, and Johnson and Newbury 2006), the power asymmetry generally holds.

Police interviews with Aboriginal suspects in North America have not yet attracted attention in the linguistic literature. In Australia, however, where many Aboriginal people speak a dialect of English quite distinct from the standard variety, a wealth of studies have concluded that a mismatch of conversational norms and inferences arises when members of the dominant cultural group (Anglo) and the non dominant cultural group (Aboriginal) come together at all stages of the legal process (Cooke 1996, Eades[2] 1992, 1993, 1994a, 1995b, 1997 and 2000, and Mildren 1999). The outcome of this interactional mismatch between people of culturally and linguistically dissimilar backgrounds is the misinterpretation of Aboriginal suspects' and defendants' accounts at every stage of the legal process.

The data explored in this paper demonstrate that Canadian Aboriginal suspects' discourse behaviour could be misinterpreted by those who do not share particular discourse features typical of the varieties of English spoken by Aboriginal people.[3] The Aboriginal suspects in this study are all from Canada's west coast, and as such are uniformly characteristic of the Aboriginal English found in the Pacific Northwest. While it is beyond the scope of this paper to provide an overview of the slight phonological and syntactic differences that exist between Aboriginal English and standard Western Canadian English, some discourse features appear to have bearing on the linguistic performance of Aboriginal speakers in the context of police interviews. In particular, in many Aboriginal speech communities there exists a high tolerance for silence, and an appreciation for brevity[4] (Ball et al. 2006, Dannenberg 2002, Leap 1993, Pye 1985 (cited in Leap 1993), Phillips 1983, Tarpent 1982, and Mulder 1982).

[2] Eades' groundbreaking and extensive work on this topic in the Australian system should inform any comparable North American study.

[3] Aboriginal English in Canada is certainly not assumed to be the same or even similar to that of Australia, and it is assumed as well, that there are varieties of Aboriginal English that vary from region to region as a result of First Nations' cultural and linguistic differences.

[4] Other characteristics which are not further addressed in this study are quieter, slower speech, less eye contact, and narratives with conceptual rather than temporal organization.

The remainder of this paper will proceed as follows: Section 2 will provide a word on the integrative methodology used in this study; Section 3 will introduce the corpus upon which the study is based; Sections 4 and 5 report on the quantitative and qualitative results respectively; and Section 6 offers a discussion and concluding remarks.

2. A dual approach to the research goal

The aim of this paper is to provide both quantitative and qualitative perspectives on discourse phenomena, comparing Aboriginal and non-Aboriginal suspects. The coupling of quantitative and qualitative analyses to present a dual view of discourse has been successfully employed in a number of discourse studies of various genres (for example, De Fina 1995, Schiffrin 2002, Sillars et al. 1992, and Van de Mieroop 2005 and 2006). Biber et al. (1998) and Schegloff (1993) have also commented on the complementarity of the two approaches. The unique benefit of this integrated approach offers the generalizing, quantificational power that comes from consulting a corpus as well as the drill-down, descriptive power afforded by discourse analysis.

3. The corpus

This study is based on video recorded interviews conducted by the Vancouver Police Department and the New Westminster Police Department between 2003 and 2005.

Extracts are drawn from six interviews with three Aboriginal suspects and three non-Aboriginal suspects.[5] The table below summarizes the subjects, their ages, and the crime for which they were questioned by police.

Group	Suspect ID	Sex	Age	Charge
Aboriginal	Ab-1	male	56	sexual assault
	Ab-2	male	50s	sexual assault
	Ab-3	female	20s	public mischief
Non-Aboriginal	nAb-1	female	19	child abuse
	nAb-2	male	34	child abuse
	nAb-3	male	31	sexual assaults, robberies

[5] The term "non-Aboriginal" was chosen because two of the non-Aboriginal suspects are Caucasian, and one is a Canadian born and raised South East Asian, who is monolingual and who speaks standard western Canadian English.

A few words on the suspects are in order to help clarify extracts in later sections. Three males are questioned for sexual assault. The first two, Ab-1 and Ab-2, are questioned for the sexual assault of young women, the third, nAb-3, was accused of the assault of several women over several days, and concurrent robberies. The two suspects questioned for child abuse are a common law couple whose five-month-old child suffered a fractured skull and internal bleeding. Medical examination concluded that there had been a severe blunt force trauma consistent with being thrown. Based on questioning by police, it was clear that the male was suspected of committing the assault, and the female was questioned for her possible involvement or for her withholding information about it. The woman questioned for public mischief, Ab-3, was accused of making a false sexual assault complaint against a man with whom she had had a one night affair that she wished to conceal from her husband. All Aboriginal suspects confessed, as did the third non-Aboriginal suspect.

Police interviews in this corpus are divided into three phases.[6] During the opening phase, the investigator collects demographic information about the suspect and often makes small talk. The investigator usually transitions to the second phase by asking the suspect if he or she knows why they are of interest to police. The questioning during this phase pertains almost exclusively to the charge or charges, and is noticeably more aggressive than questioning during the first phase. It is the second phase which is of concern in this study. In the closing phase the investigator concludes the interview and the suspect is taken back to his or her cell.

4. Quantitative results

In a dataset such as this which spans several hours of spoken dialogue, key conversational features can be accounted for by quantificational means. In this section, three quantitative analyses are presented, illustrating marked differences between the Aboriginal and non-Aboriginal suspect groups. The features to be described in quantified terms are the investigator to suspect speaking ratio, the frequency of second person pronouns as a measure of confrontation, and the use of hedges.

4.1. Investigator-to-suspect speaking ratio

Figure 1 illustrates the difference in the amount of speech produced by investigators and suspects during the questioning phase of each interview.

[6] Police interviews in general are noted to consist of three parts. See especially Heydon (2005 and this volume) for discussion.

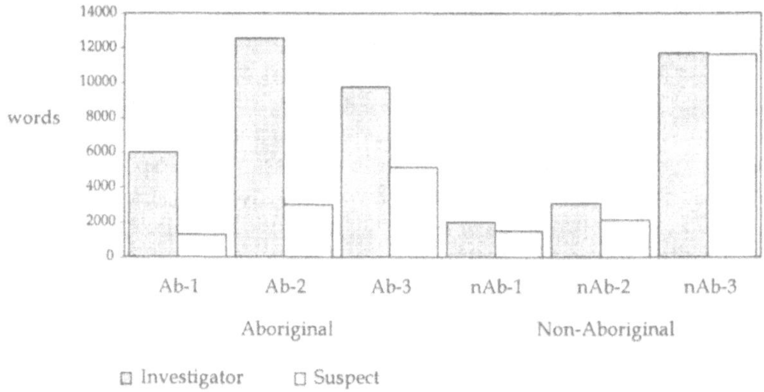

Figure 1. Investigator-to-suspect speaking ratio

In all three cases, Aboriginal suspects produce considerably fewer words overall than investigators. The most talkative of the three, Ab-3, does only slightly more than half of the talking. The other two, Ab-1 and Ab-2, produce just fewer than one word to every four produced by the investigator. The non-Aboriginal suspects, on the other hand, talk more than their Aboriginal counterparts, in the case of Ab-3 the ratio very closely approaches one to one.

The amount of talk produced by each party is of importance because the topics discussed in police interviews largely centre on events which are alleged to concern the suspect. If the investigator is doing the majority of the talking, then the majority of the details surrounding the events in question are created by him or her, rather than the suspect. Heydon (2005) discusses how the investigator's best case scenario would see the suspect generating all information relevant to the events in question without prompting by police. However, police prompting is almost always necessary to lead the suspect to talk and this prompting comes in the form of questions and assertions that contain many of the details which police have gathered from sources other than the suspect.

By producing less talk, Aboriginal suspects are allowing more of the story to be constructed by someone other than himself or herself, while the non-Aboriginal suspects are producing more of the story in their own defence. I return to this point in Section 5 when qualitative features are discussed.

4.2. Second person pronoun reference

The frequency of second person pronouns in suspects' speech demonstrates how frequently suspects directly address the investigator. Because the power hierarchy in which both parties are situated dictates that the investigator does the asking and topic selection and the suspect is in a position of responding, a turn in which the suspect directly addresses the investigator is one that might reasonably be construed as a challenge to the hierarchy, however successful or unsuccessful. Figure 2 below illustrates the number of second person references per 1000 words.[7] It makes it clear that Aboriginal suspects in this data make fewer references to the second person, and hence address the investigator between 12 and 15 times per 1000 words. Non-Aboriginal suspects, on the other hand, directly address the investigator approximately twice as often, approximately 25 times per 1000 words. Upon closer inspection of the data, it appears that second person references differ with respect to the degree to which they are confrontational. For example, second person references can be role-challenging as in extracts 01 and 02.

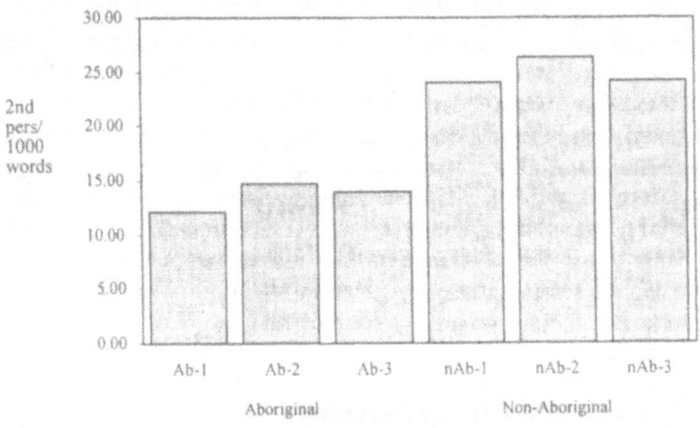

Figure 2. Second person references per thousand words by suspect

Extract 01 (nAb-02)

I We're not- this isn't making you out to be a bad person.

S Then why are you asking me if I did anything?

---

[7] Taking into account that interviews are of differing lengths, the data are normed to number of tokens per 1000 words. See Biber et al. (1998) for discussion of this technique.

Extract 02 (nAb-03)

I No, you were gonna be put there anyway. *(Regarding the suspect's location in relation to a sexual assault where he confesses to having stolen a car.)*

S Prove I raped her.[8] Where's the DNA? You don't have fucking DNA. You got no pubic hair, you've got no- Prove it!

Extracts 01 and 02 are confrontational and very typical of what is found in the interviews with non-Aboriginal suspects. These suspects appear to be pushing the institutional boundary that separates the contextually appropriate roles played by each investigator and suspect. In the first case, the suspect poses a challenging Wh-question prefaced by the discourse marker *then* linking the suspect's question to the investigator's attempt to ease the suspect's defensiveness. In the second extract, the suspect asserts that pertinent evidence from his body was not collected from the crime scene, challenging the investigator to indicate otherwise.

Second person references can be much less confrontational than those shown in Extracts 01 and 02, and are typical of those found in interviews with Aboriginal suspects. While resisting investigators' assertions, the following extracts do not have the same confrontational tone projected in the previous extracts. As such, there is less of a challenge to institutional roles:

Extract 03 (Ab-1)

I Right. So when she had too much to drink and she was lying in front of you, you were tempted. There's nothing you can do. It's biological. [SUSPECT][9]? It happened that way, didn't it.

S Whatever way you want to put it.

Extract 04 (Ab-2)

I Ok. But that's not what happened. This is what happened. And I told you ok? You came down and you checked on her, ok? What is a man to do, ok? Listen. I know guys who just bump into another girl and get aroused. You went and you touched her, flesh to flesh, and you were aroused.

S If you say so then.

In both extracts above, the suspects neither confirm nor deny the investigators' asserted information, opting instead to resist in a less challenging manner, as described in Johnson and Newbury (2006).

---

[8] As second person references were counted automatically, imperatives were not included in this study.

[9] Suspects', witnesses' and victims' names are all anonymized in the data, and are labelled in SMALL CAPS.

While both groups of suspects address the investigator using second person pronouns, non-Aboriginal suspects do so more often and when they do, present a challenge the power hierarchy that separates the institutionally defined roles played by investigators and suspects. Aboriginal suspects address investigators less often, and in a manner which presents less of a challenge to the hierarchy.

4.3. Use of hedges

Hedges in speech are generally agreed to have a softening effect on the message that they accompany. Compare for example:

Extract 05 (Ab-1)

I Ok. Now let's-and then now, did she take off her pants or did you?
S I think she probably did herself.

Extract 05a, without hedges

I Ok. Now let's-and then now, did she take off her pants or did you?
S She did herself.

In extract 05 above the hedges *I think* and *probably* signal a tentative proposition rather than an assertive one, like the hypothetical example in Extract 05a. In institutional settings, the use of hedges confirms the lack of institutional power (Johnstone 2002) held by the layperson using the hedge in conversation with the professional. In this corpus, the number of hedges used by Aboriginal suspects is considerably higher than that of non-Aboriginal suspects. Figure 3 illustrates the number of hedges per turn.

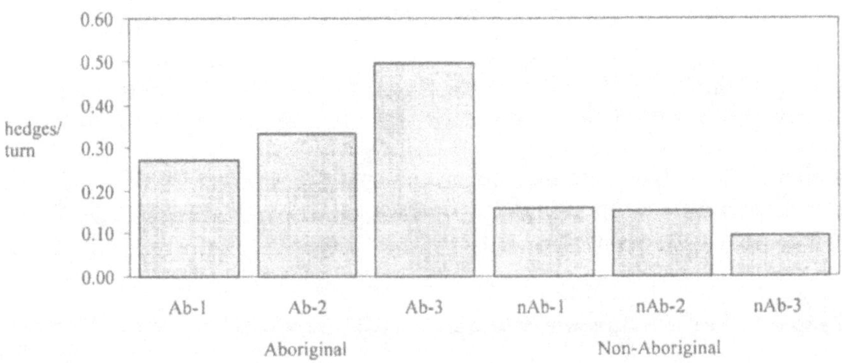

Figure 3. Number of hedges per turn by suspect

Aboriginal suspects are shown to use considerably more hedges per turn in all cases than non-Aboriginals. In the most extreme case, Aboriginal suspect Ab-3, produced on average one hedge for every two turns. On the opposite end, the non-Aboriginal suspects produced one hedge for every 10 to 15 turns. The more hedges a suspect produces, the less assertive the message. The cumulative effect of multiple hedges throughout an interview present an image of a suspect who appears less committed overall to the content of what he or she is saying, leaving more room for doubt.

The use of hedges in this context is bound to have a detrimental effect on the suspects who use them the most. Weakening one's utterances instils little or no confidence in the suspects' commitment to their utterance, to investigators and if submitted as evidence, to jury members as well.

5. Qualitative results

In Section 4 it was shown that Aboriginal suspects talk considerably less than their non-Aboriginal counterparts in relation to the amount of speech produced by the investigators. In this section, I present qualitative descriptions of discourse strategies that contribute significantly to the difference between groups in the amount of speaking each produces. First, is a comparison between Aboriginal and non-Aboriginal suspects' handling of questions and assertions from investigators: Aboriginal suspects deny details, while non-Aboriginals dispute them. Second, it is shown that non-Aboriginal suspects produce unsolicited evaluations of themselves, others, and the interview process and Aboriginal suspects do not.

5.1. Denials and disputes

The most apparent difference between the two groups of suspects in this corpus is how much or how little information is given when faced with questions and assertions put forth by investigators. In the examples that follow, chosen for their being typically representative of what takes place throughout the interviews, it will be shown that aboriginal suspects put forth very little in the way of details to counter that which is alleged by police and that non-Aboriginal suspects offer competing details.

In the two extracts below, investigators build a scenario to which the suspect is expected to respond, and in both cases, a general rejection is offered without addressing any specific details.

Extract 06 (Ab-1)

I The bottom line here is that here is a young lady, she is at your place, she is drunk, she's being flirty, she's already had sex with somebody because everybody's horny because that's what alcohol makes you do, the old lady's not around, everybody's asleep, and here she is, laying there and you're thinking ok, I've got the in, I'm gonna take the chance, and then you you did, ok? And there's no doubt in my mind that you did that.

S Yeah whatever (sarcastic).

In Extract 06, the investigator claims that the suspect was in a position which would make it easy for him to take sexual advantage of the youth who has been visiting his daughter at their home. He alleges that the victim was drunk, sexually active, presenting herself as available, and with the suspect's wife out of the home, the suspect would attempt to have sex with her. The suspect responds to the entire scenario sarcastically, without addressing any of the specific details. While some details are not necessarily disputable, the investigator's presuming to know what the suspect is thinking would be a reasonable point to dispute when the suspect has heretofore claimed innocence.

In the following extract, again, the investigator creates a detailed story, after which the suspect offers an unspecified denial.

Extract 07 (Ab-3)

I Ok, you have memories of that night. You know what you have done, ok? Now, when you realized it, maybe in the spur of the moment, you have a few drinks right? When we have a few drinks it removes our inhibitions. I know, I've been drunk before. In that moment of weakness, you have to make up a story to tell your husband, ok?

S No.

The investigator asserts that despite her claiming to have been drugged and suffering memory loss, the suspect remembers having had a sexual encounter with a man whom she met in a bar, and that her having been drinking would cause her to become uninhibited. He offers the sympathetic understanding that being intoxicated causes people to do things they would not ordinarily do. Upon going home to her husband, he suggests that she would have to conceal her affair by telling him that she had been drugged and assaulted. He appends tag questions to his points, providing openings for affirmative response, and she only responds no after the last point. It is unclear whether she is negating the last detail the investigator provides, or the entire scenario.

In both Extracts 06 an 07, the investigator paints a detailed picture to which the suspect could respond to any number of details and he or she does not. This is quite typical among the Aboriginal suspects in this data set. Extract 08 is similar, with the suspect offering a rejection of only the final detail asserted by the investigator.

Extract 08 (Ab-2)

I SUSPECT, ok, listen to me ok? You didn't hear what I said before SUSPECT and- and- and I think you need to understand, that um, you know, you woke up, and you decided that you were going go out there and try and have sex with her with this girl, alright, against her will and you went out there and you did it, and you tried to pull her pants down and she said no and there was a lot of screamin and yellin and you bailed.

S No she only screamed once.

In Extract 08, much like 06 and 07, the investigator builds a scenario composed of several details, starting with the suspect waking, deciding to have sex with the young woman, and leaving his bedroom to approach her. He tried to remove her pants, she protested, and he left the room. The only point contested by the suspect is the detail about the screaming. At other stages of the interview, before and after this exchange, he contested all of the other points, but nowhere did he offer a narrative account of what happened from his point of view, taking into account the scenario provided by the investigator.

In none of the examples above, and very seldom during their interviews do Aboriginal suspects produce a competing scenario in their own words. This trait is consistent with the notion that in maintaining institutional boundaries, the investigator introduces topics and the suspects do not. When confronted with a scenario posed by investigators, non Aboriginal suspects behave quite differently. Rather than produce unspecified denials, or denials of a small subset of the information presented by investigators, non-Aboriginal suspects in this data set frequently offer a competing scenario.

Extract 09 (nAb-1)

I And don't make this a mistake, don't make this mistake that because the baby has a fractured skull, don't make this mistake that that makes you a bad parent or a bad person. You're not.

S I didn't do it.

I No but even if you did do it you're not a bad person.

S I didn't do it.

I That doesn't make you a bad person.

S Oh yeah?

I It doesn't.

S Yeah.

I No it doesn't. It makes you somebody who's succumbed to stress like millions and millions of other people in this world.

S But not- I would never hurt my kid even if the world is on my shoulders. No I just can't see myself doing that. You know, I was- I was- my dad used to beat me up because you know, he thought I was a- a bad kid or whatever, and I promised myself God I would never do this to my kid. Ever. Cause I know the pain. He's a baby, how much [inaudible], a helpless kid that needs me, I would hurt? God no. If it was an accident why would I keep it secret? I'm not scared of anyone, I'm not here sitting in front of you, trying to please you, because I'm scared to tell you it was an accident. There was nothing, no accident. I didn't do anything intentionally. No, nothing.

In the extract above, spanning several turns, the investigator builds a scenario which suggests that the suspect could have been responsible for her child's injury. He indicates that the stress of daily life would push her to her breaking point, no differently than anyone else, suggesting that she is a victim of day to day stressful living. She counters this assertion by saying that she would be incapable of causing harm, linking to the investigator's topic, and then introducing a new topic regarding her background as an abused child as a means of saying that she herself would not be an abuser. Another strategy this suspect uses that Aboriginal suspects do not is repetition. She repeats that no accident had occurred and had one occurred, she would own up to it.

In Extract 10 below, taken from the interview of the previous suspect's common-law husband, the investigator disputes his account of the injury sustained by their child wherein the child was reported to have wiggled out of his seat and fell to the floor while the suspect was in the bathroom.

Extract 10 (nAb-2)

I But it didn't happen as you tell me. There had to be a blunt force trauma to the side of the head for that kind of an injury. It didn't happen from the chair and I'll tell you what else, like a four month, five month old baby isn't able to move too much. And you're suggesting he wiggled out of the seat.

S No no no, I swear to God, if you guys were I mean we could, we could do this, like, I mean, I don't know if we can take a staff member's time, but he has this thing where he goes like this *(mimics wiggling back and forth).* And he can slide. His grandmother has seen it, [WITNESS]'s mother. You know, but I wouldn't have left him if he was sort of energetic and doing that action. He was he was calm.

Besides a rejection of the investigator's claim that a baby of five months could indeed remove himself from a child seat, the suspect suggests that as part of the investigation, they demonstrate that the child is capable of moving side to side to slide out of his seat. He offers justification for this course of action and evidence of his credibility by claiming that others have seen the child accomplish this feat. He finishes his response by saying that had the child seemed mobile at the time, he would not have left him alone in his seat. Like the extract above, the suspect offers unsolicited information in an attempt to direct the topic in a more favourable direction for himself when confronted with the investigators' disbelief.

In the extract below, the investigator presents a simple assertion that a woman has reported a sexual assault, one for which the suspect is now being questioned.

Extract 11 (nAb-3)

I But the bottom line is, as we said before, it's just as- as, they say on the news that it's a sexual assault and you say it's not a sexual assault so that's why I want to hear your side of that.

S Prove it.

I But what you've got is a woman who says she's been sexually assaulted.

S What? When she was unconscious? She's been sexually assaulted? Let's get serious. I wanted her car. That's what I'm thinking. I want the fuckin car, I'm going out cruisin.

The suspect presents two challenges in the form of an incredulous *What?* and the clause *When she was unconscious?*, followed by the echo question *She's been sexually assaulted?* He attempts to trivialize the victim's report by suggesting it lacks seriousness. He concedes that a crime is committed, namely that he stole her car and offered the motivation that he intended to go for a joy ride, a much less serious crime than a sexual assault. Like nAb-1 in Extract 09, he uses repetition to make clear his intention.

Extracts 06 to 08 demonstrate the short answers typically produced when Aboriginal suspects are presented with allegations. By allowing investigators to "author" events and actions, and by introducing no topics or details of their own, they maintain the power hierarchy. Extracts 09 to 11 show the opposite, where non-Aboriginal suspects are verbose and present competing scenarios which challenge the power hierarchy in attempts to defend themselves.

5.2. Providing evaluative comment

In addition to offering competing scenarios of events and actions, non-Aboriginal suspects also produce unsolicited evaluative comments throughout the interview. Aboriginal suspects, on the other hand, do not. Evaluative comments can be centred on the self, other people, and the interview or interviewer. In Extract 12, the suspect takes the opportunity to extol his own virtues.

Extract 12 (nAb-3)

I When you think of the media, the media's gonna say what the media's gonna say. Where this tape is going, this is what the evidence is that goes to court. Your side of the evidence that goes to court.
S It's not just my side, it's their side. *(Referring to victims)*
I Yeah, they're gonna get their side.
S Yeah. But I just want everyone to know right now that- that- that never in my fucking life, when I've dealt with the cops, when I've done something, I've always owned it. I own what I say and I own what I do.
one minute later, a few turns about his past convictions
S If I did it, I'll own it. I'll do the time.

The investigator reminds the suspect that his recorded interview would be submitted in evidence, at which point he offers unsolicited information about his character, specifically, that he is always willing to own up to his deeds. Again, repetition appears to be a means of emphasizing his self-evaluation. The same suspect offers the following negative evaluation of another individual, one of many he produced during the interview.

Extract 13 (nAb-3)

I Where was that? *(Regarding where the suspect stole a vehicle).*
S Downtown. I went and got a bunch of dope, cus there's a guy down there, drug dealer right? Thinks he's big right? And I don't like the guy to begin with so I said fuck it, I'm gonna rob him.
I Ok.
S So I went and punched his face in in the alley.
I That night?
S Yeah, that night.
I What's his name?
S Aah, it doesn't matter what his name is.
I It is. It is kind of important what his name is because he's probably, he has probably made a complaint against you that, that uh, I don't know about yet.
S He's a drug dealer! Come on man! I'm well sure, they're fuckin rats man. Look at the heads on them!

In the extract above the suspect indicates that he does not like the drug dealer he refers to, the dealer's name is not worth reporting, and that drug dealers are rat-like, an ironic assessment coming from a self-admitted rapist. It has been suggested (Fadden 2007) that negative evaluations of others attributes and actions are a means of doing damage control during an interview, as a strategy to divert attention from the suspect's own negative actions and attributes to someone else's.

Suspects can also provide evaluations of the interview process itself. In Extract 14, the investigator has proposed that the suspect undergo a polygraph examination.

Extract 14 (nAb-1)

I So I'm gonna know whether you're telling the truth, and when I ask the machine, or we ask you a question the machine or the instrument immediately comes back and says truth or a lie, it's black and white.

S It's not. It's not accurate.

I It's very accurate.

S Well, 98% accurate

I It's very accurate, ok? So I ask you this, I'm gonna put you on this as a hypothetical, you're hooked up to the instrument, I say to you, did you accidentally or intentionally cause that injury to your son on DATE?

S That's- that's not a very good question.

In response to the proposed polygraph, the suspect provides the opinion that polygraph exams are not accurate. When the investigator disputes that claim, she concedes that the exam would be 98% accurate, but not straying far from her original opinion. The investigator then asks whether she would be found to be lying when asked about her son's injury. She dodges the question with another evaluative comment, this time indicating that the investigator's question is flawed.

Only one unsolicited opinion was found in the Aboriginal suspects' interviews, reproduced in Extract 15:

Extract 15 (Ab-1)

I I'm starting to think that maybe what you're telling me is not true.

S It is true.

I I'm starting to think that maybe there's more to this.

S Bullshit.

It is difficult to determine whether the suspect's response in the last line is a rejection of the prior assertions that the suspect is being untruthful and that he is withholding information, or that he is commenting on the investigator's manner.

The previous examples in which non-Aboriginal suspects allow themselves to provide opinions where they are not solicited demonstrate the manner in which they attempt to control certain topics and introduce others as a means of managing their otherwise powerless role. Aboriginal suspects do not use this strategy with any regularity.

6. Discussion and conclusion

This paper has explored quantitatively and qualitatively some features of Aboriginal and non-Aboriginal suspects' discourse behaviour in the context of police interviews. By no means are these three Aboriginal and three non-Aboriginal suspects intended to be representative of all suspects of those groups, and the author recognizes the limits to any conclusions to be drawn herein. However, the two groups behave differently enough to warrant further investigation on this topic.

Given the power hierarchy in effect in institutional discourse, and in particular in police interviews, the study makes clear the notion that Aboriginal suspects' discourse behaviour does little or nothing to challenge the boundaries by virtue of the fact that they say very little, are non confrontational on the infrequent occasions where they directly address the investigator, and use an abundance of hedges which contributes to a perceived lack of commitment to their message. When faced with allegations from investigators, Aboriginal suspects offer short denials and nothing in the way of alternative accounts in their own words, and they very seldom offer unsolicited opinions of themselves, others, or the investigation. Non-Aboriginal suspects are shown to push the institutional boundaries by being considerably more verbose, they are directly confrontational with the investigator, and use fewer hedges which would soften their assertions, resulting in the appearance of a stronger commitment to their words.

Discourse behaviour typical of Canadian Aboriginal speakers, namely the preference for being short on words, may give police and later on juries, the impression that aboriginal suspects are not defending themselves or that they unwittingly appear untrustworthy, or have information they wish to conceal, when instead, their discourse strategies do not align with a set of expected behaviours in the interview room. Such expected behaviours would include taking the opportunity to promote the suspect's account of what happened, signalling strong commitment to one's own account through the use of repetition, a lack of hedging, offering unsolicited opinions and taking license to advance topics not introduced by the investigator.

It is reasonable to assume that if legal professionals and jury members are not aware of Aboriginal speakers' dispreference for verbosity, then Aboriginal suspects will be at a greater disadvantage compared to non-Aboriginal suspects in an investigation. If for example a portion of an interview is shown during a trial and the defendant is shown disputing only one of several details, as was the case in Extract 08, or giving an unspecified denial as in 07, the benefit of the doubt would not likely be afforded the suspect on the basis of such evidence.

The results of a study such as this may inform Canadian agencies that are taking steps to incorporate cultural knowledge into legal practice at various stages from investigation through to trial. The contributions of linguists and anthropologists therefore, should be taken into serious consideration.

References

Ainsworth, J. (1993). "In a different register: The pragmatics of powerlessness in police interrogations". *The Yale Law Journal* 103(2), 259-322.

Ball, J., Bernhardt, B. and J. Deby (2006). "First Nations English Dialects: Implications for supporting First Nations Children's Development". In: S. McLeod (ed.), *The International Guide to Speech Acquisition*. Clifton Park, NY: Thompson Delmar Learning, 101-106.

Biber, D., Conrad, S., and R. Reppen (1998). *Corpus Linguistics: Investigating Language Structure and Use*. Cambridge: Cambridge University Press.

Cooke, M. (1996). "A different story: narrative versus 'question and answer' in Aboriginal evidence". *Forensic Linguistics*, 3(2), 273-288.

Dannenberg, C. (2002). *Sociolinguistic constructs of ethnic identity: The syntactic delineation of an American Indian English*. Durham, NC: Duke University.

De Fina, A. (1995). "Pronominal choice, identity and solidarity in political discourse". *Text* 15, 379-410.

Eades, D. (1992). *Aboriginal English and the Law: Communication with Aboriginal English-Speaking Clients: A Handbook for Legal Practitioners*. Brisbane: Queensland Law Society.

Eades, D. (1993). "The case for Condren: Aboriginal English, pragmatics and the law". *Journal of Pragmatics* 20, 141-162.

Eades, D. (1994a). "A case of communicative clash: Aboriginal English in the legal system". In: J. Gibbons (ed.), *Language and the Law*. London: Longman, 234-264.

Eades, D. (1994b). "Forensic Linguistics in Australia: An Overview". *Forensic Linguistics*, 1(2), 113-132.

Eades, D. (1997). "Language in court: acceptance of linguistic evidence about Indigenous Australians in the criminal justice system". *Australian Aboriginal Studies* 1, 15-27.

Eades, D. (2000). "I don't think it's an answer to the question: Silencing Aboriginal witnesses in court". *Language in Society* 29, 161-195.

Edwards, J. (1989). *Language and Disadvantage*. London: Cole and Whurr.

Fadden, L. (2007). "Can't stand the heat: Suspects' attention deflecting strategies". In: N. Carter, L. Hadic-Zabala, A. Rimrott and D. Storoshenko (eds.), *Proceedings of the 2006 Northwest Linguistics Conference*, Burnaby, Canada, 89-98.

Giles, H., and P. Powesland (1975). *Speech Style and Social Evaluation*. London: Academic Press.

Gumperz, J. J. (1992). "Interviewing in intercultural situations". In: P. Drew and J. Heritage (eds.), *Talk at work: Interactions in institutional settings*. Cambridge: Cambridge University Press, 302-327.

Haworth, K. (2006). "The dynamics of power and resistance in police interview discourse". *Discourse and Society* 17(6), 739-759.

Heydon, G. (2004). "Establishing the structure of police evidentiary interviews with suspects". *International Journal of Speech, Language and the Law* 11(1), 27-49.

Heydon, G. (2005). *The Language of Police Interviewing*. Basingstoke: Palgrave.

Leap, W. (1993). *American Indian English*. Salt Lake City: University of Utah Press.

Levinson, S. (1992). "Activity Types and Language". In: P. Drew and J. Heritage (eds.), *Talk at Work: Interaction in Institutional Settings*. Cambridge: Cambridge University Press.

Mildren, D. (1999). "Redressing the imbalance: Aboriginal people in the criminal justice system". *Forensic Linguistics* 6(1), 137-160.

Mulder, J. (1982). "The Tsimshian English Dialect: The result of language interference". In: G. Bartlet, S. Penfield-Jasper and B. Hoffer (eds.), *Essays in Native American English*. San Antonio: Trinity University Press, 95-112.

Newbury, P., and A. Johnson (2006). "Suspects' resistance to constraining and coercive questioning strategies in the police interview". *International Journal of Speech, Language and the Law*, 13(2), 213-240.

Phillips, S. (1983). *The invisible culture: Communication in classroom and community on the Warm Springs Indian reservation*. New York: Longman.

Pye, C. (1985). "Language Loss in Chilcotin". Paper presented at the 84th Annual Meeting of the American Anthropological Association, November 18, Washington, DC.

Schegloff, E. A. (1993). "Reflections on Quantification in the Study of Conversation". *Research on Language and Social Interaction* 26, 99-128.

Schiffrin, D. (2002). "Mothers and friends in a Holocaust life story". *Language and Society* 31, 309-353.

Sillars, A., Burggraf, C., Yost, S., and P. Zietlow (1992). "Conversational Themes and Marital Relationship Definitions: Quantitative and Qualitative Investigations". *Human Communication Research* 19(1), 124-154.

Tarpent, M.-L. (1982). "A Tsimshian English Expression: 'Them Fred'". In H. Guillermo Bartlet, S. Penfield-Jasper and B. Hoffer (eds.), *Essays in Native American English*. San Antonio: Trinity University Press, 113-121.

Thornborrow, J. (2002). *Power Talk: Language and Interaction in Institutional Discourse*. Harlow: Pearson Education.

Van de Mieroop, D. (2005). "An integrated approach of quantitative and qualitative analysis in the study of identity in speeches". *Discoure and Society* 16(1), 107-130.

Van de Mieroop, D. (2006). "The compementarity of two identies and two approaches: Quantitative and qualitative analysis of institutional and professional identity". *Journal of Pragmatics* 39, 1120-1142.

Part VI

CONTRASTIVE STUDIES

Le Cheng and **King Kui Sin**
City University of Hong Kong
Hong Kong

CONTRASTIVE ANALYSIS OF CHINESE AND AMERICAN COURT JUDGMENTS

1. Introduction

1.1. Background of the study

The transparency principle of the WTO requires member countries to publish timely and maintain transparency of trade-related laws, regulations, judicial decisions and administrative rulings (Article 10 of GATT). In accordance with the requirement of transparency, the State Council of the PRC requires that all the administrative rulings be translated into English accurately and promptly, which should also be applicable to trade-related laws, regulations, and judicial decisions (court judgments). Whether in legal practice or jurisprudence, court judgments or case briefs (the abridged version of court judgments), among the legal documents, are one of the most important legal genres for legal profession. Furthermore, legal genres are one of the top three factors causing difficulties for the lawyers involved in foreign affairs, which entail the study of court judgments, one of the most frequently-used genres in legal practice.

Moreover, it is essential for legal professionals to have a good command of the discourse conventions, which characterize legal writing. In this regard, Widdowson (1979) has propounded the idea of a universal scientific discourse, which is acquired through education. Contrastive rhetoricians maintain that different discourse communities' expectations are the primary reason for cross-cultural differences in writing styles, and that writers of second languages may transfer their L1 textual and rhetorical strategies to the new situation of the second language before they have fully absorbed the expectations of their second language audience (Connor 1996). Sub-cultural differences further entail the discourse contrast even within the same discourse community. In terms of legal community, basically, there is a dichotomy about the division of legal system: the Common Law system and the Civil Law system.

In the Common Law system, precedents constitute an essential basis in legal argument. Court judgments are cited as an example or analogy to justify decisions made for similar cases. The barrister or the litigation clerk has to search for relevant cases to support his argument. In China, the German Civil Code was introduced in the later years of the Qing Dynasty and formed the basis of the law of the Republic of China that remains in force in Taiwan. In the Civil Law system, the precedents of a higher court or a court itself don't have a binding force as those of the Common Law system do, but they do serve as a guide. Civil law later served as the foundation for socialist law used in Communist countries, which in this view would basically be civil law with the addition of Marxist-Leninist ideas. Though the Chinese legal system is claimed to be distinct from all other legal systems, jurists of the PRC follow rules of the civil law family. The legislation of the PRC reflects a structural similarity to countries in the Romano-Germanic family. Moreover, the Chinese jurists value legal doctrines and hold written law in high esteem; concrete judicial decisions are not officially considered as a source of law.

Despite the division of legal system, court judgments are noteworthy in both. Knowledge about the discourse structure of a text can increase processing precision by reducing search space, and facilitate the identification of rhetorical segments. Depending on communicative functions and genres, legal texts exhibit distinctive discourse structures and patterns of message distribution. Since the communicative goals of segments govern the distribution of content and presentation style, the identification of the discourse organization can significantly facilitate text processing.

1.2. Language and the law

The interest in language and the law is a relatively recent development. From Mellinkoff's (1963) attempts towards systematization in the 1960s, to the modern studies carried out by Bhatia (1983 and 1993) on legislative texts, and to the latest overall descriptions (Gibbons 2003) or some specific issues in legal discourse (Shuy 2002 and 2005), the emphasis has been increasingly placed on the need to define and describe the legal discourse in its own context. As a legal genre, court judgment is a written document about the decision of a court of law or a judge prepared by the judge. The length may vary from case to case. Its language style is generally less formal and technical than that found in laws. Over the years, a conventional structure of legal judgment has been developed. There are several models employed by different scholars to describe the discourse structure of a judgment. However, far from considering the legal text solely from its grammatical and semantic point of view, and, no doubt, influenced by the pragmatic flavor of other previous multidisciplinary analyses, the objective of a study should take into account the extra-linguistic communicative purposes of the text itself. In other words, a genre is more than a structure, but an intended discourse.

Bhatia has analyzed legal cases (abridged versions of court judgments) from two aspects: communicative purpose and structural interpretation. Cases in legal contexts can serve four major communicative purposes (1993: 119-120):

1. In their full form (also referred to as legal judgments), as in Law reports, cases serve as authentic records of past judgments. In this form they are taken as faithful records of all the facts of the case, the arguments of the judge, his reasoning, the judgment he arrives at and the way he does it, the kind of authority and evidence he uses and the way he distinguishes the present case from others cited as evidence either by him or by the opposing lawyers.

2. Legal judgments (including legal cases) also serve another important function. The judgments and the rule of law (*ratio decidendi*, in legal terminology) derived are meant to serve as precedents for subsequent cases, and are generally used as evidence in favour of or against a particular line of argument or decision.

3. Cases, as reported in some casebooks are meant to serve as reminders to legal experts, who use them in their arguments in the classroom or the court of law. These versions are very brief and contain nothing more than the essential material fact and the decision of the judge.

4. Cases also serve as illustrations of certain points of law. Such cases are carefully selected and appropriately abridged. They form an important part of a law student's bibliography. They are generally abridged in casebooks and are also used prominently in law textbooks in support of or against a particular point of view. Law students learn the law from such cases.

Bhatia (1993) claims that the legal case, like any other genre, also displays a typical cognitive structuring which accounts for the structural interpretation of the case. He has put forward a typical four-move structure:

1. Identifying the case
2. Establishing facts of the case
3. Arguing the case
   a) Stating the history of the case
   b) Presenting arguments
   c) Deriving *ratio decidendi*
4. Pronouncing judgment

Randall (online) holds there are seven moves in briefing a case:

Move 1 Heading
Step 1 Case Name
Step 2 Citation including court and date

Step 3 Casebook page reference
Move 2 Procedural History
Step 1 What the plaintiff sought in the trial court (the Cause of Action and Relief)
Step 2 What the trial court did
Step 3 Who the appellate is and what the appellate sought in the appellate court
Step 4 What the appellate court did
Move 3 Key Facts
Move 4 Question Presented or Issue
Move 5 Courts' Holding or Decision
Move 6 Court's Reasoning
Step 1 Facts which court concludes are true
Step 2 Law which court concludes applies.
Move 7 Disposition (obligatory ONLY in appellate cases)

Maley (1985) and Bowles (1995) also provided their versions of law report analysis (See Tables 1 and 2).

Table 1. Maley's description of the structure of law reports

Moves	Description
Facts	An account of events and/or the relevant history of the case
Issues	The issue of either fact or law or both
Reasoning	
Conclusion	The principle or rule declared applicable for the instant case
Order/finding	

Table 2. Bowles' description of the structure of law reports

Moves	Steps
1. Heading	
2. Description of court	
3. Keywords	
4. Description (of the facts)	
	4.1. List of cases cited
	4.2 Opinion of concurring judges
5. Judgment (argument of judge and principle of law)	
	5.1. Opinions of concurring judges
6. Decision (of court)	

In addition to genre analysis, some scholars focus their studies on the legal language itself. It is often said that law has its own language; it does not, but the language of law does have its distinctive characteristics. The general characteristics of a court judgment are formality, precision and the existence of a technical vocabulary. Many characteristics have their roots in the historical procedure and it is now difficult to provide a rational justification for them. They have become fossils, indicators of historical development. Other characteristics remain as justifiable attempts to reach precision in language usage. Moreover, some characteristics demonstrate the power of the legal language. Those characteristics include: a) frequent use of ordinary words with specialized meaning; b) use of words with flexible or vague meanings; c) use of legal jargons and terms; d. use of synonyms or co hyponyms. Besides, just because of the language differences, American court judgments have their own peculiar characteristics, which persist in spite of the plain language movement in legal language (Hanson 2003).

1.3 Value of the study

With the globalization of economy and interaction of legal affairs, the paper aims to analyze the structure of court judgments. The primary purpose of this study is to examine contrastively the linguistic characteristics, moves and rhetoric of judgments written in English and in Chinese, with the aim of specifying the rhetorical preferences that are characteristic of "standard" judgments. This research has an underlying pedagogical motivation as it attempts to help Chinese learners of LLP, especially Chinese law major students in colleges and practicing lawyers. They should have a good understanding of the way of writing effective judgments that meets the international legal community's expectations. Further, it helps the non Chinese legal professions to have a better understanding of the court judgments as well as legal practices in China.

2. Design of the study

2.1. Composition of the data

Our corpora contain judgments available on www.findlaw.com and www.chinacourt.com. One hundred judgments in English and Chinese, respectively, are analyzed. The average size of the English judgments that are input to the study is between 1000 and 4000 words (2 to 8 pages), which constitute 75% of the English judgments. The judgments having less than 1000 or more than 4000 words are respectively 8% or so. The average size of the Chinese documents that are input to the study are judgments between 3000 and 7000 characters long (3 to 7 pages), which form 85% of all the 100 Chinese judgments; 15% of the documents having about 2000 characters or fewer (about 2 pages); Only 5% of the judgments have more than 8000 characters. Contrary to some previous researches that focus only on limited types of judgments, my study deals with many categories of judgments covering various fields of law such as Civil law, Criminal law, Administrative law, Procedure law, Intellectual property law, Evidence law, Property law, Arbitration law, Tort law, Financial law, Maritime and Commercial law, Labour law, Consumer protection law, Securities law, Private international law etc. Moreover, this study includes the judgments handed down by first instance and second instance courts (see table 3).

Table 3. Distribution of court judgments

	American Court Judgments	Chinese Court Judgments
First Instance	50	50
Second Instance	50	50
Civil Law	25	30
Criminal Law	30	20
Administrative Law	10	15
Procedure Law	15	20
Others	20	15

Besides, we get some information from law dons and lawyers involving foreign affairs. The statements as follows are some typical ones:

> Traditionally, Chinese legal system was under the impact of the Civil Law system. Before liberation, the legal system of KuoMingTang (KMT) Administration was under the umbrella of the Civil Law system. Although most of the legislation was abolished after the foundation of the PRC, the Civil Law system still has a far-reaching effect on Chinese modern legal system. In fact, when the PRC was in good relationships with the former Soviet Union (which, of course, belongs to the Civil Law system), a lot of legislation was transplanted into China. (By a professor of jurisprudence, female, 56; translated from Chinese)

> The Chinese legal tradition was penalty-centred, official-centred and full of mysterious colour, which necessitated the vague and non-transparency of legislation and enforcement of law. Naturally, there was no much space for the existence of legal analysis in a court judgment. Therefore, a decision per se was sufficient. (By a professor of criminology, male, 48; translated from Chinese)

> To some extent, the legal system of the PRC belongs to the Civil Law system, in which legal analysis is relatively insufficient than that in the Common Law system. The major influence on the present Chinese court judgments is the legal practices

during Yan'an period (1920s-1940s)." (By an associate professor of the history of the Chinese legal system, female, 39; translated from Chinese)

Although some jurists hold that the emergence of judge's postscripts is in nature helpless, I think it is a leap toward "rule of law", because it provides additional accounts for the decision of a judgment. This at least enhances the transparency of a court judgment." (By a professor of criminal procedure law, male, 52; translated from Chinese)

2.2. Methods and procedures of the study

Our approach to analyzing and producing the results has a qualitatively and quantitatively combined basis. In combination with the literature review related to the genre analysis of court judgments and the interview of 5 jurists, a qualitative analysis is used to determine the moves of a court judgment. As to the size and percentage of each move and step, it depends mainly on a computer-based calculation and part of them needs manual computation. In order to ensure the validity and reliability of the study, the judgments are selected at random from the above-mentioned corpora; after the determination of the structure (moves and steps) of a court judgment, the law experts are interviewed about their reasons for their respective perspective. In case of conflicting responses to the same question, the law dons are invited to air their opinions to reach a consensus. Furthermore, a literature review about legal tradition and legal system is carried out in order to make the results and analysis more objective and exhaustive.

2.3. Research questions

The major research questions in this study are as follows:

a) Is there any difference in the moves and steps of Chinese court judgments and American court judgments?
b) Are the moves and steps of a judgment by a court of first instance the same with those by a court of second instance?
c) Do the judgments by courts of the same trial level follow exactly the same moves and steps?
d) Is there any difference in terms of legal analysis between Chinese court judgments and American court judgments?
e) Can any reasons be provided to account for the differences?

3. Results and discussion

Discourse analysis is viewed not simply as an act of linguistic description but more as linguistic explanation; therefore, genre analysis has become one of the major influences on the current practices in the teaching and learning of languages, in general, and in the teaching and learning of ESP and English for Professional Communication (EPC), in particular. Bhatia (1997) holds that there are at least four distinct, though systematically related, areas of competence that an ESP learner needs to develop in order to get over his or her lack of confidence in handling specialist discourse. Even if most of these learners already possess a reasonably adequate competence in the use of the language for general every day functions, they will still need to develop a) an understanding of the specialist code, b) familiarity with the dynamics of specialist genres, which includes the rhetorical forms and content, c) specific contexts they respond to and the conventions they tend to use in their responses, and d) a proficiency in the manipulation of specialist genres to respond to the exigencies of unfamiliar and novel situations. Genre analysis, thus, is an indispensable and feasible means employed in the analysis of court judgment, a discourse of professional communication and for specific purposes.

3.1. Move analysis of American and Chinese court judgments

3.1.1. Move analysis of American judgments by the courts of first instance

Move 1 Heading
- Step 1 Court
- Step 2 Written case No.
- Step 3 Parties
- Step 4 Judges

Move 2 Summary
Move 3 Facts and issues in dispute
Move 4 Legislation applied
Move 5 Arguments/ Discussion
Move 6 Decision/Conclusion

Sometimes, move 3 and move 4 cannot be clearly identified in a court judgment and some moves may have embedded steps or even sub-steps.

Example 1. Move analysis of American judgments by the trial court

	Move 1. Heading
UNITED STATES DISTRICT COURT FOR THE DISTRICT OF COLUMBIA	Step 1. Trial Organization
Civil Action No. 00-2195	Step 2. Case No.
FRANETTE McCULLOCH, Plaintiff *v.* *GEORGE W. BUSH, PRESIDENT OF THE UNITED STATES, et al. Defendants.*	Step 3. Parties
Plaintiff Franette McCulloch, an employee of the Executive Residence in the White House, alleges that... *Defendants have moved to dismiss plaintiff's claims for...*	Move 2. Summary
...The plaintiff, Franette McCulloch, has been employed as an assistant pastry chef in the White House since 1983. As an assistant pastry chef, The President, or the designee of the President, is supposed to issue regulations that define the procedures for counselling and mediation.	Move 3. Background
The President has moved under Fed. R. Civ. P. 12(b)(1) and 12(b)(6) to dismiss Count I for... *The President has moved under Rule 12(b)(1) to dismiss CountII for...* *Both the President and defendant Mesnier have moved under Rule 12(b)(6) to dismiss Count III for failing to state a claim upon which relief can be granted.*	Move 4. Discussion
...To survive a Rule 12(b)(6) motion to dismiss, "'the complaint must set forth sufficient information to suggest that there exists some recognized legal theory upon which relief can be granted.'"	Step 1. Counts I and III
FAILURE OF THE PRESIDENT TO ISSUE REGULATIONS	Sub-step 1 Reason 1
PLAINTIFF'S CONSTITUTIONAL CLAIMS	Sub-step 2. Reason 2
In CountII, plaintiff brings a discrimination claim under the First and Fifth Amendments of the Constitution rather than the PEOAA...	Step 2. Count II
Accordingly, plaintiff's complaint will be dismissed. A Final Order consistent with this Memorandum Opinion is being issued.	Move 5. Conclusion

3.1.2. Move analysis of American judgments by the courts of second instance

Move 1 Heading
  Step 1 Court
  Step 2 Written case No.
  Step 3 Parties
  Step 4 Judges
Move 2 Summary/Introduction
Move 3 Background
  Step 1 Procedural background
  Step 2 Factual background
  Step 3 Statutory background
Move 4 Standard of review
Move 5 Discussion
Move 6 Conclusion

Example 2. Move analysis of American judgments by the court of appeal

	Move 1. Heading
United States Court of Appeals *FOR THE EIGHTH CIRCUIT*	Step 1. Court Name and Trial Level
No. 03-2164	Step 2. Case No.
Taddese Lencho Gemechu v. John Ashcroft, Attorney General of the United States of America	Step 3. Parties
Before MURPHY, BRIGHT, and MELLOY, Circuit Judges	Step 4. Judges
Taddese Lencho Gemechu ("Gemechu") seeks review of a final order of removal issued by the Board of Immigration Appeals ("BIA"). The BIA affirmed the decision of the Immigration Judge ("IJ") that found Gemechu was not credible and that he failed to meet his burden of proof for establishing that he has a well-founded fear of persecution in his home country of Ethiopia.	Move 2. Summary
	Move 3. Background
Gemechu entered the United States on August 29, 1998 on a student visa with authorization to remain in the country until May 31, 2000. On August 2, 2000, Gemechu... *The IJ held hearings on the merits on January 17, 2001 and March 12, 2001.In an order dated March 12, 2001, the IJ found ...*	Step 1. Procedural Background

Gemechu testified to the following facts. Gemechu was born on November 21, 1971 in Ghinchi, Ethiopia. His ethnicity... *Gemechu testified that...* *Gemechu testified that ...*	Step 2. Factual Background
"The Attorney General may grant asylum to an alien ... if the Attorney General determines that such alien is a refugee." 8 U.S.C. 1158(b)(1). A refugee is "any person who is outside any country of such person's nationality... on account of race, religion, nationality, membership in a particular social group, or political opinion." 8 U.S.C. 1101(a) (42)(A). *The petitioner has the burden of showing refugee status. 8 C.F.R. 208.13(a) (2004). To show a well-founded fear of persecution, the petitioner "must demonstrate a fear that..."*	Step 3. Statutory Background
The BIA's decision is the final agency decision and the subject of our review. To the extent that the BIA adopted the IJ's findings, we review those IJ findings...	Move 4. Standard of Review
The IJ concluded, and the BIA affirmed, that ... *Among the reasons the IJ gave for not believing Gemechu's testimony were the following. First, Gemechu failed to ...* *Second, Gemechu failed to ...* *Third, the IJ found it implausible that ...* *Fourth, the IJ considered ...* *Fifth, the IJ found that ...*	Move 5. Discussion
Substantial evidence supports the BIA's and IJ's conclusion that Gemechu failed to demonstrate a well-founded fear of persecution. Since Gemechu... *Accordingly, we deny the petition for review.*	Move 6. Conclusion

In some court judgments, moves and steps cannot be clearly identified, that is, some of them are tangled with each other. Sometimes, some moves or steps might be missing or omitted in some court judgments.

Example 3. Move analysis of American judgments by the court of appeal

	Move 1. Heading
UNITED STATES COURT OF APPEALS *TENTH CIRCUIT*	Step 1. Court Name and Trial Level
No. 99-1045	Step 2. Case No.
PHOEBE THOMPSON, DEAN ECOFF, and MARCIA E. WADE, on behalf of themselves and all others similarly situated,	Step 3. Parties

Plaintiffs-Appellees, *v.* *STATE OF COLORADO,* *Defendant-Appellant.* *UNITED STATES OF AMERICA,* *Intervenor.*	
Appeal from the United States District Court for the District of Colorado *(D.C. No. 96-S-1791)*	Step 4. Original Court and Case No.
Before BRISCOE, Circuit Judge, REAVLEY, Senior Circuit Judge, and MURPHY, Circuit Judge	Step 5. Judges
Plaintiffs-Appellees brought a class action suit against Defendant- Appellant State of Colorado ("Colorado"). Plaintiffs claimed that...	Move 2. Introduction
Under Colorado law, a "person with a disability" may apply for a special license plate or placard. See Colo. Rev. Stat. § 42-3-121(2) (a). The license plate and the placard allow the disabled person to park in designated handicap parking spaces. See id. § 42-4-1208(3) (a)... *Plaintiffs brought a class action suit against Colorado challenging the imposition of the placard fee. Plaintiffs claimed that...*	Move 3. Facts and Procedural History *(hereby factual and procedural backgrounds are tangled and there doesn't exist statutory background)*
On appeal, Colorado argues that... *The Eleventh Amendment provides:...* *The findings section of the ADA (applicable to all titles of the Act) states that...* *This court cannot conclude that Congress "identified a history and pattern" of unconstitutional discrimination by the states against...*	Move 4. Discussion
We therefore VACATE the order of the district court granting summary judgment for Plaintiffs and denying summary judgment for Colorado and REMAND with instructions that summary judgment be entered for Colorado.	Move 5. Conclusion

3.1.3. Move analysis of Chinese judgments by the courts of first instance

Move 1 Heading
 Step 1 Headline
 Step 2 Written Judgment No.

Step 3 Parties
Move 2 Summary
Move 3 Facts and evidence
Step 1 The facts, evidence and reasons by plaintiff or prosecutor
Step 2 The facts, evidence and reasons by defendant
Move 4 Grounds of judgment
Step 1 The facts and evidence established by the court
Step 2 The reasons for judgment
Step 3 The law applied
Move 5 The results of judgment
Move 6 The time limit for appeal and the competent appellant court.
Move 7 Signature by the judge(s) and the recording clerk, and seal by the people's court.

The above-mentioned move analysis is applicable to the judgments by the court of the first instance. In the judgments by the court of second instance, *Move 6* can be omitted.

Example 4. Move analysis of Chinese judgments by the court of first instance

	Move 1. Heading
北京市第二中级人民法院 (Beijing the Second Intermediate People's Court)	Step 1. Trial Organization
民事判决书 (Civil Judgment)	Step 2. Nature of Case
（2003）二中民初字第00464号 *(2003)the second intermediate civil trial No.00464*	Step 3. Written Judgment No. and Trial Level
原告...(plaintiff) *委托代理人 (agent)* *被告...(defendant)* *委托代理人...(agent)*	Step 4. Parties
原告北京潘瑞克食品加工中心（下称潘瑞克中心）与被告北京市金天坛食品有限责任公司（下称金天坛公司）不正当竞争纠纷一案，本院于2003年1月2日受理后，依法组成合议庭，于2003年4月1日公开开庭进行了审理。潘瑞克中心的委托代理人闵学晶、高淑薇、金天坛公司的法定代表人冯志平和委托代理人戚砚英、盛建军到庭参加了诉讼。本案现已审理终结。 *(As filed by the Plaintiff A against the Defendants B with respect to the dispute over XXX, this court accepted the case on January 2, 2003. On April 1, 2003, a collegiate bench, constituted in accordance with law, heard the case*	Move 2. Summary

by public hearing. Party A's agent xxx and Party B's agent xxx participated in the proceedings. This case has now been concluded.)	
	Move 3. Facts and Evidence
原告潘瑞克中心起诉称：... 故根据我国反不正当竞争法第五条第二项、第二十二条的规定，诉至法院，请求法院判令被告： *(The plaintiff A claims:.... Therefore according to the stipulations of article 5.2 and article 22 of the Law against Undue Competition, the plaintiff filed the case to the court and asked the court to order the defendant that...)*	Step 1. Facts and Reasons by Plaintiff
被告金天坛公司辩称：...因此，原告的诉讼主张不能成立，请求法院依法判决驳回原告的诉讼请求。 *(The defendant B defended:.... Therefore, the plaintiff's claims can't be established, and the defendant asked the court to dismiss the litigation requests filed by the plaintiff in accordance with the law.)*	Step 2. Facts and Reasons by Defendant
在本案审理过程中，原告潘瑞克中心提交以下三类证据材料： *(During the hearing of this case, the plaintiff A submitted three types of evidence as follows)*	Step 3. Evidence by Plaintiff
一是证明原告权利归属方面的证据材料，即证明原告涉案产品为知名商品，原告在先使用涉案包装、装潢，包括： ...	Evidence 1
二是证明被告实施不正当竞争行为方面的证据材料，包括：...	Evidence 2
三是证明原告索赔依据方面的证据材料，包括：...	Evidence 3
被告金天坛公司对原告提交的上述证据材料发表如下质证意见：... *(As to the evidence above submitted by the plaintiff, the defendant B argued that....)*	Step 4. Defendant's Arguments against Evidence by Plaintiff
被告金天坛公司提交以下三类证据材料： *(The defendant B submitted three types of evidence as follows)*	Step 5. Evidence by Defendant
一是证明被告系在先使用涉案包装，并已就此提出外观设计专利申请方面的证据材料，包括： ...	Evidence 1
二是证明被告生产产品为合格产品，系知名商品方面的证据材料，包括： ...	Evidence 2
三是证明被告生产的涉案产品为试销产品，尚未结账，	Evidence 3

因此在法院委托审计部门进行审计的账目中不包括有关涉案产品的账目，账目中涉及的是被告生产的其他产品的账日的证据材料，包括，…	
原告潘瑞克中心对被告提交的上述证据材料发表如下质证意见：… *(As to the evidence above submitted by the defendant, the plaintiff A argued that….)*	Step 6. Plaintiff's Arguments against Evidence by Defendant
	Move 4. Grounds for Judgment
基于双方当事人的上述举证、质证意见，本院对提交的证据材料认证如下：… *经过双方当事人举证、质证和本院认证，本院查明以下事实：…* *(based on the two parties' evidence and arguments on evidence, this court authenticate the evidential materials as follows)* *(based on the two parties' evidence and arguments on evidence as well as this court's authentication, this court ascertains the facts as follows)*	Step 1. The Facts and Evidence Established by the Court
本院认为：… *(This court take the view that…)*	Step 2. The Reasons for Judgment
综上，依照《中华人民共和国反不正当竞争法》第五条第（二）项之规定， *(In Summary, according to article 5.2 of the Law against Undue Competition of the PRC)*	Step 3. The Law Applied
判决如下： *(The decision is as follows)*	Move 5. The Results of Judgment
如不服本判决，可在判决书送达之日起15日内，向本院提交上诉状，并按对方当事人的人数提交副本，上诉于北京市高级人民法院。 *(Any party which is not satisfied with this judgment may submit to this court within 15 days the Statement of Appeal with copies according to the number of the opposing parties. The appeal shall be instituted with the Higher People's Court of Beijing.)*	Move 6. The Time Limit for Appeal and the Competent Appellant Court.
审 判 长 　邵明艳 (Chief Justice xxx) *代理审判员 　张晓津 (Acting Judge xxx)* *代理审判员 　何 暄 (Acting Judge xxx)* *二○○三年五月二十六日 (May 26, 2003: the date delivering judgment)* *书 记 员 　潘 伟 (Clerk xxx)*	Move 7. Signature by the Judge(s) and the Recording Clerk, and Seal by the People's Court .

3.1.4. Move analysis of Chinese judgments by the courts of second instance

Move 1 Head
  Step 1 Headline
  Step 2 Written Judgment No.
  Step 3 Parties
Move 2 Summary
Move 3 Grounds of judgment in first instance and its holding
Move 4 Reasons and evidence for appeal
  Step 1 Reasons and evidence by appellant
  Step 2 Reasons and evidence by appellee
Move 5 Grounds of judgment
  Step 1 The facts and evidence established by the court
  Step 2 The reasons for judgment
  Step 3 The law applied
Move 6 The results of judgment
Move 7 Signature by the judge(s) and the recording clerk, and seal by the people's court.

Example 5. Move analysis of Chinese judgments by the court of second instance

	Move 1. Heading
北京市第二中级人民法院 *(Beijing the Second Intermediate People's Court)*	Step 1. Trial Organization
民事判决书 *(Civil case)*	Step 2. Nature of Case
(2003)二中民终字第 8950 号 *((2003)the Second Intermediate Civil Final No.8950)*	Step 3. Written Judgment No. and Trial Level
上诉人...(appellant) *委托代理人...(agent)* *被上诉人...(appellee)* *委托代理人...(agent)*	Step 4. Parties
上诉人中国华侨出版社（以下简称华侨出版社）因侵犯著作权纠纷一案，不服北京市朝阳区人民法院（2003）朝民初字第 13106 号民事判决，向本院提起上诉。本院依法组成合议庭审理了本案，现已审理终结。 *(For the case with respect to the dispute over xxx, the Appellant A was not satisfied with the judgment by Beijing Chaoyang District People's Court xxx (citation number of the judgment), filed an appeal to this court. In the form of a*	Move 2. Summary

collegiate bench, constituted in accordance with law, this court heard the case. This case has now been concluded.)	
北京市朝阳区人民法院经审理认定:... *(the trial court held)*	Move 3. Grounds for Judgment in First Instance and its Wording
一审判决后,华侨出版社不服,向本院提起上诉。理由是:... *(After the first trial, A, not satisfied, field an appeal to this court. The reasons are...)*	Move 4. Reasons and Evidence for Appeal
	Move 5. Grounds for judgment
本院经审理，查明的事实与一审认定的事实相同。 *在本院审理期间双方当事人均未提交新的证据。* *(After the trial, this court ascertains the facts as found in the first trial. Neither party has submitted new evidence to this court.)*	Step 1. The facts and Evidence Established by the Court
本院认为...综上，一审判决认定事实清楚、适用法律正确，应予维持。华侨出版社的上诉理由缺乏事实及法律依据，本院不予支持。(This court takes the view that.... In summary, the decision of the first trial shall be maintained for its clear ascertainment of facts and proper application of law. A's appeal is not allowed by this court for its lack of factual and legal basis)	Step 2. The Reasons for Judgment
依据《中华人民共和国民事诉讼法》第一百五十三条第一款第（一）项之规定， *(according to the prescription of article 153.1.1 of the Procedure Law of the PRC,*	Step 3. The Law Applied
判决如下：驳回上诉，维持原判... *本判决为终审判决。* *(The decision is as follows: appeal is disallowed and the original decision is maintained. This decision is final.)*	Move 6. The Outcome of Judgment
审　判　长　　刘　薇　(Chief Justice xxx) *代理审判员　　宋　光　(Acting Judge xxx)* *代理审判员　　梁立君　(Acting Judge xxx)* *二OO三年十一月十九日　(Date of delivering judgment)* *书　记　员　　郎京萍　(Clerk xxx)*	Move 7. Signature by the Judge(s) and the Recording Clerk, and Seal by the People's Court.

3.1.5. Explanations and discussion

A. Headline

The headline of a Chinese judgment, composed of title and written judgment number, includes the subject matter of the case (which is a summary of the content and nature of the case), trial institution and level of trial. The nature of the case can be criminal, civil, administrative or maritime etc. The trial level includes the trial of first instance, the trial of second instance and the trial of final distance (in China, the trial of first instance by the People's Supreme Court or the trial of second instance is the trial of final instance). As to the trial institution, it can be a trial/district court, an intermediate court, a higher court or a supreme court.

B. Names of the parties

In the civil cases, the party filing the suit is called plaintiff and the party sued is called defendant. The name of the plaintiff appears prior to that of the defendant. The criminal cases can be further divided into public-prosecution and private-prosecution ones. In a public-prosecution case, the party filing the case is called public prosecutor (in China called the People's Procuratorate) and the other party accused is called defendant; in a private-prosecution case, private prosecutor and defendant respectively. In the case where a party is not seeking money but asking the court to force the other party to do something or not do something, the parties might be called petitioner and respondent respectively. When a case moves to the appellate system, that is, the trial of second instance, the titles of the parties will be modified to reflect the corresponding status and proceedings. In most jurisdictions, the party launching the appeal is referred to as the appellant, and the other party – appellee.

C. Trial institution and level of trial

In the United States, district courts, special courts and Supreme Court can be the trial court, and courts of appeal or Supreme Court can be the appellate court. The state court structure is similar to federal one. Figure 1 is the federal court structure in the USA.

China's people's court system consists of courts at four levels: namely the grassroots, intermediate, higher and supreme people's courts, in addition to special courts such as the military, railway and water transportation courts. Grassroots/basic courts refer to tribunals in counties/autonomous counties, cities without administrative districts, or administrative districts of cities; intermediate courts are set up in prefectures, cities directly under provinces (also autonomous regions and municipalities directly under the Central Government); higher courts are those set up in provinces (also autonomous regions and municipalities directly under the Central Government).

China's trial system follows a two-hearing system in the trial process. The entire system of people's courts constitutes a four-level, two-hearing process. When litigants are not satisfied with the verdict made by any of the local people's courts at various levels after the court has gone through a first-hearing trial of the case within its jurisdiction, they may appeal to a court of the immediate higher level within the time limit prescribed by law. The court at the next higher level reviews the appeal and passes its judgment, which constitutes the verdict of the second hearing. According to the trial system, the verdict of the second hearing is the final decision against which the litigant may not appeal. The Supreme People's Court is China's highest trial organ and all of its decisions on the first- and second-hearing cases are final and shall be enforced once they are promulgated.

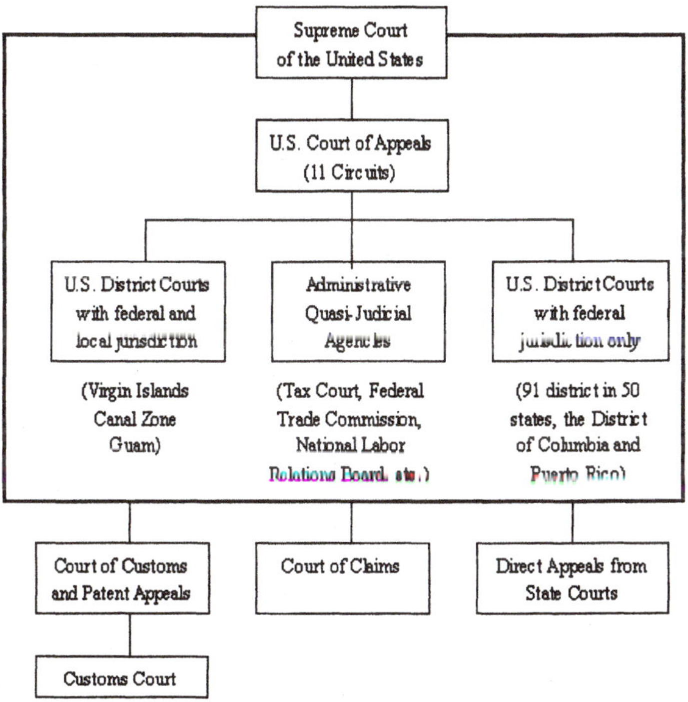

Figure 1. Federal court structure in the USA

D. Procedural background

On analyzing a court judgment, one should keep in mind whether it involves a case of the first instance or an appellate case. Appellate cases have, by definition, already had a trial stage. In fact, depending on what appeal level the case now being briefed is at, it may already have been to several appellate courts. The case brief should identify the courts that have dealt with the case and indicate the decisions those courts have made. The sections of the court opinion that help identify the procedural background will also provide information for the "roles" section above. This is another good reason to include the procedural background as part of a court judgment since it helps to clarify how the original case got to a higher court (U.S. Supreme Court or U.S. Courts of Appeals; or the intermediate people's courts, the high people's courts or the supreme people's court in China).

E. Ratio Decidendi, Obiter Dictum, Concurrence, Dissentience and Epilogue

Whether in their interpretive, common law, judicial review or rulemaking role, courts are to be bound by previous decisions or precedent. This is the doctrine of *stare decisis*, literally "to adhere to decided cases." The doctrine of *stare decisis* requires judges to align their decision with legal principles established in previously decided cases. As a result, court opinions take considerable space to show how the current decision is consistent with the established principles. The purpose of the *stare decisis* doctrine is to ensure consistency and predictability, and to save the courts time reinventing the law with each case, and to make sure judges consider the wisdom of past experience. However, courts have been known to disregard precedent if logic or changes in circumstances suggest it is a good idea to do so. Both *obiter dicta* (which appears only in Common law systems) and *ratio decidendi* are the reasons for the decision. Only the "holding" supported by the *ratio decidendi* of the case need be followed, that is, only the *ratio decidendi* (or ratio) of a case that has binding precedential force. Any other significant judicial statements not based firmly in the *ratio decidendi*, are called *obiter dicta* (things stated incidentally). Language in the opinion that is *obiter dictum* (i.e. a side comment) need not be followed, but is often viewed as persuasive depending on the reputation of the judge and level of court. In American judgments, an *obiter dictum* can be optional.

In a court judgment, the *ratio decidendi* can be found in the opinion of the court and the *obiter dictum*, or the personal opinion of a judge, can be unanimous, concurring or dissenting. The court's decision is issued in the form of an opinion setting forth its reasoning. This assists the parties in understanding the decision and preparing a further appeal, and assists later courts in deciding whether it is precedent in their cases. In addition to the majority opinion, which represents the court's ruling, there may be concurring opinions (written by judges who agree with the result but for different reasons), and dissenting opinions. The majority opinion can affirm the lower court decision, reverse the opinion, or reverse and remand the case back to the trial court for further factual findings or disposition of the case in line with the appellate court's legal ruling.

In the case of Miranda v. Arizona, we can find the dissenting opinions of the individual judges.

> MR. CHIEF JUSTICE WARREN delivered the opinion of the Court.
> *The cases before us raise questions which go to the roots of our concepts of American criminal jurisprudence: ...*
> *[We] dealt with certain phases of this problem recently in Escobedo v. Illinois, 378 U.S. 478 (1964). There, as in the four cases before us ...*
> *[We] start here, as [we] did in Escobedo, with the premise that our holding is not an innovation in our jurisprudence, but is an application of principles long recognized and applied in other settings. [We] have undertaken a thorough re-examination of the Escobedo decision and the principles it announced, and [we] reaffirm it. That case was but an explication of basic rights that are enshrined in our Constitution -- that "No person . . . "*
> *Over 70 years ago, our predecessors on this Court eloquently stated: ...*
> *[Our] holding will be spelled out with some specificity in the pages which follow but briefly stated it is this: the prosecution may not use statements, whether exculpatory or inculpatory, stemming from custodial interrogation of the defendant unless it demonstrates the use of procedural safeguards effective to secure the privilege against self-incrimination. By custodial interrogation, [we] mean questioning initiated by law enforcement officers after a person has been taken into custody or ...*
>
> MR. JUSTICE WHITE, with whom MR. JUSTICE HARLAN and MR. JUSTICE STEWART join, dissenting.
> MR. JUSTICE CLARK, dissenting.
> *It is with regret that I find it necessary to write in these cases. However, I am unable to join the majority because its opinion goes too far on too little, while my dissenting brethren do not go quite far enough. Nor can I join in the Court's criticism of the present practices of police and investigatory agencies as to custodial interrogation. The materials it refers to as "police manuals" are, as I read them, merely writings in this field by professors and some police officers. Not one is shown by the record here to be the official manual of any police department, much less in universal use in crime detection. Moreover, the examples of police brutality mentioned by the Court are rare exceptions to the thousands of cases that appear every year in the law reports. The police agencies -- all the way from municipal and state forces to the federal bureaus -- are responsible for law enforcement and public safety in this country. I am proud of their efforts, which in my view are not fairly characterized by the Court's opinion.*
>
> MR. JUSTICE HARLAN, whom MR. JUSTICE STEWART and MR. JUSTICE WHITE join, dissenting.
> *[I] believe the decision of the Court represents poor constitutional law and entails harmful consequences for the country at large. How serious these consequences may prove to be only time can tell. But the basic flaws in the Court's justification seem to me readily apparent now once all sides of the problem are considered.*

In recent judgments, we find a trend that judge's postscript (including epilogue, the content of statutes applied) which is part of the judgment but not the legal reasoning or analysis of the decision, is favoured by some courts such as Guangzhou Maritime Court (since 1999) and the Second Shanghai Intermediate People's Court (since 2002), which might indicate the influence of the Common Law practices, for multiple opinion is considered a form for transparency and fairness. As to judge's postscript/epilogue, which has appeared in Chinese court judgments (and in fact can be found in judgments of ancient China), it is no less than an expressive component. The following is a typical one (from the epilogue by the People's Court of Jianxi District, Luoyang City, China, 22 September 2002):

> *原告少年丧父，被告中年丧偶，实为人间悲剧。本案双方当事人因此而遭遇的不幸是令人同情的，但又为继承死者遗产而引发纠纷，使本来就已受到伤害的心灵雪上加霜，甚感遗憾！法律虽然可以公正地处理当事人之间的继承纠纷，但金钱毕竟无法代替亲情。死者已去矣，亲者尚生存，亲者为死者之财而起纷争，死者在九泉之下能瞑目乎？愿双方摒弃前嫌，互敬互爱，重修亲情。求家和万事兴，不亦乐哉！*
> *(The plaintiff's father died when the plaintiff was young, and the defendant's spouse died when the defendant was middle-aged, which WAS a tragedy in the secular world. The misfortune the two parties had therefore suffered was pitiable. But they came into dispute for the heritage of the deceased, adding salt to the hurt hearts, which was really a pity. Although Law can solve the dispute over heritage between the parties fairly, but money after all can't substitute passion between relatives. The deceased has gone, and the relatives are still alive but come into dispute over the property of the deceased, can the deceased rest in the Dwelling Place of the dead? May the two parties discard their past animosity, respect each other and love each other, and repair the relation. To pursue that the family are harmonious and all the things are prosperous, isn't it a pleasure!)*

F. Decision or holding

This part typically deals with the resolution of the issue(s), the outcome of adjudication, the costs to be borne or the action taken by the court. In the language of law, the decision creates, alters or terminates the legal relationships between the parties.

G. Disposition

In cases of first instance, the decision will be awarded against or for the plaintiff, prosecutor or victim. However, in appellate cases, three possible dispositions may be made (mainly in the USA and the UK):

Affirmed —The appellate court agree with the opinion of the lower court from which the appeal came.
Reversed —The appellate court disagrees with the opinion of the lower

court from which the appeal came and sets aside or invalidates that opinion. Reversals are often accompanied by a remand.
Remanded —The case is sent back to the court from which it came for further action consistent with the appellate court opinion. Remand often accompanies a reversal.

In China, after trying a case on appeal, the people court of second instance shall, in the light of the following situations, dispose of it accordingly:

a) If the facts were clearly ascertained and the law was correctly applied in the original judgment, the appeal shall be rejected in the form of a judgment and the original judgment shall be *affirmed;*
b) If the application of the law was incorrect in the original judgment, the said judgment shall be *amended* according to the law;
c) If in the original judgment the facts were incorrectly or not clearly ascertained and the evidence was insufficient, the people's court of second instance shall make a written order to set aside the judgment and *remand* the case to the original people's court for *retrial*, or the people's court of second instance may *amend* the judgment after investigating and clarifying the facts;
d) If there was violation of legal procedure in making the original judgment, which may have affected correct adjudication, the judgment shall be set aside by a written order and the case *remanded* to the original people's court for *retrial.*

3.2. Rhetorical segments and functional analysis

Every type of writing exists with an intended purpose. In scientific research, the goal is to convince the intended audience that the work reported is a valid contribution to science (Myers 1992). Court judgments are very different in this regard. They are more strongly performative than research reports, the fundamental act being a decision. Particularly, in court judgments, the judge aims to convince his professional and academic peers of the soundness of his argument. Therefore, a judgment serves both a declaratory and a justificatory function (Maley 1994). In truth, it does more even than this, for what a court judgment shows is not only its justification, but also its legitimacy. Therefore, the fact and the analysis supporting the decision or disposition are inevitably indispensable.

3.2.1 Rhetorical Segments and percentage

Under such a premise that the court judgment should include all the essential elements and in fact all the judgments chosen for the analysis in the paper deliberately exclude those without the essential elements (which do exist especially in some judgments dealing with appeal for review or mere procedural issues), a court judgment can be segmented according to the different rhetorical roles, which can easily identified by some linguistic markers as well as the content as shown in Table 4. It is easy to identify each segment in Chinese judgments for its clear structure, but the American ones sometimes need reallocation. Anyway, by using my intuitive knowledge as law major together with the help of legal experts, the task of segmenting can be successfully obtained. Epilogue has long existed in Common law jurisdictions and now we can also notice such a "transplant" of subgenre (or revival of such subgenre, for, as has been mentioned, such expressions are quite common in the court judgments of ancient China, though not necessarily in an explicitly separate segment). However, for the convenience of calculation, epilogues are also excluded when determining the percentage of segments, for epilogue only appear in 8 of the 100 court judgments on the one hand, and epilogue take a very small percentage in a court judgment on the other hand.

Table 4. Rhetorical segments, contents and linguistic markers

Rhetorical Segments	Content	Linguistic markers
Heading	To make a brief summary of jurisdiction, decision time, title of proceeding, nature of the case the parties involved, etc.	decision, judgment, reason, order; Reasons for order, Reasons for judgment and order
		人民法院(people's court), 判决书(judgment),民/刑/行 (civil/criminal/administrative),初/终字(first/final)
Introduction	To describe the situation before the court and answers these questions: who (the parties) did what (facts) to whom and how the court has dealt with the case.	introduction, summary
		提起诉讼(file a suit),开庭审理(hear),现已审理终结 (the case has been concluded)
Facts	To explain the facts in chronological order, or by description. It might include the disputed facts, the agreed facts and the found facts.	facts, background; The factual background, Agreed statement of facts
		原/被告认为(the plaintiff/the defendant thinks),经审理查明(After hearing, it is ascertained that…)

<table>
<tr><td rowspan="2">Analysis</td><td rowspan="2">To describe the comments or arguments of the judge the application of the law to the facts as found.</td><td>analysis, , discussion arguments</td></tr>
<tr><td>本院认为(this court is of the view that),依照xx规定 (according to the law xx)</td></tr>
<tr><td rowspan="2">Conclusion</td><td rowspan="2">To express the final judgment---disposition or decision made by the court (in Chinese judgments) or judge (in American judgments) and specify the effects on the parties.</td><td>conclusion, disposition, costs ,revert, remand, affirm</td></tr>
<tr><td>判决(decision),驳回 (dismiss),维持 (maintain/affirm),改判 (amend),发回重审(remand, retrial)</td></tr>
</table>

As to the size and percentage of each rhetorical segment, it depends mainly on computer-based calculation and part of them needs manual computation. A judgment is first divided into several rhetorical segment annually, the size (word numbers) for each segment is calculated by word count automatically, and put into format in the form of EXCEL as shown in Table 5; the percentage of each segment can also be processed automatically and then average percentage of each segment in all court judgments can be reached as indicated in Table 6.

Table 5. Part of statistics (word count) in terms of segment size in Chinese judgments

Heading	Intro-duction	Facts Eluci-dated	Facts Ascer-tained	Legal Analysis	Statutes	Decision	Total
204	94	1211	591	573	34	237	2944
216	102	1147	7309	493	56	143	9466
442	148	899	2728	1617	59	420	6313
552	240	888	1848	968	42	271	4809
2090	505	2568	14434	1132	290	1141	22160
198	136	416	4109	415	99	184	5557
476	192	521	2502	251	75	162	4179
821	273	880	3262	904	255	371	6766
197	126	494	1163	1163	63	155	3361
239	138	2803	1684	809	44	193	5910

Table 6. Percentage of each rhetorical segment of court judgments

Rhetorical segments		Percentage	
Label		Chinese Judgments	American Judgments
Heading		6%	1%
Introduction/summary		4%	7%
Context/Facts	Facts Elucidated	20%	20%
	Facts Ascertained	40%	
Analysis	Legal Analysis	21%	68%
	Statutes	2%	
Decision/Conclusion		7%	4%

3.2.2. Functions of rhetorical segments

For some linguists, language has to serve various purposes, as there are different types of occasions for using it, that is, language serves different functions in accordance with concrete situations. The functional approach to describing language has its roots in the traditions of British linguist Firth (1957), who viewed language as interactive and interpersonal, as a way of behaving and making others behave. Halliday (1973 and 1975) believes that language is what it is because it has to serve certain functions. In other words, social demands on language have helped to shape its structure. He provides one of the best expositions of language functions, used the term "function" to mean the purposive nature of communication and outlined seven different functions of language:

- Instrumental
  - To satisfy own material needs.
  - Serves the function *I want.*
- Regulatory
  - To regulate the behaviour of others
  - Servers the function *Do as I tell you.*
- Interactional
  - To establish and maintain contact with others
  - Serves the function of social interaction *Between you and me.*
- Personal
  - To express self or personal feeling
  - Serves the function *Here I come.*
- Heuristic
  - To learn and explore reality
  - Serves the function *Tell me why*?

- Imaginative
  - To create one's own environment
  - Serves the function *Let's pretend.*
- Informative
  - The use of language to communicate content
  - Serves the function *I have something to tell you*

Other linguists put forward different versions as to the functions of language: phatic, directive, informative, interrogative, expressive, evocative or performative (Hu 1998).

Legal documents can serve a variety of functions, including eliciting information, persuading, memorializing events such as reciprocal communications, or accomplishing performative goals, such as creating or revoking legal relationships. Court judgments, as a special genre of a legal discourse community, typically have a performative objective: they are intended to decide or alter legal relationships relevant to some controversy before the court. In fact, more exactly, we should say the decision/disposition part of a court judgment serve the performative function; the other parts of a court judgment have their own functions. Table 7 as follows is a match between the rhetorical distribution and functional analysis of a court judgment.

Table 7. Rhetorical distribution and functional analysis of a court judgment

Rhetorical Segments	Functional Analysis
Head	Informative
Introduction	Informative
Context/Facts	Informative
Analysis (ratio decidendi)	Expressive/personal (binding)
Decision/Conclusion	Performative/regulatory
Judge's Postscript/epilogue	Evocative/expressive/personal
Obiter Dictum	Evocative/expressive/personal (persuasive)

3.3. Summary

By applying the theories related to genre, rhetoric and functional linguistics to the court judgments, the findings and results are listed as follows:

a) Moves and steps of Chinese court judgments are different from those of American court judgments.

b) Moves and steps of a court judgment by a court of first instance are different from those of a court judgment by a court of second instance.
c) Judgments by courts of the same trial level do not necessarily follow exactly the same moves and steps; and some court judgments have embedded moves and steps.
d) In American court judgments, there are two types of legal analysis: *obiter dictum* and *ratio decidendi. Ratio decidendi*, having a binding force for the later decision of the same court or inferior courts, is indispensable. *Obiter dictum*, with a persuasive role but without a binding force, can be optional and usually appears in first singular person in term of linguistic feature. *Obiter dictum* can be unanimous, concurring, and dissenting.
e) In Chinese court judgments, multiple opinion and epilogue can be accounted from the perspective of legal memetics.
f) Court judgments in the two legal systems, though demonstrated in different moves and steps, have basically the same rhetorical functions for each segment and therefore basically the same communicative purposes, which implies that the mutual understanding and mutual exchange of American and Chinese court judgments are beneficial.

3.4. Legal-cultural analysis

From the analysis of the data above, we can conclude that the main differences between Chinese and American court judgments are as follows: a) legal analysis/reasoning takes much more proportion in an American court judgment than in a Chinese one; b) judge's postscript/epilogue in a Chinese court judgment is more an expressive component than a persuasive one (obiter dictum) or having binding force (ratio decidendi in American judgments); and c) *ratio decidendi* in American judgments has a binding force and *ratio decidendi* in Chinese court judgments might have a guideline function. All those differences can be accounted for in the legal culture, "the public knowledge, attitudes and behavioral patterns concerning a legal system" (Friedman 1975: 193). Contrastive legal studies in the United States have tended to focus mainly on Romano-Germanic civil law tradition, or on the law of particular geographic regions (e.g. East Asia studies, Latin American studies) (Glendon et al. 2003). Those in China mainly deal with the comparison of two legal systems. For the comparative legalists, one of the pressing tasks is try to capture how far in actual practice what is described as globalization in fact represents the attempted imposition of one particular legal culture on other societies, not just limited to the concept of legal culture. Indeed, with the economic globalization and legal cooperation, the two major legal systems overlap with and influence each other.

The development of law in China can only be understood through the prism of Chinese history, and so can the evolution of Chinese court judgments. The nexus that binds law to civil society operates differently in China from in the West. Traditionally, law in China has never been a wellspring of popular expression, nor have legal bureaucracies been Western-cast civil servants. Instead, the relationship between the law, the lawmaker, and the governed in China is quasi-fiduciary in nature and based squarely on trust (Alford 1986). The governor rather than the governed preserves social balance by harmonizing the natural and human orders, while rules are continually legitimated above and transmitted to society below (Peerenboom 1993). Chinese legal thought posits a mutually complemented two-tier system of law: the first, a formal instrument of the centralized state authority; the other, an informal code of virtue and localized community norms. In other words, there exists the contrast between *li* (conventionally translated as rites or rituals) and *fa* (conventionally translated as law), which marks a distinction in Chinese political theory as to the nature of political order and the preferred means of achieving such order. Li, closely related with Confucianism, refers to social order achieved primarily with reference to the traditional customs, mores, and norms, whereas *fa* indicates political order attained primarily through reliance on laws. The supplementary contradiction between *li* and *fa*, two dominant strategies for achieving social or political order began in the classical tradition, and that has persisted down to the present day. *Li* and *fa* help to explain present Chinese attitudes toward law and law enforcement including its concrete form-court judgments, especially the appearance of epilogue, which is full of the ideas of teaching and correction. *Fa*, a system based on punishment and force, which has far-reaching influence on the modern legal systems in China, is to some extent able to explain the relative insufficiency of legal analysis in Chinese court judgments. Legal thoughts during neo-democratic revolutionary period which emphasized "dictatorship of the proletariat" might also provide a sound account for the phenomenon that the proportion of *ratio decidendi* or legal reasoning is relatively less than that in an American judgment.

With China's post-1978 reforms and opening up, the legal system with Chinese characteristics has felt the impact of western legal system, the Common Law system, which explicates why Chinese judgment reform has attached great importance to the expansion of legal reasoning in court judgments and multiple opinions are allowed in some court judgments especially in the civil and commercial cases at lower courts. Legalists also hold that legal precedents could offer remedies to relative imprecision and vagueness of civil laws under which judges are usually allowed more freedom in their decisions. Legal precedents are not endorsed as part of legislation in China, but on some occasions typical cases that have been settled are referred to in making judgments. In 1996, the Higher People's Court of Tianjin issued three cases to which lower courts can refer in making a decision; it is the first time that a Chinese higher court has issued legal precedents (www.chinacourt.com). The Supreme People's Court has released typical cases it collected and instructions on a quarterly basis to instruct lower courts, and the Law Research Institute under the Supreme People's Court has published *Selected Cases Settled by People's Courts*. Law specialists agree that the practice of legal precedents could help to protect the integration of the law and guarantee impartiality and efficiency in administering justice.

4. Conclusion

Rapid economic and social development in China, especially after its accession to the WTO, has created a need for more legally qualified and legally aware personnel in all aspects of life. There will be an increasing demand that legal professionals have a sound understanding of the common law system and the legal system of China. However, there are not many who are bilingual and legally professional. Besides the study of foreign legislation, research in foreign court judgments, especially those of English-speaking countries, is necessary due to the requirements of the WTO transparency principles.

Despite the similarities of Chinese and American court judgments, because of the same discourse community, there exist some differences in generic and rhetorical features. The paper compares the differences of court judgments in terms of their respective moves, rhetorical segments and functions. The paper is not just limited to the genre analysis, which is of course indispensable for our study, but it goes further to cultural analysis in order to find out the underlying rationales for the differences. From the study, the authors would like to put forward the following pedagogical implications:

a) Contrastive genre analysis is a feasible and useful tool in cross-cultural discourse analysis;
b) When a generic analysis is carried out, we should not just do some superficial research such as the lexical, structural features, but go further to probe into the underlying rationales for those features from a socio-linguistic perspective, i.e. cultural angle;
c) Legal translation or legal transplant is more than a symbolic transfer, but a cross-cultural communication. Therefore, what a legal translator needs is not only solid bilingual proficiency but also a grasp of different legal contents and cultures.

References

Alford, W. P. (1986). "The inscrutable Occidental? Implications of Roberto Unger's uses and abuses of the Chinese past". *Texas Law Review* 64(5), 915-972.

Bhatia, V. K. (1983). *Applied discourse analysis of English legislative writing.* Birmingham: University of Aston in Birmingham.

Bhatia, V. K. (1993). *Analysing genre: language use in professional settings.* London: Longman.

Bhatia, V. K. (1997). "Applied genre analysis and ESP". In T. Miller (ed.), *Functional approaches to written text: Classroom applications*. English Language Programs: United States Information Agency, 134-149.

Bowles, H. (1995). "Why are newspaper law reports so hard to understand?". *English for Specific Purposes* 14, 201-222.

Connor, U. (1996). *Contrastive rhetoric: Cross-cultural aspects of second-language Writing*. Cambridge: Cambridge University Press.

Firth, J. R. (1957). *Thesis in linguistics*. London: Oxford University Press.

Friedman, L. (1975). *The legal system: A Social Science Perspective*. New York: Russell Sage Foundation.

Gibbons, J. (ed.) (1994). *Language and the law*. Harlow: Longman.

Gibbons, J. (2003). *Forensic linguistics: an introduction to language in the justice system*. Oxford: Blackwell.

Glendon, M. A., Gordon, M. W. and P. G. Carozza (2003). *Comparative legal traditions* (2nd ed.). Peking: Law Press.

Goodrich, P. (1986). *Reading the law: a critical introduction to legal method and techniques*. Oxford: Blackwell.

Halliday, M. A. K. (1978). *Language as a social semiotic*. London: Edward Arnold.

Halliday, M. A. K. (1985). *An Introduction to functional grammar*. London: Edward Arnold.

Hanson, S. (2003). *Legal method and reasoning*. London: Cavendish Publishing Ltd.

Hu, Z. (1998). *Linguistics*. Peking: Peking University Press.

Levi, J. N. (1982). *Linguistics, language and law: a topical bibliography.* Evanston: Northwestern University.

Maley, Y. (1994). *The language of the law*. London: Longman.

Myers, G. (1992). "Speech acts and scientific facts". *Journal of Pragmatics* 17(4): 295-313.

Mellinkoff, D. (1963). *The Language of the Law*. Boston: Little, Brown and Co.

Peerenboom, R. P. (1993). *Law and morality in ancient China: The Silk Manuscripts of Huang-Lao*. Albany: State University of New York Press.

Randall, V. (online) "Elements of the *Case Brief*", available at http://academic.udayton.edu/legaled/online/class/case01.htm, accessed July 2007.

Shuy, R. W. (2002). *Linguistic battles in trademark disputes*. Basingstoke: Palgrave Macmillan.

Shuy, R. W. (2005). *Creating language crimes*. New York: Oxford University Press.

Stygall, G. (1994). *Trial language: differential discourse processing and discursive formation*. Amsterdam: John Benjamins.

Tiersma, P. (1999). *Legal language*. Chicago: University of Chicago Press.

Widdowson, H. G. (ed.) (1979). *Reading and thinking in English*. Oxford: Oxford University Press.

Aleksandra Matulewska
Adam Mickiewicz University
Poland

THE MACROSTRUCTURE AND REGISTER OF ENGLISH AND POLISH TESTAMENTS

1. Types of testaments

Last Will and Testament is the name of a document in which testators dispose of their estates (real and personal property) in the event of death. The word *testament* derives from Latin *testamentum*, which means a disposition of property which is made in the contemplation of the testator's death. English and Polish have adopted the term in the form *testament*. Under early English law the term meant the disposition of personal property by will and therefore the word *will* was introduced into the name of this legal instrument. Nowadays, it is possible to use the terms *Last Will* or *Last Will and Testament*. It is due to the fact that the word *will* nowadays relates not only to personal but also to real property as well.

In general, a *Last Will and Testament* is made in writing. However, the laws of Poland, England and the USA provide for oral testaments as well. There are three main forms of written wills: holographs, allographs and notary wills.

Holographs are testaments handwritten, signed and dated by the testator. They may be executed in the presence of witnesses or without witnesses. Allographs are testaments executed in the presence of witnesses, whereas notarial testaments are those which are executed by a notary public at the request of the testator, or which are executed by the testator in the presence of a notary public.

There are also the following types of wills: i) a military testament, ii) a mutual testament, and iii) a mystic testament. A military testament is made by word of mouth. It is accepted under Polish, English and American law, but as it is an oral genre it shall not be discussed in this paper in more detail. Mutual testaments are wills which are made by two people who leave their property reciprocally to the survivor. Those wills are not lawful in Poland as Polish law allows only for the dispositions of a single person to the testaments and they must be executed by the testator's own will and either cannot be made as a contract or cannot have a reciprocal character. A mystic testament is allowed under the laws of Louisiana and California. This testament is also called a sealed testament, a secret testament or a closed testament as after its execution the testator must sign the disposition of the estate, and then the document is folded in such a way that it at the same time serves as an envelope, which is sealed in the presence of a notary and seven witnesses. The testator then declares it to be the last will and testament and the notary prepares a special document (the act of superscription) which is to accompany the will as its envelope or is made on the will itself.

A *codicil* is a kind of a supplement or an addition to an existing will which may modify it, add something to it or revoke some of its provisions. It is not a will and therefore may not provide for disposing of the entire estate of the deceased. The name codicil derives from Latin *codicillus*, which was an inferior and rather informal type of a will executed by the Romans.

What follows below is an overview of English, American and Polish testaments.[1]

2. English testaments

English and American wills are similar and therefore they will be discussed jointly. Nevertheless, it shall be borne in mind that:

i) literal wording is very important in American and British testaments;
ii) land ownership in the USA and England is understood in a completely different way.

Heading

The heading of a testament may be separated from the main body of the document or it may be blended into its first sentence.

> Last Will and Testament
> This is Last Will and Testament of ...

Testator's identification clause

This clause facilitates identification of the testator who executed the will by providing his or her name, place of residence and sometimes job or profession. Moreover, this part usually includes a declaration made by the testator as being of sound mind and memory.

> I, Michael ... of the City of Rochester in the County of Monroe and State of New York being of sound mind and memory, do make publish and declare this my Last Will and Testament, in manner following that is to say:...

[1] The corpus of testaments includes documents published in Chojnowski and Jarzęcki (1971), Kierzkowska (1998) and Poznański (1998), as well as the author's collection of original testaments.

> This is the Last Will and Testament of me Alexander John Brown, of 133 Forfar Road, Brechin, in the County of Forfar, Plumber, made this Fourteenth day of October, one thousand nine hundred and sixty-five.
>
> THIS Last Will and Testament is made by me … of …

Date

The date of the execution of a will may come at the end of the main body of the document or may be included in its first sentence as in one of the above examples. What deserves special attention is the fact that the year is written in a variety of ways and some of them are used in legal language only, e.g. *one thousand nine hundred and sixty-five*.

> In Witness Whereof, I have hereunto subscribed my name the 16th day of May in the year Nineteen Hundred and Eighty-five.

Revocation of prior will clause

A prior will may be revoked in a special clause. In English law it is very popular if the testator has already executed a will and wants to change it or simply make it void.

> I hereby revoke all Wills and Codicils made by me at any time heretofore.
>
> …hereby revoking all former wills by me made.
>
> I REVOKE all previous wills and codicils.
>
> I HEREBY revoke all former Wills, Codicils and other Testamentary instruments made by me and declare this to be my last Will.

Executor appointment clause (Alcaraz and Hughes 2002:143)

This is the part of a testament in which an executor is appointed by the testator to carry out the instructions and requests described in detail in the document and to dispose of the property in the manner described in the testamentary provisions.

> I appoint my wife, Alice Jane Brown and Thomas Watt, of Montrose Street, Brechin, aforesaid Baker, to be my Executors, and …
>
> Lastly, I hereby appoint my wife, Vanda, executrix, or if she shall not survive me or qualify, then Stanislawa, Blvd., Rochester, New York, executor of this, my Last Will and Testament with full power and authority to …
>
> I APPOINT as executors and trustees of my will … of … and … of … and … of … and should one or more of them fail to or be unable to act I APPOINT to fill any vacancy … of …

Debt clause (Alcaraz and Hughes 2002:141)
This clause provides for paying back debts and fulfilling obligations existing at the moment of the testator's death. It also encompasses the funeral expenses.

> First, I direct that all my just debts and funeral expenses be paid.
>
> ...and direct that all my Debts and Funeral Expenses shall be paid as soon as conveniently may be after my decease.
>
> ...and direct that all my debts and Funeral Expenses shall be paid as soon as convenient after my death.
>
> ...pay my debts, taxes and testamentary expenses...

Distribution clause (Alcaraz and Hughes 2002:141)
This is the clause in which the testator transfers the estate among heirs and relatives. It includes triplets (*give, devise and bequeath*; *rest residue and reminder*) (Mellinkoff 1963).

> Second: I give, devise and bequeath all the estate and effects whatsoever, both real and personal, to which I may be entitled, or which I may have power to dispose of at my decease, unto my wife, Vanda, absolutely and forever.
> I give and bequeath unto my son Robert Brown the sum of two hundred and eighty pounds, unto the said Thomas Watt, the sum of fifty pounds, unto my daughter, Alice Brown, all those two houses situated in and being Nos. 3 and 5, Queen Street, Arbroath, and all the reminder of my property unto my wife the said Alice Jane Brown.

Common disaster clause (Alcaraz and Hughes 2002:142)
This clause provides for an alternative beneficiary in the event both the testator and his or her heir die in a common disaster.

Survivorship clause (Alcaraz and Hughes 2002:142)
This clause provides for the situation in which the testator survives the beneficiary or beneficiaries named in his or her testament. It is usually a second distribution clause, which is to be applied in the event the beneficiaries predecease the testator.

What follows below is an example of the common disaster and survivorship clause:

> Third: in the event that my aforesaid wife shall have predeceased me, or that we shall both die in, or as a result of, the same accident or occurrence, then I hereby give, devise and bequeath my entire residuary estate, as aforesaid, as follows: ...
>
> PROVIDED THAT if any of my children dies before me or after me but under that age, I GIVE the share that child would have taken to his or her own children who attain

18 equally. If no person shall inherit the residue of my estate under the preceding gifts, I GIVE it to...

Guardian appointment clause (Alcaraz and Hughes 2002:143)
Parents may include a clause appointing a guardian for their child. This type of a guardian is called a testamentary guardian. There is also the institution of a guardian by election, who is chosen by a child.

I APPOINT ... of ... to be guardian of any of my children who are minors if my wife dies before me.

Saving clause (Alcaraz and Hughes 2002:143)
This clause may be included in a testament in order to keep it valid even if some part or parts of it are invalidated. This clause is also called a severability clause.

If any portion of my will shall be held illegal, invalid or otherwise inoperative, it is my intention that all of the provisions hereof shall continue to be fully effective and operative insofar as is possible and reasonable.

Derogatory clause
This clause is rather rare in testaments. "In a will, this is a sentence of secret character, inserted by the testator, of which he reserves the knowledge to himself, with a condition that no will he may make thereafter should be valid, unless this clause be inserted word for word. This is done as a precaution to guard against later wills being extorted by violence, or otherwise improperly obtained. Such a provision is anomalous" (Black, 1979: 400).

Signature (Alcaraz and Hughes 2002:144)
As far as wills are concerned, the signature clause usually has a very solemn form.

In witness whereof, I have hereunto subscribed my name the 16th day of May in the year Nineteen Hundred and Eighty-five

IN WITNESS WHEREOF, I have hereto set my hand and seal this 18th day of March, 1989.

SIGNED by the above-named testator in our presence on the 3rd day of August 1994 and then by us in the testator's presence
Testator's Signature ...
Witnesses' Signatures

____________ ____________
of ____________ of ____________
____________ ____________
Occupation ________ Occupation ________

However, it is also possible just to sign the will with the first name and family original name.

Attestation clause, testing clause or testimonium (Alcaraz and Hughes 2002:144) This clause is characteristic not only of wills but also other legal instruments such as certificates, affidavits, notarized statements etc. (which in order to be valid must be signed or executed in the presence of witnesses). In testaments, this part is to certify to the facts and circumstances concerning the witnesses attending the execution of the document in question.

We, whose names are hereto subscribed, Do Certify that on the 16th day of May 1985 Michael the testator above named, subscribed his name to this instrument in our presence and in the presence of each of us, and at the same time, in our presence and hearing, declared the same to be his last Will and Testament, and requested us and each of us, to sign our names thereto as witnesses to the execution thereof, which we hereby do in the presence of the testator and of each other, on the day of the date of the said Will, and write opposite our names our respective places of residence.

Bryan R.	residing at	Rochester, New York
Laura W.	residing at	Greece, New York

Signed by the said Testator Alexander John Brown, in the presence of us both, present at the same time, who at his request in his presence and in the presence of each other have subscribed our names as witnesses

3. Polish testaments

When talking about Polish testaments, it should be borne in mind that they differ from the English ones significantly. First of all, under statutory civil law there is less need to execute testaments for many people. Most people want to dispose of their property in the statutory way, which is why they do not bother to make a will.

The most popular seem to be holographs and notary wills. Those two types of wills should in fact be discussed separately, as they, in a way, constitute two different sub-genres. This is due to the fact that legal forms are not so popular and widespread, not to mention widely available, in Poland as they are in England or the USA. People have to seek legal help or execute their wills themselves. Thus, wills executed by the notary public are more similar to English and American ones than those made by people without legal education. Notarial, allographic and holographic testaments will be discussed here.

i) Notarial Testaments

Notarial testaments are a kind of report made by a Notary Public of what the testator wants to do. Therefore, the dispositions of the testator are expressed in the third person singular.

Heading

Testament

[Testament]

Distribution Clause

Marian Adamowicz powołuje do spadku dzieci swoje: a) Janinę Cegiełkowską, zam. w Częstochowie przy ulicy Kościelnej nr 5 m. 2, w ¼ (jednej czwartej części i b) Stefana Adamowicza, zam. w Krakowie przy ulicy Wyspiańskiego nr 6 m. 2, w ¾ (trzech czwartych) częściach, zobowiązując tego ostatniego do wypłacenia pozostałym jego dzieciom: Zofii Jankowskiej, zam. w Warszawie przy ulicy Anielewicza 5 m. 4, i Michałowi Adamowiczowi, zam. w Poznaniu przy ulicy Długiej nr 8 m. 20, po 50.000 zł (pięćdziesiąt tysięcy).
Gdyby osoby powołane do spadku albo jedna z nich nie chciały lub nie mogły być spadkobiercami, do spadku lub jego części na ich miejsce powołuje wnuka Feliks Nowaka, zam. w Krakowie przy ulicy Nowotki 6 m.1.

[Marian Adamowicz calls to succession his children (i) Janina Cegiełkowska residing at ul. Kościelna 5 flat 2 to one fourth part and (ii) Stefan Adamowicy residing at ul. Wyspiańskiego 6 flat 2 to three fourth parts, obliging the latter to pay to his other children, that is Zofia Jankowska, residing at ul. Anielewicza 5 flat 4 in Warsaw and Michał Adamowicz, residing at ul. Długa 8 flat 20 fifty thousand zlotys each.
If any person or persons called to succession did not want or could not be successors, the Testator calls to succession or its part in their place and stead his grandson, Feliks Nowak, residing at ul. Nowotki 6 flat 1 in Kraków.]

Funeral Arrangements

Syna Stefana Adamowicza zobowiązuje do urządzenia mu pogrzebu i postawieniu mu nagrobka według zwyczajów miejscowych.
Wartość tego rozrządzenia szacuje na 200.000 zł (dwieście tysięcy).

[The son, Stefan Adamowicz, shall arrange for the Testator's funeral and shall have a tombstone erected according to the local customs.
The value of this disposition is estimated at two hundred thousand Polish zlotys (PLN 200,000).]

Executor appointment clause

Na wykonawcę tego testamentu powołuje żonę swoją Bożenę Adamowicz, a w razie jej śmierci – syna Stefana Adamowicza.

[The testator appoints his wife Bożena Adamowicz executrix of this testament, and in the event of her death he appoints his son, Stefan Adamowicz, executor.]

Typical elements of a Notarial Act

Od aktu tego za dokonanie czynności pobrano 847,50 zł (§ 10 rozp. o opł not.).
Akt ten odczytano, przyjęto i podpisano
M. Adamowicz
Notariusz L. Ajewski

[The sum of eight hundred forty seven Polish zlotys and fifty groszys (PLN 847.50) has been collected as a fee for acts-in-law performed in connection with this deed (par.10 of the Regulation on Notarial Fees).
Read, accepted, and signed.
M. Abramowicz
Notary L. Ajewski]

ii) Allograph Testament

This type of testament is executed in the presence of witnesses but not the Notary Public. The particulars concerning the witnesses are given at the very end of the document. This type of testament is very similar to English testaments.

Heading

Testament

[Testament]

Identification of the Testator

Ja niżej podpisany Felicjan Fortunny, syn Piotra i Marii, urodzony 14 listopada 1925 roku w Warszawie, zamieszkały w Warszawie przy ul.XYZ10, legitymujący się dowodem osobistym seria S 25111458670 wydanym przez...

[I, the undersigned Felicjan Fortunny, the son of Piotr and Maria, born on 14th November 1925 in Warsaw, residing at ul. XYZ10 in Warsaw, holding identity document number S 25111458670 issued by...

Statement of Fact

...w ramach mojej ostatniej woli i w pełni świadomości postanawiam co następuje:
1. Wraz z moją żoną Romualdą Florentyną Fortunną z domu Kowalską jesteśmy właścicielami nieruchomości stanowiącej zagospodarowaną wspólnie działkę o powierzchni 830 m2 oraz domu jednorodzinnego, piętrowego z garażem położonego w Warszawie przy ulicy XYZ10;

[...as my last will and testament being of sound mind and memory represent the following:
1. I and my wife are together the owners of the immovable property which is composed of a developed lot of land of 830 sq. m. and a two-floor single family house with a garage located at ul. XYZ10 in Warsaw;]

Distribution Clause

2. w razie mojej śmierci do całości spadku przypadającego na mnie powołuję wyłącznie żonę moją Romualdę Florentynę Fortunną z domu Kowalską;
[In the event of my death I call to all succession, which I leave, only my wife, Romualda Florentyna Fortunna, née Kowalska.]

Exclusions

3. Wszystkie nasze dzieci (łącznie z przysposobionymi) a to:
a)Krystyna K. ur. 27.03. 1946, córka Felicjana i Eugenii,
b)Mirosław F. ur. 27.07.1946 syn Marii B., (ojciec nieznany),
c)Aleksander A. ur. 07.04.1949 syn Aleksandra i Romualdy,
d)Andrzej A. ur. 03.07.1953 syn Aleksandra i Romualdy,
zostały całkowicie i współmiernie materialnie zaspokojone i z tego tytułu nie przysługuje im prawo roszczeń do spadku po mnie.

[3. All our children (including the adopted ones) that is:
Krystyna K., born on 17 March 1946, the daughter of Felicjan and Eugenia,
Mirosław F. born on 27 July 1946, the son of Maria B, (father unknown),
Aleksander A. Born on 7 April 1949, the son of Aleksander and Romualda,
Andrzej A. Born on 3 July 1953, the son of Aleksander and Romualda,
have been financially provided for sufficiently and adequately and thus they shall not be entitled to the estate left by me.]

Attestation Clause

Testament sporządziłem osobiście i własnoręcznie, oraz jako zgodny z moją wolą podpisuję
Felicjan Fortunny
Warszawa 14 maja 1993r.
Pan Felicjan Fortunny złożył własnoręcznie podpis w mojej obecności ...

[I have executed this testament on my own and in my handwriting, and I sign it as consistent with my will
Felicjan Fortunny
Warsaw, 14 May 1993
Felicjan Fortunny has subscribed his name in my presence ...]

iii) Hollograph Testament

In this part of the article an attempt will be made to prove that there is a *quasi-legal language* that is the language used in holographs. This language can be classified as neither legal language, nor as legal meta-language nor as colloquial language due to its characteristic features, viz:

i) native speakers who use this language do not know law and legal language but attempt to create a text in the language for special purposes, and perceive the executed document as solemn, formal and written in the legal jargon;
ii) the language used is different from standard Polish due to the range of legal terms used (despite the fact that those terms are often used in an inappropriate way or an inappropriate meaning is attached to them) and the style which is perceived as highly official and formal;
iii) if interpreted literally in both the standard language or legal language, those texts would have a completely different meaning than the one which is intended.

Testament

Ja niżej podpisany, Jan Kowalski, oświadczam, że ***zapisuję*** cały swój majątek memu synowi Jackowi Kowalskiemu.

Jan Kowalski

[Testament

I, hereinunder signed Jan Kowalski, represent that I ***call to the legacy*** after me my son Jacek Kowalski.

Jan Kowalski]

As is clearly recognizable from the above example, the most common mistake is to use *zapisywać* [*to call to legacy*] instead of *powoływać do spadku* [*to call to succession*]. From the strictly legal point of view this mistake is crucial. However, in practice it does not change much under Polish law and the will remains valid and it is not treated as a codicil. Additionally, even if the wording is such the whole estate may be transferred if the will has other elements necessary for it to be valid (such as the date of its execution and the signature).

Holographs are made intuitively not only because testators do not know the law but also because they do not know legal language. Furthermore, even their knowledge of the formal standard language may be limited. As a consequence, many legal terms are mixed or used in an inappropriate way. In order to interpret those documents in accordance with the intentions of its author there is a provision in the Polish Civil Code of 23 April, 1964 which states as follows:

> Art. 65. § 1. Orzeczenie woli należy tak tłumaczyć, jak tego wymagają ze względu na okoliczności, w których złożone zostało, zasady współżycia społecznego oraz ustalone zwyczaje.
> § 2. W umowach należy raczej badać, jaki był zgodny zamiar stron i cel umowy, aniżeli opierać się na jej dosłownym brzmieniu.
>
> [Art. 65. § 1. A declaration of will is to be interpreted so as is required by the circumstances in which it is made, the principles of community life, and the established custom.
> § 2. In the case of contracts, the congruent intention of the parties and the purpose of the contract, rather than relaying on its literal wording, must be established.] (translated by Wojtasiewicz, amendments by Kierzkowska, Polish Law Collection).

This provision makes Polish testaments completely different from English ones as in the case of the latter the literal wording is what really matters. Thus, much more attention is paid to the language and terms used in English legal instruments than to those made in Polish or those to which Polish law is applicable.

4. Concluding remarks

Apart from the obvious conclusion that there are a wide variety of testaments, it needs to be emphasized that the fact that legal forms are not as popular in Poland as they are in England and the USA makes the situation even more complicated from the translator's point of view. The need to construe testaments written in quasi-legal language (under the Polish Civil Code of 23 April 1964) makes the situation even more difficult when translating wills into English, more so as it must be remembered that there are codicils in the English legal system in which legatees are called to legacies. Thus, in order not to cause misunderstandings in which a Polish testament may be understood to be a codicil, translators should construe the text in such a way that the intentions of the testator are expressed properly. Thus, the advice of Saint Jerome, patron-saint of translators, *Non verbum e verbo, sed sensum exprimere de sensu* [Not word by word, but meaning for meaning] should be applied also in such circumstances. However, if the translation was necessary to verify the authorship of the document then the mistakes may be vital, as they convey some information concerning the author of the document e.g. that the author did not know the law and was not accustomed to dealing with legal documents.

References

Alcaraz, E., and B. Hughes (2002). *Legal Translation Explained.* Manchester: St. Jerome Publishing.

Black, H. C., Nolan, J. R. and M. J. Connolly (1979). *Black's Law Dictionary.* St Paul, Minn. West Publishing Co.

Chojnowski, W. and A. Jarzęcki (1971). *Wzory aktów i innych dokumentów notarialnych.* Warszawa: Wydawnictwo Prawnicze.

Mellinkoff, D. (1963). *The Language of the Law.* Boston/Toronto: Little, Brown and Company.

Ustawa z dnia 17 listopada 1964 r – Kodeks Postępowania Cywilnego [The Code of Civil Procedure – Act of 17 November 1964].

Ustawa z dnia 23 kwietnia 1964 r. – Kodeks cywilny [The Civil Code – Act of 23 April 1964].

Part VII

THE SEMANTICS OF TRADE NAMES

Richard L. Creech
Attorney-at-Law, Washington, DC
USA

MISSING THE MARK: ASSESSING TRADEMARKS FOR DISTINCTIVENESS AND DESCRIPTIVENESS IN EUROPE'S MULTILINGUAL ENVIRONMENT

1. Introduction

Under Article 7(1) of the European Community's regulation on trademarks,[1] a trademark may not be registered if it is "devoid of any distinctive character" or if it consists exclusively of words "which may serve, in trade, to designate the kind, quality, quantity, intended purpose, value, geographical origin or the time of production of" the associated goods. Determining whether a proffered mark is either "distinctive" or merely "descriptive" can be difficult enough when the inquiry involves only one language. The European Union, however, is robustly multi-lingual. The twenty-seven Member States have twenty-three national or official languages among them, to say nothing of the dozens of regional and minority languages spoken throughout the EU. A multilingual assessment of a trademark's meaning is necessary, as Article 7(2) of the regulation states that a mark is unregisterable "notwithstanding that the grounds of non registerability obtain in only part of the Community." Consequently, before decreeing that a proffered mark is valid, a court should, in theory anyway, examine how the mark is understood by speakers of all the different languages spoken in the Community.

There is, however, a disconnect between theory and practice.[2] The judicial institutions of the European Union have preferred to take an easier route and have generally considered the meaning of a mark in only one language. For example, in a case decided in 2001, the European Court of Justice effectively ignored Europe's linguistic diversity when it ruled that Procter and Gamble was entitled to register the mark "Baby Dry" for its diaper products.[3] While the Court observed that "if a combination of words is purely descriptive in one of the languages used in trade within the Community, that is sufficient to render it ineligible for registration,"[4] the tribunal nonetheless decided that a monolingual analysis would

[1] Council Regulation No. 40/94 of 20 Dec. 1993, [1994] O. J. L11/1.
[2] The analysis of the EU's case law is based in part on Creech 2005.
[3] Case C-383/99, *Procter and Gamble Co. v. OHIM*, 2001 ECR I-6251.
[4] *Id.*, para. 41.

suffice, and stated, in a judicial *non sequitur*, that "[i]n order to assess whether a word combination such as BABY-DRY is capable of distinctiveness, it is therefore necessary to put oneself in the shoes of an English-speaking consumer."[5] After figuratively donning its anglophonic footwear, the Court concluded that the words "Baby Dry" were capable of distinctiveness in English, and that was the end of the story.

2. A methodology for assessing trademarks?

A little more intellectual rigor emerged two years later when the ECJ considered the meaning of the Wrigley Company's "Doublemint" chewing gum.[6] In particular, Advocate General Jacobs developed a methodology for assessing trademarks in a polyglot Community.[7] He noted that pursuant to Article 7(2) of the trademark regulation, "presumably a sign should be assessed in the light of the perception of consumers in all Member States,"[8] and proceeded to lay out the procedure that he believed should be followed in making such an assessment. First, he said, the mark should be viewed "from the standpoint of a native speaker of the language concerned."[9] If the words were descriptive in that language, the mark would be unregisterable and it would therefore be unnecessary to proceed any further. If, however, the words were not descriptive in the first language, one must consider the mark "through the eyes (or ears) of a Community consumer whose language is different."[10] Jacobs provided some examples of how this process should operate.

> For example, the English word "handy", meaning easy to handle, might be seen as a possible word mark, or part of a mark, for a mobile phone. Since however that word is commonly used in Germany to designate a mobile phone, it could not be registered as a Community mark. Similarly, a term derived from one language may acquire a different meaning or connotation in another: the English word "smoking" does not in

---

[5] *Id.*, para. 42.

[6] Case C-191/01, *OHIM v. William Wrigley Jr. Co.* (2003).

[7] The Advocate General is an officer of the court who conducts a preliminary examination of a case and offers an opinion to the full court. The full court can then either adopt or reject his findings, but it accepts them more often than not. In contrast to the opinions of the full court, which are often very short and elliptical, Advocates General typically issue longer, more-thoroughly reasoned opinions. While an opinion of the Advocate General can often provide insight into the thinking of the Court, it is not always clear how much of the reasoning in the opinion is adopted by the Court in any particular instance.

[8] Opinion of Advocate General Jacobs in Case C-191/01, *OHIM v. William Wrigley Jr. Co.* (2003), para. 80.

[9] *Id.*, para. 83.

[10] *Id.*, para. 85.

> English designate any characteristic of formal evening dress for men, whereas in French, German or Italian it designates what would in English be known as a dinner jacket or (by those who refer to nappies as "diapers") a tuxedo.[11]

Jacobs added a significant qualification to this procedure. Words should be analyzed through the prism of a particular language only if the words at issue "belonged" to that particular language. If a word did not belong to a particular language, it was irrelevant, in his view, how speakers of that language might understand that word. It was "inappropriate," he said, "to take as a normal yardstick a consumer struggling with an imperfect knowledge of a foreign tongue,"[12] and he dismissed as insignificant situations in which "speakers of one language, knowing a term to belong to another language, might misapprehend its originality in that other language by imposing on it features of their own language."[13] He therefore concluded that:

> Assessment under [the trademark regulation] should thus not be based on the question whether a term in a language used in one part of the Community might in another part of the Community be thought to designate product characteristics, so that any innovative or unusual feature in the grammatical or semantic structure of a mark must thus pass the test of innovativeness and unusualness in each of those parts.[14]

Strictly speaking, Jacobs's comments were unnecessary to the resolution of the case. Jacobs found, and the Court agreed, that the proffered mark "Doublemint" was merely descriptive in English and consequently ineligible for registration regardless of its meaning in any other languages, which Jacobs accordingly declined to consider.[15] Jacobs's opinion is noteworthy for several reasons. His proposed procedure appears to be a departure from the Court's approach in the "Baby Dry" case, where the Court failed to look at the mark's meaning in any other language after determining that it had distinctive character in English. Furthermore, he proposes a double standard that would treat words that "belong" to the language of the mark differently from those that do not "belong" to that language. This is problematic for a number of reasons. First, there does not seem to be any legitimate reason to make this distinction. If the aim of the regulation is, as Jacobs himself acknowledges, to ensure that words that are merely descriptive

[11] *Id.*, para. 86.
[12] *Id.*, para. 87.
[13] *Id.*, para. 87.
[14] *Id.*, para. 90.
[15] *Id.*, para. 82. The ECJ agreed with Jacobs's conclusion without elaborating on the difficulties posed by multilingualism.

may be freely used by all persons,[16] speakers of a language in which a word is regarded as descriptive of a product should not be denied the ability to use that word in connection with the product simply because the word is regarded as "belonging to" another language. Moreover, the regulation itself does not authorize any such distinction. And Jacobs does not address the threshold question of how one is to determine when a given word "belongs" to a particular language, or what that concept even means. Because languages borrow words from other languages and incorporate them into their own lexicons, it can often be fuzzy as to whether a given word is, with respect to a particular language, a foreign word or simply a word with foreign flavour. Most English speakers are familiar with eastern European dishes such as "goulash," "borscht" and even more so, "vodka." Should they be understood as "belonging" to English, or do they remain the sole lexical property of Hungarian, Russian or Polish?[17] Does *handy* "belong to" German, as Jacobs apparently believes?

In addition, Jacobs did not fully explain why he made the understanding of English speakers the touchstone of the case. Most likely he viewed this as the obvious choice in light of the fact that "double" and "mint" were words in the English language. Last year, the Court of First Instance stated expressly that when the mark at issue "is composed of English words, the relevant public ... is the average English-speaking consumer in the Community."[18] Of course, as we all know, the average English-speaking member of the Community is actually someone who has learned English as a second language, but, as noted earlier, Advocate General Jacobs stated that one should disregard the "consumer struggling with an imperfect knowledge of a foreign tongue."[19]

---

[16] *Id.*, para. 17, citing Joined Cases C-108/97 and C-109/97 *Windsurfing Chiemsee*, 1999 ECR I-2779, para. 25.

[17] The ECJ has frequently rejected claims by various Member States that they effectively own words used for certain food products and that they could, as a result, prevent foreign producers from using these terms to market products with non-traditional ingredients. See, e.g., Case 407/85, *3 Glocken GmbH v. USL Centro-Sud*, 1988 ECR 4233 (rejecting Italy's attempt to limit meaning of "pasta"); Case 178/84, *Commission v. Germany*, 1987 ECR 1227 (meaning of "beer"); Case 193/80, *Commission v. Italy*, 1981 ECR 3019 (meaning of "vinegar"). These and other related cases are discussed in Creech 2005.

[18] Case T-61/03, *Irwin Industrial Tool Co. v. OHIM* (2004), para. 27. See also Case T-183/03, *Applied Molecular Evolution Inc. v. OHIM* (2004), para. 17 (stating that "under Article 7(2) of Regulation No. 40/94 it is sufficient to establish that since the sign in question is English the relevant public comprises knowledgeable English-speaking consumers.")

[19] In Case C-498/01P,*OHIM v. Zapf Creation AG* (2004), Jacobs rejected the argument that a mark's registration in Denmark and Sweden, where the public has an "excellent knowledge" of English, precluded the need to consider the mark's meaning in "other Member States where English is the native language of the vast majority of the population" (Advocate General's Opinion, para. 56).

However, the Court of First Instance, which is the court below the ECJ in the European Union's judicial system, has also indicated that it is not always the speakers of the language of the mark that are to be considered as the relevant linguistic group.[20] A company which marketed pork products to Europeans of Southeast Asian descent applied for registration of the mark "kiap mou" with the Community's trademark office. Registration was opposed by another company which held multiple food-related trademarks for the word "mou" in the United Kingdom. Finding that there was a likelihood of confusion between the applicant's proffered mark and the older mark, the Trademark Office denied the applicant's request for registration, prompting an appeal to the Court of First Instance.

The word "mou" means "pork" in Thai, Laotian, and other languages spoken in southeast Asia, and "kiap mou" could be roughly translated as "crispy pork." The applicant argued that to its Indochinese customers, the term "mou" would be viewed as simply a descriptive term for pork but the term "kiap mou" was a fanciful creation. As a result, the applicant's mark could be registered, but its competitor's mark was invalid. Moreover, the applicant contended that its customers would find the mark "kiap mou" to be sufficiently distinctive from "mou" to prevent any likelihood of confusion.

The CFI rejected the applicant's attempt to focus on speakers of Asian languages. The court expressed doubt as to whether the goods in question were exclusively intended for the limited customer base of Europe's Indochinese community.[21] Noting that the trademark regulation proscribed registration of a mark where there was a likelihood of confusion "in the territory in which the earlier trade mark is protected,"[22] the court focused on the general population of the United Kingdom, which is where the earlier marks had been registered. The court reasoned that

> Such a public is in the very great majority anglophone. The words mou, kiap and kiap mou have no meaning in English and they bear no resemblance to the English words which have a meaning equivalent to that of these words in Laotian or Thai. Moreover, there is nothing in the case file or the applicant's arguments to suggest that a significant proportion of that public has a sufficient knowledge of the Laotian or Thai languages to understand the meaning of the words in question in those languages. It also follows from those considerations that, from the point of view of the relevant public, and contrary to the applicant's submission, mou is not

---

[20] Case T-286/02, *Oriental Kitchen SARL v. OHIM* (2003).

[21] *Id.*, para. 32. The courts have, however, ruled in other cases that some marks should be considered with respect to the understanding of a specific group of specialized consumers. See, e.g., Case T-183/03, *Applied Molecular Evolution Inc. v. OHIM* (2004), paras. 15-16 (ruling that relevant group was specialist consumers in the field of protein engineering).

[22] Council Regulation No. 40/94 of 20 Dec. 1993, Art. 8(1)(b), [1994] O.J. L11/1

> descriptive of the goods covered by the earlier mark. It will be viewed by that public as a term which is invented and inherently distinctive.[23]

The CFI accordingly upheld the denial of the registration sought, and thereby indicated that the language of a mark will not always determine the language upon which an inquiry of consumer understanding is based.[24]

3. National legal systems and trademark law

National legal systems have also grappled with the impact of multilingualism in the realm of trademark law. Several international treaties have addressed the issue, most prominently the Paris Convention for the Protection of Industrial Property of 1883[25], to which most of the world's countries, and all twenty-seven members of the European Union are signatories, provides that for trademarks considered to be "well-known" states shall prohibit the use of a translation of a competitor's translation of a prior mark.[26] Belgium, the Netherlands and Luxembourg have agreed that a party who obtains the right to a trademark in one of the national or regional languages of the Benelux area automatically obtains the exclusive right to the translation of the mark in the other area languages.[27] Several countries follow what is known as the "doctrine of foreign equivalents," a concept which was developed in the United States, under which foreign-language words in a proffered mark are compared to their translations in the country's native language in order to determine its validity.[28] Germany follows a version of this procedure,[29] and in the Wrigley case, the German government intervened to suggest that German-speakers, whose fondness for forming compound nouns knows no end, would translate "Doublemint" into the merely descriptive German term *Doppelminze*.[30]

---

[23] *Oriental Kitchen SARL v. OHIM*, paras. 41-42.

[24] The Court's decision to focus on the linguistic abilities of the majority of the country's population would seem to have ramifications for those considering the use of marks based on words derived from indigenous languages spoken in the UK such as Welsh, Scots, Scots Gaelic, or Irish.

[25] United Nations Treaty Series, Vol. 828, No. 11847, p. 108, last revised at Stockholm 14 July 1967.

[26] *Id.*, Art. 6(1).

[27] Uniform Benelux Law on Trademarks, Art. 13C(1).

[28] See, e.g., *Enrique Bernat F. SA v. Guadalajara, Inc.*, 210 F.3d 439 (5th Cir. 2000) (holding that *chupa* is Spanish-language term for "lollipop"); *Otokoyama Co. Ltd. v. Wine of Japan Import, Inc.*, 175 F.3d 266, 270 (2d Cir. 1999) (*otokoyama* is generic Japanese term for "sake").

[29] See, e.g., "House of Blues" case, Bundesgerichtshof Beschluss I ZB 27/96 of 18 Mar. 1999; "Home Depot" case, I ZB 10/94 of 7 June 1996.

[30] *Wrigley*, para. 81.

In Poland, a recent decision of the Patent Office indicated that a mark in a foreign language will be translated into Polish for purposes of determining its validity only when there is a competing mark that uses the Polish equivalent of the words at issue.[31] In 2001, Esprit International, which held a trademark in Poland for use of the French-language mark "Esprit" in connection with clothing and footwear, filed a request to cancel the English-language mark "Spirit" which had been registered by a competitor. Esprit International argued that "Spirit" infringed upon the mark "Esprit," as both words meant the same thing when translated into Polish; in fact they would both be translated by the same word in Polish (*duch*). The Patent Office rejected Esprit's argument, however, ruling in 2003 that the French and English marks were to be compared to each other, and not to their Polish equivalent. The Office stated that in Polish, the words "Esprit" and "Spirit" were both fanciful indications and would be perceived as phonetically distinct by Polish speakers. The Office did indicate, however, that it would be appropriate to consider a foreign mark's meaning in Polish when its validity was to be considered vis-à-vis a mark that was itself in Polish.[32]

4. Conclusion

Courts on both the national and European levels will increasingly confront multilingual trademark issues as the world in general, and Europe in particular, continues to experience a rapid trans-nationalization of commerce. The full impact of the recent enlargement of the EU, which brought with it many of the languages of Eastern Europe, has yet to be felt. Most, in fact all, of the languages of the new Member States are not well known by the populations of the traditional and economically dominant Member States of the west, and it will be intriguing to watch how courts grapple with the issue of Community trademarks in a territory where such a diverse range of languages, now including several non-Indo-European ones, is spoken. The recent accession of Romania and Bulgaria has complicated the EU's linguistic makeup further, and the addition of Bulgarian, with its Cyrillic script, is bound to engender all sorts of trademark and other legal issues as the EU struggles with a largely unfamiliar alphabet.[33] Even further down the line, the EU may expand to encompass Turkey and new states in the Balkans.

---

[31] *Esprit International v. L.I. Ltd.*, Decision of the Polish Patent Office of 3 June 2003.

[32] For a discussion of the analysis of foreign-language marks in Poland during the Communist era, see Szwaja 1984.

[33] Several legal issues arose when the Greek alphabet was introduced to the European Community upon the admission of Greece in 1981. See, e.g., Case C-168, *Konstantinidis*, 1993 ECR I-1191 (addressing legal problems connected with the transliteration of a Greek national's name into Roman letters by German authorities).

The relevance of multilingualism to trademark law, and indeed to all areas of law, is certain to grow considerably in the years to come.

References

Creech, R. (2005). *Law and Language in the European Union: The Paradox of a Babel "United in Diversity"*. Groningen: Europa Law Publishing.

Szwaja, J. (1984). "Pologne". In: M.-A. Perot-Morel (ed.), *Le Droit des Marques dans les Pays Socialistes d'Europe de l'Est*. Grenoble: Centre universitaire d'enseignement et de recherche en propriété industrielle.

Syûgo Hotta
Ritsumeikan University
Japan

MORPHOSYNTACTIC STRUCTURE OF JAPANESE TRADEMARKS AND THEIR DISTINCTIVENESS: A NEW MODEL FOR LINGUISTIC ANALYSIS OF TRADEMARKS[1]

1. Introduction

In this paper, a new analytical model for the morphosyntactic structure of trademarks will be proposed. It exploits a well-known linguistic concept called *markedness*, redefined in terms of Grice's (1975) Cooperative Principle and the cognitive load theory (Sweller 1988). In conjunction with this new model, this paper will discuss a Japanese trademark infringement case in which the morphosyntactic structure of two trademarks was at issue. The court seems to have come up with an erroneous linguistic analysis of what counted as a "distinctive part" of compounds in the trademarks. Identifying a distinctive part of trademarks is of great significance, since it is that part that often determines the result of a case. For example, since trademark law protects a mark that is distinctive from others, if one of the morphemes of the linguistic expression of a mark is by itself a distinctive part of the trademark (e.g. *Lion* for oral care products), the use of the morpheme in another trademark will not be allowed (e.g. *Superlion*). On the other hand, if the word or compound of a trademark is a distinctive part as a whole (e.g. *Kozoo-zushi*, "boy-sushi", for take-out sushi), the use of a part of the word, i.e. a morpheme (e.g. *Kozoo* for rice balls), may not be judged an infringement, because it is the whole expression, not a part of it, that is distinctive and thereby granted legal protection. Japanese courts have used a misleading, less scientifically grounded method to decide the distinctive part of a trademark without recourse to expert analysis. I will challenge one of such analyses by the courts with empirical evidence based on a survey. The analytical model to be proposed in this paper is designed to help non-linguistic experts

[1] The research reported in this paper is financially partly supported by the Grant-in-Aid for Young Scientists (B), The Ministry of Education, Culture, Sports, Science and Technology, Japan. I would like to express my gratitude to Professor Masaharu Miyawaki at Ritsumeikan University for his helpful advice on my legal discussion on the Japanese Trademark Act. I am also grateful to Professor Alber Ting at Ritsumeikan University and Mohsen Ahmed, a lawyer and colleague at Osgoode Hall Law School, York University, Canada, for their valuable comments on an earlier version of this paper. All remaining errors are my own, nonetheless.

identify the distinctive part of a trademark more systematically and "elegantly" than the current conventions and standards provide. It will also be shown that the new model is in fact applicable not only to marks involving compounds but also to those with a wide variety of linguistic structure, and beyond Japanese language. For example, I will look at the *McSleep Inn* case in the US in which the use of the bound morpheme *Mc-* was disputed, and demonstrate that the model can be applied to it.

This study has both practical and theoretical implications: it contributes to the legal practice in trademarks by offering a model that will provide a more consistent, empirically-grounded, and easily-applicable standard for the analysis of linguistic structure of trademarks, which accordingly facilitates the just administration of law[2]; the morphosyntactic analysis proposed in this paper incorporates the three independently developed theories mentioned above, namely markedness conventions, Grice's Cooperative Principle and the cognitive load theory. The integration of these three theories is novel in linguistic theory and therefore adds to the scholarly discourse of linguistics as well.

2. Markedness and Cognitive Load

Markedness, a classical notion in linguistics, constitutes the central pillar of the analysis of trademark language to be developed here. It originally meant that a thing is *marked* if it contains a certain distinctive feature, while it is *unmarked* if it lacks that feature. We will follow McCawley's (1985) definition of markedness: something is marked if it is not normal, or is deviant, idiosyncratic, or specific in a given group or, more generally, a *context*, whereas something is unmarked if it is general, standard, or neutral in the context. Markedness is a relative notion. For example, if a short hairstyle is the standard hairstyle of a given group, a long-haired member of that group is marked. Conversely, if only one member is short-haired while all other members are long-haired, the short-haired member is marked. Another example from language illustrates the point further. When you want to know the height of your friend, you will ask "How *tall* are you?" as opposed to "How *short* are you?" in a normal situation. The use of *tall* is normal,

[2] There are two types of distinctiveness: *inherent* distinctiveness and *acquired* distinctiveness. The former is used to refer to a mark's inherent capacity to be distinguished from other marks, while the latter is used to refer to the distinctiveness that a mark has acquired through exposure to the market. So, secondary meaning, the source indicating function, and the quality-guarantee function of trademarks are all realized by acquired distinctiveness. Some marks, e.g., those with secondary meaning, lack inherent distinctiveness. Registrability of marks typically depends heavily on inherent distinctiveness: only the marks that are distinguishable from others can be registered. The linguistic analysis to be proposed in this paper will, in principle, offer an insight into inherent distinctiveness of marks.

and therefore it is unmarked. The use of *short*, on the other hand, is not neutral or normal, and therefore it is a marked question. The latter in fact presupposes that the speaker believes the hearer is short, and, from a cognitive point of view, it imposes more "load" on our cognition, because understanding the presupposition is an additional process in comprehension, which is not required in understanding the unmarked equivalent of the expression that lacks such a presupposition[3] (cf. Sweller 1988)[4].

Such a cognitive viewpoint is important, since confusion of trademarks is essentially a matter of cognition. For example, it is often important to identify the "distinctive part," or *yoobu*, of a trademark in Japanese trademark courts. The distinctive or salient part of a trademark is defined as a part of a trademark that draws consumers' attention most (Kakuta and Tatsumi 2000) and is likely to qualify for legal protection. Attending to something is an extra cognitive process. Therefore, a part that "draws attention" is, in other words, the part that imposes some additional load on cognition. Then, recognizing a marked element and "drawing attention" share a very important feature: they both involve cognitive load. Put differently, the distinctive part of a trademark is a marked part of a mark, since it incurs cognitive load. Under the present trademark law practice in Japan, the definition of "the part that draws consumers' attention" is not based on any scientific ground and even lacks definitive standards. However, if the distinctive part of a trademark is redefined in terms of markedness, we can identify it in a more systematic, predictable way with scientific grounding.

The proposed analysis also captures one of the mechanisms of trademark confusion. The more marked the language of a mark is, the greater the load on cognition that results, and therefore the harder to remember the exact mark (Sweller 1988). If the language of the mark is hard to remember, consumers often have difficulty recalling the exact name of the product. Some manufacturers take advantage of this and confuse consumers into buying their product bearing a name similar to another company's product. Thus, highly marked marks involve such a cost, or risk, for (original) manufacturers, while ensuring distinctiveness.

---

[3] Such cognitive load manifests itself upon human memory and perception. For example, a psychological study by Harris (1973) shows that, when subjects were told to guess the height of a basketball player, those who were asked the question with a marked adjective, i.e., *how short*, tended to estimate the height far lower than those who were asked the question with an unmarked adjective, i.e., *how tall*. Thus, the result of this experiment shows that the marked linguistic expression has some influence on our cognition. Hotta & Fujita (in preparation) is conducting experimental research on the relationship between markedness of morphemes and cognitive load.

[4] Sweller's proposal is for learning processes, but the idea of cognitive load is applicable to many other fields including the cognitive aspects of trademarks.

3. Grice's Cooperative Principle

The analysis of linguistic properties of trademarks in terms of markedness can be elaborated by incorporating the Cooperative Principle proposed by Grice (1975). This concept reveals the mechanism of how we understand *implicature*, i.e. what is implied in conversation. The Cooperative Principle, in short, refers to a general principle that participants in a conversation are expected to observe in the mutual cooperative efforts to understand each other. Along with the Cooperative Principle, the following four maxims of conversation that a speaker is expected to fulfill are postulated (Grice 1975: 45-47):

Maxim of Quantity:
1. Make your contribution to the conversation as informative as necessary.
2. Do not make your contribution to the conversation more informative than necessary.

Maxim of Quality:
1. Do not say what you believe to be false.
2. Do not say that for which you lack adequate evidence.

Maxim of Relevance:
Be relevant (i.e., say things related to the current topic of the conversation).

Maxim of Manner:
1. Avoid obscurity of expression.
2. Avoid ambiguity.
3. Be brief (avoid unnecessary wordiness).
4. Be orderly.

Failure to observe these maxims leads to hardship in communication. For example, suppose you were trying to find a person at a party, whom you know only by his/her first and last name. There are a few people there who have an identical first name and they only tell you their first name and refuse to say their last name or say only the first initial of their last name. These pieces of linguistic information do not help differentiate them from each other. Then, the communication would fail for lack of the necessary information. This is a violation of the Maxim of Quantity, since those people do not provide a sufficient amount of information to identify the person that you are looking for. Similarly, if you purchase something for 8 dollars with a ten-dollar bill and a clerk gives you back two dollars by saying "A million dollars is your change," you will simply have trouble understanding what information s/he is trying to convey with that utterance. This violates the Maxim of Quality. Similarly, you ask a person about her/his age, but s/he changes the topic and starts talking about the weather without answering your question. Her/his utterance is of no relevance to your question. Therefore, it fails to meet the Maxim of Relevance. Finally, if you ask your partner what s/he has bought for your beloved daughter for her birthday, but s/he answers in French, the Maxim of Manner gets violated. Violating Grice's maxims gives rise to confusion in linguistic communication. They are fundamental rules to follow in establishing effective communication.

These maxims are fundamental, but they do not always have to be observed. It is quite often the case that they are violated. Intentional violation is particularly important for our discussion on language in trademarks here: it suggests the existence of an implicature, i.e. an implied message, in communication. When we find a violation of these maxims in conversation, we try to identify the reason. In other words, we try to find out what extralinguistic message is implied by the violation. For example, if you ask someone about his/her age but s/he intentionally changes the topic to something else such as weather without answering the question (which violates the Maxim of Relevance), you will try to guess why s/he does so. (The most likely implied message being that s/he would not want to be asked about his/her age.)

This mechanism of understanding implicature pertains deeply to messages contained in language in trademarks. For example, when we see the mark *Bisquick* for baking mixes, we try to decompose the word into *Bis-* and *-quick*, since we immediately notice from its contextual information such as a picture on the package, the place where it is displayed etc. that the whole word does not refer to a class of products, i.e. baking mixes, which is a violation of the Maxim of Relevance. Then, we recognize that the morpheme *Bis-* is incomplete, since it is not in our lexicon and no such morpheme would go well semantically with the adjective or adverb *quick* in English. Since the use of the short form of *biscuit* is a violation of the Maxim of Quantity, we start figuring out the implied message(s). Then, from its phonetic or sound similarity with (the pronunciation of) the word *biscuit* and contextual information such as association of the name with baking mixes, we can reconstruct the missing part of the word and understand that it has something to do with the word *biscuit*.[5] Finally, when this morpheme is combined with *quick*, we can guess that we can make biscuits or the like quickly with this product.

The mechanism of understanding implicature pertains to markedness. A linguistic expression that violates the Cooperative Principle is not a normal,

---

[5] I am thankful to participants of the *Language and Law 2005: East Meets West* conference at the University of Łódź, Poland, for various comments and suggestions regarding this paper. I am especially grateful to Loren Billings for comments on the analysis of *Bisquick*. As Loren pointed out to me, *Bisquick* is a fusion of the words *biscuit* and *quick* from a phonetic and phonological point of view. However, as far as the graphical information or spelling of the word is concerned, *quick* is complete, whereas *Bis-* is incomplete. The former is more easily recognizable than the latter, because there is no violation of the Maxims in the former and no extra cognitive calculation is required to understand the language. Therefore, while it is true that the resulting mark sounds like a fusion of two words, it is better to analyze the mark as it is analyzed here.

standard utterance. Hence, it is marked. As argued in the preceding section, markedness is associated with cognitive load. It imposes some additional load on our cognitive process of understanding the messages conveyed in the linguistic expression of trademarks. In simpler terms, if there is a violation of maxims in the linguistic expression of a trademark, it is marked. In the discussion below, it will be shown with a few examples how the Conversational Maxims discussed here help determine the markedness of the linguistic expression of a given mark.

4. A linguistic model of distinctiveness of trademarks

Distinctiveness of trademarks is so complex an issue that it must be examined multi-dimensionally; the same is true of the markedness of trademarks. Although there surely are many dimensions that should be considered to capture the properties of trademarks with regard to their distinctiveness, two primary dimensions of trademarks, namely, the structural dimension and the associative dimension, will be explored to assess the markedness and distinctiveness of marks in this section.

4.1. Structural markedness

It will be of help to take an example to sketch out how the notions discussed in the preceding sections work in analyzing trademarks. In the US case of *McDonald's v. McSleep Inns*[6], the use of the prefix *Mc-* was disputed. Quality Inns International Inc., a large hotel chain company that intended to market a new economy line of hotels under the name, filed an action seeking a declaratory judgment that their use of the prefix *Mc-* does not infringe on McDonald's registered marks, after they received a letter from McDonald's Corporation demanding that they not use the proposed mark. The court held that Quality Inn's use of the *Mc-* prefix is infringing on McDonald's trademarks, since the proffered evidence convinced the court to conclude that the mark *McSleep Inns* is confusing enough for the public to believe that "*McSleep Inns* is sponsored, associated, affiliated, connected, or endorsed by McDonald's."[7] Let us see how this tricky case can be captured by our approach. The following represents the structural dimension of the trademarks. In the structural dimension, all factors that have

---

[6] *Quality Inns International, Inc. v. McDonald's Corp.*, 695 F. Supp. 198 (D.Md. 1988).
[7] Ibid. at 221

something to do with the structure of words, e.g. syntax, morphology, phonology, semantico-syntax[8], spelling, pronunciation etc.

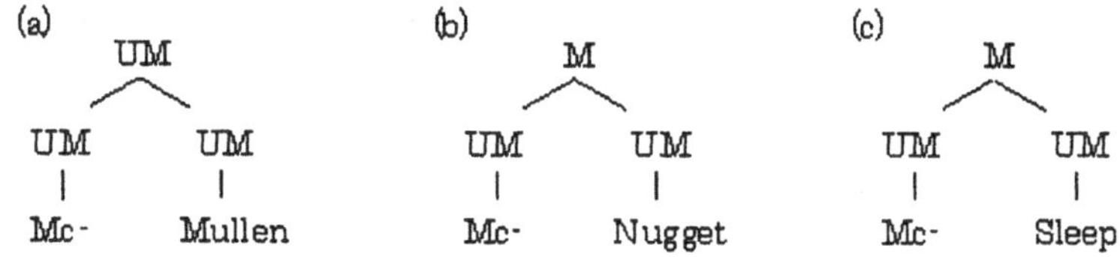

(UM = unmarked; M = marked)

Figure 1. Structural dimension of linguistic expressions

The prefix *Mc-* is a patronym which is often found at the beginning of some names of Irish and Scottish origin (Shuy 2002). It is a common morpheme, denoting "a son of". For example, *McMullen* originally meant "son of Mullen." So, the use of the prefix *Mc-* is unmarked, and so is the personal name *Mullen*. The combination of the prefix and a person's name is a regular, ordinary use, and therefore the whole expression is unmarked. (Figure 1a)

On the other hand, McDonald's Corporation has developed and invested in the use of the prefix in combination with non-personal names, e.g. *McFries*, *McNuggets*, *McShake* etc. The prefix *per se* is again unmarked, and the words *fries*, *nuggets* or *shake* are common English words and therefore unmarked. However, the combination of the prefix and non-personal names is marked, since it is an irregular use and violates the Maxim of Relevance (Figure 1b). As argued above, a marked part of a trademark is a distinctive part of the mark, which is likely to qualify for legal protection. Although the mark in question is thus marked and distinctive by nature, it involves additional efforts to strengthen its eligibility for legal protection. McDonald's has advertised and invested in the use and acquired a reputation. The use of *Mc-* on non-personal names has gained public recognition such that a substantial number of people associate and connect it to McDonald's business and goodwill, as the court remarked.[9] Also, *Mc-* is associated with cheap, convenient and fast service. Such an association is not what the prefix inherently conveyed, but was created and cultivated by McDonald's through its business ideas and efforts. In the case of *McSleep Inns*,

[8] The term *semantico-syntax* here should be understood to refer to the pseudo-structural relations of semantic units. For example, in the analysis of the words in Figure (1a-c), semantic relations of the morphemes are examined. Thus, the representation of the structure of words here should not be confused with the representations of morphological, syntactic, or other grammatical components in existing linguistic frameworks.

[9] *Quality Inns International, Inc. v. McDonald's Corp.*, *supra* note 18 at 221. The court based this opinion on the survey evidence presented by McDonald's.

then, the prefix *Mc- per se* is unmarked, and *sleep* is a regular English word and therefore unmarked. However, the combination of that patrimonial prefix and a non-personal noun is a violation of the Maxim of Relevance and is marked, as argued above (Figure 1c). Such a marked use is difficult for independent persons to come up with. It is McDonald's, as argued above, that created and developed that particular linguistic pattern, i.e. the marked combination, and the cognitive paths in association with their goodwill. Trademark law should serve to protect it. This analysis and claim concurs with the court's holding that *McSleep Inns* was infringing on McDonald's trademarks. McDonald's trademarks were thus infringed by *McSleep Inns*.[10]

4.2. Associative markedness

Markedness extends to another dimension of trademarks - namely, the *associative dimension*. Trademarks do not stand by themselves. They must be associated with goods and services. The associative dimension can be captured by the following representation:

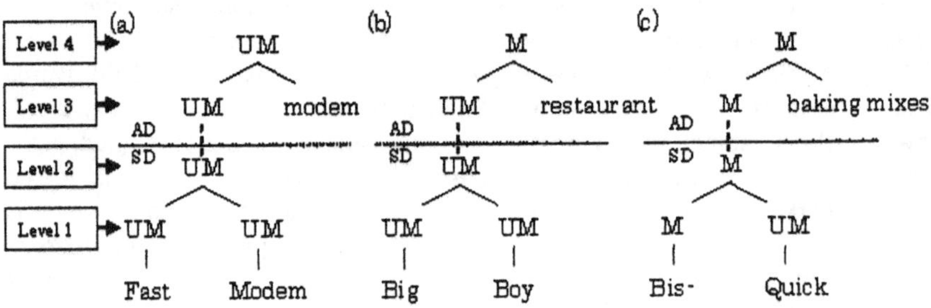

(AD = Associative Dimension; SD = Structural Dimension)

Figure 2. Representations of Associative and Structural Dimensions

Below the horizontal line between Levels 2 and 3 in Figure 2 are representations of the three marks, *Fast Modem*, *Big Boy*, and *Bisquick* in the structural dimension, whereas above the line are those in the associative dimension. In Figure 2a, both morphemes at Level 1, *Fast* and *Modem*, are existing English words and therefore

[10] It is interesting that, in a Canadian case of *McDonald's Corp. v. Coffee Hut Stores Ltd.*([1994] 3 C.F. F 44), the court held that the Coffee Hut Store Ltd.'s use of a mark *McBeans* in association with coffee and tea is not likely to cause confusion with McDonald's (use of *Mc-*) and hence the mark is registrable.

unmarked. The combination of those morphemes, which is at Level 2, is quite normal in every respect, e.g. semantically, morphologically, syntactically etc. Therefore, it is also unmarked. The markedness of the whole expression determined in the structural dimension is taken over as it is to the associative dimension as seen at Level 3. Then, the association between the term and the ware or service is assessed at Level 4. Since the association is straightforward and has nothing deviant in it, it is unmarked.

In Figure 2b, the morphemes *Big* and *Boy* are both existing English words (Level 1), and the combination of these morphemes is also quite normal. So, there is nothing deviant structurally and therefore it is unmarked at Level 2 (and also at Level 3). However, the association of the term and the ware/service which is represented at Level 4 is marked, since the term *Big Boy* has nothing to do with a restaurant business, which violates the Maxim of Relevancy.

In Figure 2c, one of the morphemes, namely, *Bis-*, is already marked at Level 1. The morpheme does not exist in English. As discussed above, it is part of the word *biscuit*. This shortening of the word violates the Maxim of Quantity. Therefore, the marked markedness is taken over to upper levels. Since the word is already marked, its association with goods is also marked at Level 4.

The same line of argument works for marks that go beyond word or phrase level. An illustrative example is the mark "*I Can't Believe It's Not Butter*" for margarine. *I Can't Believe It's Not Butter* may be regarded as unmarked in its structural dimension, because there is nothing marked in its structure, e.g. grammar, combination of morphemes, spelling etc. However, it is clear that the manner of describing the product is not straightforward. This non-straightforwardness lies in its markedness in the associative dimension. The association of the mark with the product is marked since the combination of the words does not mention the generic or purely descriptive term for the product directly. That is, it violates the Maxim of Quality. It requires a cognitive leap to associate the name with the product. Hence, it is marked. Since the length of a sentence is a matter of structure, the long sequence of words can be marked in terms of structure as well as its association.

The proposed analysis of markedness serves as a helpful guide to the elucidation of tacit properties of trademarks. The following table illustrates categories of trademarks:

Table 1. The Distinctive Spectrum (Categories and 1-3 are cited from Shuy 2002)

Categories	generic	descriptive	suggestive	arbitrary	fanciful
1) definition	class of goods	only describes characteristics or ingredient of goods	suggests a characteristics or ingredient of goods	an arbitrary word as applied to goods	a made-up word
2) example	CAR	TASTY BREAD	STRONGHOLD	APPLE	KODAK
3) goods	car	Bread	nails	computers	photograph ic supplies
4) structural markedness	Unmarked	Unmarked	Unmarked	Unmarked	Marked
5) associative markedness	Unmarked	Unmarked	Marked	Marked	Marked

Trademarks can be roughly divided into five categories according to their meaning and association with goods or services – from *generic* to *fanciful*. A basic definition of each type is provided in the table. Generic marks and descriptive marks are less distinctive than the rest of the categories, i.e. suggestive, arbitrary, and fanciful marks, and unlikely to qualify as trademarks. Conversely, the other three categories are more distinctive and more likely to be given trademark protection than the remaining two categories. Among the three categories, arbitrary marks are more likely to be registrable as trademarks than suggestive marks, and fanciful marks are even more so than the other two. Suggestive marks require a "leap of imagination" (Shuy 2002: 65) to associate the wares or services with them. In other words, they impose some cognitive load. Hence, they are marked. Arbitrary marks and fanciful marks require even more cognitive load, since the mark typically has little connection with the wares or services and requires an effort (e.g. to memorize the association) for consumers to link them. Hence, they are also marked. Markedness is not a bipolar scale, but a gradient one, assessed in terms of degree. Associative markedness will be higher in degree, i.e. more marked, with suggestive marks than with arbitrary marks, since the latter would require more cognitive load than the former. Put simply, the more marked a mark is in either or both dimensions, the more distinctive it will be and accordingly the more likely it will obtain legal protection. This is partly because, as markedness increases, it would require a greater cognitive leap, and therefore it is less likely for independent language users to come up with the same mark for the same kind of association independently and coincidentally.

The table above shows that, when either the structure or association of a trademark, or both, are marked, the mark is more likely to be distinctive as a trademark. The examples used in Figure 2 illustrate this point. *Fast Modem* for a modem in Figure 2a is unmarked in both the structural and associative dimension. Therefore, it is not distinctive, nor is it registrable as trademark. *Big Boy* for a restaurant is marked in the associative dimension, although no structural markedness is observed. Thus, it is distinctive and registrable. *Bisquick* for baking mixes is marked in both dimensions. It is distinctive and registrable as a trademark, too.

Introducing markedness into the traditional spectrum thus has at least two implications: first, although standards or thresholds for distinctiveness and registrability are rather obscure and complex under the traditional scheme, the proposed analysis offers a systematic, simplified analytical scheme of the properties of trademarks, which would help practitioners, judges, juries etc. to understand and determine the properties of the trademarks they examine. Second, the proposed scheme is well-grounded from the perspective of linguistic and cognitive science, which in turn provides scientific justification for the traditional classification or spectrum of trademarks.

5. A Japanese case

This section examines a Japanese case in which the court came up with a dubious analysis of disputed trademarks. In this case, the confusing similarity was between a mark for software that connects a cell phone to a computer to transfer data, which is called *Keitai-setsuraku 7,* which literally means "cell-phone contact-easy 7" and another company's mark for software for constant connection with the internet, called *Jooji-setsuraku,* which literally means "constant contact-easy." They are both non-existent in the vocabulary of Japanese language, i.e. coined words. The court held that the distinctive part of the mark was *the expression as a whole* in both cases and therefore they were not confusingly similar in terms of their sound, appearance, and meaning, which I dispute.

I conducted a simple survey on this case, testing 21 subjects (including 9 undergraduates and 9 graduate school students). The question that was asked after exposing them to the two marks can be translated into English as "Do you think these are products of the same company or different companies only on the basis of their linguistic aspects?”[11] The results showed that 16 of the subjects thought the products were of the same company, whereas 5 of them thought they came from different companies. The Chi Square test was applied to this result: ($\chi^2(1)=5.76$, $p<.05$). In general, if probability (p) is smaller than 0.05, values are considered to be significantly different. The actual value of our result is $p = 0.016$. Therefore, there indeed is a significant difference. This result suggests that it is very likely that people find these marks as belonging to the same company, i.e. they are confusingly similar. The court's decision, which I strongly disagree with on the basis of the survey results, was based on its wrong analysis of the “distinctive part” of the marks. As mentioned above, the court found that the whole expression was the distinctive part, and then the structure and meaning were different between the disputed marks and therefore these marks were not confusingly similar. However, there is a good reason to believe that it is not the case.

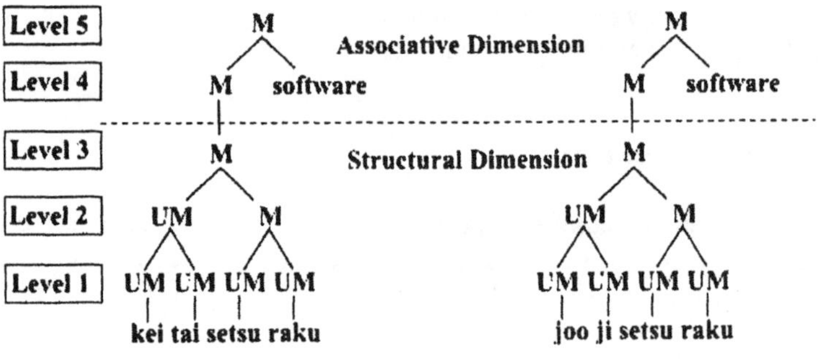

Figure 3. a) b)

Figure 3a is the representation for *keitai-setsuraku*. All the four morphemes in the first example, namely, *kei*, *tai*, *setu*, and *raku*, are found in the regular vocabulary of Japanese, and therefore unmarked. The same is true of the morphemes of *jooji-setsuraku* on Level 1 in Figure 3b. At Level 2, the first two morphemes *kei*

[11] This survey takes a format similar to the one called the *Squirt* format used in *Squirt Company v. Seven-Up Company* (207 USPQ 12, 20-21 [ED Mo 1979], affd 628 F2d 1086, 207 USPQ 897 [CA 8 1980]). In this format, the subjects are typically asked 1) whether they thought the junior and senior brands were put out by the same or different companies and 2) what made them think so. The *Squirt* format may be, as often criticized, not an ideal measure to assess the likelihood of confusion. However, since the purpose of this survey is not to tender it to the court as evidence but to simply show that there are a substantial number of people who believed these would be the products of the same manufacturer, it would be sufficient. A good critical review of popular survey formats including the *Squirt* format can be found in Simonson (1993).

and *tai* constitute a compound that refers to a cell phone, which is also in the regular vocabulary of Japanese. Hence, it is unmarked. On the other hand, the second pair of the morphemes, *setsu* and *raku*, also constitutes a compound, but the resulting compound is not found in the Japanese vocabulary. So, the combination of these two morphemes is very odd to native speakers of Japanese. It violates the Cooperative Principle in two ways: the morpheme *setu* is a bound morpheme and must be combined with another morpheme but *raku* is not one that it is usually combined with. So, it is a violation of the Maxim of Relevance. Also, when we look at the combination of those two morphemes, we try to figure out its implied meaning. Then we recognize from the context that it will be a short form of *setuzoku*, which means "connect." In this sense, the morpheme violates the Maxim of Quantity as well, since it is not a full form of the word. Thus, the combination of the two morphemes in Figure 3a is marked in either way. At Level 3, the two compounds are combined, and the resulting combination is, again, marked, since it involves a marked part. Then, the marked property of the whole expression is carried over to Level 4, which is in the associative dimension. Then, it goes further up to Level 5, and the association of the mark with the product is, again, marked, since the word *keitaisetsuraku* is not a regular term for such software. It should be noted here that the second half of the word, *setsu-raku*, is marked and is the distinctive part of the mark by itself, contrary to the court's analysis. It is not the whole expression but this part that draws the consumers' attention, i.e. *yoobu*, and should be protected from being copied or used by others, according to Japanese trademark law.

Now consider the other mark, *joojisetsuraku*. At Level 1 in Figure 3b, the first two morphemes *joo* and *ji* are of the regular vocabulary of Japanese and therefore unmarked. And so are *setsu* and *raku*. At Level 2, the first two morphemes *joo* and *ji* are combined. The word is in the regular vocabulary of Japanese, and means "constant" or "always." Nothing is deviant. Therefore, it is unmarked. However, as we have seen with *keitaisetsuraku* in Figure 3a, the combination of the two morphemes *setsu* and *raku* is marked. Hence this is the distinctive part of the mark. The rest works in the same way as *keitai-setsuraku*.

As can be seen, *setsuraku* is the part that is marked and draws consumers' attention most in both cases. The two marks share that part. This is why a substantial number of people find that these two marks are confusingly similar. Thus, the proposed analysis captures the real property of trademarks with regard to their distinctiveness, which the Japanese court failed to identify.

6. Conclusion

In this paper, a new approach to assess distinctiveness (and registrability in some cases) of trademarks has been proposed based on markedness, the

Cooperative Principle, and the cognitive load theory. There will be cases that cannot be well captured by it. The analysis proposed is targeted at the structural and associative dimensions of trademarks. Although only two dimensions of trademarks have been examined in this paper, more research needs to be conducted to determine the markedness of marks. The distinctiveness of trademarks is often determined by non-linguistic factors as well, e.g. the guise of the product. Those factors will be left open here because they are beyond the scope of this paper. Nonetheless, as has been demonstrated above with a few case studies, the proposed approach to trademarks should be a good first approximation toward a systematic analysis of the distinctiveness of trademarks.

References

Grice, H. P. (1975). "Logic and Conversation". In: P. Cole and J. L. Morgan (eds.), *Syntax and Semantics*, Vol. 3, *Speech Acts*, New York: Academic Press, 41-58.

Harris, R. J. (1973). "Answering questions containing marked and unmarked adjectives and adverbs". *Journal of Experimental Psychology* 97, 399-401.

Hotta, S. and M. Fujita (2006). "A Cognitive Linguistic Model of Trademarks: An Experimental Research". Paper presented at the annual meeting of the Law and Society Association, 6th July 2006

Kakuta, M. and N. Tatsumi (2000). *Chiteki Zaisanho* [Intellectual Property Law]. Tokyo: Yuhikaku Aruma.

McCawley, J. D. (1985). "Kuhnian paradigms as systems of markedness conventions." In: A. Makkai and A. Melby (eds.), *Linguistics and Philosophy: Studies in Honor of Rulon S. Wells.* Amsterdam: Benjamins, 23-43.

Shuy, R. (2002). *Linguistic Battles in Trademark Disputes*. New York: Palgrave.

Simonson, I. (1993). "The Effect of Survey Method on Likelihood of Confusion Estimates: Conceptual Analysis and Empirical Test". *Trademark Reporter* 83, 364-392.

Sweller, J. (1988). "Cognitive load during problem solving: Effects on learning". *Cognitive Science* 12, 257-285.

Part VIII

FORENSIC LINGUISTICS

Susan Blackwell*, **Willem Meijs**** and **Jess Shapero***
*University of Birmingham
**Language Consultancy Desk, Birmingham
England

TEXTS OF MURDER AND MARTYRDOM

1. Introduction

The Dutch political climate in the past few years has been characterised by provocative statements concerning Islam by a number of public figures, and the subsequent assassinations of two individuals associated with such statements. These events have undoubtedly contributed to a deterioration in community relations within the Netherlands and a rise in tensions between its various ethnic and religious groups; they have nonetheless placed a number of documents in the public domain which are of interest to forensic linguists because of their unusual nature and the challenges they pose to any attempt at linguistic analysis.

2. The characters

2.1. Victim No. 1: Pim Fortuyn

The texts discussed here need to be understood in their political context. In order to do so, it is necessary to begin with Pim Fortuyn, a sociology lecturer at the University of Rotterdam who decided to trade in his academic career for a political one, with startling success. He first came to the attention of the Dutch media as the leader of a local party called Leefbaar Rotterdam ("liveable Rotterdam"). There had been a series of local "Leefbaar" initiatives, starting with Jan Nagel's Leefbaar Hilversum in 1994 and followed by Leefbaar Utrecht in 1999. Building on a number of successes in local elections, the "Leefbaar" parties decided to pool their resources and go national, establishing Leefbaar Nederland in 1999.

On 25 November 2001, Fortuyn was selected at the congress of Leefbaar Nederland to head its electoral list in the forthcoming General Election. He had always been a flamboyant character: openly gay, and vociferous in his condemnation of Islam, which he characterised as homophobic and reactionary, "a backward culture". Initially, these traits were regarded as an asset by his party as it watched its ratings soar in the opinion polls. However, on 9 February 2002

Fortuyn gave an interview in De Volkskrant which went a step too far. Describing the Netherlands as "full", he asserted that he wanted "geen islamiet meer" (not one single Muslim more) to enter the country and added that he hoped to see the abolition of Article 1 of the Constitution, which prohibits discrimination. The leadership of Leefbaar Nederland unceremoniously dumped Fortuyn the next day, and he responded by setting up his own party.

On Monday, 6 May 2002, Fortuyn was shot dead as he left the Hilversum media park after giving a radio interview. The unspoken assumption was that he had been killed by a Muslim organisation in response to his pronouncements about Islam. It came as something of a relief to the nation when the assassin turned out to be Volkert van der Graaf, a white animal rights activist. The General Election went ahead on 15 May 2002 and Fortuyn's party gained 26 seats, becoming the second largest party overnight. Its success proved to be short-lived: in the wake of its leader's death it fell apart due to internal faction-fights, causing the collapse of the governing coalition and leading to fresh elections on 22 January 2003.

2.2. Victim No. 2: Theo van Gogh

The fears which had proved unfounded at the time of Fortuyn's death came to be realised two and a half years later. Theo van Gogh, a great-great grandnephew of the artist Vincent van Gogh, was a well-known journalist and film-maker, notorious and popular at the same time for his unrepentant chain-smoking and outrageous pronouncements. Like Fortuyn – about whom he made a film – he described Islam as "a backward culture"; and if possible he went even further to insult its adherents, describing the hijab (headscarf) as "invented by backward goat-fuckers from the Middle Ages who restrict our freedoms". Van Gogh described the Belgian Muslim leader Abu Jahjah as "the prophet's pimp" and termed Muslims in general "the religious fascists of Islam". In his defence it should be said that he did not reserve his venom solely for Muslims, but delighted in giving gratuitous offence to practitioners of all religions and none.

In 2004 van Gogh enabled Ayaan Hirsi Ali, a member of the Dutch parliament, to make a short film entitled "Submission", a fictional portrayal of violence against Muslim women. "Submission" featured semi-naked females, some in see-through veils, with texts from the Qur'an concerning the position of women written on their lacerated and bruised bodies. Not surprisingly, this piece of creative art endeared neither van Gogh nor Hirsi Ali to certain sections of the Dutch community.

As van Gogh cycled from his Amsterdam house on 2nd November 2004, he was shot eight times; then, while on the ground pleading for his life, he was repeatedly stabbed and his throat was cut. According to witnesses, the killer calmly took a piece of paper out of his rucksack and fixed it to his victim's chest with a second knife. Hirsi Ali, never lost for words even at a time like this, termed it an act of "ritual slaughter".

2.3. The home-grown killer: Mohammed Bouyeri

This time the assassin did indeed turn out to be a Muslim, but probably not one who conformed to the expected stereotype. In many ways, "Mohammed B."[1] was the Dutch public's worst nightmare: the home-grown terrorist. Born to Moroccan parents in the Netherlands on 8th March 1978, thus 26 years old, he held dual, Moroccan and Dutch, nationality. He had Dutch as his first language and had completed his secondary education with a respectable "HAVO" school leaving certificate. He became involved in various kinds of community work, but became frustrated with officials who refused support and funding to his projects. According to some who knew him, he turned to increasingly extreme forms of Islam after the death of his mother. He wrote poems and religious essays on various Islamic websites and associated with a network of religious extremists whom police later dubbed the Hofstad Group.

This is the man, then, who brutally murdered van Gogh and pinned a letter to his body with a knife. The letter, however, was not addressed to van Gogh but to Ayaan Hirsi Ali.

2.4. Intended victim No. 1: Ayaan Hirsi Ali

Hirsi Ali was born in Somalia and raised as a Muslim. Her family sent her to Europe for an arranged marriage, but she fled and came to the Netherlands as an asylum seeker. Initially undertaking menial jobs, she eventually became a member of the Dutch Parliament representing the PvdA (Labour Party). She received death threats after speaking out about the oppression of Muslim women within the family and describing herself as an "ex-Muslim". In October 2002 she left the PvdA and became a candidate for the right-wing VVD in the 2003 general election. After regaining her seat she became even more outspoken, making the film "Submission" with van Gogh.

[1] Under Dutch law, all suspects have to be given anonymity in the media, even after conviction. However, the names of all the suspects named in this paper – who have all now been convicted – are by now widely known around the world via the Internet and the international press.

2.5. Intended victim No. 2: Geert Wilders

At around the same time as the murder of van Gogh, an "open letter to Wilders" was placed on the website www.Marokko.nl. It has since been removed from that site but has been widely circulated. It threatens Dutch member of Parliament Geert Wilders. Bouyeri is alleged to be the author of this letter, too, due to its strong similarities with the Open Letter to Hirsi Ali left on van Gogh's body.

Wilders was originally a member of the VVD, but left it to set up his own party. Many of his pronouncements echo those of Fortuyn: he has called for a halt to "the import of Islam through migration and family reunion" and accuses Islam of "preaching fascism". He has called for mosques which "promote terror" to be closed. Like Hirsi Ali, he has received death threats.

3. The texts[2]

3.1. The "Open Letter to Hirsi Ali" (henceforth OLHA)

The letter which was left on van Gogh's body was headed "Open Brief aan Hirshi Ali" (Open Letter to Hirshi[3] [sic] Ali). It describes her as "an unbelieving fundamentalist ... of the Thaghoet [*idolatrous*] Party VVD". The letter continues for five pages, making detailed references to Dutch politicians and proposed legislation affecting Muslims. It contains quotations from the Talmud and accuses politicians of being under Jewish control. It also contains quotations from the Qur'an written in the Arabic script followed by their Dutch translations, and numerous religious Islamic expressions.

3.2. The "Open Letter to Wilders" (henceforth OLW)

The text which appeared on the "Marokko.nl" website describes itself as "an open letter to the filthy faggot: Wilders", implying that Wilders is homosexual[4]. Like the letter to Hirsi Ali, it appears to be a death threat, ending with a quotation from the Qur'an: "[Allah] says: 'Die in your rage, in truth, Allah knows the innermost secrets of people's hearts.' (3:119)"

---

[2] We gratefully acknowledge the assistance of Carole Bebawi of the University of Birmingham with the translation of the Arabic expressions in these texts.

[3] The politician's surname is spelt incorrectly: "Hirshi" instead of "Hirsi".

[4] It is unclear whether this is true: unlike Fortuyn, Wilders has never to our knowledge made a public issue of his sexual orientation.

3.3. The "martyrdom letter" (henceforth MA)

Bouyeri did not make a very serious attempt to escape after the murder of van Gogh and was quickly arrested after a shoot-out with the police. He was then discovered to have a letter on his person, which we have dubbed the "martyrdom letter" because from its contents it is clear that Bouyeri expected to die in the course of killing van Gogh and thus regarded himself as a martyr. The letter, like the others, is written in Dutch; unlike the others, however, it is in verse. It contains numerous Islamic religious expressions referring to paradise as well as condemning "the hypocrites".

3.4. Further texts

There is believed to be at least one further letter placed on a website which resembles the "open letters" to Hirsi Ali and Wilders. Further farewell/martyrdom letters thought to be written by Bouyeri were found in the flat of another member of the Hofstad Group, "Rachid B." (Racid Belkacem, alias Abu Fadel). One witness told the police that Bouyeri even recorded a "martyrdom video" of the type described in 4.7 below, but this has never been found. He is also alleged to be behind the pseudonym Abu Zubair, who translated a number of texts into Dutch including one entitled "De Ware Moslim" (The True Muslim). At Bouyeri's trial, expert evidence was given concerning over 40 documents allegedly written by him over a period of several years and illustrating his increasing radicalisation.[5]

The language of the three available texts will be discussed in more detail below. First, though, let us consider whether they can be situated in any existing category of written discourse. Can MA be regarded as a type of suicide note or is there an existing genre of martyrdom texts? Is anything comparable to OLHA known from previous murder cases?

4. Suicide notes and murder notes

4.1. Proportions of suicides leaving notes

The percentage of suicides who leave notes is considerably higher than folklore might suggest. When Salib et al. (2002: 189) reviewed previous studies they found that figures ranging from 15% to 42% were cited, as shown in Table 1 below. Toshiki et al. (2005) apparently found that 23.4% to 36.2% of suicides in

[5] At the time of writing, the authors do not have access to any of these additional documents.

Kobe between 1981 and 2001 left notes (apparently, this range was "static", despite an increased suicide rate and economic depression). Shapero (forthcoming) examined suicides in Birmingham, UK, who died between 1995 and 1999 and found figures of 41.30% for males and 31.17% for females.

Table 1. Percentages of suicides leaving notes in studies from 1957 to 1999[6]

Author(s)	**Year**	**Subjects**	**Place**	***% notes***
O'Conner et al.	1999	142	N. Ireland	38
Ho et al.	1998	169	Hong Kong	20
O'Donnell et al.	1993	242	London	15
Heim & Lester	1990	3,121	W. Berlin	30
Asgard	1990	104	Stockholm	42
Symonds	1985	82	S. England	20
Chynoweth	1911	135	Australia	20
Beck et al.	1914	194	Philadelphia	24
Edland et al.	1913	1,418	New York	23
Capstick	1960	881	Wales	15
Tuckman et al	1959	142	Philadelphia	24
Shneidman et al.	1951	121	Los Angeles	15

4.2. Characteristics of suicide notes

Suicide notes tend to be written to partners, family and friends, rather than to strangers. They are typically signed, but not dated. Much of their content can be described as instructions (often of a trivial domestic nature) or references to events. Suicide notes tend to address, or refer to, the writer's mother or occasionally someone else's: in the Birmingham corpus (Shapero, forthcoming), 40% of the subjects used "mother" lexis. Shapero also observed a tendency to say "sorry", and to a lesser extent, "thanks". Somewhat surprisingly, suicide notes have a more positive than negative outlook (Houston 2003).

4.3. Murder-suicides

When people kill others, and proceed within a matter of days to kill themselves (or contrive to get themselves killed), the scenario is classified in the

[6] Adapted from Salib et al. 2002: 187. "Year" indicates year of publication of the study in question. The O'Donnell and Symonds studies were described as "probable suicides on the London Underground" and "probable railway suicides", respectively. The Asgard suicides were, apparently, all female.

academic literature as a "murder-suicide". There is no consensus on the number of days qualifying as a limiting period for this term to apply: some studies use a time limit of 3 days, others a week.

According to van Wormer and Odiah (1999: 365), citing Marzuk et al. (1992), 42% of murders in Denmark, but only 5% in the USA, are murder-suicides. Barraclough and Harris (2002: 577) concluded that most of the murder-suicide cases involved "lower social class" males killing their family members, and women killing their children. It seems that single-event mass murderers are more likely to be suicidal than are serial killers (see below). However, it is not clear how many murder-suicides leave notes.

4.4. A murder-suicide text: Terres

In Wisconsin, USA, in 1993, Dion Terres shot and killed two people, injured a third, and then shot himself in a McDonald's restaurant. This was described by Palermo (1997: 1) as "The unique case of a mass murderer who left, as a suicide "note", a video-taped soliloquy". The tape, found in his car, was 40 minutes long. Palermo says that it did not contain any explicit statements of intent to kill, only implicit ones.

On the tape Terres talked about his "traumatic childhood", "feelings of rejection", "wanting to kill his employer, his relatives, [his parents] and his psychiatrist", "admiration for Hitler and understanding for the serial killer Jeffrey Dahmer", his conviction that "many serial killers were caught because of stupid mistakes", and his "belief that it would be better to end it all, fearing that he would become a serial killer" (Palermo 1997:4).

4.5. Murder notes

Mass murderers tend to be making a political or social point by their acts (Palermo 1997), so a higher proportion of notes is not surprising. In the case of mass-murderers, "their notes, when present, and their statements, when given, bespeak their deep frustration with perceived wrongs" (Palermo 1997: 2). Murder notes, as such, seem to be fairly common from serial killers. They are often addressed to the police or the press.

4.6. A murder text: "Son of Sam" letter

Serial killer David Berkowitz taunted the New York City police with a series of letters in which he referred to himself as the "Son of Sam". The first letter was found at a crime scene in 1977, and was addressed to Captain Joseph

Borrelli (Bardsley, n.d.: 1). It read, "However, to stop me you must kill me. Attention all police: Shoot me first - shoot to kill or else keep out of my way or you will die!" (p.2); "Police: Let me haunt you with these words: I'll be back! I'll be back!" (p.3).

Berkowitz's text appears to be a typical example of a "murder text". It seems that notes to the victim or intended victim are rare and (apart from OLHA) we have not yet encountered an example of one.

4.7. Martyrdom texts

In cases of suicide bombings in the Middle East, it is common for the attackers to leave a video testament explaining their motives. This is spoken, not written, discourse. It is left with friends, not at the scene of the attack (the very nature of which would destroy the text), and released to the media after the successful execution of the terrorist action in question. The victims in such cases are usually chosen opportunistically, so names are not mentioned.

Previous examples of such texts have hitherto been mainly in Arabic, but since August 2005 a "martyrdom video" exists in English. The tape was made by Mohammed Siddique Khan, a nursery school teacher from Leeds, in the North of England, who went on to take part in the suicide bombings on the London public transport system on July 7th, 2005.

Khan is apparently addressing the citizens of Western European states when he alleges:

> Your democratically elected governments continuously perpetuate atrocities against my people all over the world. And your support of them makes you directly responsible, just as I am directly responsible for protecting and avenging my Muslim brothers and sisters.
>
> Until we feel security you will be our targets and until you stop the bombing, gassing, imprisonment and torture of my people we will not stop this fight. We are at war and I am a soldier. Now you too will taste the reality of this situation.

5. Analysis and discussion of the van Gogh texts

5.1. A unique case?

Notwithstanding the suicide, murder and martyrdom texts described above, we believe the van Gogh texts provide the first example of a case where someone planning a "martyrdom operation" writes *separate* texts about their expectations of killing and dying, and in a European language at that.

5.2. The "martyrdom letter"

Let us now compare MA with a typical suicide note (see 4.2 above). It is not addressed to family or friends but to "the fighter" and "the enemy" respectively, neither of whom is named. It contains no instructions and makes no reference to specific events; rather it consists of a string of religious pronouncements. Despite the importance of Bouyeri's mother in his life and the distress her death is known to have caused him, the letter does not mention her. There is no element of thanks or of apology to anyone. It cannot be said to have an overall "positive outlook" since it contains both positive and negative elements. Finally and most obviously, it is written in verse. In short, it has none of the usual characteristics of a suicide note. However, according to press reports the letters discovered at Belkacem's flat do appear to have more features of typical suicide notes: Bouyeri states that he does not want his organs to be donated and gives instructions as to who should get his saucepan set.

If it is not accurate to describe MA as a suicide note, can it be characterised as a murder-suicide or murder note? There are not many examples of murder-suicide texts, so we cannot tell whether it resembles these. Murder notes are typically addressed to the police and may taunt them for their inability to catch the perpetrator. By definition they are written by people who have not yet been caught, and do not expect to be. As such they are opposite in nature to the text found on Bouyeri at the time of his arrest, which indicates that he expected to die in a hail of bullets.

We probably need a special category for the genre of martyrdom texts. MA has some characteristics in common with the "suicide video" of Mohammed Siddique Khan. However, despite a common theme of Islamic struggle against oppression, Khan's language is more direct and down to earth than the language of Bouyeri's martyrdom letter. The Khan tape seems to have more in common with the Open Letters to Hirsi Ali and Wilders, to which we now turn.

5.3. The "murder letters"

OLHA and OLW begin identically, "In the name of Allah the Beneficent, the Merciful", and continue:[7]

> Peace and blessings to the Emir of the Mujahideen, the smiling killer Mohammed Rasulu Allah (Sala Allaho alahie wa Sallam), his family and companions and those who follow them sincerely until the Day of Judgement .

[7] All translations from the Dutch texts are our own.

> There is no aggression except against the aggressors.
> The following:
> Peace and blessings to everyone who follows the Leaders.

From this point on the text of the two letters differs. OLHA ends with a curse which is notable for its parallel structure:

> I know for sure that you, O America, will be destroyed.
> I know for sure that you O Europe, will be destroyed.
> I know for sure that you O Holland will be destroyed.
> I know for sure that you, O Hirshi Ali will be destroyed.
> I know for sure that you, O unbelieving fundamentalist, will be destroyed.

OLW ends:

> Wilders: may Allah destroy you!
> The flag of Tawheed will also, with Allah's will, wave in your place[8]. It is only a question of time before Allah makes good His promise to His servants. Allah, the most Exalted, says: [...]
> [He] says: 'Die in your rage, in truth, Allah knows the innermost secrets of people's hearts'. (3:119)

Both letters are signed "Saifu Deen alMuwahhied" ("The sword of religion, believer in the One God"); in the case of OLHA this is preceded by "Hasboena Allah wa nima alwakeel / Nima alMawla wa Nima anNasseer" ("May we be held to account by God and by the grace of the One who appoints, / the grace of the Controller and the grace of the One who gives victory").

5.4. Shared lexis between the texts

The prosecutors at Bouyeri's trial had little doubt that he was the author of all the three texts under discussion; but is there linguistic evidence to support this assertion? An obvious starting point for any forensic linguistic analysis is to examine the texts for shared lexis. It is conventional to make a distinction between "content words" (nouns, lexical verbs, adjectives and adverbs) and "function words" (prepositions, articles, modal verbs, all closed-set word classes) (Padley 1976: 12, Blackwell 1999), and this has been done in tables 2 and 3 below:

---

[8] The word translated as "place" here, Dutch "zetel", is the term for a Parliamentary seat, and may indicate a wish that Wilders will be replaced in the Dutch Parliament by a Muslim.

Table 2. Shared lexis between the Open Letter to Hirsi Ali and the Open Letter to Wilders

OLHA	OLW	Shared types:
Total types: 673 Total tokens: 1,836	Total types: 317 Total tokens: 701	63 + 3 content 76 + 2 function

Table 3: Shared lexis between the Open Letter to Hirsi Ali and the "Martyrdom letter"

MA	OLHA	Shared types:
Total types: 91 Total tokens: 139	Total types: 673 Total tokens: 1,836	11 + 5 content 33 function

It can be seen that the number of lexical items in the Hirsi Ali letter is much larger than in either of the others, which is to be expected since the number of tokens is also much greater.

Sixty-three content word tokens are shared between OLHA and OLW, plus an additional 3 words whose lemmas are shared but which appear in different variants. This constitutes almost 10% of OLHA's lexis for content words and some 20% of OLW's lexis. In addition, 76 function words (plus two lemmas) are shared between the two documents. This is an impressively high level by any standard and one might consider the case for common authorship to be closed. However, a closer inspection of the texts reveals that 27 of the shared content words and 20 of the shared function words are to be found in the formulaic opening section which is identical in both texts.

It now has to be asked whether the opening passage is attributable to the idiolect(s) of its author(s) or whether it is so standard that any Muslim writing in Dutch could be expected to open such a letter in the same way. The answer is a complex one. The opening phrase "In Naam van Allah de Barmhartige, de Genadevolle" is absolutely formulaic. As Sardar and Davies (2004: 30) put it, "The most common attributes of God are contained in the statement Muslims utter every time they undertake an action: 'In the name of God, the Beneficent, the Merciful'". Likewise "Mohammed Rasulu Allah" ("Mohammed the messenger of Allah") is completely predictable. However, the epithet which precedes it, "de lachende doder" ("the smiling killer") is certainly *not* a standard name for the Prophet Mohammed, and Muslims confronted with this phrase have told the authors that they are both bewildered and offended by it.

The name of the Prophet is conventionally followed by the phrase "peace be upon Him", which is so standard that in English it is commonly abbreviated in writing to "pbuh". However, Muslims have a choice of language in which to utter or write this phrase. It is common to use the vernacular, and indeed later in OLW the author does so, using "vzmh" ("vrede zij met hem"); but here at the beginning of both texts the formula is expressed in Arabic. Does that indicate fluency in the Arabic language? Or perhaps the choice of Arabic by someone who is not a native speaker of that language is indicative of a more fundamentalist interpretation of Islam?

Given the shortness of MA, it is unwise to attribute any great significance to the fact that 11 of its 91 content words are shared with OLHA. One striking feature they do have in common is the phrase "wenst de dood" ("wish for death"), with capitalisation of the word "DOOD" (death):

> Martyrdom text:
> "Wenst de DOOD of hou anders je mond en ... zit."
>
> Murder text 1:
> "Mevrouw Hirshi Ali: WENST de DOOD als u werkelijk van uw gelijk OVERTUIGD bent."
> (*Ms. Hirshi* [sic] *Ali: WISH for DEATH if you are really CONVINCED that you are right.*)

5.5. Stylistic constraints on the texts

Benschop (2005) goes so far as to claim that OLHA follows the pattern of a fatwa, beginning with an opening prayer, then listing the crimes for which Hirsi Ali must be punished, and culminating with the pronouncement of the death penalty. This, however, is interpreting the term "fatwa" in a very narrow sense. A fatwa is any legal opinion by a Mufti, a scholar trained in Islamic law. It may concern matters such as divorce or inheritance and is comparable to a written opinion by a Western lawyer. In only a minority of cases will a fatwa be concerned with actions viewed as criminal and with their appropriate punishments: it will not necessarily end with the pronouncement of any kind of penalty, let alone the death penalty.

The extent to which the authors of OLHA and OLW have restricted stylistic options is therefore highly debatable. In any event they have put *themselves* under these constraints and thus are still, paradoxically, expressing a personal choice. This kind of interpretive dilemma goes to the heart of forensic stylistic analysis and is explored at length by Goutsos (1995).

We are on somewhat more solid ground with MA, whose author has undoubtedly constrained himself by writing the text in verse. He is not a very good poet, and at times the rhyme seems to dictate the lexis:

Tegen de hypocrieten zeg ik tenslotte dit:
Wenst de DOOD of hou anders je mond en ... zit.
("To the hypocrites, finally, I say this:
Wish for DEATH or else shut up and ... sit [still].")

The reader has the impression that the author was at a loss for anything to rhyme with "dit" and the best he could come up with was "zit".

5.6. Similarities at the pragmatic level

In fact, the most convincing similarities are at the pragmatic level: sudden switches of genre and of formality in all the texts.

OLHA addresses Hirsi Ali extremely politely at first:

I would like to begin with your recent proposal to screen Muslims for their ideology when they apply for jobs.

It then switches abruptly to a more confrontational style:

Your proposal is very interesting, all the more so because its introduction brings to the fore the rotten face of your political masters.

At one point the writer explodes:

Ayaan Hirshi Ali je zal jezelf stuk slaan op de Islam!"
("Ayaan Hirshi Ali you will break yourself to pieces on Islam!")

At this point the writer, who has used the polite second-person "u" form throughout, switches to the familiar "je" which he continues to use throughout the rest of the letter. This is a further example of pragmatic inconsistency. Similar stylistic incongruities occur in OLW:

A couple of truths will be brought to light in this letter about the sort of rotten soul of the kind of people who deserve Allah's wrath. With the following verses from Allah, the Most High, I remind you and all the Hanses and Mieps of those likeminded people who were destroyed.[9]

[9] By "likeminded people" the author appears to mean gays and lesbians, and this is perhaps also the intended meaning of "Hansen en Miepen" which is not a standard expression in Dutch: the passage he goes on to quote concerns "Loeth" (Lot) and seems to refer to the destruction of Sodom and Gomorrah.

The same kind of stylistic clashes can be seen in the Martyrdom text:

> Accept the offer ...
> And Allah will give you free range ...
> He will give you the garden ...
> In place of earth's ruins ...
> To the enemy I also have something to say...
> You are sure to bite the dust ...

Notwithstanding the similarities we have noted above, the evidence is not conclusive. Leemhuis (cited in Luyendijk 2004) believes that the writer of OLHA is *not* the same as that of MA. While he accepts that Bouyeri authored MA himself, he is of the opinion that "Saifu Deen alMuwahhied" is a Syrian whose language has been influenced by English translations of the Qur'an. He also believes that some of the more formulaic passages are translations. "Saifu Deen" on its own is not an unusual name, meaning literally "the sword of religion". Saifu Deen alMuwahhied is also, according to Leemhuis, the name of a fundamentalist group from North Africa which conquered a part of Spain in the Middle Ages. It is entirely possible that it is being used today by a new fundamentalist group and not a single individual.

The pragmatic inconsistencies noted above could indicate that all three texts were written by the same highly disturbed individual; on the other hand, they could constitute evidence of multiple authorship. It is now established beyond doubt that Bouyeri had a network of contacts with Islamic cells around the world and that some of the texts were circulating widely on the Internet. It is quite possible that the murder letters were produced jointly, or that earlier versions served as models for later variants, with a number of authors involved who may not even have known each other.

6. Conclusion

The mere presence of significant lexical and stylistic differences between two texts does not make it safe to conclude that they have different authors: the differences between our murder and martyrdom letters may be attributable to factors such as the former being focused on specific individuals and proposed government policies, or the latter being written in verse. Conversely, similarities between the texts may be due to universal Islamic formulaic expressions and so are not a secure basis for inferring common authorship. Further study is needed to establish the extent of the parts played by religious and linguistic background on the one hand, and individual style and idiolect on the other.

What is clear from the van Gogh case is that martyrdom texts deserve a genre of their own, distinct from both suicide and murder texts. We have already seen from the London suicide bombings that the Bouyeri martyrdom letter was the first, but not the last, of this genre to be produced in a Western European language. Unfortunately, it seems likely that further examples of such texts will be forthcoming in the near future to expand the amount of material available for forensic linguistic analysis.

References

Asgard, U. (1990). *Suicide among Swedish women: psychiatric and epidemiological study.* Stockholm: Karolinska Institute.

Bardsley, M. (n.d.). "The Letter". *Court TV's Crime Library: Serial Killers; Most Notorious; Son of Sam.* (Ch.1, p.1-3), http://www.crimelibrary.com/serial/son/sonmain.htm

Barraclough, B. and E. C. Harris. (2002). "Suicide preceded by murder: the epidemiology of homicide-suicide in England and Wales 1988-92". *Psychological Medicine* 32, 577-584. [Online journal, accessed May 2005].

Beck, A., Morris, J. and D. Lester (1974). "Suicide notes and risk of future suicide". *Journal of the American Medical Association* 228, 495-496.

Benschop, A. (2005). *Chronicle of a Political Murder Foretold: Jihad in the Netherlands.* Amsterdam University, http://www.sociosite.org/jihad_nl_en.php

Blackwell, S.A. (1999). "Looking up *Look:* Discourse markers in the Bank of English". In: J. M. Kirk (ed.), *Corpora Galore: Analysis and Techniques in Describing English.* Amsterdam: Rodopi.

Capstick, A. (1960). "Recognition of emotional disturbance and the prevention of suicide". *British Medical Journal* 1, 1179-82.

Chynoweth, R. (1977). "The significance of suicide notes". *Australian and New Zealand Journal of Psychiatry* 11, 197-200.

Edland, J. F. and C. E. Duncan (1973). "Suicide notes in Monroe County; a 23-year look (1950-72)". *Journal of Forensic Sciences* 18, 364-369.

Goutsos, D. (1995). Review article: "Forensic Stylistics", *Forensic Linguistics* 1(1), 99-113.

Hirsi Ali, A., (2004). "'Ik ben de dorpsgek, jij de afvallige vrouw'", opinion piece in *NRC Handelsblad*, 3rd November 2004, http://www.nrc.nl//opinie/artikel/1099461610109.html

Poorthuis, F. and H. Wansink. (2002). "De islam is een achterlijke cultuur", interview with Pim Fortuyn in *De Volkskrant*, 9 February 2002, http://www.volkskrant.nl/denhaag/8761028966812.html

Heim, N. and D. Lester (1990). "Do suicides who write notes differ from those who do not? A study of suicide in West Berlin". *Acta Psychiatrica Scandinavica* 82, 372-373.

Ho, T. O., Yip, P. S. F., Chiu, C. W. F. and P. Halliday (1998). "Suicide notes: what do they tell us?". *Acta Psychiatrica Scandinavica* 98, 467-473.

Houston, M. (2003). "Final Notes found to be far from despairing." *Irish Times*, 8th March, 2003, p. 1.

Lyendijk, W. (2004). "Pamflet product uit de polder", report in *NRC Handelsblad*, 6th Nov 2004, http://www.nrc.nl/binnenland.artikel/1099636221651.html

Marzuk, P., Tardiff, K. and C. Hirsch (1992). "The epidemiology of murder-suicide". *The Journal of the American Medical Association* 267(23), 3179-83.

O'Conner, R., Sheehy, N. P. and D. B. O'Conner (1999). "A thematic analysis of suicide notes". *Crisis* 20(3). Toronto: Hogrefe and Huber Publishers.

O'Donnell, I., Farmer, R. and J. Catalan (1993). "Suicide notes". *British Journal of Psychiatry* 163, 45-48.

Padley, G. A. (1976). *Grammatical Theory in Western Europe 1500-1700.* Cambridge: Cambridge University Press.

Palermo, G. B. (1997). "The Berserk Syndrome: A Review of Mass Murder". *Aggression and Violent Behaviour* 2(1), 1-8. [Online journal, accessed May 2005].

Salib, E., Cawley, S. and R. Healy (2002). "The significance of suicide notes in the elderly". *Aging and Mental Health* 6(2), 186-190.

Sardar, Z. and Davies, M. W. (2004). *The no-nonsense guide to Islam*, London: Verso.

Shapero, J. J. (forthcoming). "Suicide notes: language and authorship attribution". Doctoral thesis, University of Birmingham.

Shneidman, E. S. and N. L. Farberow (1957). "Some comparisons between genuine and simulated suicide notes in terms of Mowrer's concepts of discomfort and relief. *Journal of General Psychology* 56(25), 1-256.

Symonds, R. L. (1985). "Psychiatric aspects of railway fatalities". *Psychological Medicine* 15, 609-621.

Toshiki, S., Akiyoshi, N., Kohei, A., Ryo, A., Hideyuki, N., Yasuhiro, U., Maki, K. and S. Toshiyuki (2005). Abstract from "Incidence of note-leaving remains constant despite increasing suicide rates". *Psychiatry and Clinical Neurosciences* 59(2), 226-228.

Tuckman, J., Kleiner, R. J. and M. Lavell (1959). "Emotional content of suicide notes". *American Journal of Psychiatry* 116, 59-63.

van Wormer, K. and C. Odiah (1999). "The psychology of suicide-murder and the death penalty". *Journal of Criminal Justice* 27(4), 361-370. [Online journal, accessed May 2005].

Burns Cooper
University of Alaska Fairbanks
USA

IDEA DENSITY AS A MARKER OF AUTHORSHIP: A PRELIMINARY STUDY

1. Introduction

This paper is a preliminary investigation of the possibility of using a psycholinguistic measure, "idea density," for forensic linguistic work. Although it should be considered a progress report on an ongoing study, the early work has produced some interesting, suggestive results.

The idea for this project was sparked by a widely-publicized paper in the Journal of the American Medical Association (JAMA) in 1996: "Linguistic Ability in Early Life and Cognitive Function and Alzheimer's Disease in Late Life: Findings from the Nun Study" (Snowdon et al 1996). The Nun Study is a multi-variable, long-term study of an order of nuns in Wisconsin (the School Sisters of Notre Dame), comparing factors in their lifestyle with outcomes in their long-term health. The JAMA article focused on just one aspect of the study: all the women had written autobiographies when they entered the order (mostly in their late teens or early twenties), and the study compared features of these autobiographies with their cognitive function decades later, and specifically with their likelihood of getting Alzheimer's disease.

What is surprising is that there *was* a relationship. The authors, led in this part by the psycholinguist Susan Kemper, analyzed the autobiographies for two "indicators of linguistic ability": *grammatical complexity* and *idea density*. Both indicators correlated significantly with the later diagnosis of Alzheimer's, but the stronger correlation was with idea density. (Idea density is also called semantic or propositional density, and because *propositional density* (PD) is a more precise term, I will use that term in the rest of this paper). Specifically, the group of nuns with the lowest PD had the highest likelihood of later developing Alzheimer's. The implications of this are truly amazing: in effect, writing style at 22 is a predictor of dementia at 70 or 80.

More directly relevant for forensic linguistics is the fact that writing style at age 22 is also apparently a predictor of writing style at 70 or 80, at least in these two parameters. The researchers had the same women write similar autobiographies in 1995, and compared them. They conclude, "The linguistic scores for the autobiographies written in the 1930s and those written in 1995 were highly correlated (i.e. 0.73 for idea density and 0.62 for grammatical complexity)" (1996: 529).

The paper, then, implies (though it doesn't explain) a long-term relationship between propositional density and neurology. It occurred to me that this might be useful for authorship studies--a way of getting at the basic problem of whether writers maintain elements of their style over time. Clearly some things change, not only from year to year but from text to text, but is there anything that remains relatively constant, that is tied to the writer rather than the circumstances? As one way of addressing this question, this study analyzes personal letters from different years, and in fact, different decades, by the same authors, to see if PD is more consistent within the same author's writing than across different authors.

Even if individual authors do have characteristic idea densities, that does not necessarily make it a useful marker for questioned authorship analysis. The goals of the JAMA article are quite different from those of forensic linguists. They used propositional density to classify a relatively large sample of people (93) into just 3 categories: low, average, and high. Low propositional density correlated highly with later Alzheimer's disease. By contrast, authorship studies normally try to classify a small sample of people into categories of only one member each. (Or, at least, the most important category, "Author of the questioned document," has only one member.) This is a much harder task, and one that no one has completely solved yet. This paper will not pretend to solve that problem. My goal is simply to get a first idea of whether the author/density correlation exists, how strong it is, and how consistent it is over time.

2. Methods

Analyzing propositional density seems clear in principle: it is the number of propositions in a sentence, divided by the number of words, multiplied by 10. (Multiplying by 10 serves simply to produce a more readable, non-fractional number; it is irrelevant to the comparative statistics). Propositions are "'idea units' or basic predicates expressing actions or states, modifications of these actions or states such as qualifications, quantifications, and negations, and connections between them such as conjunctions, disjunctions, and contrasts" (Kemper et al. 1995, 156). To get an initial idea of what this means, look at these two examples from the Nun Study:

> Sister A: I was born in Eau Claire, Wis., on May 24, 1913 and was baptized in St. James church. (PD=3.9)

> Sister B: I visited the capitol in Madison and also the Motherhouse of the Franciscan Sisters of Perpetual Adoration at Duluth which visit increased my love for Notre Dame, because it was and is Notre Dame. (PD=9.1)

The JAMA paper authors present this analysis of the propositions in the first sentence: *1) I was born; 2)born in Eau Claire, Wis.; 3)born on May 24, 1913; 4)I was baptized; 5)was baptized in church; 6) was baptized in St. James Church; and 7) I was born...and was baptized* (530). In effect, any predication by a lexical verb, prepositional phrase, adjective, adverb, or adjunct noun, plus any conjunction-like relationship such as *and, but,* or *if*, will add one proposition. Sister A's sentence has 7 propositions, 18 words, and therefore a propositional density of 3.9.

However, things are not always this straightforward. Intuitively, the second sentence seems more complex, but complexity and density are not necessarily the same thing. Sister B's sentence is 32 words long (if we count *Notre Dame* as one word), so to have a PD of 9.1, it must have 29 propositions. The JAMA paper gives no analysis of this sentence, but it is not easy to find 29 propositions there. One can force out 29, but some of them seem dubious (see Appendix for more on this).

In fact, working out a system of analysis that will give reasonably consistent results turns out to be quite difficult and complicated; several of the authors who have worked on propositional density have commented on these difficulties. However, although I am quite sure my analysis is not identical with that of the authors of the JAMA paper, I believe I worked out a method that has a reasonable amount of internal consistency of its own. Based on the coding manual from the Nun Study (which is based primarily on Turner and Greene (1977)) and other published material in this area of psycholinguistics and textual analysis, I think reasonable internal consistency is actually the best one can hope for – a lot of these analytical decisions are worked out on the fly, not *a priori*. It's just not possible to anticipate all the possible questions that come up. This methodological difficulty makes it even more impressive that the Nun Study got results that correlated both with cognitive tests and with hard physical results from autopsies.

A big part of the complication is that we count not only explicitly expressed propositions, but also presupposed and implied propositions. This leads to the question of just how to establish that a proposition is implied.

As an example, take this analysis of a sentence from Hemingway's *The Sun Also Rises*, given in Turner and Greene (1977, 59-69). I have simplified the format slightly in order to more closely match that of the Nun Study. The formalism here is that, in each proposition, the predication goes first, followed by any arguments. So, in a canonical simple sentence, the lexical verb goes first, followed by the subject and object(s) or other complement(s): "The cat caught the vole" = catch: cat, vole. Information in parentheses is explanatory, not a predication or argument *per se*. Implied propositions are marked with ">". The sentence to be analyzed is:

"The stream was clear and shallow but it did not look trouty." Here is Turner and Greene's analysis (simplified):

1) clear: stream
2) shallow: stream
3) and (conjunction): 1, 2
4) >possess: stream, trout
5) > if (condition): >4, 3
6) "Trouty": stream
7) if: 4, 6
8) not (negation): 6
9) but (concession): 3, 6

The implied, as opposed to explicit, elements in this sentence are in the word "trouty" and its relationship to the first half of the sentence. "Trouty" here seems to mean, not "trout-like," but "full of trout" or "likely to have trout". The word "but" implies some kind of contrast with the first clause, so we are left to infer that *(7)* if a stream possesses trout, it is trouty; and *(5)* if it is clear and shallow, *(4)* it (likely) possesses trout; *(9)* but *(8)* not in this case.

Another example from the same passage is, "[He] went down toward the stream to try and dig some worms for bait". Turner and Greene argue that this includes an implied proposition ">obtain: he, worms". One might argue about whether other propositions are also implied, but it is at least clear that as readers we do understand that the character intends to obtain the worms (not just dig in the dirt where they are) and that if we failed to understand that, we could not be said to understand the sentence.

A key question here is how strongly something must be implied to be counted; that is, how crucial an implication must be to the interpretation. Clearly a literary critic might find all sorts of possible implications that would have no place in this kind of analysis. To clarify where the line is, we might distinguish several levels of certainty, although there are no sharp boundaries between them:

1) The text is uninterpretable without this inference; there is no other way to make sense of it.
2) The text has an unexplained juxtaposition, and thus a gap in coherence, unless you make this inference. (e.g., "Why does sentence 9 follow sentence 8, unless this inference links them?")
3) A "normal" reader would make this inference, and it makes sense with the content and with accepted pragmatic principles.
4) A knowledgeable reader (one familiar with the writer and/or circumstances) would make this inference; it makes sense with pragmatic principles and with the content and perceived intentions of the author.

In practice, the choice of which standard to use is really between levels 1 and 2; the others are too difficult to be consistent about from one text to another. Levels 3 and 4 are part of a reader's interpretation, but are too subjective to quantify.

Based on published work from practitioners such as Kemper, Kintsch, Van Dijk, Turner, and Greene, as well as the relatively high average density scores the JAMA paper reports, it seems that they are working from something like level 2.

Similar to implied propositions are presuppositions, in which the standard meanings of words entail other propositions. For example, Kemper uses this principle for causatives; the sentence "Chocolate pie is fattening" has four propositions (personal communication, 2005):

1) chocolate: pie;
2) eat: (you), pie;
3) gain: you, weight;
4) cause: 2, 3 (PD = 4 words / 4 propositions * 10 = 10)

That is, "fattening" is not just an attribute of the pie, like being chocolate, but a causative relationship: eating the pie *(1)* causes *(4)* you to gain weight *(2)*. Again, this leads to questions about which kinds of presuppositions and entailments count and which don't; causation and negation do, deictic reference, anaphora, and modality apparently do not. The system doesn't claim to break all predications down to the most basic semantic primitives (which would have its own problems), so the analyst simply has to make a decision and try to be consistent.

There is not space in this paper to go into many of the analytical problems that have to be worked out; I will discuss just a few. Some are low-level decisions about how to count words and sentences, but they must be decided for the sake of consistency. Others run into very thorny theoretical issues about how to analyze propositions (see Appendix).

An example of the low-level kind is the question of what counts as a sentence: is it the stretch from capital letter to period, or is it an independent clause with all its free modifiers (a "T-unit")? Should single words ("Doubtful."), or even non-words ("Grrr!") be analyzed as sentences, if they are written that way?

An example of a thornier issue is that, according to the Nun Study coding manual, we are to ignore all auxiliary verbs, including modals, and count only lexical ones, so "She might have been going" is the same proposition as "She went" (but with a very different PD). But since only the canonical modal verbs are ignored, not all words with similar semantic content, this leads to oddities: "She can come" and "She must work" are one proposition each, but "She is able to come" and "She has to work" are two.[1] There is also the problem of ellipsis; one letter in my study contains the sentence: "He enjoys volleyball when he can."

[1] Logicians might also have trouble with this analysis, since the truth conditions for "He can cook" and for "He is cooking" are quite different. But we must remember that this system was developed for psycholinguistic, not philosophical, ends; the true test is whether "She might have been going" takes the same amount of mental processing as "She went."

Representing this as equivalent to "He enjoys volleyball when he enjoys volleyball" makes no sense; it has to be something like "He enjoys (playing) volleyball when he is able (to play volleyball)," or even "If he is able to play volleyball, he enjoys it."

Perhaps the trickiest question of all has to do with figurative language. The coding manual, like Turner and Greene, says to treat "idioms and other figurative expressions as figurative," so that "lose your head" = "lose: you, control"; but often it's not that simple. Metaphors can be extended and work on more than one level, and are not all conventional. One letter in my study contains an anecdote concluded by the sentence "Which bird are we?" Another says, "We hope that this 'thread' we send will help bind us until we meet each other again." There are no simple or context-free paraphrases for these, although in context they are not difficult to understand.

There are many more systematic issues to be resolved, as well as problems with individual words and sentences. In many cases experience and careful reasoning lead one to a clear choice. However, in some cases, there is no obvious reason to prefer one solution over another; the crucial thing is to keep careful records and be consistent.[2]

2. Samples

Once the methodological problems have been resolved one way or another, the next question is which *texts* to apply these methods to. The end goal is to use them in forensic applications, but I did not use documents from actual forensic cases. I wanted to start with as controlled a situation as possible, to try to limit the number of variables. For this reason, as well as the availability of data, I chose to look at annual Christmas letters, the kind people make multiple copies of to send to all their friends and relations. My own relatives provided one set, going from 1964 to 2002. A Web search turned up two more fairly long sets, which went back to 1985 and 1986 respectively. It would be nice to have three sets from 1964 on, but a time depth of 20 years should still be enough to show changes over time, if there are any.

The advantage of these texts is that they share a fairly narrowly-defined genre, a common purpose, a similar audience, and even some subject matter. The

[2] Perfetti and Britt (1995) discuss some of the uncertainty in identifying propositions; they report asking three experts in the field to analyze several sentences and getting widely varying results. For the sentence "Lyle pushed Paris out of his mind for three months" (where Paris refers to the city, not a person) the three experts come up with three, five, and seven propositions, respectively. However, Perfetti and Britt still argue for the usefulness of propositions as a level of analysis, because it has proved so useful in experimental work.

authors so far are also demographically similar (which may have to do with what kind of people archive their Christmas letters and put them on the Web). They are all English-speaking men, married with grown children, middle class, with postgraduate degrees and university-related careers (although only one is a professor). One is from the United States and two are from England (one of whom now lives in New Zealand), but the English they write is all very standard and shows no obvious differences other than spelling and topical references.

So far, six letters from each set have been analyzed. Where possible, I selected the same years for all three authors: one letter from 1985 or 86 and one each from 1990, 1995, 1999, and 2002. I also included 1964 and 1975 from the longest set to look for longer-term changes, and 2004 from the two shorter sets to give the longest possible time spread.

From each letter the salutation and any anomalous material such as quotations were skipped, and then the first 10 sentences analyzed. This is the same size sample as the Nun Study used. One might ideally like large samples, but there are several reasons to limit the size. Because propositional analysis is extremely time-consuming and cannot be done by a computer, keeping sample size down is an important consideration.[3] Also, many documents in actual cases of questioned authorship are quite short, so if the method of analysis shows reliability on relatively small samples it is more potentially useful. To check the assumption that 10 sentences is enough, in the first phase of the research I analyzed 20 sentences from 3 letters of each author, but found no consistent difference between the first 10 sentences and the second 10: they were not identical, but the second 10 were sometimes more dense and sometimes less. The two samples from the same letter were also not much more similar to each other, on average, than samples from different letters by the same author. Although one would ideally have many sentences from many texts, it seemed more useful for now to concentrate on adding more letters, rather than longer samples from each.[4]

Ideally there would be more than one "coder" who could spot-check each other's work. That was not possible in this case, but I did go back and re-analyze them all a second time in case my criteria had drifted in the course of handling more texts. In addition to the danger of random inconsistencies, there is a serious danger of bias if the coder knows which texts belong to which author (as is inevitable in this case), and this must be guarded against by rigorously checking to be sure that similar structures are all analyzed the same way.

Once the raw scores were compiled, the twenty-sentence and ten-sentence groups were compared in various ways. I compared the mean, median, standard

---

[3] Cheung and Kemper 1992 discuss the labor-intensive nature of propositional analysis (72-73).

[4] Sentences were not selected randomly, for several reasons. The most important of these is that consecutive sentences are not necessarily independent of each other, and these relationships can be important in analyzing propositions.

deviation, and standard error. I used a t-test to check various pairings, both comparing letters by the same author to each other, and letters by different authors. I also ran a one-way ANOVA test on the mean scores for all the letters from all the authors.

4. Results and discussion

Table 1 summarizes the results by giving the mean score for each letter.

Table 1. Mean propositional densities

Author	1964	1975	1985/6	1990	1995	1999	2002	2004
A	6.39	6.86	6.69	6.27	7.21	6.92	6.56	
C			6.03	5.19	6.49	6.10	6.22	5.94
B			5.73	5.70	6.17	6.12	5.97	5.99

Author A's PD is higher than the other two; the differences are statistically significant at the $P<.01$ level. Authors C and B, however, have a very similar overall mean density; they are not significantly different from each other, although there is another difference we will see in a moment. The clearest difference is between author A and author B, as Figure 1 shows. (Note that the x-axis should be considered merely a sequence of data points, not a representation of time, since the time intervals are inconsistent.) For the most part, the two authors occupy two different ranges, although author A's 1990 letter appears to be a bit of an outlier, and is almost as low as author B's highest score. So far, though, the consistent ranges of the scores make Propositional density look promising as a potential marker of authorship. Although the overall mean is virtually the same for authors B and C, C is much more variable; he has by far the lowest score (1990) but also one (1995) that is higher than any of author B's, and higher than the two lowest of author A. (It is possible that variability itself – both from text to text and from sentence to sentence – is idiosyncratic and could be a marker of authorship, but that will have to wait for another study.)

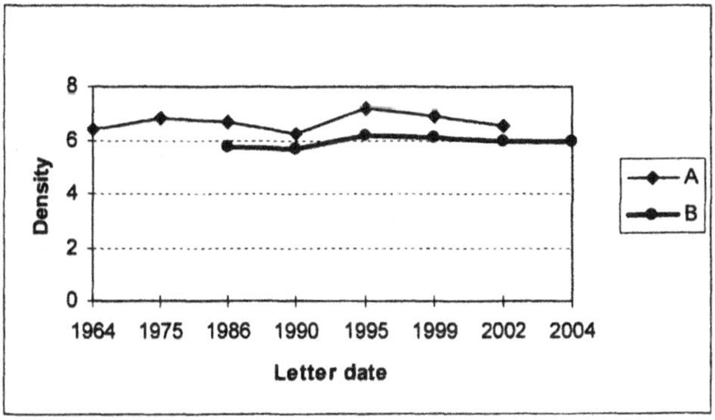

Figure 1. Comparison of propositional density for Authors A and B

Things get a bit messier, though, when we add in author C (see Figure 2).

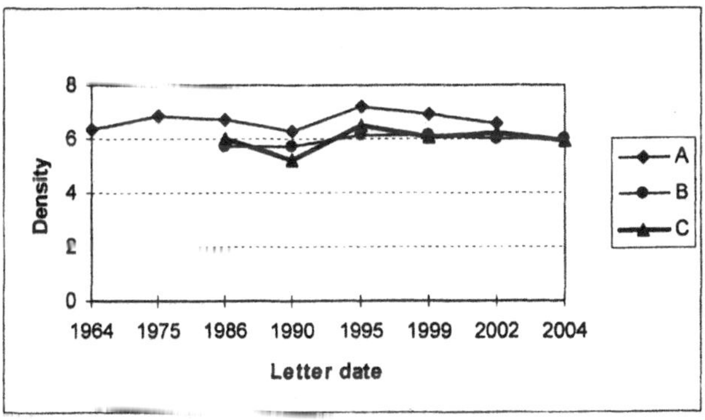

Figure 2. Comparison of propositional density for Authors A, B, and C

In a forensic task of author identification, it would be impossible to tell C from B by propositional density alone. Perhaps more troubling, there would also be a good chance of error even for distinguishing A from C, even though the average difference between these authors was statistically very significant ($P<.01$). Although with a large enough sample we could probably make a correct identification, imagine being given A 1990 as a questioned document: it could easily result in an identification that was either inconclusive or simply wrong.

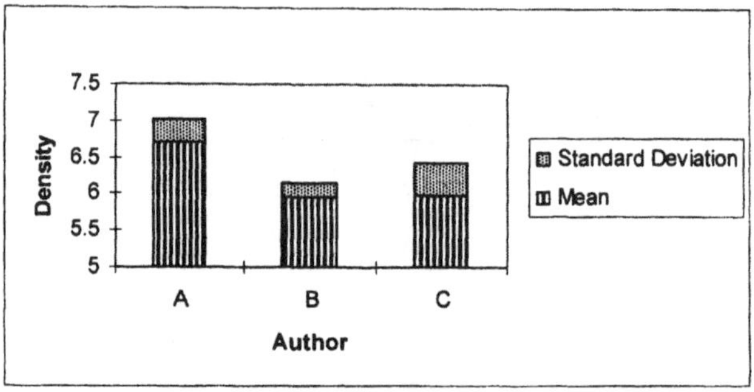

Figure 3. Comparison of variability of authors A, B, and C

A second issue this study was designed to address is whether a given author's PD changes over time, or remains relatively stable. The results so far provide no support for authors' PD changing over time. Although there are fluctuations in scores, the direction of change from one letter to the next is inconsistent and unpredictable. This looks more like variation within a range than sustained change in style or cognitive ability. However, we don't yet have enough data to make a strong claim that density is stable over time, even for these three authors. Once more letters are analyzed and the time intervals are smaller, we can get a better idea.

5. Conclusions

The results so far have led to some tentative conclusions. First, PD does correlate with individual authors; to put it another way, individual authors do have characteristic propositional densities. However, PD does not necessarily distinguish authors robustly enough to be used as a sole determinant of authorship, especially if the sample is small. For example, if we were given a letter with a PD of 5.9 and asked to say on that basis if it came from author C or author B, we couldn't do it. On the other hand, PD could be a factor along with other measures. There *is* a correlation, just not a very precise one. Keep in mind that this is a deliberately homogeneous sample both in genre and in demographics, one that was least likely to produce major differences between authors. It is possible, even likely, that bigger differences in density might show up in cases where the authors are more demographically diverse, where the genre (text type) is less predictable, or even in a different group of authors of annual Christmas letters chosen the same way. Even in the very small number of texts by other authors I have examined so far, there are some scores outside the range (from 5.2 to 7.2) of the three authors in this paper. The Nun Study found a range from 3.9 to 9.3 for their written autobiographies.[5]

There was no evidence of the authors' PD changing over time, although we would need more data before we could say that it is definitely stable from year to year. If it does turn out to be stable, though, that would make PD potentially especially useful in certain cases; for example, in comparisons of documents written some years apart.

There is something satisfying about the idea of using an indicator of authorship for which there is evidence that it may be linked not just to preference or force of habit, but to the writer's total cognitive capacity. On the other hand, the very complexity of PD as a feature leads to challenges that may make it harder to use than more mechanical measures such as lexical frequency counts, collocation, mean length of utterance, error analysis, and so on. Grammatical complexity, the other linguistic indicator used in the Nun Study, and one which linguists have already used in some forms for author identification, may occupy a middle ground of sorts--easier to quantify than PD, but harder than some other measures. Nevertheless, despite its difficulties, propositional density shows enough promise, both for practical applications and for theoretical investigation of the factors underlying style, that it is worth further research. The ideas in this paper need to be tested, possibly with refinements to the methodology, with a bigger and more varied sample.

References

Cheung, H. and S. Kemper (1992). "Competing complexity metrics and adults' production of complex sentences." *Applied Psycholinguistics* 13, 53-76.

Kemper, S., Rice, K., and Y.-C. Chen (1995). "Complexity metrics and growth curves for measuring grammatical development from five to ten." *First Language* 15, 151-166.

Kintsch, W. (1974). *The Representation of Meaning in Memory*. Hillsdale, NJ: Lawrence Erlbaum Associates.

Kintsch, W., and J. Keenan (1973). "Reading rate and retention as a function of the number of propositions in the base structure of sentences." *Cognitive Psychology* 5, 527-274.

Kintsch, W., and T. A. Van Dijk (1978). "Towards a model of text comprehension and production." *Psychological Review* 85, 363-394.

[5] My scoring is not precisely calibrated with theirs, which is why I have not used their figures for detailed comparison. However, their total range gives a better idea of what could be expected from a wider population, even though their sample itself (the nuns) was chosen partly for its homogeneity.

Lyons, J. (1998). "Sentences, clauses, statements and propositions." In: P. Collins and D. Lee (eds.), *The clause in English: in honour of Rodney Huddleston.* Amsterdam: Benjamins, 149-175.

Mitzner, T. L., and S. Kemper (2003). "Oral and Written Language in Late Adulthood: Findings From the Nun Study." *Experimental Aging Research* 29, 457-474.

Perfetti, C. A., and M. A. Britt (1995). "Where Do Propositions Come From?" In: C. A. Weaver III, S. Mannes and C. R. Fletcher (eds.), *Discourse Comprehension: Essays in honor of Walter Kintsch.* Hillsdale, NJ: Lawrence Erlbaum Associates, 11-34.

Snowdon, D. A., Kemper, S. J., Mortimer, J. A., Greiner, L. H., Wekstein, D. R., and W. R. Markesbury (1996). "Linguistic Ability in Early Life and Cognitive Function and Alzheimer's Disease in Late Life: Findings From the Nun Study." *Journal of the American Medical Association* 275:7, 528-532.

Turner, A., and E. Greene (1977). *The Construction and Use of a Propositional Text Base.* Institute for the Study of Intellectual Behavior, University of Colorado, Technical Report No. 63.

Appendix

Look again at Sister B's sentence. Simply looking for words that convey a predication, in an automatic way, produces only 15 propositions:

1. visited: I, 2
2. and: capitol, Motherhouse
3. in: Madison, capitol
4. of: sisters, Motherhouse
5. Franciscan: sisters
6. of: Adoration, sisters
7. Perpetual: Adoration
8. at: Duluth, Motherhouse
9. increased: 1, love
10. my: love
11. for: Notre Dame, love
12. because: 15, 9
13. is: it, Notre Dame
14. was: it, Notre Dame
15. and: 13, 14

*(PD = 15/29*10 = 5.17)*

To come up with more requires several kinds of more sophisticated (and more subjective) analysis. We can break down some words into component and/or implied meanings; for example, "visited" can be re-analyzed as "traveled (in order) to see". Certain words, such as "also," seem not to add much meaning, but could be considered predicates (perhaps in this case emphasizing that there are 2 visits, not 1). We can find implied propositions that are needed in order to make sense of the text; for example, "capitol" may imply "of Wisconsin" and/or "capitol building". Finally, and most problematically, we can supply propositions to make sense of vague parts of the text; for example, "because it was and is Notre Dame" doesn't really explain why the visit increases her love; we may infer (among several possibilities) that she prefers Notre Dame over the Franciscan Sisters and the visit confirmed this preference. Some of these elaborations are probably more defensible than others.

An elaborated version.

1. travel: I, 3
2. >capitol: building
3. to: 2 (capitol building)
4. in: Madison, 2
5. see: I, 2
6. to (purpose): 5 (see), 1 (traveled)
7. travel: I, 8
8. to: Motherhouse
9. see:, I, Motherhouse
10. to (purpose): 9 (see), 7 (traveled)
11. adore: sisters, X (someone/thing)
12. perpetual: 11 (adoration)
13. of: 12, sisters
14. Franciscan: 13
15. of: 14, Motherhouse
16. at : Duluth, Motherhouse
17. and: 1, 7
18. also: 17
19. > *reference*: visit = 7 ("which visit")
20. cause: visit, 21
21. increase: 22
22. love: I, Notre Dame
23. was: it, Notre Dame
24. is: it, Notre Dame
25. and: 23,24
26. because: 25, 20
27. >prefer: I, Notre Dame
28. >over: Franciscan Sisters, 27
29. >and: 27, 25

Godfrey A. Steele
University of the West Indies
Trinidad and Tobago

COURSE CONTENT FOR LANGUAGE AND THE LAW AND INTERPRETATION OF THE LAW

1. Introduction

This paper addresses the issue of identifying and organizing course content for an undergraduate course on language and the law. A theoretical framework is presented for the sample course outline presented. Using the first ten volumes of *Forensic Linguistics: the International Journal of Speech, Language and the Law* as a base, an attempt was made to classify the articles according to various areas of the field of forensic linguistics. Afterwards, the articles that dealt specifically with language and the law were examined to identify themes and/or topics that could be included in an undergraduate course of study for law students, legal communication students and perhaps students of linguistics. However, no background in linguistics was assumed. Such a course would perhaps be of interest also to practicing attorneys, judicial officers and other persons in the legal profession.

An introduction to the tenth volume signalled a name change in the title of the journal to *The International Journal of Speech, Language and the Law*[1]. The slightly modified new title was meant to reflect a changing trend in the discipline (Cotterill, Coulthard and French 2003). So, in a sense, the tenth volume marked an explicit redefining of the focus of the journal. For this reason, it seems timely and useful to chart the progress of the journal in those first ten years and reflect on the journal's contribution to the debate as to what constitutes the relationship between language and law. This contribution is used to inform the proposal for an undergraduate course.

2. Language and the law or language *of* the law?

The questions emerging from the language issues raised in a previous paper (Steele 2005: 5-6) point to the way that the language of the law and the

[1] I will henceforth use the abbreviation *IJSLL* to refer to the journal before and after the title change.

interpretation of the law have come to be treated in the discipline of forensic linguistics. For example, the term "language of the law" relates to a concern with clarity and brevity in the language used in law (Melinkoff 1963), and more recent emphases on legal language (Goodrich 1987, Conley and O'Barr 1998) and plain language (Tiersma 1999) as summarized by McMenamin (2002). In fact, McMenanim (2002: 42) defines the language of the law in this way: "Language of the law is concerned with assuring that the legal language of statutes and of legal and consumer writings be clear, brief, and simple, i.e. plain language". In a Privy Council judgement analyzed in Steele (2005), references to the language of the law focused on three issues: intention and meaning, language and intention, and legal language. A later section of that paper focused on the interpretation of the law.

The interpretation of the law is characterized as an attempt to determine the intention of a statute. However, this enterprise, though often regarded as a primary purpose of interpretation, is often influenced by other factors such as the scope of interpretation.

In November 2003, the then final court of appeal in Trinidad and Tobago, based in England, found that contrary to a long practice, the imposition of the death penalty for the crime of murder was discretionary, not mandatory. In relation to the interpretation of the law, consider the overall approach to the treatment of the following issues in the Privy Council's majority ruling delivered by Lord Steyn. Paragraph 77 is instructive in defining an approach to interpreting the language of the constitution. In undertaking the task of constitutional interpretation, it is important for a court to use "a generous and purposive interpretation" in dealing with "constitutional provisions protecting human rights".[2]

- Approach to interpreting the law (paragraph 77)
    - The role of judges (paragraph 76)
    - The unity of the legal system (paragraphs 8-14)
- Interpretation issues
    - Interpretation and construction of the statute (paragraph 16)
    - Interpretation and modification (paragraph 23)
    - Interpretation and intention (paragraph 24)
- Interpretation contexts
    - Narrow and broad construction (paragraph 26; see paragraph 16 above)
    - Scope of interpretation: International legal context (paragraphs 28-31)
    - Scope of interpretation: Social and Constitutional Contexts (paragraph 32)

[2] The judgment is available at www.privy-council.org.uk/files/other/balkissoon%20roodal.rtf.

Given these examples, what does the actual scholarly work in the IJSSL contribute to the discussion on the interrelated issues of the language of the law and the interpretation of the law?

Other sources such as textbooks provide definitions of the sub-fields in forensic linguistics. For example, statements on the language of the law, semantics and pragmatics appear below.

> "Language of the law is concerned with assuring that the legal language of statutes and of legal and consumer writings be clear, brief, and simple, i.e. plain language" (McMenamin 2002: 42)

> "[Forensic] Semantics focuses on the comprehensibility and interpretation of written and spoken language that is difficult to understand e.g. e.g., consumer product warnings, jury instructions, trademarks, etc." (McMenamin 2002: 42)

> "Pragmatics is the analysis of a speaker's intended meaning in contexts of actual use. Forensic linguists use the tools of theoretical tools of provided by discourse analysis and pragmatics to analyze the function of language used in specific contexts, such as dictation, conversations, hearings, questioning, and the language of specific speech acts, e.g., threats, promises, warnings, etc" (McMenamin 2002: 42).

2. Analysis

Over the ten-year period 1994-2003, 184 items in three main categories were published on all topics, divided into research articles (61.4%, n=113), case studies or reports (9.8%, n=18), and book reviews (28.8%, n=53) in the International Journal of Speech Language and the Law. The frequency pattern for these three main categories of items on language of the law was similar: research articles (44.2%, n=19), case studies or reports (5.6%, n=2) and book reviews (51.2%, n=22). Overall, almost one-quarter of the content of the Journal dealt with the language of the law. Of the 113 research articles, the language of the law content comprised 16.8% (n=19). Of the 18 case studies or case reports, 11.1% (n= 2) and of the 53 book reviews, 41.5% (n=22) pertained to the language of the law. The trends indicate that the language of the law was a significant topic in the journal.

The significance of the topic would have been of interest to curriculum developers, academics and researchers on the subject of language and the law. In this paper, the focus is on research articles, case studies or reports, and book reviews. Essays, commentaries and rejoinders, and bibliographies were excluded because of the small number of items. See Table 1 for a summary of the main categories of published items.

Table 1. Summary of Articles Published in IJSSL 1994-2003

Category of publication	All Topics		Language and the law and/or language of the law topics	
	N	%	N	%
Research article	113	61.4	19	44.2
Case study or report	18	9.8	2	5.6
Book review	53	28.8	22	51.2
Total	184	100.0	43	100.0

2. 1. Areas of forensic linguistics

A review of the topics covered in the journal suggests an inductively generated grouping of related topics. These topics are presented and coded in alphabetical order below. A rudimentary attempt is made to outline 13 categories and 33 subcategories of classification.

- Authorship Studies [AS]
  - Attribution [AA]
  - Disputes [AD]
- Confession Statements [CS]
- Expert Opinion [EO]
- Forensic Morphology [FM]
  - Historical Dialectology [HD]
  - Trademark Law [TL]
- Forensic Phonetics [FPH]
  - Speaker Identification [SI]
  - Speaker Recognition [SR]
  - Speaker Authentication [SA]
  - Speaker Discrimination [SD]
  - Tape Authentication [TA]
  - National Origin [NO]
  - Physical Attributes [PA]
- Trademark Law [TL]
- Forensic Pragmatics [FPG]

    - Linguistic context [LC]
    - Extralinguistic context [EC]
- Forensic Semantics [FSM]
    - Lexical [LS]
    - Sentential [SS]
- Forensic Syntax [FSY]
    - Word Level [WL]
    - Sentential Level [SL]
    - Discourse Analysis [DA]
- Interpreting [II]
    - Utterances [ITU]
    - Text [ITT]
- Language and the Law [LL]
    - Judicial Process [JP]
    - Legislation Process [LP]
    - Evidence [EV]
    - Language Rights [LR]
    - Corpus Linguistics [CL]
- Transcription [TT]
    - Speech to Text [TST]
    - Text to Speech [TTS]
- Vulnerability [VV]
    - Witnesses [VVW]
    - Disadvantaged [DA]
    - Manipulation [MM]
- Witness Statements [WS]
    - Expert [EW]
    - Naïve [NW]

An index of the topics published in the IJSLL shows the development of various interests in the forensic linguistics field over the period 1994-2003. The main clusters of research, case studies or case reports and book reviews were: authorship studies, confession statements, expert opinion, forensic morphology, forensic phonetics, forensic pragmatics, forensic semantics, forensic syntax, interpreting of texts (spoken and written), language and the law, transcription of texts (speech to text and text to speech), vulnerable persons, and witness statements

3. Course Outline

Using the classification above as a framework for the selection of the course content, I have attempted to provide a sample course outline as shown in Appendix 1. A number of observations, and criteria for evaluation as well as potential limitations of the course are suggested. The proposed course outline is offered for comment and feedback.

The rationale for the course is based on the need to define the scope of studies in language and the law and the interrelationship between language and law as explored in a variety of sources (Maley 1994, Gibbons 1994, O'Barr and Conley 1997). The course objectives are designed to help participants explore the scope and interrelationship of language and the law from cognitive and affective perspectives in six modules.

Following a modular format, the first three topics include: the nature and study of the language of the law; an exploration of linguistic and communication issues; concepts, models and frameworks associated with the language and interpretation of the law; applications of knowledge of the law to the practice of interpreting the law; case studies and reports. Topics 4 and 5 include a practical investigation of a language and interpretation of the law problem, and presentations based on selected approaches to investigating a practical problem. Topic 5 consists of a review of course content and the provision of feedback on Assignments 2 and/or 3.

The course schedule requires 39 contact hours (13 weeks at three hours per week) in one semester. The course will be assessed by two or three coursework assignments (50%) and a final written examination (50%). The first coursework assessment (an individual essay) occurs after the first three modules at the end of week 6, and one-two (oral and/or written) assessments occur after two more modules at the end of week 10.

4. Discussion

Selecting and organizing a suitable range of topics is the first main issue in designing the course outline. The range of the topics will be influenced by the range of topics covered in published research articles, book reviews and case studies or case reports in a scholarly journal. IJSLL provides a suitable range of topics on the language and the law. These range from the nature and use of evidence (Coulthard 1994 and 1997, Levi 1994, Eades 1994, Storey-White 1997, Newbrook and Curtain 1998, Kredens and Góralewska-Łach 1998, Thompson 2002); the judicial and the legal processes (Hale 1997), the use of texts (Tiersma 2001); legislation (Penny et al. 1995), to the use of threats (Fraser 1998, Storey 1995). These examples provide useful background material.

The depth of coverage will be determined by the learner's knowledge and experience of the law and understanding of the study of language, as well as the overall goals and objectives of the course. For example what background knowledge of the law and of linguistics should participants be expected to have? First year linguistics and/or communication and law courses would be helpful but should not be a requirement. Since the intention is to provide an undergraduate learning experience that can become the basis for graduate work in forensic linguistics and/or communication studies, no previous knowledge beyond Level 1 should be expected. It would be helpful to combine this course with other relevant courses of study in linguistics, communication and law.

4.1. Rationale: Theoretical/empirical, philosophical/professional, and socio-cultural and legal bases

The rationale for the course and the selection and organization of the course content rests on three pillars. The first pillar is the authority derived from theoretical and empirical bases and justifications for inclusion of content. In other words, are the content topics based on the scholarly work investigated in a journal such as IJSLL (FL) under the rubric of the language and the law? This paper provides an index of suitable sources (Table 2).

The second pillar is derived from the philosophical and professional reasons for the selection and organization of the course content. Do the topics address issues that are important to forensic linguists and legal professionals? How can an exploration of the selected topics equip forensic linguists and legal professionals to obtain, examine, sift, evaluate and use language evidence in legal contexts in the interest of justice?

The third pillar is based on the socio-cultural and legal bases for selecting and organizing the course content. How do the topics address significant socio-cultural issues such as perceptions of justice, fairness, confidence in the rule of the law, and the use of language evidence in the judicial and legal system, and issues related to the rights and treatment of the accused, witnesses and vulnerable persons, the conduct of police interviews, the use of oral and written texts, and the use of linguistic and communication experts.

4.2. Objectives: achievement and relevance

Two issues should be taken into account in considering the suitability of the objectives. Is there a reasonable expectation that the objectives can be achieved? Are the objectives relevant to the course of study and the underlying rationale for the course? The objectives appear to have content validity, but may need to be modified in the light of experience and the backgrounds of participants.

4.3. Schedule: coverage and balance

Is there sufficient time to adequately cover the proposed course content? Is there adequate balance and pacing in the time allocated to the content areas? Are the content areas appropriately sequenced to support learning? These questions need to be applied to the proposed schedule. An effort has been made to proceed incrementally with six modules. The modules begin with foundational concepts and continue with critical exploration and application of knowledge experiences characterized by reflective practice.

4.4. Assessment: Weighting and balance

Are the assessments adequately weighted and balanced? The assessments occur at the end of Weeks 6 and 10. The weighting of the first assessment ranges from 10 to 25% depending on the three options presented in Appendix 1. It consists of an individual conceptual essay (25%), which will be complemented by an oral presentation of a practical investigation (25%). The alternatives are to have two different weightings for the essay (20 or 10%), and the oral and written presentations based on the practical investigation (15+15 or 15+25%). The first option is less rigorous than the last two. The last two provide higher rewards as the participants make progress through the course of study.

5. Conclusion

Ultimately, the value of the course will be based on the extent to which there are teaching/learning opportunities to explore, explain and articulate the relationship between the language of the law and the interpretation of the law and to consider the attendant communication issues in a legal context. Another criterion for assessing the course is to consider the extent to which the goal of encouraging participants to relate the study of the language and the law to the various sub-fields of forensic linguistics and communication has been achieved. The rationale for selecting and organizing the course content or a course on language and the law benefited from an analysis and review of IJSSL articles.

References

Conley, J. M. and W. M. O'Barr (1998). *Just Words: Law, Language and Power*. Chicago: University of Chicago Press.

Cotterill, J., Coulthard, M., and P. French (2003). "Editorial foreword". *Forensic Linguistics* 10: v.

Coulthard, M. (1994). "Corpora in forensic texts". *Forensic Linguistics* 1: 27-44.

Coulthard, M. (1997). "A failed appeal". *Forensic Linguistics* 4: 287-302.

Eades, D. (1994). "Forensic linguistics in Australia: An overview". *Forensic Linguistics* 1: 113-132.

Fraser, B. (1998). "Threatening revisited". *Forensic Linguistics* 5: 159-173.

Gibbons, J. (ed.) (1994). *Language and the Law*. Harlow: Longman.

Goodrich, P. (1987). *Legal discourse: Studies in Linguistics, Rhetoric and Legal Analysis*. New York: St. Martin's Press.

Hale, S. (1997). "Clash of world perspectives: The discursive practices of the law, the witness and the Interpreter". *Forensic Linguistics* 4: 197-209.

Kredens, K. and G. Góralewska-Łach (1998). "Language as sole incriminating evidence: The Augustynek Case". *Forensic Linguistics* 5: 193-202.

Levi, Judith N. (1994). "Language as evidence: The linguist as expert witness in North American courts". *Forensic Linguistics* 1: 1-26.

Maley, Y. (1994). "The language of the law". In: J. Gibbons (ed.), *Language and the law*. Harlow: Longman, 3-50.

McMenamin, G. R. (2002). *Forensic Linguistics: Advances in Forensic Stylistics*. London: CRC Press.

Melinkoff, D. (1963). *The Language of the Law*. Boston: Little, Brown.

Newbrook, M. and J. M. Curtain (1998). "Oates' theory of Reverse Speech: A critical examination". *Forensic Linguistics* 5: 174-192.

Penny, L., Fitzhardinge, S. and H. Materne (1995). "The language of the suffrage debates in the South Australian Parliament, 1883-94". *Forensic Linguistics* 2: 56-64.

Steele, G. A. (2005). "The language of the law and the interpretation of the law". Paper presented at IAFL 7, Cardiff University, Wales, July 1-4.

Storey, K. (1995). "The language of threats". *Forensic Linguistics* 2: 74-80.

Storey-White, K. (1997). "KISSing the jury: Advantages and limitations of the 'keep it simple' principle in the presentation of expert evidence to courts and juries". *Forensic Linguistics* 4: 280-286.

Thompson, J. K. (2002). "'Powerful/powerless' language in court: A critical re-evaluation of the Duke Language and Law Programme". *Forensic Linguistics* 9: 153-167.

Tiersma, P. M. (1999). *Legal Language*. Chicago: University of Chicago Press.

Tiersma, P. M. (2001). "Textualizing the law". *Forensic Linguistics* 8: 73-92.

Appendix 1

Language and the law and interpretation of the law: A sample course outline

Rationale

This course seeks to define the scope of studies in language and the law and establish their interrelationship. Participants will explore the relationship between language and the law and the approaches used to study this relationship. One approach to exploring this relationship was described as the role of language in constructing the law (Maley 1994). Another approach is based on the comprehension and production of law in relation to a simple model of language and extended in an analysis of the levels of language (Gibbons 1994).

Some of the work in forensic linguistics distinguishes between the language of the law and the language and the law (O'Barr and Conley 1997). Such a distinction has not always been adequately considered in practical situations facing legal professionals. The distinction between the two emphases may have implications for the work of forensic linguists as they seek to interact and communicate with legal professionals. This course explores this dynamic tension. This course also explores the language of the law and its relationship to the interpretation of the law. It also establishes the relationship of this sub-field of forensic linguistics, the language and interpretation of the law to its other sub-fields such as authorship studies and speaker identification studies.

Objectives

Participants will:

- Describe and explain the nature and scope of the field of the language and the law
- Explore and explain concepts, models and frameworks for defining the field of the language and the law
- Consider the linguistic and communication implications of the impact of the language of the law on the interpretation of the law and produce reflective statements on their interrelationship.
- Consider and articulate the interrelationship between the language and interpretation of the law and other sub-fields of forensic linguistics. These sub-fields appear in Table 2.

Course Schedule

An undergraduate Level 2/3 three-credit course taught normally in a 13-week first semester programme

Week	Module	Hours
1-2	The nature and study of the language and interpretation of the law: Linguistic and communication issues.	6
3-4	Concepts, models and frameworks associated with the language and interpretation of the law.	6
5-6	Applications of knowledge of the language of the law to the practice of interpreting the law: case studies and reports	6
	Assignment 1 due at the end of Week 6	
7-8	Investigating a practical language and interpretation of the law problem	6
9-10	Presenting an approach to an investigation of a practical problem	
	Assignment 2 (Individual or team oral presentation in Weeks 9-10)	6
	Assignment 3 (Written submission of Assignment 3)	
11-12	Review of course and feedback on projects	6

Assessment

Two or three in-course assignments 50%

AND

One final two-hour examination with two questions to be done 50%

Table 3. Summary of Assessment

Assessment	% Weighting		
	Option 1	Option 2	Option 3
In-course essay	25	20	10
Oral presentation of project	25	15	15
Written presentation of project	0	15	25
Subtotal	50	50	50
Final Examination	50	50	50
Total	100	100	100

ŁÓDŹ
Studies in Language

Vol. 1 Barbara Lewandowska-Tomaszczyk / Patrick James Melia (eds.): PALC'99: Practical Applications in Language Corpora. Papers from the International Conference at the Universtiy of Łódź, 15-18 April 1999. 2000.

Vol. 2 Lou Burnard / Tony McEnery (eds.): Rethinking Language Pedagogy from a Corpus Perspective. Papers from the third international conference on Teaching and Language Corpora. 2000.

Vol. 3 Barbara Lewandowska-Tomaszczyk / John Osborne / Frits Schulte: Foreign Language Teaching and Information and Communication Technology. 2001.

Vol. 4 Piotr Cap: Explorations in Political Discourse. Methodological and Critical Perspectives. 2002.

Vol. 5 Ewa Waniek-Klimczak / Patrick James Melia (eds.): Accents and Speech in Teaching English Phonetics and Phonology. EFL perspective. 2002.

Vol. 6 Barbara Lewandowska-Tomaszczyk / Kamila Turewicz (eds.). Cognitive Linguistics Today. 2002.

Vol. 7 Barbara Lewandowska-Tomaszczyk (ed.): PALC 2001: Practical Applications in Language Corpora. 2003.

Vol. 8 Corpus Linguistics by the Lune. A Festschrift for Geoffrey Leech. Edited by Andrew Wilson, Paul Rayson and Tony McEnery. 2003.

Vol. 9 Barbara Lewandowska-Tomaszczyk (ed.): Practical Applications in Language and Computers. PALC 2003. 2004.

Vol. 10 Imagery in Language. Festschrift in Honour of Professor Ronald W. Langacker. Edited by Barbara Lewandowska-Tomaszczyk and Alina Kwiatkowska. 2004.

Vol. 11 Seana Coulson / Barbara Lewandowska-Tomaszczyk (eds.). The Literal and Nonliteral in Language and Thought. 2005.

Vol. 12 Piotr Cap (ed.): Pragmatics Today. 2005.

Vol. 13 Jacek Waliński / Krzysztof Kredens / Stanisław Goźdź-Roszkowski (eds.): Corpora and ICT in Language Studies. PALC 2005. 2007.

Vol 14 Krzysztof Kosecki (ed.): Perspectives on Metonymy. Proceedings of the International Conference "Perspectives on Metonymy", held in Łódź, Poland, May 6–7, 2005. 2007.

Vol. 15 Barbara Lewandowska-Tomaszczyk / Tomasz Płudowski / Dolores Valencia Tanno (eds.): The Media and International Communication. 2007.

Vol. 16 Krzysztof Kredens / Stanisław Goźdź-Roszkowski (eds.): Language and the Law: International Outlooks. 2007.

Kolibri 360 GmbH
Ferdinand-Jühlke-Straße 7
99095 Erfurt, Deutschland
produktsicherheit@kolibri360.de

Druck:
CPI Druckdienstleistungen GmbH
im Auftrag der
Kolibri 360 GmbH
Ferdinand-Jühlke-Str. 7
99095 Erfurt